ILDÁNACH ILDÍRECH

An t-Ollamh Proinsias Mac Cana

CELTIC STUDIES PUBLICATIONS IV

ILDÁNACH ILDÍRECH

A Festschrift for

Proinsias Mac Cana

edited by

John Carey, John T. Koch, & Pierre-Yves Lambert

CELTIC STUDIES PUBLICATIONS, INC.

ANDOVER & ABERYSTWYTH

1999

ISBN 1–891271–01–6

Cover design by John T. Koch, Celtic Studies Publications, Andover & Aberystwyth

Typeset in the Cynrhan type family by Celtic Studies Publications, Inc.

Printed by Gomer Press, Llandysul, Ceredigion, Wales

Celtic Studies Publications, Inc.

business office:

P. O. Box 639
Andover, MA 01810–0011
USA

CelticSP@aol.com
www.celticstudies.com

editorial correspondence:

Celtic Studies Publications
Centre for Advanced Welsh and Celtic Studies
National Library of Wales
Aberystwyth, Ceredigion SY23 3HH

Wales

PREFACE

OUR title alludes to the maxim *Bes ildánach bid ildírech* 'He who will have many skills will have many honour-prices', from the early Irish tract on status *Uraicecht Becc*. A similar pronouncement is found in *Bretha Nemed Toísech*; and some manuscripts of *Lebar Gabála* echo the phrase in their account of the omni-competent god Lug. *Díre* 'honour-price' is of course a legal concept rooted in the social specificities of pre-Norman Ireland. But we do not think that it is too fanciful to discern in this precept the basic idea that someone whose gifts have enabled him to serve his fellows in many ways is deserving of correspondingly many tokens of recognition. This book, while it cannot hope to fulfil this ideal to the letter, is offered in its spirit.

The cover art is a detail of the top rear panel of the Clonmore or Blackwater Reliquary and appears by the kind permission of the Ulster Museum, Belfast. It dates to the late sixth or early seventh century. We selected it as an instance of a Christian artefact displaying a style of ornamentation of pre-Christian Celtic origin, thus analogous to some dimensions of literature examined in this volume, as well as in the work of Proinsias Mac Cana. We thought it fitting for this tribute also in that the piece comes from roughly the same corner of Ireland as does the honorand.

We wish especially to thank the following, who are among the many people who generously assisted us at various stages in the production of this book: Cormac Bourke, David Dumville, Siân Evans, Andrew Hawke, Pamela S. Hopkins, Glenys Howells, Fergus Kelly, Beverly Koch, Anne Lea, James Leonard, Marion Löffler, Réiltín Mac Cana, Máirín Ní Dhonnchadha, Patrick Sims-Williams, Edgar Slotkin.

JOHN CAREY

JOHN T. KOCH

PIERRE-YVES LAMBERT

CONTENTS

TABULA GRATULATORIA

G. M. Adam, *Penrhyndeudraeth ger Porthmadog, Gwynedd, Cymru*

Dorothy Africa, *Bedford, Massachusetts, USA*

Anders Ahlqvist, *Ollscoil na hÉireann, Gaillimh, Éire*

Bo Almqvist, *Shankill, Co. Dublin, Ireland*

Fernando Alonso, *Facultad de Filologia, Universidad de Santiago de Compostela, España*

Rhian M. Andrews, *Celtic Studies, School of Modern Languages, Queen's University, Belfast, Northern Ireland*

Frank Battaglia, *College of Staten Island, City University of New York, Staten Island, New York, New York, USA*

Helmut Birkhan, *Institut für Germanistik, Wien, Österreich*

Jacqueline Borsje, *Scoil an Léinn Cheiltigh, Institiúid Ard-Léinn Bhaile Átha Cliath, Éire*

Thomas P. O'Neill Library, *Boston College, Chestnut Hill, Massachuetts, USA*

D. J. Bowen, *Adran y Gymraeg, Prifysgol Cymru, Aberystwyth, Cymru*

John Bradley, *Roinn na Nua-Staire, Ollscoil na hÉireann, Baile Átha Cliath, Éire*

M. T. Brasseur, *Bruxelles, Belgique*

Dorothy A. Bray, *Department of English, McGill University, Montreal, Quebec, Canada*

Nancy J. Breen, *Arlington, Massachusetts, USA*

Rachel Bromwich, *Aberystwyth, Ceredigion, Cymru*

Marie-Thérèse Brouland, *Versoix-Genève, Suisse*

J. P. Brown, *Geufron, Llangollen, Clwyd, Cymru*

Andrea Budgey, *Pontifical Institute of Mediaeval Studies, Toronto, Ontario, Canada*

Francis John Byrne, *Roinn na Staire, Ollscoil na hÉireann, Baile Átha Cliath, Éire*

C. Cachia, *University of Toronto, Ontario, Canada*

Prifysgol Cymru Caerdydd

Thomas Gildea Cannon, *Mequon, Wisconsin, USA*

Canolfan Uwchefrydiau Cymreig a Cheltaidd, *Llyfrgell Genedlaethol Cymru, Aberystwyth, Ceredigion, Cymru*

John Carey, *Roinn na Sean agus na Meán-Ghaeilge, Ollscoil na hÉireann, Corcaigh, Éire*

Melita Cataldi, *Torino, Italia*

Celtic Studies Foundation, *University of Sydney, New South Wales, Australia*

Thomas Charles-Edwards, Jesus College, Oxford, England

Paula Powers Coe, Los Angeles, California

M. J. Connolly, Department of Slavic and Eastern Languages, Boston College, Chestnut Hill, Massachusetts, USA

Mary-Ann Constantine, Adran y Gymraeg, Prifysgol Cymru, Aberystwyth, Cymru

Raymond Cormier, Longwood College, Farmville, Virginia, USA

Johan Corthals, Universität Hamburg, Deutschland

Aedeen Cremin, Celtic Studies, University of Sydney, New South Wales, Australia

Bernadette Cunningham, Drumcondra, Dublin, Ireland

Gregory J. Darling, John Hay College of Criminal Justice, Fordham University, New York, New York, USA

K. R. Dark, London, England

Sioned Davies, Adran y Gymraeg, Prifysgol Cymru, Caerdydd, Cymru

Patrizia de Bernardo Stempel, Bonn, Deutschland

Department of Anglo-Saxon, Norse and Celtic, Cambridge University, England

Scheherazade Downey, Littleton, Colorado, USA

Seán Duffy, Roin Stair na Meánaoiseanna, Coláiste na Tríonóide, Baile Átha Cliath, Éire

David N. Dumville, Girton College, Cambridge, England

D. R. Edel, University of Utrecht, Doorn, The Netherlands

Lawrence Eson, Denver, Colorado, USA

D. Ellis Evans, Jesus College, Oxford, England

Dewi Wyn Evans, Aberdaron ger Pwllheli, Gwynedd, Cymru

Fachgebiet Vergleichende Sprachwissenschaft/Keltologie der Philipps-Univerität, Marburg, Deutschland

Gillian Fellows-Jensen, Copenhagen, Denmark

Joanne Findon, Department of English, Simon Fraser University, Burnaby, British Columbia, Canada

Verlyn Flieger, Department of English, University of Maryland, College Park, Maryland, USA

Patrick K. Ford, Department of Celtic Languages and Literatures, Harvard University, Cambridge, Massachusetts, USA

Katherine Forsyth, Department of Celtic, University of Glasgow, Scotland

Philip M. Freeman, Department of Classics, Washington University, St Louis, Missouri, USA

Brian Frykenberg, Andover, Massachusetts, USA

Anne Germain, Norwood, Massachusetts, USA

William Gillies, Department of Celtic, University of Edinburgh, Scotland

William Grant, Department of Celtic, University of Edinburgh, Scotland

Eamon Mary Greenwood, University of Abertay, Dundee, Scotland

Toby Griffen, University of Southern Illinois, Edwardsville, Illinois, USA

Cozette Griffin-Kremer, Issy-les-Moulineaux, France

R. Geraint and E. Eluned Gruffydd, Aberystwyth, Ceredigion, Cymru

David G. Guild, Russian Department, The University of Edinburgh, Scotland

Marion Gunn, Everson Gunn Teoranta, Baile Átha Cliath, Éire

Nigel Hackney, Lenton, Nottingham, England

Ann Hamlin, Belfast, Northern Ireland

Joseph Harris, Department of English, Harvard University, Cambridge, Massachusetts, USA

Alan Harrison, Roinn na Nua-Ghaeilge, Ollscoil na hÉireann, Baile Átha Cliath, Éire

Harvard College Library, Cambridge, Massachusetts, USA

Anthony Harvey, Royal Irish Academy, Dublin, Ireland

Andrew Hawke, Geiriadur Prifysgol Cymru, Aberystwyth, Ceredigion, Cymru

Marged Haycock, Adran y Gymraeg, Prifysgol Cymru, Aberystwyth, Ceredigion, Cymru

Dara Hellman, University of California at Berkeley, California, USA

Máire Herbert, Roinn na Sean agus na Meán-Ghaeilge, Ollscoil na hÉireann, Corcaigh, Éire

Barbara Hillers, Department of Celtic, University of Edinburgh, Scotland

Gary Holland, Linguistics Department, University of California at Berkeley, California, USA

Pamela S. Hopkins, Department of Celtic Languages and Literatures, Harvard University, Cambridge, Massachusetts, USA

David Howlett, Dictionary of Medieval Latin from British Sources, Bodleian Library, Oxford, England

Benjamin T. Hudson, Department of History, Pennsylvania State University, University Park, Pennsylvania, USA

Baden Hughes, Australian National University, Canberra, Australia

Dafydd Ifans, Llyfrgell Genedlaethol Cymru, Aberystwyth, Ceredigion

Rhiannon Ifans, Canolfan Uwchefrydiau Cymreig a Cheltaidd Prifysgol Cymru, Aberystwyth, Ceredigion, Cymru

An Leabharlann, Scoil an Léinn Cheiltigh, Institiúid Ard-Léinn Bhaile Átha Cliath, Éire

Colin A. Ireland, Beaver College, Dublin, Ireland

Graham R. Isaac, Bonn, Deutschland

Nicolas Jacobs, Jesus College, Oxford, England

Christine James, Adran y Gymraeg, Prifysgol Cymru, Abertawe, Cymru

Dafydd Jenkins, Aberystwyth, Ceredigion, Cymru

Geraint H. Jenkins, Canolfan Uwchefrydiau Cymreig a Cheltaidd Prifysgol Cymru, Aberystwyth, Ceredigion, Cymru

Jesus College, Oxford, England

Diarmuid Johnson, Gaillimh, Éire

R. M. Jones, Aberystwyth, Ceredigion, Cymru

Bríd Hennigan Jouzier, Paris, France

Joann Keesey, Malden, Massachusetts, USA

Fergus Kelly, Scoil an Léinn Cheiltigh, Institiúid Ard-Léinn Bhaile Átha Cliath, Éire

J. F. Killeen, Galway, Ireland

Peter Kitson, Stoke Prior, Bromsgrove, Worcestershire, England

David Klausner, Centre for Medieval Studies, University of Toronto, Ontario, Canada

John T. Koch, Canolfan Uwchefrydiau Cymreig a Cheltaidd Prifysgol Cymru, Aberystwyth, Ceredigion, Cymru

Harald Krahwinkler, Universität Klagenfurt, Institut für Geschichte, Klagenfurt, Österreich

Pierre-Yves Lambert, Centre Nationale de la Recherche Scientifique/École Pratique des Hautes Études, Paris, France

Donatien Laurent, Brest, Bretagne, France

Anne E. Lea, Department of English, Anderson House, Clark University, Worcester, Massachusetts, USA

Leabharlann Náisiúnta na hÉireann, Baile Átha Cliath, Éire

Gwenaël Le Duc, Université de Haute Bretagne, Rennes 2, Bretagne, France

Ceri W. Lewis, Treorci, Morgannwg Canol, Cymru

Michael D. Linkletter, Department of Celtic Languages and Literatures, Harvard University, Cambridge, Massachusetts, USA

Emily Lyle, School of Scottish Studies, University of Edinburgh, Scotland

Henar Velasco López, Scoil an Léinn Cheiltigh, Institiúid Ard-Léinn Bhaile Átha Cliath, Éire

Ceridwen Lloyd-Morgan, Adran Llawysgrifau, Llyfrgell Genedlaethol Cymru, Aberystwyth, Ceredigion, Cymru

Derec Llwyd-Morgan, Prifysgol Cymru, Aberystwyth, Ceredigion, Cymru

Llyfrgell Genedlaethol Cymru, Aberystwyth, Ceredigion, Cymru

Donald MacAulay, Department of Celtic, Glasgow University, Scotland

Bill McCann, Aberdyfi, Gwynedd, Cymru

Kevin A. McCarthy, Kings Park, New York, USA

Gearóid Mac Eoin, Ollscoil na hÉireann, Gaillimh, Éire

Uáitéar Mac Gearailt, Coláiste Phádraig, Druim Conrach, Baile Átha Cliath, Éire

John MacInnes, School of Scottish Studies, University of Edinburgh, Scotland

Catherine McKenna, City University of New York, New York, USA

Liam Mac Mathúna, Coláiste Phádraig, Druim Conrach, Baile Átha Cliath, Éire

Clare Macrae, Edinburgh, Scotland

William J. Mahon, Adran y Gymraeg, Prifysgol Cymru, Aberystwyth, Ceredigion, Cymru

Laurance Maney, Department of Celtic Languages and Literatures, Harvard University, Cambridge, Massachusetts, USA

Ursula Marmé, Bonn, Deutschland

Toshi Matsuoka, Hosei University, Chiyoda-ku, Tokyo, Japan

Michael Meckler, Department of Greek and Latin, The Ohio State University, Columbus, Ohio, USA

Ruth Megaw and J. V. S. Megaw, Archaeology, Flinders University, Adelaide, South Australia

Daniel Melia, Celtic Studies Program, University of California at Berkeley, California, USA

Bernard Merdrignac, Université de Haute Bretagne, Rennes, Bretagne, France

Anne Michel, Université de Liège, U. D. Germanique, Liège, Belgique

Stephen Mitchell, Department of Germanic Languages and Literatures, Harvard University, Cambridge, Massachusetts, USA

Tadaaki Miyake, Okayama-shi, Japan

Musée Cantonal d'Archeologie et d'Histoire, Lausanne, Suisse

Ichiro Nagai, Chofu-shi, Tokyo, Japan

Gregory Nagy, Department of the Classics, Harvard University, Cambridge, Massachusetts, USA

Joseph Falaky Nagy, Department of English, University of California at Los Angeles, California, USA

Muireann Ní Bhrolcháin, Roinn na Sean-Ghaeilge, Ollscoil na hÉireann, Má Nuad, Co. Chill Dara, Éire

Próinséas Ní Chatháin, Roinn na Sean-Ghaeilge, Ollscoil na hÉireann, Baile Átha Cliath, Éire

Cáit Ní Dhomhnaill, Scoil na Gaeilge, Ollscoil na hÉireann, Gaillimh, Éire

Máirín Ní Dhonnchadha, Scoil na Gaeilge, Ollscoil na hÉireann, Gaillimh, Éire

Máire Ní Mhaonaigh, St John's College, Cambridge, England

Meidhbhín Ní Úrdail, Roinn na Nua-Ghaeilge, Ollscoil na hÉireann, Baile Átha Cliath, Éire

Úna Nic Éinrí, Roinn na Gaeilge, Coláiste Mhuire gan Smál, Luimneach, Éire

Kenneth E. Nilsen, Department of Celtic Studies, St Francis Xavier University, Antigonish, Nova Scotia, Canada

Colm Ó Baoill, Department of Celtic, University of Aberdeen, Scotland

Dónall P. Ó Baoill, Institiúid Teangeolaíochta Éireann, Baile Átha Cliath, Éire

Feargal Ó Béarra, An Spidéal, Gaillimh, Éire

Máirtín Ó Briain, Scoil na Gaeilge, Ollscoil na hÉireann, Gaillimh, Éire

Elizabeth O'Brien, Dundrum, Dublin, Ireland

Séamus Ó Catháin, Roinn Bhéaloideas Éireann, Ollscoil na hÉireann, Baile Átha Cliath, Éire

Seán Ó Coileáin, Roinn na Nua-Ghaeilge, Ollscoil na hÉireann, Corcaigh, Éire

Tomás Ó Concheanainn, Deilgne, Co. Chill Mhantáin, Éire

Breandán Ó Conaire, Port Mearnóg, Co. Bhaile Átha Cliath, Éire

Donnchadh Ó Corráin, Roinn na Staire, Ollscoil na hÉireann, Corcaigh, Éire

Dáibhí Ó Cróinín, Roinn na Staire, Ollscoil na hÉireann, Gaillimh, Éire

Gearóid Ó Crualaoich, Béaloideas, Ollscoil na hÉireann, Corcaigh, Éire

Brian Ó Cuív, Scoil an Léinn Cheiltigh, Institiúid Ard-Léinn Bhaile Átha Cliath, Éire

Caitríona Ó Dochartaigh, St Edmund's College, Cambridge, England

Mícheál Ó Flaithearta, University of Uppsala, Sweden

Cathal G. Ó hÁinle, Scoil na Gaeilge, Coláiste na Tríonóide, Baile Átha Cliath, Éire

Ruairí Ó hUiginn, Roinn na Nua-Ghaeilge, Ollscoil na hÉireann, Má Nuad, Co. Chill Dara, Éire

Dáithí Ó hÓgáin, Roinn Bhéaloideas Éireann, Ollscoil na hÉireann, Baile Átha Cliath, Éire

Diarmuid Ó Laoghaire, Cherryfield Lodge, Ranelagh, Dublin, Ireland

Lillis Ó Laoire, Roinn na dTeangacha, Ollscoil Luimnigh, Éire

Philip O'Leary, Irish Studies, Boston College, Chestnut Hill, Massachusetts, USA

Thomas O'Loughlin, Theology and Religious Studies, University of Wales, Lampeter, Ceredigion

Breandán Ó Madagáin, Ollscoil na hÉireann, Gaillimh, Éire

Peadar Ó Maoláin, An Tulach Mhór, Co. Uíbh Fhailí, Éire

Mícheál A. Ó Murchú, Ionad na Gaeilge, Faculty of Humanities, University of Ulster, Coleraine, Co. Derry, Northern Ireland

Pádraig Ó Riain, Roinn na Sean agus na Meán-Ghaeilge, Ollscoil na hÉireann, Corcaigh, Éire

H. J. T. O'Sullivan, Sevenoaks, Kent, England

Ann Parry Owen, Canolfan Uwchefrydiau Cymreig a Cheltaidd Prifysgol Cymru, Aberystwyth, Ceredigion, Cymru

Oliver Padel, Peterhouse, Cambridge, England

Patrick Périé, Reims, France

Thérèse Petit, Bruxelles, Belgique

Jean-Michel Picard, Roinn na Fraincise, Ollscoil na hÉireann, Baile Átha Cliath, Éire

Erich Poppe, Fachgebiet Vergleichende Sprachwissenschaft/Keltologie der Philipps-Universität, Marburg, Deutschland

The Library, The Queen's University of Belfast, Northern Ireland

Barry Raftery, Roinn na Seandálaíochta, Ollscoil na hÉireann, Baile Átha Cliath, Éire

Levraoueg ar Gevrenn Brezhoneg ha Keltieg, Skol-Veur Roazhon, Breizh Uhel

Annalee Rejhon, Celtic Studies Program, University of California at Berkeley, California, USA

Jean-Claude Richard, Centre Nationale de la Recherche Scientifique, St Guilhem-le-Désert, France

Michael Richter, Universität Konstanz, Deutschland

Brynley F. Roberts, Aberystwyth, Ceredigion, Cymru

Roinn Bhéaloideas Éireann, Ollscoil na hÉireann, Baile Átha Cliath, Éire

Hans Rössing, Cölbe, Germany

Jenny Rowland, Ollscoil na hÉireann, Baile Átha Cliath, Éire

Paul Russell, Radley College, Abingdon, Oxfordshire, England

The Father Charles Brewer Celtic Collection, Angus L. MacDonald Library, St Francis Xavier University, Antigonish, Nova Scotia, Canada

Nicholas R. Scheetz, Special Collections Division, Georgetown University, Washington, DC, USA

Karl-Horst Schmidt, Sprachwissenschaftliches Institut der Universität Bonn, Deutschland

R. Mark Scowcroft, Department of English, Catholic University of America, Washington, DC, USA

Richard Sharpe, Faculty of Modern History, University of Oxford, England

Patrick P. Sims-Williams, Adran y Gymraeg, Prifysgol Cymru, Aberystwyth, Ceredigion, Cymru

Edgar Slotkin, Department of English and Comparative Literature, University of Cincinnati, Ohio, USA

Sprachwissenschaftliches Institut der Universität Bonn, Deutschland

Lisa L. Spangenberg, Santa Monica, California, USA

Robin Chapman Stacey, Department of History, University of Washington, Seattle, Washington, USA

Nathalie Stalmans, Fonds National de la Recherche Scientifique, Université Libre de Bruxelles, Belgique

Claude Sterckx, Institute des Hautes Études de Belgique, Bruxelles, Belgique

Frederick Suppe, History Department, Ball State University, Muncie, Indiana, USA

Dorothy D. Swartz, Lexington, Massachusetts, USA

Eve Sweetzer, Department of Linguistics, University of California at Berkeley, California, USA

Charles Thomas, Lambessow, St Clement, Truro, Cornwall

David Thomas, Taylor Institution Library, St Giles, Oxford, England

Graham C. G. Thomas, Aberystwyth, Ceredigion, Cymru

Owen Thomas, Canolfan Uwchefrydiau Cymreig a Cheltaidd Prifysgol Cymru, Aberystwyth, Ceredigion, Cymru

Derick S. Thomson, Cathcart, Glasgow, Scotland

Nikolai Tolstoy, Southmoor nr. Abingdon, Berkshire, England

Anne Trindade, History Department, University of Melbourne, Parkville, Victoria, Australia

Hildegard L. C. Tristram, Freiburg, Deutschland

Maria Tymoczko, University of Massachusetts, Amherst, Massachusetts, USA

The Ulster Museum, Botanic Gardens, Belfast, Northern Ireland

Kees Veelenturf, Zoeterwoude-Dorp, The Netherlands

D. B. Walters, Les Facultés Universitaires Saint-Louis, Bruxelles, Belgique

Calvert Watkins, Department of Linguistics, Harvard University, Cambridge, Massachusetts, USA

T. Arwyn Watkins, Abertawe, Cymru

Seosamh Watson, Dámh an Léinn Cheiltigh, Ollscoil na hÉireann, Baile Átha Cliath, Éire

Andrew Welsh, Rutgers University, New Brunswick, New Jersey, USA

Máire M. West, Horsley, Rochester, Northumberland, England

Dan Wiley, Department of Comparative Literature, Harvard University, Cambridge, Massachusetts, USA

G. Aled Williams, Adran y Gymraeg, Prifysgol Cymru, Aberystwyth, Ceredigion, Cymru

J. E. Caerwyn Williams, Canolfan Uwchefrydiau Cymreig a Cheltaidd Prifysgol Cymru, Aberystwyth, Ceredigion, Cymru

D. S. Wodtko, Institut für Sprachwissenschaft, Universität zu Köln, Deutschland

Donna Wong, Madison, Wisconsin, USA

Jonathan Wooding, Theology and Religious Studies, University of Wales, Lampeter, Ceredigion

Stefan Zimmer, Sprachwissenschaftliches Institut der Universität Bonn, Deutschland

The Finding of Arthur's Grave: A Story from Clonmacnoise?

John Carey

NATIONAL UNIVERSITY OF IRELAND, CORK

I T would be difficult to enumerate all of the ways in which Proinsias Mac Cana has broadened and deepened our understanding of the links between the languages, cultures, and traditions of the Celtic peoples of Ireland and Britain: casting about among a multitude of examples, one might instance his careful and influential study of the Irish influences in the tale of *Branwen*;[1] his sensitive comparisons of Welsh and Irish syntax;[2] and his exploration of Welsh analogues to the Irish topos of the poet as king's lover.[3] In the present paper I shall suggest that Ireland exercised a potent, but hitherto I think unsuspected, influence upon Brittonic tradition in yet another area, contributing significantly to the development of the Arthurian legend.

---

1 *Branwen Daughter of Llŷr: A Study of the Irish Affinities and of the Composition of the Second Branch of the Mabinogi* (Cardiff, 1958).
2 E.g. his recent article 'The Historical Present and the Verb "To Be"', *Ériu* 45 (1994), 127–50.
3 'The Poet as Spouse of his Patron', *Ériu* 39 (1988), 79–85.

The alleged discovery of the remains of King Arthur at Glastonbury, in the year 1190 or 1191, was the occasion of considerable excitement at the time and has been a topic of continuing interest down to the present day. In what follows I shall be adding a further item to the relatively limited dossier of evidence upon which analysis and discussion of this event have so far concentrated; before doing so, however, it may be useful to give a brief overview of the current state of the question.

We are fortunate in having several accounts of the circumstances: Gerald of Wales's *De principis instructione* (begun before 1192) and *Speculum ecclesiae* (written *c.* 1217); the *Chronicon Anglicanum* of Ralph of Coggeshall (written *c.* 1223); the chronicle of Margam Abbey (written *c.* 1234); and Adam of Domerham's *Historia de rebus gestis Glastoniensibus* (written *c.* 1290). Antonia Gransden has argued that these works reflect the testimony of two lost, contemporary sources: a description of the discovery commissioned by the Glastonbury community, and very likely written by Gerald himself (drawn upon subsequently by Gerald in his other writings, as well as by Adam); and an account which circulated among Cistercian monasteries (used by Ralph and by the Margam chronicler).[4] For a general impression of the medieval narratives, we can consider one representative of each of these two groups: Ralph of Coggeshall's *Chronicon* for the Cistercians, and Gerald's *De principis instructione*.

First Ralph, writing *sub anno* 1191:[5]

> In this year, moreover, there were found at Glastonbury the bones of the most famous Arthur, once king of Britain, hidden in a certain most ancient coffin flanked by two ancient pyramids, standing erect, on which certain letters had been carved which however could not be read because of their excessive barbarousness and defacement. [The bones] were found in this way. When they dug up the earth there so as to bury a certain monk, who in his life had with fervent desire chosen this as the place of his burial, they found a coffin, above which a leaden cross had been placed, on which this was written: 'Here lies the famous king Arthur, buried in the island of Avalon'.[6]

4   'The Growth of the Glastonbury Traditions and Legends in the Twelfth Century', *Journal of Ecclesiastical History* 27 (1976), 337–58 (pp. 350–2).
5   *Radulphi de Coggeshall Chronicon Anglicanum*, ed. J. Stevenson, Rolls Series (London, 1875), p. 36; see also E. K. Chambers, *Arthur of Britain* (London, 1927), p. 268.
6   'Hic iacet inclitus rex Arturius, in insula Auallonis sepultus.'

Gerald, who evidently visited the site himself, gives a more circumstantial account. Speaking of Arthur's alleged patronage of Glastonbury, he continues:[7]

. . . His body, moreover, has been found in these our days, at Glastonbury between two stone pyramids set up in a certain holy cemetery, hidden deep in the earth in a hollow oak tree, and marked by wondrous and almost miraculous signs. And it was transferred with honour into the church, and fittingly consigned to a marble tomb. Wherefore too a leaden cross attached to a stone buried [there] — not set above it as is customary in our days, but rather affixed to the under side — which we too have seen and indeed handled, bore this inscription (not plain and facing outward, but rather turned inward toward the stone): 'Here lies buried the famous king Arthur, with Guenevere his second wife, in the island of Avalon' . . . .[8] And her bones were found together with her husband's, but nevertheless distinct: two parts of the coffin, so to speak, toward the head, were assigned to the bones of the man; while the third part, at the foot, held the woman's bones separately. And a bit of woman's hair was found there, yellow, still intact and retaining its colour, which when a monk snatched it up and lifted it with eager hand fell instantly all to dust.

There were, then, some indications that the body was to be found there [preserved] in their writings, others on the pyramids carved with inscriptions (which however were mostly rubbed away on account of their great age), others again which had been received through visions and revelations granted to good and religious men. Most of all, however, and most plainly, it was the king of England, Henry the Second, who informed the monks of everything even as he had heard it from an ancient Briton, a singer of histories: that deep in the earth, sixteen feet at least, they would find the body, and not in a stone coffin but in a hollowed-out oak tree . . . .

His shin-bone, set next to the shin of the tallest man of the place — whom the abbot also showed us — and fixed in the earth beside [this man's] foot, extended three inches beyond his knee. And his skull, as if it were a prodigy or an omen, was so roomy and large that the space between his eyebrows, and between his eyes, was the width of a palm. In it there appeared ten or more wounds; all of them, apart from one bigger than the rest, which had made a great gap and which seemed the only mortal one, had grown together in a solid cicatrice.

7 *Giraldi Cambrensis Opera*, ed. J. S. Brewer et al., Rolls Series, 8 vols (London, 1861–9), VIII, 127–9; also Chambers, *Arthur of Britain*, pp. 269–71.

8 'Hic iacet sepultus inclitus rex Arthurus cum Wenneueria uxore sua secunda in insula Auallonia.' The word order is somewhat different in the *Speculum ecclesiae*: 'Hic iacet sepultus inclytus rex Arthurius, in insula Auallonia, cum Wenneuereia uxore sua secunda' (*Giraldi Cambrensis Opera*, Brewer et al., IV,50; Chambers, *Arthur of Britain*, p. 273).

In the *Speculum ecclesiae* Gerald retells the story at still greater length. He adds two further details: that an excavation to find the remains was undertaken as the result of a direct command from King Henry himself to the abbot Henry de Sully;[9] and that the stone to which the lead cross was attached was not found with the coffin but above it, only seven feet below the surface. Adam of Domerham tells substantially the same story again; it should be noted, however, that he agrees with the Cistercian chroniclers in giving a version of the inscription on the cross which does not mention Guenevere. He also states that, while the digging was going on, curtains or screens were set up around the hole to shield it from the view of onlookers.

Predictably, this colourful story has provoked very different reactions, running the gamut from complete scepticism to fervent belief.[10] The sceptics have pointed out that it would have been very convenient for the monks of Glastonbury to have discovered Arthur's remains at just this time, for at least two reasons. A catastrophic fire had destroyed most of the monastery in 1184, and Henry II had contributed generously to the costs of rebuilding. But his death in 1189 had brought an end to this support: it would have been natural enough to seek some fresh stimulus for the generosity of his son Richard, and of pilgrims to the monastery.

The discovery could also have been politically motivated. The idea that Arthur was, at some time of crisis, to return from the Otherworld was an inherently subversive one: thus Herman of Laon describes how an argument as to whether or not Arthur was still alive sparked a riot in a Cornish monastery in 1113;[11] while the doctrine's propaganda potential is reflected in the poem *Draco Normannicus* (*c.* 1169), where the threat that Arthur might come back from Avalon is invoked against Henry's attempts to dominate Brittany.[12] 'Proof' that the Celtic saviour

---

9   This cannot be literally true, as the latter only became abbot on the occasion of the former's death in 1189. Discussion in W. A. Nitze, 'The Exhumation of King Arthur at Glastonbury', *Speculum* 9 (1934), 355–61 (p. 358).

10 A particularly cogent exposition of the case for scepticism appears in Gransden, 'Growth of the Glastonbury Traditions'. For a concise statement of some of the considerations invoked on the other side, see G. Ashe, 'Glastonbury', in *The Arthurian Encyclopedia*, ed. N. J. Lacy et al. (London, 1986), pp. 237–43 (pp. 241–2).

11 R. S. Loomis, 'The Oral Diffusion', in *Arthurian Literature in the Middle Ages: A Collaborative History*, ed. R. S. Loomis (Oxford, 1959), pp. 52–63 (pp. 53–4); text in Chambers, *Arthur of Britain*, p. 249.

12 Loomis, 'The Legend of Arthur's Survival', in *Arthurian Literature*, pp. 64–71 (p. 69); text in Chambers, *Arthur of Britain*, pp. 264–5.

hero was truly dead, on the other hand, would strengthen the position of the English king; and the Glastonbury grave could prove exceptionally useful in dampening the hopes of dissident Britons. Such reasoning clearly lay behind Edward I's solemn reburial of the remains in front of the high altar, a ceremony performed in connection with his own final and decisive campaign against the Welsh in 1278.[13]

The lead cross too has come in for criticism: the description of the body as that of a 'famous king' does not sound contemporary with Arthur himself,[14] nor does the identification of Glastonbury with the fabulous 'island of Avalon'. The story's defenders have pointed out that, even if much of the inscription's wording seems problematical, its script is decidedly archaic, with a square *c* and *h*-like *n*. The lettering cannot, admittedly, be as old as that of Arthur's own time, but could very well be that of the tenth or eleventh century. Leslie Alcock has suggested accordingly that the stone with the lead cross may have been placed there after an earlier monument had been destroyed in the tenth century, when Saint Dunstan refurbished the old cemetery south of the Lady Chapel in which the two 'pyramids' stood.[15] But this scenario is of necessity, as Alcock acknowledges, 'a structure of hypothesis'; and easier interpretations of the evidence can be proposed. There would have been nothing to prevent the monks, had they been intent upon faking such a find, from copying old documents or inscriptions available in the monastery: for inscriptions they would have needed to look no further than the famous 'pyramids' themselves, the writing on which is mentioned by Ralph and Gerald, and was examined carefully by William of Malmesbury.[16] Indeed, Philip Rahtz has pointed out that 'an inscription on the twelfth-century tympanum in the entrance porch of nearby Stoke-sub-Hamdon has lettering that is very similar'.[17]

The most telling evidence in the story's favour was produced by C. A. Ralegh Radford's excavation in 1962. Digging at the site of the old cemetery, between what he took to be the bases of the two 'pyramids', Radford found

13 Nitze 'Exhumation', p. 360; Rahtz, *Glastonbury*, p. 44.
14 'The adjective *inclitus* is not known to have been applied to Arthur before the time of Geoffrey of Monmouth, in the earlier twelfth century' (Rahtz, *Glastonbury*, p. 46, citing Philip Morland).
15 *Arthur's Britain: History and Archaeology AD 367–634* (Harmondsworth, 1971), pp. 77–80.
16 *The Early History of Glastonbury: An Edition, Translation and Study of William of Malmesbury's De Antiquitate Glastonie Ecclesie*, ed. and trans. R. Scott (Woodbridge, 1981), pp. 84–5. The 'pyramids' — probably funerary monuments with tapering shafts — seem to have been removed in the eighteenth century (Rahtz, *Glastonbury*, pp. 33–6 and 90–1).
17 Rahtz, *Glastonbury*, p. 46.

. . . a large irregular hole, which had been dug and filled in after standing open for a very short time. At the bottom this hole had destroyed two, or perhaps three, of the slab-lined graves belonging to the earliest stratum. One of these destroyed graves was set against the wall of the mausoleum: a position likely to have been granted only to a person of importance.

The earth used to fill the hole contained chips of the same stone which was used in the facing of the Lady Chapel, a building erected immediately after the 1184 fire.[18]

It would seem, then, that digging did indeed take place in Glastonbury at the time and on the spot indicated by the medieval writers: a fact which, if true, is of cardinal importance in assessing the historicity of their accounts. It should be noted, however, that these details of time and place are the only features of the story which the 1962 excavation confirms. The hole does not appear to have been as deep as Gerald states,[19] and for that matter there is no indication that an oak-log coffin was found there: the available evidence suggests, rather, that the monks found only a few slab-lined graves of the type common in the cemetery.

This, much compressed, is where the matter now stands, with the balance of likelihood tending to discourage acceptance of the medieval descriptions at face value. My own rather prosaic contribution to the debate is a further piece of evidence on the side of scepticism: an anecdote concerning the prominent Irish monastery of Clonmacnoise.

The story in question occurs in the Liber Flavus Fergusiorum, a fifteenth-century manuscript in the Royal Irish Academy, where it forms part of a little cluster of Clonmacnoise legends. It is sufficiently brief to be quoted in its entirety:[20]

---

18 C. A. R. Radford, 'Glastonbury Abbey', in *The Quest for Arthur's Britain*, ed. G. Ashe (London, 1968), pp. 97–110 (pp. 107–8).

19 Radford's account is unfortunately not at all specific here; it may however be inferred from his warning (ibid., p. 100) that 'too much reliance cannot be placed' on Gerald's statement that the grave was a very deep one that this feature of the story was not confirmed by his own findings. The slab-lined graves in the old cemetery seem in fact to have been quite shallow, roofed with slabs at the old surface level (Rahtz, *Glastonbury*, p. 88) — i.e. now about 3½ feet underground (Radford, 'Glastonbury Abbey', pp. 107–8). Since Radford states that the late twelfth-century hole had destroyed some of these graves 'at the bottom', it seems likely that it was less than 2 metres deep.

20 'Elfenbegräbnis', ed. Kuno Meyer, *Zeitschrift für celtische Philologie* 8 (1912), 559–60.

One day [the poet] Mac Coise was on the shore of Loch Léibinn, when he saw a lone woman sitting above the lough lamenting wildly. She wore a green mantle, and had shining tresses on her head. All the beauty of the women of the world was in her form. In size she was huge and immeasurable, beyond the women of her time. 'Why are you lamenting?' said Mac Coise. 'I have reason to', said she. 'My first love and dearest lover was killed today in Síd Codail, and taken for burial to Clonmacnoise, so that he has been buried there'. Then Mac Coise bade her farewell, and went to Ruba Conaill where the king of Ireland was, that is, Congalach son of Mael Mithig; and he told him the whole story. 'Let us go to Clonmacnoise tomorrow', said Congalach, ' to see whether the story is true'. Next day Congalach and Mac Coise went to Clonmacnoise. They asked the clerics whether a man of that description had been buried among them at that time. The clerics said that no one had been buried among them within the last three months. Congalach began to contradict Mac Coise, and to make game of him. They went into Clonmacnoise that night.

They heard the bell for the dead next morning. A monk had died in the place, and was taken to be buried, so that a hole was dug for him where the Stone of the Druids is today. When they had dug some way down, they found blood and fresh birch leaves there. They marvelled greatly at that. The deeper the grave, the more blood and leaves were found. The story was told to everyone; everyone came to see, so that they were standing above the grave. Congalach said to them, 'Dig the grave for as long as you find the blood and the leaves'. The digging went deep. At the bottom they found a bundle [?; literally 'broom'] of birch, and a man in the midst of it, his face downward. That was told to Congalach and to Mac Coise and to everyone else; they went and stood above the grave. Then they lifted the body up out of the grave. He was the fairest of the men of the world in shape and form. Yellow hair upon his head. A single huge wound in his flesh. He was twenty-five feet tall. They gazed on him for a while, and then the grave was filled in over him. Everyone came next day to see him, and to determine what they should do about him. The grave was dug up again, and his body was not found there, and nothing is known of him since.

The resemblances between this account and those relating to the Glastonbury find are striking, and in my own view too detailed to be plausibly explained as mere coincidence. Here, as in Gerald's version, a king learns from a poet that a remarkable warrior lies buried in a famous monastery. As in the Cistercian version, the digging is undertaken in order to provide a grave for a monk of the community, at a spot marked by an ancient monument. Gerald, again, states that the grave was dug to a great depth, and that when found the remains were those of an extremely tall man, bearing the mark of a single fatal wound. Both at Glastonbury and at Clonmacnoise, the mode of burial is unusual. The lock of yellow hair mentioned by Gerald may perhaps be compared with the Irish story's statement that the giant corpse was blonde; and Gerald's description of the female skeleton in the coffin, and his claim that Guenevere was named on the lead cross — neither point, incidentally, confirmed by the Cistercian chroniclers — with the beautiful heartbroken giantess who tells Mac Coise of her lover's death. Even if we exclude these more distant analogies from consideration, however, the overall correspondence between the Irish and the English evidence is undeniable.

Is the English account the source of the Irish one, or vice versa? Several considerations seem to me to render it likely that the latter is the case. Let us consider the evidence which can be brought to bear in trying to get a sense of the age and background of the Irish story.

Our first *terminus post quem* is provided by the king in the anecdote, Congalach Cnogba son of Mael Mithig, who reigned between the years 944 and 956: the story as we have it cannot, therefore, conceivably be earlier than the middle of the tenth century. Any attempt to estimate the text's age on the basis of language is complicated by the fact of its occurring only in a single manuscript: it is accordingly impossible to be certain which features are original, and which are the results of later copying. I can see nothing, however, which would militate against a date in the later Middle Irish period — that is, somewhere in the eleventh or twelfth century. This leaves the anecdote's chronological relationship to the Glastonbury find unclear: it would seem likeliest that it is older, but I cannot think of any linguistic argument which would rule out its having been written in the years immediately following the discovery.

Fortunately, this is not the end of the road: there is another account of the giant buried at Clonmacnoise. The version of the treatise *De Ingantaib Érenn* ('On the Wonders of Ireland') found in the Book of Ballymote (late fourteenth century) includes the following among the 'three marvels' of that monastery:[21]

> The grave that was dug in Clonmacnoise, moreover; and no grave had been known or heard of there. And a man with a great beard was found in it, and drops of blood were on him, and the tops of fresh birch bound in bundles (?; literally 'of brooms of fastening') around him. He was fifteen feet long, and there were thirty feet of earth above him.

21 Dublin, Royal Irish Academy 23.P.12, p. 256 col. b lines 30–3: 'INt adnacul foclas i Cluain beus, ⁊ ni fess ⁊ ni closs do adnacul ann ⁊ fofrith fer morulcach índ ⁊ bræna fola derge tairis. Barrach uirbeithi do scuabaib cengail ime. Cuig traigi deg ina fod ⁊ .xxx. troiged do talmain uasu'. The tract is printed in *Leabhar Breathnach annso sis: The Irish Version of the Historia Britonum of Nennius*, ed. J. H. Todd and A. Herbert (Dublin, 1848), pp. 192–219: our passage appears on pp. 206–7.

Clearly, this is a shorter variant of the same story: can it help us in our inquiry? While a thorough study of the various collections of Irish *mirabilia* texts remains to be undertaken, even a cursory examination shows that three of them are closely interrelated: the Ballymote text of *De Ingantaib Érenn* which I have just cited; another, significantly divergent text in Trinity College MS H.3.17 (1336);[22] and Bishop Patrick of Dublin's Latin poem *De mirabilibus Hiberniae*.[23] The poem is much closer to Ballymote than it is to H.3.17. Since Patrick was drowned in the year 1084, the source shared by these three texts must be earlier than that date.

The story of the gigantic corpse found at Clonmacnoise appears in neither of the other collections: where Ballymote lists three 'wonders of Clonmacnoise', the others speak only of the first of these: a headless man named Ambacuc. We may suppose, then, that our episode is an addition on the part of that recension of *De Ingantaib Érenn* which the Book of Ballymote's copy represents. What is the time-frame within which this addition might have been made?

Twelve *mirabilia* are peculiar to the Ballymote list: an immortal couple residing near Clonard, otherwise known to us from the hagiography of Patrick;[24] the invulnerable ducks of Senboth Fola, mentioned in the glosses to *Féilire Oengusso*;[25] two wonders associated with Clonmacnoise (our own item, and a blind man able to catch eels in the Shannon); and eight marvels taken from the Clonmacnoise family of annals. The annalistic items appear, with one exception, in chronological order: six relate to events in the ninth century, the remaining two to a pair of prodigies recorded for the year 1054.[26] It seems reasonable to suggest that this group was added to the Ballymote version not too long after the date of the last of the events mentioned. If they joined the text significantly later — late enough, that is, for an oblique reflection of the Glastonbury exhumation to be included

22 The text of this version is printed piecemeal in the notes to Todd and Herbert's version of the copy in Ballymote (see preceding note).

23 *The Writings of Bishop Patrick 1074–1084*, ed. and trans. Aubrey Gwynn (Dublin, 1955), pp. 56–71.

24 *Bethu Phátraic*, ed. Kathleen Mulchrone (Dublin, 1939), lines 1379–80; *The Tripartite Life of Patrick, with Other Documents Relating to that Saint*, ed. and trans. Whitley Stokes (London, 1887), 2 vols, II,478.

25 *Féilire Óengusso Céli Dé*, ed. and trans. Whitley Stokes (London, 1905), p. 228.

26 The Annals of Ulster (AU), *Chronicon Scotorum* (CS), Annals of the Four Masters (AFM), and Annals of Clonmacnoise (Clon.) give the following dates for items in the Ballymote list: (xv) AU 804, AFM 799, Clon. 801; (xvii) CS 850, AFM 847; (xviii) AU 866, CS 866, AFM 864; (xix) AU 878, CS 878, AFM 875, Clon. 863; (xx) AU 885, CS 885, AFM 882, Clon. 870; (xxvii) CS 1052, AFM 1054; (xxviii) CS 849, AFM 847; (xxx) AU 1054, CS 1052, AFM 1054. Items xxvii and xxx are assigned to the same year in the 'Annals of Tigernach'.

among them — then it would be odd to find no mention made in Ballymote of the two mermaids captured in 1118;[27] or of the unearthing of the skull of Eochaid mac Luchta, 'the size of a large caldron', in 1157.[28]

Of course, it is not necessarily the case that the story of the corpse at Clonmacnoise joined the text tradition at the same time as the items from the annals — although, inasmuch as it appears that the annals in question were in fact being compiled at Clonmacnoise in the eleventh century, the temptation to make such an association is a strong one.[29] We do, however, have another clue to the date of the Ballymote recension as a whole. The copy of De Ingantaib Érenn in the Book of Ballymote is one of three consecutive texts said in that manuscript to derive from the Book of Glendalough. In an influential article published in 1981, Pádraig Ó Riain argued that this manuscript can be identified as Rawlinson MS B 502 in the Bodleian Library, a codex written c. 1130.[30] If this identification is correct, then the story of the body found at Clonmacnoise must obviously be considerably older than the alleged exhumation of Arthur at Glastonbury; and in fact Professor Ó Riain's arguments have found general acceptance in the years since they were first advanced. Just last year, however, Caoimhín Breatnach has challenged this consensus: his own discussion has only recently appeared in published form, and it is too early to tell how it will be assessed by the scholarly community as a whole.[31] While it does not seem to me that Dr Breatnach's objections dispose of the most telling points in Ó Riain's case, I must acknowledge that I have not personally examined the various texts around which the debate revolves: it seems best to acknowledge that the question of the Book of Glendalough's date is again, at least for the present, an open one.

The annalistic borrowings peculiar to the Ballymote version of De Ingantaib Érenn suggest that it may have received its additional material between the years 1054 and 1118; if Ó Riain's identification of the Book of Glendalough is correct, then the Book of Ballymote's source for this text was a manuscript written c. 1130. Both of these considerations would seem to indicate that the story of the dead giant already existed in Ireland some generations before the Glastonbury exhuma-

27 *Sub anno* 1118 in the Annals of Ulster and the Annals of the Four Masters.
28 *Sub anno* 1157 in the Annals of the Four Masters and the Annals of Clonmacnoise; cf. *The Annals of Tigernach*, ed. and trans. Whitley Stokes (Felinfach, 1993), 2 vols, II,397.
29 Gearóid Mac Niocaill, *The Medieval Irish Annals* (Dublin, 1975), pp. 22–3.
30 Pádraig Ó Riain, 'The Book of Glendalough or Rawlinson B 502', *Éigse* 18 (1981), 161–76; our text is mentioned on p. 171.
31 'Rawlinson B 502, Lebar Glinne Dá Locha and Saltair na Rann', *Éigse* 30 (1997), 109–32.

tion; but we cannot be certain of either of them. The case for such a view can be strengthened, however, by taking another look at the version of the story in Liber Flavus Fergusiorum.

What gives this version particular importance is the circumstance that it is far closer than the one in the Book of Ballymote to the Glastonbury accounts. In Ballymote, the only parallels are that a giant corpse is found deep in the earth, in a spot on the grounds of a monastery where no grave was known to exist. It is the Liber Flavus which tells us that the king heard of the burial from a poet, that the body was found when a grave was being dug for a monk, that a monument stands at the spot, that the body bore the mark of a single deadly wound. We may posit one of two scenarios: either the Liber Flavus version was based on some account of the Glastonbury find, and itself served as a source for the Ballymote *De Ingantaib Érenn*; or the *mirabilia* item is the most primitive version, the Liber Flavus anecdote was based upon it, and the Glastonbury stories derive from the latter. For various reasons, I believe that we are obliged to choose the second of these options.

First: certain features in the Liber Flavus story seem to echo *other* items in the exemplar shared by the three *mirabilia* lists. Thus all three lists include an anecdote which tells of the sighting of a ship in the air at an assembly convened by none other than Congalach Cnogba;[32] and another anecdote in which the protagonist is his poet Mac Coise. Here is the Book of Ballymote's version of the latter:[33]

> One day Mac Coise was on the brink of the Boyne, when he saw a flock of swans, and cast a stone at them. It went through the wing of one of them. He ran to catch it then, and saw that it was a woman. And he asked tidings of her: what had happened to her, and whence she had come. She said that she had been sick, and that it had seemed to her household that she had died, but that it was demons who had carried her off. And he restored her to her household.

Many intriguing parallels to this little story could be adduced. Its relevance to us, however, is that it resembles the opening of the Liber Flavus anecdote in portraying Mac Coise's encounter, beside a body of water, with a supernatural woman in distress. It appears that whoever put the Liber Flavus version of the story together drew in the course of doing so upon several of the items in the Ballymote

---

32 I discuss this story in 'Aerial Ships and Underwater Monasteries: the Evolution of a Monastic Marvel', *Proceedings of the Harvard Celtic Colloquium* 12 (1995), 16–28.

33 Dublin, Royal Irish Academy MS 23.P.12, p. 256, col. b, lines 39–45. Cf. *Leabhar Breathnach*, pp. 208–11 (with the text of the H.3.17 version in n. y); and *Writings of Bishop Patrick*, pp. 64–5.

version of *De Ingantaib Érenn*. It may be worth noting in this connection that the story of Congalach and the air-ship, and the story of Mac Coise and the swan-woman, are grouped together in H.3.17 and in Patrick's poem (though not, curiously, in Ballymote).

We need not look far to find another instance of conflation of just this kind. In an article published a few years ago, I argued that the story of Congalach and the air-ship, as it appears in *De Ingantaib Érenn*, was combined with a legend about Saint Brigit to produce a new version of the air-ship tale, this one relocated to Clonmacnoise. Further evidence that the Brigit story had entered the orbit of Irish *mirabilia* and come to be associated with Clonmacnoise is to be found, precisely, in the Book of Ballymote version of *De Ingantaib Érenn*.[34]

Granted that the path of its transmission was more or less as I have suggested, can we ascertain the ultimate source of the story of the giant corpse? Not with any certainty, I suspect; but there is the intriguing chance that it may reflect — at whatever remove — the details of an actual chance find. Throughout the Germanic countries bodies have been found lying face downward, covered with birch twigs or wattles, or pegged down with birch stakes: a reference to a similar custom in Tacitus's *Germania* suggests that it was malefactors who were interred in this fashion.[35] Did such burials also take place in Ireland at some point, and did one of these — preserved perhaps by favourable soil conditions — come to light in the early Middle Ages? Or did the story come from farther afield? We can only remain agnostic, while acknowledging the possibility that — however news of the discovery of such a burial might have reached Clonmacnoise — the legend may have a factual basis.

I would like to mention one further piece of Irish evidence. As we have seen, the Glastonbury and Clonmacnoise stories share a remarkable number of details, for which I can suggest no parallels elsewhere: this is, of course, my reason for proposing that there is a direct connection between them. On the other hand, the Clonmacnoise anecdote does also exhibit some similarities to the curious tale *Tochmarc Becfhola*, the oldest version of which appears to date from the tenth century. Becfhola, wife of the king of Tara — herself, as it transpires, originally a denizen of the Otherworld — becomes enamoured of an Otherworld hero with whom she spends the night on an unknown island. A year later, monks from the island monastery of Devenish bring to her husband the king the ornaments found on the corpses of this warrior's brothers and cousins, who have just slain one

---

34 Carey, 'Aerial Ships', pp. 22–3.
35 P. V. Glob, *The Bog People*, trans. R. Bruce-Mitford (London, 1969), pp. 104–5 and 148–53.
    I am grateful to Jonathan Wooding for this reference.

another there. There are many fundamental differences between the stories; but both involve the romance of an Otherworld couple, together with the king of Tara's involvement in the discovery, at a major monastery, of the bodies of splendid Otherworld warriors killed in battle.[36] This, the closest analogue which I have been able to find for our two excavation accounts, is older than either, and is set in Ireland: further confirmation, I would suggest, of the views already proposed.

Remarkably, we find still more evidence to this effect in Glastonbury itself, where an account of another exhumation some centuries later recalls the Clonmacnoise story in ways to which the story of Arthur's grave provides no parallel. The abbot Nicholas Frome, describing an excavation carried out in 1419 in search of the remains of Joseph of Arimathea, wrote of the discovery of coffins 'at a depth of about 17 feet'. Near the skull of one of the corpses was 'an abundance of grains of green and scented herbs with their seeds', near the head of another 'a great abundance of fluid, which appeared as fresh blood to those present in that place both by its colour and substance'.[37] This looks very much like an echo of the 'blood and fresh birch leaves' said to have been found at Clonmacnoise: it seems that a version of the Clonmacnoise story was preserved at Glastonbury throughout the Middle Ages, and that the monks made use of it on more than one occasion as an aid to their own none-too-scrupulous imaginations.

In the article mentioned above, I discussed the migration to England of another Clonmacnoise wonder: the same aerial ship which *De Ingantaib Érenn* associates with Congalach Cnogba. As it happens, the relevant evidence again clusters around the close of the twelfth century: a French chronicle written in 1184 states that an air-ship appeared over London in 1122; and Gervase of Tilbury, an Englishman writing in Germany *c.* 1211, describes a similar incident happening somewhere in Britain.[38] If one Clonmacnoise *mirabilia* anecdote can be shown to have travelled to England by the later twelfth century, and a tale closely resembling another appears in England at the same time, it seems reasonable to suppose that the process of transmission has been the same.

In the present case, the hypothesis that Irish legendary material was transferred to Glastonbury fits in well with what we know of the monastery's history: its Irish connections are already mentioned in *Sanas Cormaic*, a glossary whose compiler

36 'A New Edition of *Tochmarc Becfhola*', ed. and trans. Máire Bhreathnach, *Ériu* 35 (1984), 59–91, especially pp. 76, 80–1.

37 Rahtz, *Glastonbury*, p. 89.

38 Carey, 'Aerial Ships', pp. 19–20 and 24.

died in 908;[39] and by the early tenth century the monastery was advancing its audacious claim to possess the relics of Saint Patrick. Dunstan's earliest biographer, who derived much of his information from men who had known the saint personally, speaks of Irish monks visiting Glastonbury and instructing the community there in his hero's youth.[40]

If, as I see every reason to believe, the bulk of the Glastonbury story was deliberately modelled on an anecdote imported from Ireland, it is difficult to feel much confidence in the find itself — especially as the monks had already discovered another prestigious grave, that of Saint Dunstan, under highly suspicious circumstances just a few years earlier.[41] The account offers us a wealth of tantalising and in a few instances persuasive detail;[42] as a whole, however, it must be assigned to legend rather than to history. It seems ironic that whoever engineered the find, seeking to undermine the belief that Arthur's body had been, in Gerald's words, 'borne far off by spirits, and not subjected to death',[43] should have modelled his account upon a tale of the vanishing corpse of a warrior of the Otherworld.[44]

39 This evidence seems to have been overlooked by L. Abrams, 'St Patrick and Glastonbury Abbey: *Nihil ex Nihilo Fit?*', in D. N. Dumville et al., *Saint Patrick A.D. 493–1993* (Woodbridge, 1993), pp. 233–42. It is acknowledged rather dismissively by Michael Lapidge, 'The Cult of St Indract at Glastonbury', in *Ireland in Early Mediaeval Europe*, ed. Dorothy Whitelock et al. (Cambridge, 1982), pp. 179–212 (p. 183 n. 24). His objection that 'it is far from certain that *Glassdimbir* is identical with Glastonbury' is hypersceptical; and the observation that it is called 'of the Gaels' only in some manuscripts is scarcely a telling one, inasmuch as the passage in question is an enumeration of sites in Britain occupied by the Irish.

40 Lapidge 'Cult of St Indract', pp. 182–3; Abrams, 'St Patrick', *passim*.

41 Gransden, 'Growth of the Glastonbury Traditions', pp. 347–8.

42 I am thinking here specifically of the coffin made of a hollowed oak, which cannot be accounted for on the basis of the Irish parallel. Jonathan Wooding informs me that burials of this type are known to have been made in Britain in the first millennium A.D.; examples were found in the Northumbrian cemetery at Whithorn in 1987. Despite the lack of archaeological evidence at the site, it is perhaps not impossible that such a coffin was indeed found at Glastonbury.

43 *Giraldi Cambrensis Opera*, ed. Brewer et al., VIII,126; Chambers, *Arthur of Britain*, p. 269.

44 I am grateful to Jonathan Wooding for many indispensable references, and for discussion of the archaeological dimension of the question considered in this paper; also to those who attended the presentation of an oral version at the Centre for Advanced Welsh and Celtic Studies, Aberystwyth, on 7 May 1998.

Britons in Ireland, *c.* 550–800

T. M. Charles-Edwards

JESUS COLLEGE, OXFORD

PROINSIAS MAC CANA, through his scholarship and his teaching, has been an interpreter of the Irish to the Welsh and of the Welsh to the Irish. This paper, on Britons in Ireland in the post-conversion and pre-Viking period, is offered in gratitude to a teacher of Irish among the Britons and of Welsh among the Irish.[1] My concern, however, is not with the most important contribution of Britons to Irish history — their role in the conversion of the Irish to Christianity — but with evidence for the continued presence of Britons in Ireland after the period of conversion. Nor shall I discuss that other major area of interaction between Irish and Britons, the Irish settlements in Britain. Dál Riata is a more difficult case, since, though a settlement in Britain, it seems not to have been a settlement in British territory;[2] moreover, the part of Dál Riata in Britain, approximately the modern Argyll, was colonial land long attached to its Irish mother-kingdom in the north-east of Antrim.[3] Unlike the Irish settlements further south, it remained Irish-speaking and would eventually construct a new Scotland, a

---

1 I am very grateful to the editors for suggested improvements.
2 I assume that the peoples of western Scotland north of the Clyde basin did not perceive themselves as Britons, though, equally, they may not have considered themselves Picts, since the latter, a confederation of peoples created after the establishment of the Roman frontier in Scotland, were based mainly in eastern Scotland.
3 J. Bannerman, *Studies in the History of Dalriada* (Edinburgh, 1974), 7, suggests that the Scottish and Irish sections of Dál Riata 'began to go their separate ways' after the battle of Mag Roth in 637, but the evidence is unclear.

new 'Irish-land', overseas. The creation of Scotland was accomplished, however, in the Viking period, and it thus lies outside my remit. Finally, I shall limit myself largely to the ecclesiastical presence of Britons in Ireland, thus neglecting such issues as the use of British mercenaries or the attacks of Britons on Ulster.[4]

Two developments brought to an end the period of British leadership in the conversion of the Irish. The first was the end of British authority over the Irish Church, probably exercised by a synod.[5] Patrick's *Confessio* indicates that his mission, predominantly in the west of the island, remained under ultimate British supervision: his conduct as bishop and even his worthiness to be a bishop were subject to scrutiny and judgement by *seniores* — by which he probably meant the members of a synod — in Britain.[6] Later evidence and contemporary continental parallels suggest that, at the period of conversion, it was assumed that the tier of authority above a bishop was constituted by a synod, headed by a metropolitan bishop, and that the normal synod exercised its authority within a province.[7] So far as it goes, the British evidence cites only the synod, while that from Frankish Gaul stresses rather the metropolitan;[8] but both corresponded to the layer of late-Roman government represented by the province rather than the diocese, by 'Britannia Prima' rather than Britain as a whole. It is unlikely, therefore, that all Britain was subject to a normal synod; perhaps the British missionaries in Ireland were subject to one British synod, but this is a matter of guesswork.[9] What is evident is that, probably towards the end of Patrick's mission — a phase that

---

4 Mercenaries: AU 709. 2. Conflict between Britons and Ulstermen: AU 682. 2, 703. 1 (but apparently allies in 697. 10). Britons in conflict with the Uí Néill of Brega: AU 702. 2.

5 On synods see D. N. Dumville, *Councils and Synods of the Gaelic Early and Central Middle Ages*, Quiggin Pamphlets on the Sources of Mediaeval Gaelic History, 3 (Cambridge, 1997).

6 Patrick, *Confessio*, cc. 26–9, 32; E. Malaspina, *Patrizio e l'acculturazione latina dell'Irlanda* (Rome, 1984), 133–5.

7 Council of Nicaea, c. 5; Hilary of Poitiers, *Liber de synodis*, is addressed, among others, to 'the bishops of the British provinces'; *Statuta Ecclesiae Antiqua*, c. 9 (ed. C. Munier, *Concilia Galliae, A. 314 – A. 506*, CCSL 148 [Turnhout, 1963], 167); Council of Agde, cc. 3, 35, 49 (ed. Munier, *Concilia*, 193–4, 208, 212); the British synods ('The Synod of North Britain', 'The Synod of the Grove of Victory') in L. Bieler, *The Irish Penitentials* (Dublin, 1963), 66–9; *Collectio Canonum Hibernensis*, Bk. xx, De provincia (ed. H. Wasserschleben, *Die irische Kanonensammlung*, 2nd edn., Leipzig, 1885), 60–3).

8 Gregory of Tours, *Hist*, ix. 20, the legates of Childebert II (Including Gregory himself) argue against the idea of holding a national council: 'Sed iuxta consuetudinem canonum placebat gloriosissimo nepoti vestro, ut unusquisque metropolis cum provincialibus suis coniungeret'; cf. Council of Orléans, AD 533, cc. 1–2, 7 (ed. C. de Clercq, *Concilia Galliae, A. 511 – A. 695*, CCSL 148A [Turnhout, 1963], 99–100).

9 The name of the western province of Britain appears to have been Britannia Prima: P. Salway, *Roman Britain* (Oxford, 1981), Map VII.

itself may be dated to the late fifth century — Irish Christianity remained under British tutelage.[10] The end of this relationship is likely to have come approximately between 490 and 550, since the Irish Church remembered by Columbanus, that is, the Irish Church of the decades before 590, appears to have progressed well beyond the stage of dependence.[11]

Apart from the end of the formal authority of a British synod or synods in Ireland, the other major reduction in British influence will have been slower: the decrease in the numbers of British clergy working in Ireland. This will have occurred naturally as Irish clergy and nuns, already attested in Patrick's writings, took the places of British missionaries. It is, however, the contention of this paper that the reduction in numbers of Britons in Ireland was not merely slow but incomplete.

The last major British figure in sixth-century Ireland may have been the principal teacher of Columba. This remains uncertain, partly because of the difficulty in deciding whether the Findbarr/Finnio/Uinniau who taught Columba was the Finnian who founded Movilla (Mag mBili) in Co. Down or his namesake who founded Clonard in Co. Meath, or even some combination of the two. Finnian of Movilla was described as a bishop in his obit in 579;[12] Finnian of Clonard is not known to have been a bishop and his obit is s.a. 549 (or 551).[13] Unless an unnecessary emendation is made to the text of Adomnán's Life of Columba, Columba's teacher was still alive at the beginning of the 560s;[14] moreover, Adomnán describes him as a bishop.[15] The ascription of Finnian of Movilla in the annals to Dál Fiatach (approximately east Co. Down) appears to be a later addition;[16] evidence to the same effect in the genealogies is rendered suspect because it allies Findbarr with the clerical family of the church of Saul, which seems to have been especially active in claiming other churches' saints for itself.[17]

---

10 In favour of a date for Patrick late in the fifth century, see, for example, the evidence assembled by D. N. Dumville, *St Patrick, A.D. 493–1993* (Woodbridge, 1993), esp. 51–7.

11 Columbanus, *Ep.* v (ed. and trans. G. S. M. Walker, *Sancti Columbani Opera* [Dublin, 1957], 38–9).

12 AU 579. 1 (also AT, CS).

13 AU 549; the equivalent to AU 551 in AT and CS.

14 T. M. Charles-Edwards, 'The New Edition of Adomnán's *Life of Columba*', CMCS, 26 (Winter 1993), 71.

15 Adomnán, *Vita S. Columbae*, i. 1; ii. 1.

16 In using the Latin phrase *filius nepotis* the annalist was thinking of the later interpretation of *maccu/moccu* as *macc uí*.

17 *CGH* i. 411 (LL 330 a 10); *CGSH* §§ 115.2 (alternative pedigree for Breccán mac Sáráin); 136. 2 (the seven sons of Trichem); 184 (Da Beóc of Glenn Gerg/Derg, now Lough Derg, Co. Donegal, was his descendant); 185 (Samthand of Cluain Brónaig was his descendant).

Professor Ó Riain has gone further and has argued that the Finnian of Clonard was really the same person as Finnian of Movilla.[18] According to him, the existence of two separate local cults of one and the same saint was likely to stimulate a dispute as to which church had the body of the saint.[19] If both were unwilling to give way, this dispute might easily lead to the emergence of two separate *personae* for the saint, with attendant feastdays and genealogies. Whether or not this argument is accepted, it remains probable that Columba's teacher was the saint of Movilla. There is also a reasonable chance that this Finnian was the 'Vennianus auctor' who corresponded with Gildas, whose own obit is given in the annals as 570, nine years before that of Finnian of Movilla.[20] Columbanus, who is our source for this information, had been a monk of Bangor until he left for the continent *c.*591; Bangor is only a few miles from Movilla. For the same reason, Columbanus's use of the Penitential of Vinnian is easier to explain if that Vinnian was the patron-saint of Movilla.[21] Finally, Finnian of Movilla later had a high reputation as a scholar, consonant with a role as the teacher of Columba.[22]

The late Léon Fleuriot assembled some impressive evidence that Vinnian (Finnian) was a Briton, although, for him, the saint in question was the patron of Clonard.[23] His claim, however, has been disputed by Ó Riain partly on linguistic grounds.[24] Ó Riain points out that the British symptoms appear in the pet-forms, whereas Adomnán's full form, Findbarr is purely Irish. Yet the pet-forms are derived from the full-form rather than the other way around. Moreover, the pet-names so widely used in the Irish and British Churches in the sixth century were influenced by British (unsurprisingly, given the general influence of British Christi-

---

18 P. Ó Riain, 'St Finnbarr: A Study in a Cult', *Journal of the Cork Archaeological and Historical Society*, 82 (1977), 63–82.

19 Compare Muirchú, *Vita S. Patricii*, ii. 13 (ed. and transl. L. Bieler, *Patrician Texts in the Book of Armagh*, 120–1).

20 Columbanus, *Ep.* i. 7 (ed. and trans. Walker, 8–9).

21 Although it must be admitted that Columbanus, who was a native of Leinster, may have had some personal knowledge of Clonard, which lay on the boundary between Leinster and Mide.

22 e.g. *Fél.*[2] 10 Sept., Ó Riain, 'St Finnbarr: A Study in a Cult', 78.

23 L. Fleuriot, 'Le "saint" breton *Winniau* et le pénitentiel dit "de Finnian" ', *Études Celtiques*, 15 (1976–8), 607–14. On arguments for Movilla and for Clonard, see D. N. Dumville, 'Gildas and Uinniau', in M. Lapidge and D. N. Dumville (eds.), *Gildas: New Approaches* (Woodbridge, 1984), 207–14.

24 P. Ó Riain, 'Finnian or Winniau?', in P. Ní Chatháin and M. Richter (eds.), *Irland und Europa: Die Kirche im Frühmittelalter* (Stuttgart, 1984), 52–7; idem, 'Finnio and Winniau: A Question of Priority', in R. Bielmeier and R. Stempel (eds.), *Indogermanica et Caucasica: Festschrift für Karl Horst Schmidt* (Berlin, 1994), 407–14, replying to D. N. Dumville, 'Gildas and Uinniau', 207–14.

anity in Ireland at that period, as shown in the Latin loan-words). It would, therefore, be entirely possible for an Irish saint to be given a partially British pet-name. For Ó Riain, therefore, the crucial indicator of the ethnic background of a person was his full name rather than his pet-name(s). On this principle, a saint known as Findbarr or Uinniau or Finnio should have been Irish. The difficulty of this argument is that a British counterpart to Findbarr existed (VENDVBARI, *CIIC* 368 = *ECMW* 150, an inscription of which Professor Ó Riain is well aware). In the sixth century the British form would have required little change to make it purely Irish (approximately **Winnvarr* to **Windvarr* with a shift of the stress from the final syllable to the penultimate). Ó Riain also argues that it was only in Irish that we can see both the full forms and pet-forms for Findbarr being used at the same time for the same person. But this is perhaps to undervalue the more general evidence posed by the British influence on Irish ecclesiastical pet-names: it is hard to see how this influence could have occurred if the formation of pet-names from full names was not a living process in British (as in Eliudd: Teilo). Ó Riain's linguistic argument is thus not as conclusive as it may seem. Elsewhere in this volume, however, he has made a highly attractive suggestion to reconcile the opposed symptoms of Britishness and of Irishness in the saint's dossier.[25] Since the Irish had long been settled in western Britain by the time of Findbarr, there is every possibility that Findbarr was from Britain but of Irish descent.

Between the arrival of Palladius in 431 and the death of Uinniau in 579, many individual churches will have been founded by Britons, such as Louth by Maucteus (Mauchte, Mochta).[26] The way early Irish law dealt with the succession to headship of a church excluded the possibility that aliens would have family interests in a church, unless the alien in question was the *érlam*, the patron-saint (often, but not always, the founder).[27] Even, however, when a founding patron-saint was a Briton, any continuance of his family's interest was unlikely to persist, given their probable geographical remoteness from the site. Moreover, stories could be framed to exclude them, as may have happened at Trim, where the British founder-saint, Lommán, was said to have made Fedelmid of the local royal dynasty, Cenél Lóegairi, his heir and thus the ancestor of an ecclesiastical as well

25 Below, 185ff.

26 R. Sharpe, 'Saint Mauchteus, *discipulus Patricii*', in A. Bammersberger and A. Wollmann (eds.), *Britain 400–600: Language and History* (Heidelberg, 1990), 85–93.

27 T. M. Charles-Edwards, '*Érlam*: The Patron-Saint of an Irish Church', in R. Sharpe and A. Thacker (eds.), *Local Saints* (forthcoming).

as a lay lineage.[28] Moreover, not all churches were in the possession of any lineage: examples are Clonfertmulloe and Clonmacnois.[29] In such cases, also, no claim by the kindred of the *érlam* would arise, since all claims stemming from kinship had been excluded, theoretically by the will of the founder.

These considerations suggest that two questions need to be put. First, there is the issue whether any churches founded by Britons continued to have British connections. Secondly, there is the converse question, whether any churches founded by Irishmen nevertheless contained British monks or had connections with British churches.

Two churches that remained distinctively British were 'the Durrow of the Britons' in southern Brega,[30] and Gallen, Gailinne na mBretan, 'Gallen of the Britons' (or 'the Gallen of the Britons' if there was another Gailinne).[31] Gallen bore this name when, in 823, it was burnt by Fedelmid mac Cremthainn, king of Munster, on one of his harrying raids into Mide.[32] It lay a few miles east of Clonmacnois, in the same frontier kingdom of Delbnae Bethra, and thus exposed to attack like several other major Mide churches lying on or close to the frontier with Munster. The patron-saint appears to have been Mo Chonóc.[33] He was later identified with St Cynog, the principal saintly offspring of Brychan of Brycheiniog.[34] The site of the church is marked by an early cross and gravestones.[35] The designation of the church as being 'of the Britons' is evidence for an enduring British element. One may compare, on the one hand, a church such as

28 *Patrician Texts in the Book of Armagh*, ed. and transl. L. Bieler (Dublin, 1979), 166–71.
29 *Vita I S. Lugidi*, c. 30 (ed. W. W. Heist, *Vitae Sanctorum Hiberniae* [Brussels, 1965], 137), J. Ryan, 'The Abbatial Succession at Clonmacnois: From the Foundation of the Monastery to the Coming of the Norse', in J. Ryan (ed.), *Féilsgribhinn Eóin Mhic Néill* (Dublin, 1940), 490–507.
30 AU 836. 7 (to be distinguished from Columba's Durrow and from Dairmag Ua nDuach).
31 Grid ref.: N 11 23, townland and parish of Gallen, barony of Garrycastle, Co. Offaly.
32 AU 823. 9.
33 19 Dec., *MG, MD*.
34 *CGSH* § 722. 89 (= Bartrum, *Early Welsh Genealogical Tracts*, 32–3): *CGSH* § 722. 89 shows that he was then thought to be the saint both of Gallen and of Cell Muccraissi (perhaps Kilmuckridge, tl. and par., Co. Wexford: Hogan, *Onom.*); § 169 refers only to Cell Muccraissi; § 706. 626 is of Mo Chonóc Gailinne, distinguished, perhaps wrongly, from Mo Chonóc ailithir, § 707. 628. He is included among the forty saints in Glendalough in the Litany of Irish Saints I, ed. C. Plummer, *Irish Litanies* (London, 1925), 56; this may be because his supposed brother, Mo Goróc, was the saint of Deirgne / Delgne (Delgany, Co. Wicklow, close to Glendalough). On this text, see A. S. Mac Shamhráin, *Church and Polity in Pre–Norman Ireland: The Case of Glendalough*, Maynooth Monographs 7 (Maynooth, 1996), 174–9.
35 Lord Killanin and M. V. Duignan, *The Shell Guide to Ireland*, 2nd edn. (London, 1967), 277.

Tuilén (Dulane), founded by the Briton Cairnech.[36] The British origins of Cairnech were not forgotten, but that did not mean that Tuilén was called 'Tuilén of the Britons'.[37] On the other hand, we may compare Mayo, Mag nÉo na Saxan, where the phrase 'of the English' described continuing English membership of the community and continued English connections;[38] the founder, in this case, had been an Irishman, Colmán, formerly bishop of the Northumbrians.[39] The same continued English connections are known to have been true of Tulach Léis na Saxan,[40] and may have been true of Tech Saxan (Tisaxan), two miles west of Kinsale, since an annotator of the *Félire Óengusso* thought it a plausible place to situate Ichtbricht (Wihtberht).[41] The formation of the name Tech Saxan, Tisaxan, is exactly paralleled by Tech mBretan (Tibradden townland, parish of Cruagh, Co. Dublin; compare Tibradden Mountain at O 14 22) mentioned in the *Martyrology of Tallaght* as the church of Da Loe or Do Loe.[42] A further point of comparison is the prominent midland churchman, Colmán of the Britons, that is, 'the British Colmán', the founder of a major clerical dynasty at Slane.[43] His name, Colmán, may have been given him when he entered a clerical life and is consistent with his having had British descent, but the name of his father, Fáelán, suggests that he is unlikely himself to have come from Britain.

Although the British character of Tech mBretan is only attested by the name — nothing is known of Do Loe — its situation is significant in two ways. By the late eighth century it was on the edge of the small kingdom of Uí Chellaig Cualann, ruled by the descendants of Cellach Cualann (ob. 715), the last king of

---

36 Grid ref.: N 73 78.

37 *Fél.*[2] Notes, 16 May. Cf. the reference to Dulane in the *Vita Prima Carantoci*, c. 6, ed. and transl. A. W. Wade–Evans, *Vitae Sanctorum Britanniae et Genealogiae* (Cardiff, 1944), 146–7.

38 Grid ref.: M 26 79; cf. the obit of Garald, AU 732; Alcuin, *Epp.* 2, 3, 287, ed. E. Dümmler, *Epistolae Karolini Aevi*, ii, MGH Epp. iv (Berlin, 1895).

39 Bede, *HE* iv. 4.

40 Tullylease, townland and parish, Co. Cork, R 34 18; I. Henderson and E. Okasha, 'The Early Christian Inscribed and Carved Stones of Tullylease, Co. Cork', *CMCS* 24 (Winter 1992), 1–36.

41 Tisaxan townland, barony of Kinsale, Co. Cork; the old graveyard is W 610 507; *Fél.*[2] Notes, 8 Dec.

42 *MT* 7 Jan.

43 Obit: AU 751. 9; he is a party to a complex set of exchanges recorded in a document in the Book of Armagh, *Additamenta*, 11 (ed. and transl. Bieler, *The Patrician Texts in the Book of Armagh*, 174–5); on his family, see K. Hughes, *The Church in Early Irish Society* (London, 1966), 163; compare Virgno Brit, 'Virgno, a Briton', with Colmán na mBretan, 'the British Colmán' (as opposed to the many other Colmáns).

Leinster to come from the Uí Máil / Uí Théig.[44] Uí Chellaig Cualann, together with the kingdoms of the Uí Théig and Uí Máil, were isolated fragments of what had, in the seventh century, been one of the major powers of the province, before the Uí Dúnlainge consolidated their grip on northern Leinster in the decade after Cellach Cualann's death. Tech mBretan was in a doubly unfavourable position, on the mountainous edge of a declining kingdom; it was probably recorded in the Martyrology of Tallaght only because the two churches were so close. The situation of Tech mBretan is also significant, however, simply because it was in Leinster and thus in the southern half of Ireland, which had conformed to the Roman Easter in the 630s. While some Britons, probably those of Strathclyde, conformed c. 690, the Welsh of Dyfed remained adherents of the Celtic Easter when Aldhelm wrote to the king of Dumnonia, Geraint, c. 672–5, and those of Gwynedd did not conform until 768.[45] Moreover in the second half of the seventh century many in the Roman party believed that their opponents were not merely wrong but heretical.[46] As a consequence, the Roman party in Ireland was inclined to look upon Britons with deep suspicion.[47] The paschal controversy, therefore, could have had the power to cause a rupture between the Britons and the southern half of Ireland. Such a development would have left Dairmag na mBretan and Gailinne na mBretan untouched, since they lay within the lands of the southern Uí Néill and thus in the northern half of Ireland. Again, although a major monastery such as Taghmon, whose founder probably belonged to northwest Ireland, may have withstood the authority of Leinster synods for a time, it is very unlikely that a minor church could have done the same.[48] Tech mBretan might have been founded in the period between the conversion of the Britons to the Roman Easter and the composition of the Martyrology of Tallaght, but this is made less likely by the form of the patron-saint's name, Do Lue. Personal names of this type are occasionally found in the late eighth and early ninth century, but

44 His British links are discussed by Mac Shamhráin, *Church and Polity in Pre-Norman Ireland*, 67–8.

45 Bede, *HE* v. 15; Aldhelm, *Ep.* 4 (ed. R. Ehwald, *Aldhelmi Opera*, MGH AA 15 (Berlin, 1919), 480–6; transl. M. Lapidge and M. Herren, *Aldhelm: The Prose Works* (Ipswich, 1979), 155–60; for the date, see 140–3); AC s.a. 768.

46 This harsh standpoint appears with the letter of the pope-elect John in Bede, *HE* ii. 19; Theodore, Penitential, I. v. 3–5, II. ix. 1–3 (ed. P. W. Finsterwalder, *Die Canones Theodori Cantuariensis und ihrer Überlieferungsformen* [Weimar, 1929], 295, 323–4); Stephen, *Vita S. Wilfridi*, cc. 12, 14, 15 (ed. and transl. B. Colgrave, *The Life of Bishop Wilfrid by Eddius Stephanus* [Cambridge, 1927], 24–7, 30–3).

47 *Collectio Canonum Hibernensis*, xx. 6, ed. H. Wasserschleben, 2nd edn. (Leipzig, 1885), 61–2.

48 Cf. *Vita I S. Fintani seu Munnu*, cc. 29–30, ed. W. W. Heist, *Vitae Sanctorum Hiberniae ex codice olim Salmanticensi nunc Bruxellensi* (Brussels, 1965), 207–8.

they appear to be isolated revivals of an ancient mode of naming.[49] On the assumption, therefore, that Tech mBretan was an early foundation, its situation offers evidence that links between the Britons and the southern half of Ireland were not broken by the paschal controversy.

A comparable church was Tech na mBretan in the *termonn* of Kells, very possibly, but not certainly, founded after the foundation of Kells itself (alternatively, it might have beeen an older church made into a satellite of Kells).[50] The name with the definite article, Tech na mBretan, may be explained on the grounds that, since there was more than one church within the *termonn* of Kells, this one was identified as the house of the Britons as opposed to other houses inhabited by Irish (or others), the Britons being one group within the wider community attached to Kells and Tech na mBretan being their sole house. Tech mBretan, on the other hand, was not within an obvious cluster of churches belonging to one *familia* and so could be sufficiently distinguished by being called 'British House' without so direct an implied contrast with other nationalities or any implication that there were no other British houses within Leinster.

As well as those churches that continued to be recognized as British, there were also Irish foundations that attracted British monks. It is well known that Iona had a British element because Adomnán records a story according to which the first monk to die on Iona was a Briton.[51] Moreover the fourth abbot, Virgno, is likely himself to have been a Briton.[52] A British participation in other Hebridean churches is attested by the Oan (Owain), abbot of Eigg, who died in 725.[53]

The same phenomenon can also be observed in Ireland. The Litany of Pilgrim Saints includes 'fifty Britons accompanying the son of Moínán in Land Léiri'.[54] The Martyrology of Tallaght, under 21 October, commemorates 'Fintan, that is, the son of Tulchán, together with his monks who were under his yoke, 233 of them, whom the fire of Judgement will not burn, whose names are as follows'. The list that follows, probably derived from Tech Munnu, Taghmon, contains

---

49 Examples are in AU 763, 771, 838.
50 *Fél.*[2] Notes, 26 Oct.
51 Adomnán, *Vita S. Columbae*, iii. 6.
52 *MT, Fél.*[2] 2 March; M. Herbert, *Iona, Kells, and Derry* (Oxford, 1988), 39–40; his pedigree is not included among the group of genealogies of abbots of Iona belonging to Cenél Conaill, probably of eighth-century date, later slightly expanded, in *CGSH* §§ 336–48 (see Herbert, *Iona, Kells, and Derry*, 36–7, for this collection).
53 AU.
54 *Irish Litanies*, ed. C. Plummer, HBS 62 (London, 1925), p. 66: *Coica fer de Bretnaib la mac Móinain i lLaind Léri.*

223 names, of which between 15 and 20% may be non-Irish.[55] It is difficult to be exact because the names are preserved in only one twelfth-century manuscript, and many of them will have been transmitted *via* the Martyrology of Tallaght from the seventh century. The compiler of the Martyrology evidently took the list to be of monks who were under the personal authority of Fintan (Munnu) himself in the early seventh century. It is, however, possible that names of later monks were attached to the list. The following are those most likely to be British (they are all given in the genitive, '(the day) of X':

Rioli: compare RIALOBRANI, *CIIC* 468 (Madron, Cornwall), Rioual, *The Text of the Book of Llan Dâv*, ed. J. Gwenogvryn Evans and J. Rhŷs (Oxford, 1893), 178.

Conani: 2 exx.: probably the later Welsh Cynan, Breton Conan.[56]

Rioci: 2 exx.: perhaps Riōc < *Rīgākos*; cf. Rióc of Inchboffin, Lough Ree, *VT*² 897; Riothamus etc., *LHEB* §§ 79, 82.

Gurdoci: Cf. *Book of Llan Dâv*, 158, 183, 215, 228; W. *gwrdd*, perhaps from Lat. *gurdus*, but the latter is said by Quintilian, *Instit. Orat.* 1, 5, 57 to be a borrowing into Latin from Spain, and therefore possibly Celtic.

Uali: compare CVNOVALI, *CIIC* no. 468.

Eboci: perhaps for Ebroci rather than *eb-* 'horse' (as in *ebol*, *ebran* etc.)

Gurgaile: the second element is inflected as an Irish *ā*-stem (*gal*, *gaile*); it may therefore be a half-Gaelicized British Gurgal; for the latter, see *Book of Llan Dâv*, 167.

Condoci: this may be for Conōc (later Cynawc, Cynog) with *Con-* assimilated to Irish *cond*.

Cantani: compare CANTIORI, *CIIC* no. 394 = *ECMW* no. 103;

<hr>

55 The principal church of Munnu was Tech Munnu, Taghmon in Co. Wexford, T 92 19, for which see M. J. Moore, *Archaeological Inventory of Co. Wexford* (Dublin, 1996), no. 1468, but there was also a Taughmon in Co. Westmeath at N 46 60.

56 D. McManus, *A Guide to Ogam* (Maynooth, 1991), 63, § 4. 13, regards Ir. Conán (cf. CONANN, *CIIC*, no. 74) as the equivalent of W. Cynin (CVNIGNI), but Conán is not attested in *CGH*; the only examples of Conán in *CGSH* are two in the list of *sacerdotes*, § 705. 93, 248; there are none among the names of persons other than saints, which contain fewer foreign items. Welsh Cynan and Breton Conan, however, are very common. The person commemorated in *CIIC* no. 74 may also be British.

and the tribal name Cantii, Cantiaci.

Eloci: cf. Eloc, *Book of Llan Dâv*, 163, 202, Eluc, 205, Elioc, 178, 182;
          the first element may be the *El-* found in Eliud (Eliudd,
          Teilo).

Iunerti: perhaps for Iudnerti (Old Welsh Iudnerth, later Idnerth, with
          Irish loss of *d* before *n*).

Some of these names could well belong to the lifetime of Munnu (ob. 635), although the evidence of the suffix *-ōc* is perhaps not conclusive since it may have become conventional to use this old spelling in forms with Latin terminations.[57] On the other hand, there is evidence that the names are not all of the same date. If Gurgaile is correctly explained as containing the equivalent of the later Welsh *gwr* 'man' (Gurgal: Ir. Fergal), initial *w-* had already developed to *gw-*.[58] Since, however, the name *Uali* retains the initial *w-*, the form Gurgaile may be evidence that monks of a generation later than that of Munnu were included in the list.[59] Since the better-known Tech Munnu, Taghmon, was in Co. Wexford, just across St George's Channel from Dyfed, which itself was ruled by an Irish dynasty at this period, a long-term British participation in the community would not be surprising.

The assumption behind this argument is that the Irish kept to their own names and did not adopt those of their neighbours. Any acquaintance with the genealogies and the annals will show that, by and large, this assumption is true. An exception, however, is the dynasty of Cenél nGabráin (of Dál Riata) in the generations immediately after Áedán mac Gabráin (ob. 606). As is well known, Áedán called one of his sons Artúir (Arturius);[60] another example is the Rígullon son of Conaing of AU (and AT) 629 said to have been one of 'the grandsons of Áedán'. Rígullon has rightly been interpreted as a borrowing from the Cumbrian form of the name that gave Middle Welsh Rhiwallawn.[61] These appearances of British names in an Irish royal

---

57 According to *LHEB* § 11, *ō* > *aw* occurred in the eighth century; cf. P. Sims-Williams, 'The Emergence of Old Welsh, Cornish and Breton Orthography: The Evidence of Archaic Old Welsh', *BBCS* 38 (1991), 63–71.

58 According to *LHEB* § 49, this occurred in Welsh at the latest by the late eighth century, but probably earlier. P. Sims-Williams, 'The Emergence of Old Welsh, Cornish and Breton Orthography', 71–2, uses the name *Uebrersel* as evidence that *u-* survived into the seventh century.

59 The name Uindici may be an early form of Ir. Findech. Irish *w-* > *f-* may have occurred *c.*600, in which case this, if it derived from St Munnu's time, would be a somewhat conservative spelling.

60 Adomnán, *Vita S. Columbae*, i. 9; cf. Artúr in the AT version of AU 625. 6, the obit of Mongán mac Fíachnai.

61 *LHEB* 393 n.

kindred are, however, quite exceptional; they suggest that Áedán had a policy of alliance with the Britons of Strathclyde, an alliance which may lie behind the battle of Degsastan, but which broke down in the years of crisis for Dál Riata after the battle of Mag Roth in 637.[62] The few later examples of Artúir in Ireland are likely to be imitating the son of Áedán mac Gabráin.[63]

There were, therefore, British monks in Irish foundations from at least Eigg in the north to Taghmon in the south, while there were distinctively British communities in both the northern and southern halves of Ireland. All these links will have served to maintain the strong ecclesiastical connections across the Irish Sea created in the fifth and sixth centuries. They were not broken by the paschal controversy, by the fading of the Irish presence in Wales, or indeed by the Vikings. As later British saints' lives attest, notably those of Cybi, Cadog and David, they endured into another era.

62 Bede, *HE* i. 34. Cf. AU 642. 1.
63 Mac Shamhráin, *Church and Polity in Pre-Norman Ireland*, 67–8.

Onomaris: Name of Story and History?

D. Ellis Evans

JESUS COLLEGE, OXFORD

T HE enticing study of proper names, not least for antiquity, is full of perils, but can also be remarkably rewarding. In this discussion my purpose is, on the one hand, to draw attention to one comparatively early personal name with a, perforce, brief discussion of its perplexing form and noteworthiness and, on the other hand, to consider how it reflects the peculiar status of names of this kind in its special context. This name is attested only once, occurring in a remarkable Classical Greek text recently edited and highlighted anew. It occurs nowhere else. Its Celticity is far from certain, but its context can be confidently claimed as 'Celtic' or 'Galatian', despite the mounting and quite often irrational hesitation displayed by a number of scholars nowadays (especially in Britain) over the use of old labels such as these. Finally and all too briefly, due consideration will be given to the character of the source and the entry in which the name occurs.

The name Ὀνόμαρις occurs in a brief anonymous Greek text known by a Latin title as *Tractatus De Mulieribus Claris in Bello* (henceforth *DM*), consisting of a series of short notices naming and describing the accomplishments of fourteen women from the broadly Near Eastern world, some well known, others more or less obscure. These notices are based on accounts to be found in the works of authors of the fifth and sixth centuries BC in the main (the source for the Onomaris entry is unknown and is likely to be later). The text has been published four times, by Heeren in 1789,[1] by Westermann in 1839,[2] by Landi in 1895,[3] and by Gera in 1997 in an important monograph devoted entirely to detailed analysis of the text.[4]

My main purpose in this brief contribution is to discuss the name Onomaris itself, indicating its particular status as a proper name, and to consider its remarkably interesting context. That context suggests at once that Onomaris had a powerful connection or function which undoubtedly has to be regarded as Celtic or Galatian.[5]

I quote first the relevant part of the eclectic Greek text as presented by Gera, followed by her English translation:

1   A. H. L. Heeren, 'Tractatus Anonymi de Mulieribus quae Bello claruerunt', *Bibliotheek der alten Litteratur und Kunst*, 6 (1789), 3–24.

2   In A. Westermann, ΠΑΡΑΔΟΞΟΓΡΑΦΟΙ: *Scriptores Rerum Mirabilium Graeci* (Brunswick and London, 1839) [repr. Amsterdam, 1963], 218.

3   C. Landi, 'Opusculus de fontibus mirabilibus, de Nilo etc. ex Cod. Laur. 56.1 descripta', *Studi italiani di filologia classica*, 3 (1895), 531–48.

4   Deborah Gera, *Warrior Women. The Anonymous Tractatus de Mulieribus* [*Mnemosyne*: Bibliotheca Classica Batava, Supplementum 162] (Leiden – New York – Köln, 1997). Gera's work should be consulted for fuller information on a number of aspects of the significance and interpretation of the text overall. I am grateful to Dr Jane Lightfoot, All Souls College, Oxford, for stimulating my interest in this text and in the name *Onomaris* in particular, and for kindly drawing my attention to the new edition by Gera.

5   I am well aware of the difficulties connected with these terms and know that these difficulties are often exaggerated and misrepresented. I have discussed some relevant aspects in my 'Celticity, Celtic Awareness and Celtic Studies', *Zeitschrift für celtische Philologie*, 49–50 (1997–8), 1–27, and 'Linguistics and Celtic Ethnogenesis', *Proceedings of the Tenth International Congress of Celtic Studies*, vol. I (in press). For a new and clearly well considered approach to the analysis of Celticity in antiquity see the 1994 University of Oxford D.Phil. dissertation by Jonathan Creer Williams of the British Museum, entitled 'Rome and the Celts of Northern Italy in the Republic', an important historical and historiographical examination of its theme. I am grateful to Dr Williams for the opportunity to read his stimulating and enlightening paper on 'Celtic Ethnicity in Northern Italy — Problems Ancient and Modern' (now published in *Gender and Ethnicity in Ancient Italy*, ed. Tim Cornell and Kathryn Lomas [Specialist Studies on Italy, 6] (London: Accordia Research Inst., University of London, 1997), 69–81). Relevant also is the truly caring and sensitive book by the social anthropologist Sharon Macdonald (now at Sheffield University), entitled *Reimagining Culture: Histories, Identities and the Gaelic Renaissance*, which I have, through the author's kindness, had the opportunity to read in typescript (now published, Oxford/New York: Berg, 1997). Writings on the Celts and on Celticity and Celticism, greatly varying in quality, are growing apace.

Ὀνόμαρις μία τῶν ἐν ἀξιώματι Γαλατῶν, καταπονουμένον ὑπ'
ἀφορίας τῶν ὁμοφύλον καὶ ζητούντων φυγεῖν ἐκ τῆς
χώρας. παραδιδόντον δὲ αὐτοὺς ἐν ὑποταγῇ τῷ θέλοντι
ἀφηγεῖσθαι, μηδενὸς τῶν ἀνδρῶν θέλοντος τήν τε οὐσίαν
πᾶσαν εἰς μέσον ἔθηκε καὶ τῆς ἀποικίας ἀφηγήσατο, πολλῶν
ὄντων ὡς εἰς . . . διαβᾶσά τε τὸν Ἴστρον καὶ τοὺς ἐπιχωρίους
μάχῃ νικήσασα τῆς χώρας ἐβασίλευσεν.

Onomaris, one of the distinguished Galatians. Her fellow tribesemen were
oppressed by scarcity and sought to flee their land. They offered to obey whoever
wanted to lead them, and when none of the men was willing, Onomaris placed
all their property in common and led the emigration, with many people,
approximately . . . She crossed the Ister and, after defeating the local inhabitants
in battle, ruled over the land.[6]

She is described, then, as μία τῶν ἐν ἀξιώματι Γαλατῶν, one of the Galatians
who was an honoured person or a person of high repute or rank or position. Her
figure is the most elusive in the list of fourteen women's names in *DM*. As with
Rhodogyne, no other person is named in the notice concerning her. She is
depicted as a leader of the people of her own race or kin. There is a suggestion
in the text that the people wished to flee their land because they were worn out or
wearied or oppressed by scarcity or barrenness or sterility.[7] After placing all their
property in common she led many (the number is unspecified or lost) in an
emigration or flight, crossed the river Ister (the Middle or Lower Danube?),
defeated the local inhabitants in battle and ruled over the land. We cannot
determine what her exact status would have been.

This tantalisingly brief account, found in this source only, has attracted
remarkably little attention. It is not the prime purpose of this note to try to
interpret its historical significance, even if indeed we were inclined to justify an

6 See Gera, op. cit., 5–11 (the Onomaris text and translation are given on pp. 10–11). Gera is
  the first scholar to produce a full translation of the entire text of *DM*. For a French
  rendering of the Onomaris section see Dottin, *Revue des Études Anciennes* 8 (1906), 123.
  Variant readings in the manuscript sources are slight and, in general, insignificant. The
  lacuna after 'ὡς εἰς . . .' is a problem. Landi (op. cit., 544) claims that there is space for
  five or six letters in that lacuna. Gera has drawn attention to a number of interesting points
  with regard to the Onomaris section. She points out that Onomaris is chronologically the
  latest woman found in the text, that it is the last of the fourteen sections in the text, and
  that it may indeed be incomplete so that the lack of a source quotation for it may indicate
  that a part may have been lost (possibly in the lacuna) and that this section may at one time
  not have been the final one in the original (see Gera, op. cit., 29, 30, 219–20).
7 The rendering of the Greek is, I think, less certain here than Gera's version suggests. The
  exact nature of the people's distress is not clear. See further below.

interpretation of it as essentially historical.[8] However, I do want to refer to some
earlier consideration of it. It first attracted attention in Celtic scholarly writing, as
far as I can make out, in a short note entitled 'Le passage du Danube par les
Galates' by Georges Dottin in 1906,[9] accompanied by a brief comment by the then
towering scholar Camille Jullian.[10] Dottin surmised that the source for the passage
might be Timaeus. He declared that the name Onomaris was not Celtic and
suggested that it might reflect the influence of a Greek formation such as
Ὀνόμαρχος. But he added 'On peut toutefois reconnaître dans le second terme
le mot celtique bien connu -*mara* "grande", un peu défiguré'. Jullian related the
Onomaris text to the Scordisci, 'le peuple celte établi autour de Belgrade, dans la
région des grands confluents danubiens'. He toys with the idea that the source
may have been Posidonius or Phlegon, declares that the name Onomaris may be
Celtic and that the Galatian ruler bearing the name may be 'simplement la
transformation en femme de quelque fétiche, de quelque virago mythique du
peuple, ou même, plutôt. de sa grande déesse, la Victoire ou la Bellone des
Scordisques'.[11] There is no reference to the name Onomaris in Alfred Holder's
copious *Altceltischer Sprachschatz* (Leipzig, 1891–1913) or K. H. Schmidt's 'Die
Komposition in gallischen Personennomen' (*ZCP* 26 (1957) or indeed my own
Gaulish Personal Names (*GPN*; Oxford, 1967).[12]

8   Not a great deal can be added to Gera's concise and generally reliable comments (especially
    pp. 219 ff.). However, we can now include a reference to the important 1994 University of
    Vienna doctoral dissertation by Kurt Tomaschitz, entitled 'Die Wanderungen der Kelten in
    der antiken literarischen Uberlieferung' (maschinschrift.), soon to be published as a
    monograph (giving the Greek text after Westermann, with commentary, pp. 102–05 — I am
    particularly grateful to Dr Tomaschitz for generously according me the privilege of a xerox
    copy of his work; this was made possible through the good offices and kindness of
    Professor Helmut Birkhan, through whose rich and wide–ranging work on *Die Kelten.
    Versuch einer Gesamtdarstellung ihrer Kultur* (Wien, 1997) I first became aware of
    Tomaschitz's work).
9   See *Revue des Études Anciennes*, 8 (1906), 123.
10 See *Revue des Études Anciennes*, 8 (1906), 124.
11 See also Jullian, 'Les conquêts gauloises en Europe', in his *Histoire de la Gaule*, 4 Vol. I
    (Paris, 1920), 281–332, especially 283, 285 with n. 2. Gera (op. cit., 223) is rightly inclined to
    reject the view that Onomaris was viewed in *DM* as a priestess or goddess because this
    would run counter to what we know of the other thirteen women included in the text. See
    also Tomaschitz, op. cit., p. 103.
12 It is not surprising that it is not mentioned in surveys of Celto-Galatian names of Asia
    Minor, in the work of Leo Weisgerber ('Galatische Sprachreste', in *Natalicium Johannes
    Geffcken* (Heidelberg, 1931), 151–75), Wolfgang Dressler, 'Galatisches' in *Beiträge zur
    Indogermanistik und Keltologie*, hrsg. Wolfgang Meid (Innsbruck, 1967), 147–54), O. Masson
    ('Quelques noms celtiques en Grece et en Asie Mineure', *EC*, 19 (1982), 129–35), and
    Stephen Mitchell (*Anatolia. Land Men, and Gods in Asia Minor*. Vol. I: *The Celts and the*

I see no way in which one could *confidently* claim the formation of the name as Celtic or even quasi-Celtic or some other more or less exotic type. However, we do need to take account of both its notional (and uncertain) location and possible comparable formations or elements, Celtic and non-Celtic, in both proper names and other designations.

I have mentioned already that the learned and perceptive Camille Jullian was quick at the outset to assign Onomaris to the well-attested Scordisci[13] (commonly regarded as Celtic or Celto-Thracian) in a central Balkan area roughly corresponding to the region in which ancient Singidunum (in the vicinity of modern Belgrade) was situated. Much has been written on the partly Celtic and in general complex and shadowy linguistic evidence in antiquity, especially the evidence of fragmentary languages, in the Balkans.[14] This in general is an area for which scholars dally with a number of 'Restsprachen' or 'Trümmersprachen',[15] for which

---

Impact of Roman Rule (Oxford, 1993), 50–51, 173–5). I should add that L. Zgusta's renowned *Kleinasiatischer Personennamen* (Prague, 1964) has not revealed comparable forms.

13 For classical literary sources on the Scordisci see Holder, op. cit., ii. 1399–1405 (see also the following note).

14 See Radoslav Katičić, 'Zur Frage der keltischen und pannonischen Namengebiete im römischen Dalmatien', *GABiH*, 3 (1965), 53–76; id., 'Keltska Osobna imena u antickoj Slovenij', *Arheoloski Vestnik*, 17 (1966), 145–68; id., op. cit., 6 (1968), 61–120 (cf. Hamp, *Acta Neophilologica*, 9 (1976), 3–8); id., op cit., xi (1978), 57–63; id., *Ancient Languages of the Balkans*, Parts 1 and 2 [Trends in Linguistics. State of the Art Reports, ed. W. Winter, vol. 4] (The Hague/Paris, 1976 (on the pre-Greek evidence and what Katičić terms 'The Thracian complex' and 'The Illyrian complex'); id., 'Die Balkan Provinzen', in *Die Sprachen im römischen Reich der Kaiserzeit. Kolloquium vom 8. bis 10. April 1974* [Beihefte der Bonner Jahrbucher, Bd. 40] (Köln / Bonn, 1980), 103–20; G. Alföldy, 'Les territoires occupés par les Scordisques', *Acta Antiqua Academiae Scientiarum Hungaricae*, 12 (1964), 107–27; id., *Die Personennamen in der römischen Provinz Dalmatien* (Heidelberg, 1969); F. Papazoglu, *Srednjobalkanska Plemena u Predrimsko Doba* (Sarajevo, 1969) [for the section on the Scordisci see pp. 209–98, with resumé in French pp. 402 f. — for an English version see id., *The Central Balkan Tribes in Preroman Times* (Amsterdam, 1978), 271 ff.]; the author, 'The Labyrinth of Continental Celtic', *Proceedings of the British Academy*, 65 (1979), 497–538 (especially 520–23 on the difficulties in Central European and Danubian regions). See further Josef Bujma and Miklós Szabó, 'The Carpathian Basin', in *The Celts* (Milan: Bompiani, 1991), 277–84; Borislav Jovanović, 'The Scordisci', op. cit., 337–46; Miklós Szabó, 'The Celts and their movements in the third century B.C.', op. cit., 303–19; id., *Les Celtes de l'Est. Le seconde âge du fer dans la cuvette des Karpates* (Paris, 1992) [dealing with the Scordisci in the second century B.C. on pp. 47–56]. For a good summary see Miklós Szabó, 'Le monde celtique au IIIe siècle av. J.-C. Rapport sur les recherches récentes', *Études celtiques*, 28 (1991), 11–31.

15 For these terms see especially Jürgen Untermann, 'Zu den Begriffen, Restsprache und Trümmersprache', in *Germanische Rest- und Trümmersprachen* hrsg. v. Heinrich Beck [Ergänzungsbände zum Reallexikon der Germanischen Altertumskunde, hrsg. v. Heinrich

labels such as Illyrian, Thracian, Dacian, and Scythian (not to mention other more vague and probably more unsatisfactory terms) are adopted.[16] Jullian's linking of Onomaris with the Scordisci is, on the face of it, reasonable and attractive, but is bound to be *more* than a little uncertain. Nevertheless, it is noteworthy and not surprising that his suggestion has been accepted by other scholars. W. W. Tarn seems to have taken this for granted.[17] Tomaschitz links the Onomaris account with the expansive and relatively early phase of Celtic intrusion into Eastern Europe and comments 'Hier könnte man mit Jullian an die keltischen Skordisker denken, die an der unteren Save bis zur Donau hin siedelten'.[18] Birkhan hesitantly echoes the view expressed by Tomaschitz and, like him, tends to regard the name Onomaris as apparently non-Celtic.[19]

There is little or nothing to be gained from indulging in inconclusive etymological games here in an effort to determine whether the name can reasonably be counted Celtic.[20] I refer to only a few formations or elements which may be relevant. The name may be dithematic *Ono-maris*. The elements *maro-* [maːro-] 'great' and *mori-* 'sea' are well attested in Old Celtic names.[21] However, we know that a number of forms in *maro-*, *mari-*, *-maros*, *-mara*, *maris*, etc. have been claimed, for example, as Thracian.[22] But here too there are difficulties, partly because of the apparent equivalence or correspondence of some forms claimed as Thracian or Celtic (or even Thraco-Celtic) items and features, as Vladimir Orel[23] and Rolf Ködderitzsch[24] have shown.

It may be that a fair case could be made out for the Celticity of *ono-* in a form such as Onomaris, although this too does present problems. I mention for

---

Beck, et al., Band 3] (Berlin / New York, 1989), 15–19.

16 See my comments in *Proceedings of the British Academy*, loc. cit. Note 14 above draws attention to some of the extensive and ever growing literature on this area. On the use of the term 'Galatian', especially for the Celts in eastern Europe and Asia Minor, see G. Nachtergael, *Les Galates en Grèce et les Sôteria de Delphes* (Bruxelles, 1977).

17 See W. W. Tarn, *Antigonos Gonatas* (Oxford, 1913), 142.

18 See Tomaschitz, op. cit., 104 f. For a recent survey of opinion on Celtic expansion to Eastern Europe see Helmut Birkhan, *Kelten* (Wien 1997), 130–48.

19 See Birkhan, op. cit., 337, 1024.

20 Dr Lightfoot quite rightly commented to me that 'more research on onomatology here is likely to lead to a series of frustrating "non liquets"'.

21 See, for example, the author, *GPN* 223 ff., 233 f.

22 D. Detschew, *Die thrakischen Sprachreste* (Wien, 1957), 288, 289.

23 Orel, 'Thracian and Celtic', *BBCS*, 34 (1987), 1–9.

24 Ködderitzsch, 'Keltisch und Thrakisch', *Akten des ersten Symposiums deutschsprachiger Keltologen (Gosen bei Berlin, 8.–10. April 1992)*, hrsg. v. Martin Rockel und Stefan Zimmer (Tübingen, 1993), 139–57 (arguing for the prehistoric contact of Celtic and Thracian and Dacian).

possible comparison the Gaulish personal name Ουνα (or Ουνακουι) attested in a Cavaillon Gallo-Greek inscription.[25] There are some other forms which may be Celtic and remotely relevant here: (1) *onna-* or *onnum* from the Ravenna Cosmography and the Notitia Dignitatum;[26] (2) Gaulish *onno* 'flumen' and possibly *on(n)a* 'stream, water' (both problematic);[27] (3) *onobiia* of uncertain meaning, in a graffito of Banassac;[28] (4) the perplexing *onodieni* of Marcellus of Bordeaux.[29] More importantly perhaps, it should be noted that there is a goodly sprinkling of other *on(n)-* forms in 'Celtic' areas, especially in Gaul, but also in Spain.[30]

It *is* idle speculation to try to perceive both the origin and, worse, the etymological 'meaning' of this particular proper name. I cannot see that it is helpful to wrest a 'meaning' for it from any of the potentially significant Celtic forms I have mentioned above. The grammatical primacy and nuclearity of names really make them too special for that kind of obsessive attention.[31] On the other hand, Dr. Carey has rightly declared to me that it does not seem 'self-evident that

25 See Michel Lejeune, *Recueil des inscriptions gauloises*, vol. I, *Textes gallo-grecs* (Paris, 1985), 159–62 (especially 161 f.); the author, *Gaulish Personal Names* (Oxford, 1967) [hereafter *GPN*], 370–1.

26 For some recent views see A. L. F. Rivet and Colin Smith, *The Place-Names of Roman Britain* (London, 1979), 431–3.

27 For some references see the author, op. cit., 371

28 Léon Fleuriot (*EC*, 14/2 (1975), 444–7) interpreted it as 'vifs liquides' or 'liquides de vie' (even perhaps 'eaux de vie'), whereas P.-Y. Lambert (*La langue gauloise*, Paris, 1994), 140) interpreted it as meaning 'coupe-soif' (a compound of **pono-* 'fatigue, soif' and an agent derivative of **bhei-H-* 'couper').

29 See most recently Wolfgang Meid, *Heilpflänzen und Heilsprüche. Zeugnisse gallischer Sprache bei Marcellus von Bordeaux* (Innsbruck, 1996), 58–9.

30 For some of these see Holder, op. cit., ii.854–59; the author, op. cit., 371; María Lourdes Albertos Firmat, *La Onomástica Primitiva de Hispania Tarraconense y Bética* (Salamanca, 1966), 173 (with correction, *Emerita*, 45/1 (1977), 37); Helmut Birkhan, *Germanen und Kelten bis zum Ausgang der Römerzeit* (Wien, 1970), 156 n. 191. To the Insular Celtic forms referred to in *GPN*, loc. cit., reference should be made also to the conceivably relevant Irish forms *on* 'blemish, disfigurement' (also the less certain *on* (?*ón*) 'idiot', *ond* (*onn*) 'stone, rock', and *onn* 'pine-tree, furze-bush, or ash' (also the name used for the letter *o* in Ogham)). See, for example, *RIAContr.*, *N-O-P*, 143 ff., *LEIA*, O–22 ff. Dr. John Carey has kindly reminded me that, in Celtic as in other languages, names variously connected with words meaning 'repulsiveness' or 'ugliness' or the like are not uncommon

31 I have dealt briefly (displaying my altogether strong conviction) with this topic in a paper entitled 'Some Remarks on the Study of Old Celtic Proper Names', in *Indogermanica et Caucasica. Festschrift für Karl Horst Schmidt zum 65. Geburtstag*, hrsg. v. Roland Bielmeier und Reinhard Stempel (Berlin/New York, 1994), 306–15, and in another on 'Rex Icenorum Prasutagus', in *Ir sult sprechen willekomen: grenzenlose. Mediävistik; Festschrift für Helmut Birkhan*, hrsg. v. Christa Tuczay et al. (Bern, 1998), 99–106.

speculation regarding the etymology of the name of a legendary figure is *a priori* chimerical. If a character's name has been invented to match his/her role or traits, then the legend or cult itself can potentially give us valuable clues — even if we knew much less Irish, Latin, and Greek than we do, the stories about them would surely be a great aid in arriving at the etymologies of the names of the Dagda, Jupiter, and Demeter.' [32] As a quite minor postscript I should add that I have noted how Peter Berresford Ellis recently and, maybe, dangerously toyed with the name on which this paper focuses and was tempted to put forward the suggestion[33] that it may mean 'like a great mountain-ash or rowan tree'.[34] Gera prudently resisted the contextual temptation to relate the name to the senses 'great' and 'river', although her dalliance with that perception is *no* more shaky than several others that could be put forward.

I have highlighted this name and the brief narrative which accompanies it for two reasons. The Galatian or Celto-Thracian connections are its prime relevance for me, as a focus for a contribution to a volume in honour of a distinguished Celtic scholar. It holds a special interest, firstly, because it is a notable example of the peculiarly strong *referential* role and significance of a proper name in communication. Secondly, the specific context in which this unique name occurs has a particular attraction because the notice pertaining to the name can, maybe should, be understood and interpreted in more than one way, enhancing its interest and significance.

John Lyons opened a section on 'naming' in his detailed study of semantics[35] with the remarkable and telling (though perhaps not, on reflection, all that original) statement that 'As far back as we can trace the history of linguistic speculation, the basic semantic function of words has been seen as that of naming'. He goes on to elaborate on the referential and vocative functions of names, their assignment and associations, their special denotative qualities and

32 I quote from his helpful letter to me dated 24 April 1998.
33 See his *Celt and Greek: Celts in the Hellenic World* (London, 1997), 64.
34 This relates to the etymology of Welsh *onn(en)* 'ash tree(s) or ash wood', Old Irish *(h)uinnius,,* etc. (see J. Pokorny, *Indogermanisches etymologisches Wörterbuch*, Bd. I (Bern, 1949–59), 782). On trees and woodland in early Irish economy and especially the veneration of trees and the cult of sacred groves in Celtic tradition overall see now Fergus Kelly, *Early Irish Farming* [Early Irish Law Series, vol. IV] (Dublin, 1997), 279–90. See also Marged Haycock, 'The Significance of the "Cad Goddau" Tree-list in the Book of Taliesin', in *Celtic Linguistics/Ieithyddiaeth Geltaidd, Festschrift for T. Arwyn Watkins*, ed. Martin J. Ball *et al.* (Amsterdam/Philadelphia, 1990), 297–331; Bernhard Maier, *Lexikon der keltischen Religion und Kultur* (Stuttgart, 1994), 248 f., s.v. *nemeton* (with references); James MacKillop, *Dictionary of Celtic Mythology* (Oxford, 1998), s.vv. 'ash', 'rowan', 'tree', etc.
35 John Lyons, *Semantics*, Vol. I (Cambridge, 1977), 215–23.

sense-relations. In the Onomaris text the origin of the given name is unknown and the person named is otherwise unknown to us. In a paper entitled 'Proper Names and Intentionality', first published in 1982, John R. Searle[36] considers the question 'How do proper names work?'. There he recognizes in particular the merit of Gottlob Frege's emphasis on the 'intentional content of a name in virtue of which it refers' and considers different sorts of cases of intentional reference involving proper names. In the case of our test-case (the Onomaris text) there is little point in wondering whether the 'author' of the entry naming her in *DM* (or the source author or authors) would have had personal contact with Onomaris. It is perhaps more than likely that the acquaintance was indirect, dependent on other people's prior usage of the name, so that the occurrence of it in *DM* is, in Searle's special terminology, 'parasitic'. Indeed the name may even have been coined or imagined for the entry, although a view taken of *DM* overall might induce us to come to a different conclusion. We cannot tell at this remove. Onomaris has a special connotation (in the non-philosophical sense) because of its clear association with an account, uniquely and briefly preserved in *DM*, of a woman's courage and initiative in leading her troubled 'Galatian' people, considerably more than two thousand years ago, to a new territory across the river Danube. It has been rightly pointed out that this depiction of her in *DM* is consonant with what we know from other classical sources with regard to the independence and warlike quality of other Celtic women in more or less early Celtic tradition.[37] This view of women has been linked with various well documented and well considered perceptions of Celtic matriarchy or 'Mutterrecht' and of the status and recognition of women in Celtic lands.[38]

36 In his volume *Intentionality. An Essay in the Philosophy of Mind* (Cambridge, 1983), 231–61 (reprinted in *The Philosophy of Language*, second edition, ed. A. P. Martinich (Oxford/New York, 1990), 330–46). There is a somewhat contentious but stimulating and *very* extensive literature on the philosophical, logico-semantic, and pragmatic aspects of 'Namenforschung'. I use that term in contra-distinction to the study of the grammar of names and the, at worst, superficial and, at best, inconsequential para-linguistic discipline of onomastics. I single out for mention here only three significant discussions: John McDowell, 'On the Sense and Reference of a Proper Name' *Mind*, 86 (1977), 159–85 (reprinted in *Meaning and Reference*, ed. A. W. Moore (Oxford, 1993), 111–36); Gareth Evans, *The Varieties of Reference*, ed. John McDowell (Oxford, 1982), Chapter 11 on 'Proper Names'; Ariel Shisha-Halevy, *The Proper Name: Structural Prolegomena to its Syntax — a Case Study of Coptic* [Beihefte zur Wiener Zeitschrift für die Kunde des Morgenlandes, Band 15] (Wien, 1989), especially the preliminary section (pp. 1–43), preceding his pilot study of proper-name grammar in Coptic.
37 See, *inter alios*, H. D. Rankin, *Celts and the Classical World* (London, 1987), 245–58; Gera, op. cit., 221–2 (with references).
38 See, for example, Helmut Birkhan, *Germanen und Kelten bis zum Ausgang der Römerzeit* (Wien, 1970), 487–557; id., *Kelten: Versuch einer Gesamtdarstellung ihrer Kultur* (Wien,

Gera has claimed that *DM* is a sub-literary text of fourteen brief notices, each following a fixed pattern 'typical of catalogue writing' and suggested that it was 'probably compiled at the very earliest at the end of the second century or the beginning of the first century BC'.[39] She has drawn attention to the fact that it 'can be viewed in several ways — as an assemblage of brief biographical anecdotes, a collection telling of unusual figures, a series of *exempla* or παραδείγματα, . . . a collection of stratagems, or a catalogue of women' and sums up with the rightly hesitant view that '*DM* may have been compiled for curiosity's sake, as part of a rhetorical exercise or argument, to point to historical precedents to powerful Hellenistic queens, to buttress a philosophical position on women's capabilities, or simply by a learned woman'.[40]

We here, finally, need to consider how the Onomaris entry itself is to be interpreted. The account is so brief, for all its telling phrases, that we are left wondering what really lies behind it other than the depiction of the heroism, the courage, the independence, the initiative, and the interest in power and possibly political sovereignty of Onomaris herself.[41] Finding a precise and secure historical context for it is, I fear, impossible. No hint is given in the text with regard to a date for the intrepid action taken by Onomaris. The only proper name other than that of Onomaris herself in the text is that of the river Ister or Istros (i.e. the Danube). We cannot tell whether the reference to the river is introduced as a marker of a border between an established Celtic territory and a non-Celtic one, another territory sought for by the troubled people led by Onomaris. The Hellenic aura and the Greek language of *DM* overall *may* point to an eastern Celtic thrust or intrusion on the Lower Danube. The dating has to be uncertain, but is likely to be the fourth or (early?) third century B.C.[42] Did Onomaris seek a refuge or a new opportunity elsewhere across the Danube in order to join other (possibly more northerly)[43] Celtic people, following a lack of vision and leadership and an unspecified distress among her own people? We cannot really tell what kind of deprivation or suffering is indicated by the term ἀφορία in the text. It most

---

1997), 1022–36.

39 Gera, op. cit., 26–7, 30.

40 Op. cit., 32, 61.

41 Kurt Tomaschitz (op. cit., 102–05) presents a full and careful attempt at assessing its significance. However, the frustration occasioned by its terseness has troubled him too. Gera (op.cit., pp. 11 ff.) has discussed carefully the depiction of the women of *DM* overall, stressing that 'the collection as a whole points to the power of women' and claims that it 'is in essence a statement on gender roles'.

42 See Gera, op. cit., 219.

43 See Tomaschitz, op. cit., 104.

probably refers to a lack of adequate resources.[44] What *is* certain is that the entry is included in *DM* as an account of a heroic deed successfully performed by a courageous Galatian woman. Does it reflect a historical event? Tomaschitz, following Jullian's early lead, is inclined to interpret it as an account of a credible and acceptable historical development in a central Danubian, a central Balkan, region which we can equate with that in which the Celto-Thracian Scordisci held sway.

On the other hand, I am inclined to think that this account, for all its terseness and unadorned directness, is to some extent akin in tone to what we associate with the old tradition of heroic storytelling in the world of the Celts. It could be related to some old heroic motifs, now lost, from a quite early Celtic oral tradition. I recall here that Professor Mac Cana, in a typically well considered paper on the heroic ethos of the Celts,[45] concluded with the suggestion that 'There are elements in the Celtic commentaries of Posidonius and other classical authors which smack of heroic storytelling rather than of anthropological observation, and one suspects from some of the classical accounts of the Celtic migrations . . . that some of them had already become the stuff of heroic story'. I suspect that the Onomaris account closing the anonymous Γυναῖκες ἐν πολεμικοῖς συνεταὶ καὶ ανδρεῖαι' (to quote the succinct and significant Greek title of *DM*) had drawn more than a little upon material which had become 'the stuff of heroic story'.

At the same time we know that scholars commonly and properly seek to perceive the historical background of heroic tales.[46] To be sensitive to such a perception does not diminish the importance, above all, of also properly valuing and appraising stories as artistic and imaginative creations or constructions. They can, for sure, be quite special and exciting windows on life, both contemporary life and life in the past.

---

44 See Gera, loc. cit.
45 See Proinsias Mac Cana, 'Celtic Heroic Tradition', in *The Celts* (Milan: Bompiani, 1991), 649–56.
46 It is well known, for example, how study of the heroic tales of early Ireland, especially *Táin Bó Cúailnge*, has often concentrated on their background, development, meaning, and purpose. See especially of late, inter alia, *Aspects of the Táin*, ed. J. P. Mallory (Belfast, 1992); *Studien zur Táin Bó Cuailnge*, hrsg. v. Hildegard L. C. Tristram *Scriptoralia* 52 (Tübingen, 1993); *Ulidia. Proceedings of the First International Conference on the Ulster Cycle of Tales, Belfast . . . 1994*, ed. J. P. Mallory and Gerard Stockman (Belfast, 1994). The great interest in so many aspects of the study of the Ulster Cycle of heroic tales continues to be strong. They are still, I suspect, story in the main, but also with many-faceted and abiding connections with history.

A Welsh 'Dark Age' Court Poem

R. Geraint Gruffydd

UNIVERSITY OF WALES CENTRE FOR ADVANCED WELSH
AND CELTIC STUDIES, ABERYSTWYTH

MY ESTEEMED FRIEND Proinsias Mac Cana's distinguished contributions to both Irish and Welsh studies make this volume long overdue, but it is all the more welcome for that reason. Because his first book in either field was *Branwen Daughter of Llŷr* (1958), and because he has remained at the forefront of Mabinogion studies ever since — witness his authoritative monograph in the 'Writers of Wales' series, *The Mabinogi* (1977, revised edition 1992) — it seems appropriate to offer in his *Festschrift* an account of a poem which displays an awareness, all the more telling because it is in a sense incidental, of the thought-world of these remarkable tales.

The poem occurs in Aberystwyth, National Library of Wales MS. Peniarth 2, 'The Book of Taliesin', one of a group of five manuscripts written by the same scribe during the first half of the fourteenth century in the middle or southern marches of Wales, perhaps at the Cistercian Abbey of Cwm-hir.[1] The manuscript

---

1 Reprinted as BT; see M. Haycock, 'Llyfr Taliesin', NLWJ 25 (1987–8), pp. 257–86. I wish to thank Professor Emeritus J. E. Caerwyn Williams for his comments on an early draft of this

purports to be a collection of poems by, or about, Taliesin. There appears to have been a historical Taliesin, a late sixth-century court poet in the British kingdoms of southern Scotland and northern England — the Old North —, but he later became the chief character of a vivid and evolving folk-tale. He appears in both guises in the Book of Taliesin, as the labours of Sir Ifor Williams, with Professor J. E. Caerwyn Williams, and Dr Marged Haycock have made amply clear.[2]

The poem I wish to discuss is on pp. 68–9 of the manuscript and consists of 29 lines in the *rhupunt* metre. It was first edited by Sir Ifor Williams in the *Transactions of the Anglesey Antiquarian Society and Field Club* in 1941; his edition was reprinted by Dr Rachel Bromwich in her collection of Sir Ifor's papers, *The Beginnings of Welsh Poetry*, in 1972. Sir Ifor established beyond reasonable doubt that the poem was an elegy for an Anglesey magnate named Aeddon (although when he wrote his article he thought his name was Cynaethwy), who had come to Môn (Anglesey) from Arfon and who had unfortunately brought with him four young women — whether daughters or concubines is not stated — who had an undue influence upon him and who remained influential after Aeddon and his wife Llywy had died; unhappily, that influence was not exerted in favour of the poet. As Sir Ifor drily comments, 'Such things have happened'!.[3] Unfortunately, there is no Aeddon at all in Dr Peter Bartrum's comprehensive and invaluable collections of genealogies (nor, for that matter, is there a suitable Cyn(h)aethwy).[4] One might hypothesise that Aeddon is a by-form of Aeddan, a fairly common name in the genealogies, but of the ten persons bearing that name in Dr Bartrum's two earliest corpora of genealogies, only two can be connected with Gwynedd west of the river Conwy (*Gwynedd Uwch Conwy*), and of these two Aeddan ap Caw of Twrcelyn is almost certainly legendary, and Aeddan ap Rhodri Mawr is otherwise unknown.[5] One should perhaps hesitate to dismiss the latter Aeddan out of hand, however, since the movement of the poem's subject from Arfon to Anglesey might be thought to reflect the hegemony of both Gwynedd dynasties over the lands conquered, according to tradition, by Cunedda Wledig and his descendants.[6] Aeddan could first have been invested with lands in Arfon, and then moved to

---

paper, and also the editors for their helpful suggestions.

2   See PT, LITARA; some recent work on the legend is documented in R. G. Gruffydd, 'Why Cors Fochno?', THSC, 1995, pp. 5–19 (p. 17n65).

3   BWP 179. It should be noted that a somewhat different interpretation is proposed in OCLW 162.

4   See EWGT, indices; WG 1, indices.

5   EWGT 47, 85.

6   R. G. Gruffydd, 'From Gododdin to Gwynedd: reflections on the story of Cunedda', StC 24/25 (1989–90), pp. 1–14.

Anglesey as sub-king, by his father or his brother Anarawd. On the other hand, if our Aeddon was really Rhodri Mawr's son, why is this not mentioned in the poem? Perhaps a more likely explanation of the silence of the genealogies is that Aeddon, although clearly of high status, was of less than royal rank: he would then be a great lord in Anglesey, but not king or sub-king. If such was the case, it would make his poem unique among the five Welsh court poems that have survived from the period between the early seventh century and the late eleventh: the other four are all in praise of kings or scions of kings.[7]

As was hinted above, the factor that guaranteed the survival of Aeddon's elegy, generally known as 'Echrys Ynys' from the opening phrase of the two monorhyme sequences or *awdlau*, was the fact that its maker was familiar with the legend of Taliesin and made use of it in his poem. Because Aeddon came from Arfon to Môn, it was possible to describe his journey in legendary terms, as from 'Gwydion's land' to 'Seon's stronghold': the country south of Caernarfon was traditionally the playground of the legendary wizard Gwydion and his siblings, together with his uncle Math; and Dr Brynley F. Roberts has demonstrated conclusively that Caer Seon is to be located in Anglesey, although we do not know precisely where.[8] This recollection of traditional geography prompted the poet to refer to another segment of the tradition, that Math and Eufydd (whom we must now surely recognise as another of Dôn's progeny)[9] brought into being a craftsman or artist, whom we know from another poem in the same manuscript to have been Taliesin himself,[10] the implication being that the poet's calling was in some sense divine. The point is further made that at the time of Gwydion and Amaethon order and justice reigned, a state of affairs which was presumably meant to contrast with present disorder. It is remarkable to find this awareness of figures assigned by tradition to the pagan past in what is otherwise a thoroughly Christian poem, but a similar split consciousness is found in several other poems in the Book of Taliesin.[11] It may also be salutary to recall that in a recent television programme the apparently serious claim was made that Gwydion still has over a thousand devotees in Anglesey!

As mentioned at the beginning, the poem is in the *rhupunt* metre, which occurs in the earliest Welsh poetry and has Irish parallels.[12] At the risk of seeming to

7   Editions in AAYH 23–34 (R. G. Gruffydd); SGS 17 (1996), pp. 172–8 (idem); EWSP 174–9; BWP 155–72.
8   TYP 400–2 and cross-references; AAYH 318–25.
9   The facts are set down in PKM 252–3.
10 BT 23.8–27.12 (25.26–26.1); commentary in LITARA 121–65.
11 E.g. BT 33.1–34.14; commentary in LITARA 187–98.
12 CD 312, 331–3; Bardos 180–6 (David Greene).

indulge in rash generalisation, it may be stated that the poem displays the metre in an intermediate stage of development between the relatively simple examples in the Book of Aneirin and the intricately crafted poems of the earlier Poets of the Princes[13]; it corresponds best therefore to the half-dozen or so examples in the Book of Taliesin and the Red Book of Hergest which may tentatively be dated to the three centuries between the ninth and the eleventh.[14] In particular, two points may be noted.

1. The tendency to combine rhyme and alliteration in the last two metra of the line in a manner approximating to *cynghanedd sain*, while already apparent in 'Echrys Ynys' (*c.* 10.3% of all lines), is rudimentary compared with the position in the two anonymous *awdlau* 'Marwnad Hywel ap Goronwy' of *c.* 1100 (24.5%) and 'Mawl Cuhelyn Fardd' of *c.* 1130 (34%), and in Seisyll Bryffwrch's 'Canu i'r Arglwydd Rhys' of *c.* 1170 (31.8%).[15] This tendency is scarcely apparent at all in the Book of Aneirin, Book of Taliesin and Red Book of Hergest examples of the metre,[16] but this may be due in some cases to difference of *genre* as much as to difference in the date of composition.

2. The use of generic rhyme in the main rhyme sequence (lines 14, 16) cannot be paralleled at all in the work of the early Poets of the Princes, but again it appears sporadically in the poems in the *rhupunt* metre found in the Book of Aneirin, the Book of Taliesin and the Red Book of Hergest.[17]

Nor does the language of the poem, as far as I can see, preclude a date in the ninth or tenth centuries. Sir Ifor detected a lone example of the definite article in line 5, but the form, in my view, is far more likely to be a preposition. He also remarked that 'rhymes like *da, gowala, terra* . . . cannot be very early', but later work has shown that they would have been perfectly acceptable in the Old Welsh

---

13 CA 11, 50–2; CBT I poems 1 and 2, CBT II poem 24.

14 BT 44.17–45.9, 46.5–47.18, 52.6–17, 53.3–54.15, 67.9–17 (editions in LITARA 355–60, 361–8, 369–71, 372–80, 299–305); RBH 1049.7–1050.6 (edition in AWPVT 120–40). I have chosen not to include in the discussion various fragments in the same metre from the Book of Aneirin and the Book of Taliesin, and have also set aside the religious poem from the Black Book of Carmarthen edited in BBGCC 234–7 because of its seeming relative lateness: see also A. Breeze, 'Master John of St David's, a new twelfth-century poet?' *BBCS* 40 (1993), 73–82 (78).

15 See references in the second part of note 13 above. I wish to record my indebtedness to Dr Peredur Lynch's discussion of the metre in BaTh 258–87 (pp. 269–70).

16 See references in the first part of note 13 above and in note 14.

17 As in the previous note.

period (*c.* 800–1150).[18] The curious form *[B]retonia* (line 20) may also be a pointer to a relatively early date, since kindred forms (*Brettones, Brettonici; lingua Brettonum*) seem to occur only in Bede (*c.* 730) and a Cornish charter (*c.* 870).[19] The present indications are that 'Echrys Ynys' is indeed a 'Dark Age' court poem, to be dated to either the ninth or tenth centuries, although a date in the first half of the eleventh century, as suggested by Sir Ifor, certainly cannot be precluded. If only we knew who Aeddon was!

There follows a text of the poem, with line-divisions, capitals and punctuation supplied, as literal a translation as possible, and minimal annotation. My debt to Sir Ifor Williams's earlier edition will be apparent throughout.

18 LHEB 445, 458–9, 466–8.
19 DMLBS 218.

ECHRYS YNYS
(NLW Peniarth MS. 2, pp. 68–9)

Echrys ynys gwawt huenys[1]: gwrys gobetror.
Mon mat gogei[2] gwrhyt eruei; Menei y dor.
Lleweis wirawt gwin a bragawt gan vrawt escor
Teyrn wofrwy; diwed pop rwy[3]; rewinetor!
5 Tristlawn deon yr archadon[4] kan rychior.
Nyt uu, nyt vi, yg kymelri y gyfeissor.
Pan doeth Aedon o wlat Wytyon Seon tewdor
Gwenwyn pyr doeth pedair pennoeth meinoeth tymhor.
Kwydynt kyfoet, ny bu clyt coet, gwynt ygohor.
10 Math ac Euuyd hutynt[5] geluyd, ryd eluinor.
Ymyw Gwytyon ac Amaethon atoed kyghor.
Twll tal y rodawc; ffyryf ffo diawc; ffyryf diachor.
Katarn gygres; y varanres ny bu warthuor.[6]
Kadarn gyfed ym pop gorsed gwnelit y vod.
15 Cu kyn aethyw[7], hyd tra uwyf uyw kyrbwylletor.
A'm bwyf i gan Grist, hyt na bwyf trist, ran ebostol.
Hael archadon[8] gan egylyon cynwyssetor.

Echrys ynys gwawt huenys[9]: gwrys gochyma.
Y rac budwas, Kymry dinas, aros ara.
20 Dragonawl[10] ben, priawd[11] perchen yMretonia.
Difa gwledic, or bendefic, a'e tud[12] terra.
Pedeir morwyn, wedy eu cwyn, dygnawt eu tra,
Erdygnawt wir: ar vor, ar tir, hir eu trefra
O'e wironyn na ddigonyn dim gofettra.
25 Kerydus wyf na chyrbwyllwyf a'm rywnel da.
Y lwrw Lywy, pwy gwahardwy, pwy attrefna?
Y lwrw Aedon, pwy gynheil Mon mwyn gowala?
A'm bwyf i gan Grist, hyt na bwyf trist, o drwc o da,
Ran trugared y wlat ried, buched gyfa.

Manuscript readings

1	huynys	5	Hutwyt	9	huynys
2	goge	6	werthuor	10	draganawl
3	rwyf	7	kynaethwy	11	priodawr
4	archaedon	8	archaedon	12	tu

'DESOLATE IS THE ISLAND'

Desolate is the island of splendid panegyric: there is strife on all sides.
Auspiciously did Anglesey arise [through] surpassing valour; Menai is its gate.
I consumed strong drink of wine and bragget with my true brother
[Having] the handsome mien of a lord; now is the end of all pomp; all is destroyed!

5   Full of sorrow are the noblemen on account of the most just one, now that he is fallen.
There has not been, there will not be, his equal in battle.
When Aeddon came from Gwydion's land to Seon's stronghold
It is cruel that there came [also] four bare-headed women in the midnight hour.
Companions fell, woods were no refuge, [with] the wind contrary.

10   Math and Eufydd fashioned by magic an artist, a generous utterer.
During the life of Gwydion and Amaethon counsel used to prevail.
The front of his shield was shattered; he was strong and reluctant to flee; he was strong [and] unyielding.
Mighty [his] attack, in the fury of battle he was no mercenary.
Mighty in carousal, in every assembly his will was done.

15   Beloved was he before he departed, as long as I shall live he shall be praised.
May there be to me from Christ, so that I shall not be sorrowful, an apostle's lot.
The generous and most just one by angels shall be received.

Desolate is the island of splendid panegyric: the slaughter of battle.
In the presence of the victor, the refuge of Welshmen, it was pleasant to remain.

20   A ferocious chief, a rightful possessor in the land of Britain.
The ruler is perished, the governor of a coast, earth covers him.
The four maidens, after their feasting, grievous was their oppression,
A cruel truth: on land, on sea, their deceit is long-lasting
That for his faithful henchman they will do nothing at all.

25   I am guilty were I not to praise him who might have done me good.
In the manner of Llywy, who may prevent it, who will restore order?
In the manner of Aeddon, who will defend Anglesey of abundant wealth?
May there be to me from Christ, so that I shall not be sorrowful, from [my] evil and [my] good,
The lot of mercy in the land of majesty, life fulfilled.

NOTES

1. **huenys**: MS. *huynys*. < *huan* 'light, sun' + *-ys*. Contrast GPC 1928 which in addition proposes a derivation < ?*hu-*, *hy-* + *ynys* 'island'; if this interpretation were to be accepted, the first two metra could be translated 'The great island of song is a desolate island'.

2. **gogei**: MS. *goge*: the *-i* must be supplied to save the rhyme. Dr John T. Koch reminds me that the spelling is Old Welsh. A baffling form, as previous discussions, or their lack, show, see G 160, 548 but nothing in GPC or in BWP 172-80. G 548's proposed emendation to *gwgei* is attractive; but here a connection is tentatively assumed between a verb **cogi* and the Welsh and Breton nouns *cogwrn* (but contrast GPC 541), *kogell*: see SCHP 52-3.

3. **rwy**: MS *rwyf*: the *-f* must be deleted to save the rhyme, but the forms *rhwyf/rhwy* in fact alternate freely: see CA 241-2. The word here is assumed to bear its specialised meaning of 'pomp, &c'; see CBT II 26.29n, V 23.193, VI 25.3, VII 41.18, 42.20n.

    Menei: The arm of the sea which separates Anglesey from the mainland.

4. **archadon**: MS. *archaedon* (also line 17). On the emendation see GPC 179. In view of the example here and at line 17, compared with C 71.5, it seems likely that *archaddon* was an honorific title; thus *Llyn Archaddon* at SH 467851 may well be significant, as Sir Ifor surmised: see BWP 180 and references.

5. **Aedon**: See introductory note (also line 27).

    Gwydion: See introductory note (also line 11).

    Seon: See introductory note.

9. **Kwydynt kyfoet**: Cf. CA 7 *kwydyn gyuoedyon* (line 171).

10. **Math**: See introductory note.

    Euuyd: See introductory note.

    hutynt: MS. *Hutwyt*. On the emendation, see BWP 174-6.

    eluinor: G 755 proposes a derivation from *gyluin* 'beak, &c' + *gôr* 'pus'; here it is assumed that *gyluin* is rather combined with the nominal termination *-or*.

11. **Amaethon**: See introductory note.

12. **Twll tal y rodawc**: cf. CA 43 *twll tal y rodawc* (line 1080).

13. **warthuor**: MS. *werthuor*. I follow GPC 1588 rather than G 623 which gives only the meaning 'gwarth, cywilydd' [disgrace, shame]; note however the comment in CBT IV 2.10n that 'môr cywilydd' [a sea of shame] would be a more natural construction. Even more natural would be to treat the form as a compound of *gwarth* + *mawr*, with vowel mutation as a result of the accent shift: the meaning would be 'greatly disgraced'.

    [As the probable date of composition is rather early for reduction of *-fawr* > *-for* and there are no other instances of old *aw* in the seventeen occurrences of the *prifodl*, we might consider the possibility that the compound here is *gwarth* + *bor*, with the second element as the Celtic cognate of the Greek compounding suffix -φόρος 'bearing'; see J. Pokorny, *Indogermanisches etymologisches Wörterbuch*, vol 1 (Bern, 1959) 129. Thus, translate 'in the fury of battle he was no bearer of disgrace'; cf. CA (A47) 561, (B¹.10) 1142. –JTK]

15. kyn aethyw: MS. *kynaethwy*. The emendation is necessary to save the rhyme. This consideration rules out the personal name *Cynaethwy* which G 243 favoured and with which Sir Ifor toyed in BWP 180 (GPC 179, however, represents his retraction on this point, since he was the Consulting Editor of the fascicule in which the article appeared). With the metron as a whole, cf. PT 5 *ys cu kyn eithyd* (V 11).

20. dragonawl: MS. *draganawl*. The emendation follows the implicit suggestion in G 389.

priawd: MS. *priodawr*. The emendation is necessary to save the metre.

21. or: Neither G 556 nor GPC 1495-6, 2651 comment on this form. Sir Ifor takes it to be a lenited form of *gor* 'super', with *or bendefic* forming a noun phrase in apposition to *[g]wledic*. It seems more natural to assume that *or* 'border, limit' is here meant, which for Anglesey is equivalent to 'coast'.

tud: MS. *tu*. Sir Ifor in BWP 178 assumes this emendation, but does not supply it in *id.* 173.

22. tra: With Sir Ifor, this is taken to be a syncopated form of *traha* 'arrogance': see the discussions in CBT I 9.163n, II 22.50n and cf. *id.* VII 38.10

23. trefra: Sir Ifor translates this word as '(shame?)' but does not discuss it. Here it is assumed that we have a form either cognate to, or derived from, Old Irish *trebrad* 'act of plaiting, weaving', DIL 285, used figuratively. A connection with *tref* 'settlement' cannot however be ruled out.

24. wironyn: Sir Ifor is followed in taking this form to be a diminutive of *gwirion* 'innocent; innocent one', although otherwise there is no early attestation of it; contrast G 685 which proposes a derivation < *gwirion + hynt* 'course'.

gofettra: GPC 1430 rather than G 546 ('?anghyfiawnder, anuniondeb') is followed here, but some such meaning as 'something extraordinary' is also possible.

26. Lywy: With Sir Ifor, BWP 180, this is taken to be a reference to Aeddon's wife (queen?). Unlike Sir Ifor, *Llywy* is here taken to be a proper name.

ABBREVIATIONS

AAYH   *Astudiaethau ar yr Hengerdd*, ed. R. Bromwich and R.B. Jones (Caerdydd, 1978).

AWPVT   M. B. Jenkins, 'Aspects of the Welsh prophetic verse tradition in the Middle Ages' (Ph.D. thesis, Cambridge, 1990).

Bardos   *Bardos*, ed. R.G. Gruffydd (Caerdydd, 1982).

BaTh *Beirdd a Thywysogion*, ed. M.E. Owen and B.F. Roberts (Caerdydd & Aberystwyth, 1996).

BBCS *Bulletin of the Board of Celtic Studies.*

BBGCC M. Haycock, *Blodeugerdd Barddas o Ganu Crefyddol Cynnar* ([Abertawe,] 1994).

BT *The Text of the Book of Taliesin*, ed. J.G. Evans (Llanbedrog, 1910).

BWP *The Beginnings of Welsh Poetry: Studies by Sir Ifor Williams*, ed. R. Bromwich (Cardiff, 1972).

C *The Black Book of Carmarthen*, ed. J.G. Evans (Pwllheli, 1907).

CA *Canu Aneirin*, ed. I. Williams (Caerdydd, 1938).

CBT 'Cyfres Beirdd y Tywysogion' [Poets of the Princes Series], gen. ed. R.G. Gruffydd (seven volumes; Caerdydd, 1991-6).

CD J. Morris-Jones, *Cerdd Dafod* (Rhydychen, 1925).

DIL *Dictionary of the Irish Language* (Dublin, 1983).

DMLBS *Dictionary of Medieval Latin from British sources* (London, 1975-).

EWGT P. C. Bartrum, *Early Welsh Genealogical Tracts* (Cardiff, 1966).

EWSP J. Rowland, *Early Welsh Saga Poetry* (Woodbridge, 1990).

G J. Lloyd-Jones, *Geirfa Barddoniaeth Gynnar Gymraeg* (Caerdydd, 1931-63).

GPC *Geiriadur Prifysgol Cymru* (Caerdydd, 1950-).

LHEB K. Jackson, *Language and History in Early Britain* (Edinburgh, 1953).

LlTARA M. Haycock, 'Llyfr Taliesin: Astudiaethau ar rai agweddau' (Ph.D. thesis, Wales [Aberystwyth], 1982).

NLWJ *National Library of Wales Journal.*

OCLW *The Oxford Companion to the Literature of Wales*, ed. M. Stephens (Oxford, 1986).

PKM *Pedeir Keinc y Mabinogi*, ed. I. Williams (Caerdydd, 1930).

PT *The Poems of Taliesin*, ed. I. Williams with J. E. Caerwyn Williams (Dublin, 1968).

RBH *The Poetry in the Red Book of Hergest*, ed. J. G. Evans (Llanbedrog, 1911).

SCHP P. Schrijver, *Studies in Celtic Historical Phonology* (Amsterdam & Atlanta, GA, 1995).

SGS *Scottish Gaelic Studies.*

StC *Studia Celtica.*

THSC *Transactions of the Honourable Society of Cymmrodorion.*

TYP *Trioedd Ynys Prydein*, ed. R. Bromwich (Cardiff, 1961).

WG 1 P. C. Bartrum, *Welsh Genealogies AD 300-1400* (eight volumes; Cardiff, 1974).

Old Irish *Credne, cerd,*
Welsh *cerdd*

Eric P. Hamp

DEPARTMENT OF LINGUISTICS, UNIVERSITY OF CHICAGO

I HAVE DISCUSSED *Goídil, Féni,* and *Gŵynedd* and their relation as a partition of a single IE paradigm **ueidh-H̆/uidh-n-* ~ *ueidh-l-* (→ *ueidh-n-ā* > Irish *fían^L*), *uidh-u-* 'wood(s)' in an earlier volume dedicated to our loved and admired friend[1]. I have outlined the scope of this unrecognised IE noun class in a contribution to the Festschrift for Karl Horst Schmidt on *Indogermanica et Caucasica* (Berlin 1994). I have also continued the theme with additional observations from a number of IE branches.[2]

Some years ago (*Ériu* 39, 1988, 192–3) I considered the divine (or, at any rate, supernatural) name *Credne* with the resourceful and often perceptive help of T. F. O'Rahilly (*Ériu* 13, 1942, 159–60). Having earlier (1977) thought about *cerd* and Welsh *cerdd*, I made some progress with the phonological reconstruction and with

---

1 *Proceedings of the Harvard Celtic Colloquium* XII, 1992 (1995), edd. B. Hillers and J. Hunter, 43–50. See also 'Fian^L', *Studia Celtica Japonica* 8, 1996, 87–95 (with some harmless misprints).
2 'Βλέφαρον', *Glotta* 72, 1994 (1995) 15; Skt. *kṣaṇa, Indo-Iranian Journal* 38, 1995, 369; Lithuanian *akýlas, Baltistica* 30 (1), 1995, 40; *CDIAL* 13073 *sakthán-*, nom. *sákthi, Indo-Iranian Journal* 40, 1997, 259; Venetic *Ostila, Ostiala/*OSTIALAE, *Glotta* 73, 1997, 79; Two regular milk products, *Mír Curad*, edd. J. Jasanoff, H. C. Melchert, L. Oliver, Innsbruck 1998, 241–2; Slavic *oko* 'eye', *In memoriam: Zbigniew Gołąb, Balkanistica* 10, 1997, 1–6; Ὄκελον, *Studia Celtica* 31, 1997 (1998) 276.

the narrowing of suffixal possibilities; but I failed to reach a uniquely motivated solution. More recently (*Glotta* 72, 1994, 18–19) I saw that Greek κερδώ (related to κέρδος) is plausibly best associated through κερδαλέος with the class of substantives exemplified by μέγα ~ ἀγα- ~ *mag-n-us* (Mid.Ir. *maighne*) ~ Mycen. *me-zo-e* ~ μεγάλο- ἀγάλλω (**mĝ-l-i e/o -*), British and Gaulish *Maglo-* = OIr. *mál,* Welsh *mael, Mael-* (→ *mael*) (cf. *Studia Celtica* 26/27, 1991/2, 18–19), i.e.

$$*meĝ\text{-}H_a ~ mĝH_a\text{-} ~ m(H)ĝ\text{-}n\text{-} ~ meĝ\text{-}(ios\text{-}) ~ m(e)ĝ\text{-}l\text{-}$$

or for 'head'

$$*kep\text{-}H ~ *kp\text{-}H\text{-} (→ k(e/H)\text{-}p\text{-}H\text{-}) ~ *k(e)p\text{-}n\text{-} (> \text{Welsh } cun) ~ -kep\text{-} ~ kp\text{-}l\text{-} (→ k(e/H)p\text{-}l\text{-}).$$

Our task now is to fit the attested forms and functions of κερδώ, κέρδος, Irish *cerd,* Welsh *cerdd,* etc., and *Credne* into this structure. I hope this little effort might please our old friend Proinsias.

LÉIA (1987) C–71–2 s.v. 1 *cerd* (fem.) usefully assembles and reviews earlier literature and attested forms, but it falls short of reaching an explanatory formulation. The feminine gender of this (these) noun(s) is assured by the gen. sg. *inna cerdae* (animate) 'du potier', though both *na cerda* and *in cherda* are found. Without rehearsing the detail of documented derivatives, note *cerdach* 'artistique' and *cerdaigecht* ~ *cerdacht* 'work of art, atelier, forge'. Surely Pedersen was right that *cerdach* → *cerdchae* (fem.) *iā*-stem > nasal-stem. Here we see the results of disambiguation of homonyms.

Pokorny *IEW* 579 simply lists routine Greek, Irish, and Welsh forms; we ignore the Germanic **hort-ska-.* *LÉIA* remarks that only Old Irish and Greek equivalence 'parait solide'. But the forms and equations offered are insufficient. I have already (1988) rejected O'Rahilly's **kʷreda-.* And *RC* XII 78 on *Credne* is out of date today.

Recently A. Bammesberger (*Études celtiques* 32, 1996, 139–41, apparently without seeing my 1994) discussed *cerd* and *cerdd;* his main purpose was to reconcile the semantics of the Celtic and Greek equation, which he finds plausible. Bammesberger notes the poverty of cognates, and the Germanic zero-grade; but he does not exploit all the testimony, in my opinion, offered by Greek and Celtic. He observes attentively the double semantics 'métier' and 'artisan' of OIr. 1 *cerd* (fem.) *ā*-stem. Bammesberger concludes (140) that the basic IE source of meaning for these nouns is 'heart', in the transferred sense 'thought, sentiment', giving a thematic derivative -o- 'artisanat' in the feminine — an unnecessarily complex derivation, I think.

A. and B. Rees (*Celtic Heritage*, 1961, 34, 37, 53) identify Credne as the *cerd* (agent) who supplies small, but essential metal spare parts (unlike Goibniu of the heavy weaponry); he is **clever**, wily with Homer's δόλος.

Thus we have the set of related direct derivations:

κερδώ ~ όος f. 'thief, fox' = OIr. *cerd* f. 'craftsman' < *kerd-óH (H₀ ?)

(κέρδος *-s- n. 'profit' (= OIr. *cerd* f., Welsh *cerdd* 'craft' < *kerd-ā

κέρδεα pl. 'gain(s)') < *kérd-es-)

κερδαλέος 'shrewd' < *kerd-l-

κερδαίνω, Ion. -ανέω 'gain' = OIr. *Credne* < *kridan-iV- < *krd-n-

Quite properly, the agentive *-io- '±-ach' is suffixed to the heteroclite weak n-state of the stem '(il-)dán-'.

Some Observations on Celtic-Latin Name Formation[*]

Anthony Harvey

ROYAL IRISH ACADEMY

IT is to be hoped that among his many valuable contributions to Celtic studies Professor Mac Cana will wish to number his chairmanship of the Editorial Board of the Royal Irish Academy's multi-faceted Dictionary of Medieval Latin from Celtic Sources (DMLCS) project, a position he has held since 1980 with conspicuous benefit to all aspects of the enterprise. The present paper arises from work on one of these aspects, and it can usefully begin with an explanation of the background thereto.

For almost twenty years the DMLCS staff have been devoting part of their effort to constructing a full-text, marked-up computer database of the materials on which the lexicographical side of their operation draws. When completed, this database will consist of something over thirteen hundred separate medieval Latin texts, varying in length from fragmentary inscriptions to learned treatises that extend to hundreds of pages when printed; and it will total perhaps eight million words. Geographically, the project covers texts written in the Celtic-speaking countries or by Celts abroad. This means that as well as authors from Ireland, Scotland, Wales, Brittany, Cornwall and the Isle of Man, writers are encompassed from those parts of the former Roman Britain that were Celtic-speaking at the

---

[*] This paper is a revised version of one given at the Tenth International Congress of Celtic Studies, Edinburgh in July, 1995; I am grateful to all who took part in the subsequent discussion on that occasion, and particularly to Dr John Carey for his helpful suggestions since.

time, even if they are now in England; for example, the sixth-century Briton Gildas is included, wherever he may have lived. Encompassed too is the output of the Hiberno-Latin continent, meaning to say the works of the Irish *peregrini* such as Columbanus of Luxeuil and Bobbio, Cellanus of Péronne, Frigulus, the two Sedulii, Virgil of Salzburg, the Joseph, Clement, Donatus and John Eriugena all traditionally dubbed Scottus, the cosmologist Dicuil and so on. The database also includes the numerous anonymous verses, letters, and scholastic, theological, legislative, hagiographical and liturgical works emanating from the circles that included men such as these, principally in the eighth to tenth centuries. The rough outer date limits are shown by the full title of Michael Lapidge and Richard Sharpe's well-known Ancillary Volume to DMLCS,[1] the primary purpose of which was to define the parameters for the project.

As texts are entered into the database, no attempt is made to standardize spellings or any other characteristics, far less to normalize everything to Classical Latin usage, since one of the main interests of DMLCS is precisely the investigation of what it is that makes Celtic latinity different from other Latin registers and dialects. However, in a collaborative venture with the Academy, the Belgian firm Brepols has recently published the first of three editions of the database on compact disk (CD-ROM);[2] and in order to enable users to interrogate the archive using the search software provided, it was necessary to compile a series of electronically-stored indexes that cross-referenced authors, titles of works, Lapidge and Sharpe numbers, period, and edition used, in all possible combinations. This involved translating into Latin those names of authors and texts that in the Lapidge and Sharpe *Bibliography* appear in English, a task that was undertaken because the *Archive* offers users a choice of English, French, German and Italian interfaces, and Brepols wanted to avoid a bias towards any particular modern language in the various listings obtainable on the screen. In these indexes, as opposed to within the texts themselves, a degree of standardization was called for, so that closely related items would not be scattered around the alphabetical listings; thus the five Lives of the two distinct saintly figures called Ciarán from three different medieval collections will all be found listed next to each other as *Uita S. Ciarani* (*sic*), though the name might otherwise have been

1 *A Bibliography of Celtic-Latin Literature 400–1200* (Dublin, 1985); it may be worth noting that the main reason for these date-limits is that Latin material from much before 400 A.D. would probably have to be regarded as more or less classical, or at least Roman-dominated; while texts from much after 1200 probably owe as much to Norman influence as to Celtic throughout the DMLCS area.
2 *Royal Irish Academy Archive of Celtic-Latin Literature: First (Preliminary) CD-ROM Edition (ACLL-1)*, compiled by Anthony Harvey, Kieran Devine and Francis J. Smith (Turnhout, 1994).

entered spelled variously, as in the manuscripts, with initial *Cy-*, *Ki-*, *Ky-* or even *Que-*.[3] In determining what spellings to use, an endeavour was made to take into account in each case etymology, manuscript attestation, non-ambiguity, established scholarly practice, and consistency. This task falling to me, what I found myself effectively doing was defining norms for late twentieth-century Celtic-Latin ortho-graphy, prescriptive linguistics of this kind proving to be an unexpected aspect of the task for a lexicographer of a medieval tongue. However, the research involved was interesting, particularly since patterns did seem to emerge by which Celtic names were latinized in medieval times and since, within the wider patterns, other features seemed to distinguish a Hiberno-Latin from a Brythonic-Latin way of doing that. In saying this I am not necessarily claiming that the Hiberno-Latin world and the Brythonic-Latin world each had a deliberately constructed, unified set of conventions, lasting for centuries, by which latinization of names was carried out. Perhaps it is just that, with similar mother-tongue backgrounds and faced with similar problems of latinization, the composers of our texts in each Celtic speech-area happen to have responded in somewhat similar ways. While keeping an open mind on this, I have nevertheless felt it worthwhile in the meantime to try to describe what some of the patterns seem to be. The Andersons and J.-M. Picard, particularly, have done valuable work in this area as regards Adomnán,[4] but the computerized *Archive* provides the opportunity to survey the material more widely.

To speakers of major languages nowadays, the practice of translating proper names seems quaint (except in the rare circumstances in which they do it them-selves, as with the names of popes and foreign university departments and some place-names); but it is, of course, still widespread in some minority languages like the various Gaelic tongues and Catalan, and was general in medieval times. It is certainly overwhelmingly present throughout our corpus, even in the circumstances in which one would have considered it least necessary. Gildas was a Briton surely writing for fellow Britons, yet in his tract *De excidio Britanniae* he dutifully addresses Maelgwn in the Latin vocative as *Maglocune* and Cynlas as *Cuneglase*[5];

---

3 The works in question are those numbered 386, 417, 442, 488 and 499 in the Lapidge and Sharpe *Bibliography* (henceforth L&S).

4 Jean-Michel Picard, '*Eloquentiae exuberantia*: Words and Forms in Adomnán's *Vita Columbae*', *Peritia*, 6–7 (1987–88), 141–57; Alan Orr Anderson and Marjorie Ogilvie Anderson (eds and transls), *Adomnan's Life of Columba* (London, 1961), pp. 1–175 (particularly pp. 124–61). The quality of the Andersons' linguistic discussion is variable (see the comments in my article 'Retrieving the Pronunciation of Early Insular Celtic Scribes: The Case of Dorbbène', *Celtica*, 22 (1991), 48–63 (p. 50, n. 9)), and most of it is omitted completely from the new edition (Oxford, 1991).

5 T. Mommsen (ed.), 'Gildae sapientis De excidio et conquestu Britanniae', in *Chronica*

while in the late seventh century, Adomnán (or Adomnanus), a native speaker of archaic Old Irish, wrote a Life of Columba (or ColumCille)[6] that contains hundreds of names translated into Latin from his own native language, even though most of his intended readers may be presumed to have had the same mother tongue. As I say, even in such cases the latinizing habit is the rule rather than the exception. There seems to be little doubt that the reason had something to do with the perceived high status of Latin in the Middle Ages (at least in some fields of discourse) as compared with the vernacular, and perhaps even with a feeling that the vernacular should not, or even could not, be used when writing (though this second reason is of questionable validity in the Celtic realms with their considerable vernacular literacy throughout most of our period).[7] But the question of why the latinizing was done is not one to address further here, the plan being rather to concentrate on how it was accomplished; and in that connection one should note that the status-raising associated with a translation into Latin is itself a consideration that often affects what forms our authors adopt. For example, Adomnán renders the native name of the island of Coll, in Modern Gaelic 'Colla', as case-forms of the impressive-looking *Colosus*; and of Tiree ('Éth' in Old Irish, 'Tìr Iodh' in Modern Gaelic) as forms of *Ethica insula/terra*.[8] As the Andersons point out,[9] there seem to be no special reasons why Adomnán gave the islands these epithets; he may have awarded them 'fancifully' (as they put it), merely basing them on the Gaelic names. If so, this habit of using the vernacular

Minora III, Monumenta Germaniae Historica: Auctores Antiquissimi 13 (Berlin, 1898), pp. 1–85 (p. 44). The text is L&S no. 27.

6   L&S no. 305.

7   Though the contribution containing them needs revision, some observations may be considered relevant at pp. 18–22 of my paper 'Latin, Literacy and the Celtic Vernaculars around the Year AD 500', in *Celtic Languages and Celtic Peoples: Proceedings of the Second North American Congress of Celtic Studies . . . Halifax . . . 1989*, edited by Cyril J. Byrne, Margaret Harry and Pádraig Ó Siadhail (Halifax, 1992), pp. 11–26. The point as regards names is that it would appear to have been felt appropriate for these to be in identifiably the same language as the text in which they were embedded; compare the compiler's remarks at the end of the *Additamenta ad Collectanea Tirechani* (L&S no. 358) published at pp. 178–9 of *The Patrician Texts in the Book of Armagh*, edited and translated by Ludwig Bieler (Dublin, 1979).

8   My slightly non-standard notation is to distinguish forms that are primarily to be read or read out, which I write in normalized spelling and enclose in quotation marks, from specific Roman-letter written types where the orthography is the important consideration, which I italicize in the usual way; on the advantages of making this distinction see Anthony Harvey, 'Suggestions for Improving the Notation Used for Celtic Historical Linguistics', in *Hispano-Gallo-Brittonica: Essays in Honour of Professor D. Ellis Evans on the Occasion of his Sixty-Fifth Birthday*, edited by Joseph F. Eska, R. Geraint Gruffydd and Nicolas Jacobs (Cardiff, 1995), pp. 52–57.

9   *Adomnan's Life of Columba* (1961), p. 156.

form (if at all) as a springboard for launching a Latin form with impressive resonances is one that can be traced throughout our corpus. The exact form of the vernacular eponym of Monasterboice, the settlement in Co. Louth famous for its high crosses, seems difficult to determine precisely because it has been attracted when latinized to the name of the famous philosopher Boethius.[10] The name of St Carthach of Lismore is latinized with a *g* instead of the expected *ch* after the second syllable throughout the Lives of him and of Ciarán of Saigir in the *Collectio Dublinensis*,[11] and this seems unmotivated at first (after all, we do not find spellings with *g* in the treatment of similar names like Cainnech or Berach); but then we find its probable explanation as a back-formation from the desire to describe Carthach's monastic foundations as being Carthaginian, as if associated with famous Carthage in North Africa; and Dáibhí Ó Cróinín has kindly pointed out that we find this done as early as 655 in the text *De mirabilibus sacrae scripturae*,[12] written by an equally impressively-named Irishman calling himself Augustinus. Along the same lines, the names of the two writers in our corpus who would now be called Siadhal were latinized as Sedulius presumably because there was sufficient resemblance between them and that of the early fifth-century Christian Latin poet of that name. I imagine that Virgil of Salzburg may have been Fergal; and who knows what presumed connection with the composer of the Aeneid meant that Virgilius Maro Grammaticus came to be referred to in Latin in that guise? One could continue; the point is that a perceived resemblance between a vernacular name and a well-known Latin one could suffice, often apparently with an element of humour, to over-ride the tentative phonological rules for regular latinization to which we shall turn in a minute, and this is a consideration that must always be born in mind.

The opposite side of the coin of status-consciousness seems detectable within the Hibernian part of our corpus: vernacular hypocoristic names tend to be the exception to the convention that names must be latinized. What one has in mind here particularly (and what I mean, if over-restrictively, by the use of the term 'hypocoristic' in what follows) are those nicknames, nearly always for saints, that in both branches of Celtic took the form of an initial first- or second-person possessive adjective followed by a modified version of the actual name (rather like today's North of England custom within families of calling a boy named John 'our Jack' or a girl called Elizabeth 'our Beth', both of which, incidentally, one

---

10 The witnesses vary so much that alternative Latin forms had to be offered in the index to the *Archive*, whose entry for L&S no. 469 accordingly reads *Uita S. Boecii (Buithi)* in order to span the range that might be searched for. See further below, n. 21.

11 L&S nos 486 and 488 respectively.

12 L&S no. 291; the relevant form (the genitive plural *Carthaginensium*) is found on p. 2149 of the Patrologia edition referenced there.

hears even in the vocative). Thus in early Irish one has 'Mo-Chutu' from 'Carthach', 'Mo-Laise' from 'Laisrén' and 'Mo-Lua' from 'Lugaid', in Welsh 'Teilo' ('T-Eilo') from 'Eliud', in Breton 'Devenneg' ('De-Venneg') from 'Winwaloe', and so on. Within Hiberno-Latin texts at least, such vernacular nicknames tend to stay as they are; among the rare latinizations notable in the *Archive* are case-forms of *Mochulleus* for 'Mo-Chuille'[13] and first-declensional case-endings added to 'Mo-Lua',[14] and after all these two names are perhaps less obviously hypocoristics (in the narrow sense defined above) than are some others. The reason for the rest being left non-latinized may be (it seems to me) that there would be a perceived mismatch between the informality of the hypocoristic name, on the one hand, and the high register implied by latinizing it, on the other. However, another possible reason might be that these names are indeclinable in Irish, and to latinize such a form might be felt to involve declining the indeclinable. Against this is the consideration that, as we shall see, there was no convention within Hiberno-Latin that attempted to match Latin declensions up to their Irish equivalents, so perhaps it is unlikely that a distinction between declinable and undeclinable was deliberately transferred from one language to the other either. On the other hand, the medieval Brythonic languages had abandoned case-distinctions centuries before the composition of any of the relevant hagiographical texts in our manuscripts,[15] and in their case a distinction between declinable and non-declinable would therefore have been meaningless. Is it then coincidence that hagiographers who were native speakers of one of these languages seem somewhat more willing than Hibernian authors were to latinize their hypocoristics and thus decline them? To take a few indicative examples, the Life of St Teilo in the Book of Llandaf[16] refers regularly to *sanctus Teliaus* (genitive *Teliaui*, dative *Teliauo*), and *Maidocus* (the latter also fully declined by Gerald of Wales in various works, and in the twelfth or thirteenth-century Kalendarium sanctorum Wallensium[17]); while much earlier, in the ninth century, we have the Breton writer Bili in his life of St Malo (or Maclouius) systematically latinizing and declining the obviously hypocoristic form

---

13 Just under forty instances are to be found in the Austrian Great Legendary and Codex Salmanticensis Lives of this saint (L&S nos 370 and 429 respectively).

14 A few instances appear scattered around the hagiographical works catalogued as L&S nos 403, 409, 423 and 486, while an aberrant ablative *Moluo* appears in no. 414 (p. 339 of Heist's edition as referenced there).

15 John T. Koch is hardly exaggerating the position when he speaks of 'a key era in the breakdown of the inherited declensional system that was somewhat earlier than that of the drastic Brittonic phonological changes in the mid fifth to late sixth centuries' ('The Loss of Final Syllables and Loss of Declension in Brittonic', *Bulletin of the Board of Celtic Studies*, 30 (1982–83), 201–33 (p. 233)).

16 L&S no. 93.

17 L&S no. 126.

'Machutu' as a third-declension Latin noun with genitive *Machutis*, dative *Machuti*, and ablative *Machute*. He is a little puzzled about what nominative to use, varying between his usual *Machu* and *Machutus* (the latter looking less strange, but involving a shift to the second declension). In the accusative case his regular third-declension *Machutem* seems on one occasion to be rendered more elevated still by the substitution of *n* for the final *m*, Greek-style, giving *Machuten*;[18] but even if this is a mistake, the hundreds of regularly declined occurrences of the name enable us at least to say that this particular Brythonic author had no reluctance to latinize and decline a hypocoristic form, and that with some imagination. More generally we can say that, whatever the reason may be, there is some detectable contrast within Celtic-Latin practice in this regard: by and large, Irish authors do not latinize their hypocoristics, while native speakers of Brythonic languages often do.

Bili's application of the Latin third declension to a vernacular name proves to be another feature that in practice tends to distinguish British-Latin from Hiberno-Latin works. My findings being what they were with Bili, I decided to investigate the occurrence of third-declension personal names throughout the *Archive* database. I went about this by searching it for all examples of *sancti*, *beati* or *regis* followed immediately by a word ending in *-is*. Looking for genitive singulars in this fashion seemed a good way of selecting for the third declension, and requiring that the forms should follow *sancti*, *beati* or *regis* ensured that this is what the software found (rather than, say, verbal endings or first- or second-declension plural datives and ablatives). It also helped to weed out the thousands of occurrences of ordinary Latin common nouns ending in *-is* which the search would otherwise have produced. The result was that I found regular occurrences (about a hundred and twenty examples all told) of third-declension genitives *Conuuoionis*, *Danielis*, *Dauidis*, *Dogmaelis*, *Hamonis*, *Ismaelis* and *Samsonis/Sansonis* as well as *Machutis*, all of these being Brythonic saints. (Daniel, David and Sampson are of course Biblical names; but in the Bible, David and Sampson are indeclinable; and an electronic search of the Cetedoc Library of Christian Latin Texts for *Dauidis* as opposed to *Dauid* indicates that this name was generally left undeclined in patristic and early medieval Continental Latin practice too.) What I did not find, in contrast, was any Gaelic names that had been latinized as third-declension in this way (that is, with genitives in *-is*) when following *sancti*, *beati* or *regis*; and the Andersons imply that of all the hundreds of occurrences of Irish vernacular names latinized by Adomnán that do not follow *sancti*, *beati* or *regis*, only four are assigned by him to the Latin third declension. These are the genitives *Cerbulis* from 'Cerball', *Conallis* from 'Conall', *Domnallis*

---

18 This form occurs on p. 258 of *Annales de Bretagne*, 24, in Lot's edition as referenced in L&S no. 825.

from 'Domnall', and *Nellis* from 'Néill'; but only one of these occurs more than once, two occur in the same sentence, and Adomnán renders the names of other men called Conall and Domnall as Latin second-declension forms, so his third-declensional ones must be regarded as exceptional.[19] Adomnán's universal practice otherwise is to latinize masculine vernacular names as second declension and feminine ones as first declension, and this is in line with Hiberno-Latin usage as a whole. Again one must ask whether it is merely coincidence that Brythonic Latin authors, whose own vernaculars had no case system, felt free to use the Latin third declension in their adaptations of names, whereas Irish writers, whose own language had several declensions (including ones that were cognate with the composite Latin third),[20] kept their Latin case system as simple as possible.

Now we must home in on the Latin second declension. This is the one that Hiberno-Latin authors impose almost universally on their vernacular names, and that even Brythonic authors use far more often than the third declension. But here too, a distinction in usage between the Gaelic and the Brythonic-speaking areas seems to emerge, and it is this. Standard Latin, of course, has second-declension nominatives of proper names ending in *-us*, and many of these end in *-ius*. In the realm of western Saints' names, the same applies: alongside forms terminating in consonant plus *-us* (such as Augustinus, Aurelianus, Germanus, Petrus, Paulinus, Tertullianus etc.), one has only to open at random a few pages of a directory such as the *Clavis Patrum Latinorum* to find plenty of names ending in *-ius* (such as Ambrosius, Evagrius, Auspicius, Prudentius, Remigius, Sulpicius and so on). Within the Celtic-Latin corpus, it is clear that our authors were well aware of such names, and we have numerous instances from all places and periods of *-ius* forms such as Gregorius, Hilarius, Demetrius, Remigius, Palladius and Laurentius — and of course Patricius — together with the appropriate endings in other cases. But those examples are all of non-Celtic names. What about latinizations of names of Celtic origin? I again searched the database for genitives following *sancti*, *beati* or *regis*, this time looking for ones ending in *-ii* (this being the most striking element in the paradigm of *-ius* forms). However, since the non-distinctive contracted form in single *-i* is also still current in Celtic-Latin texts, I looked too for the nominatives *sanctus*, *beatus* or *rex* followed by names ending in the sequence *-ius* itself. The outcome was that in texts written in Britain or Brittany, there was no clear reason that I could detect why any particular name had come to be latinized

---

19 Andersons, *Adomnan's Life of Columba* (1961), pp. 136–37. Adomnán's *Finnionem* is also clearly of the third declension, but that name is known to constitute, at some level, a Brythonic loan. For a different view, see below Ó Riain, 185ff.

20 The details are provided by Rudolf Thurneysen, *A Grammar of Old Irish*, revised and enlarged edition, with Supplement, translated by D.A. Binchy and Osborn Bergin (Dublin, 1946), pp. 176–217.

as an -*ius* rather than as a consonant-plus-*us* form. The names that did come to be latinized as -*ius* forms are rare but, putting them into the nominative for reference, we regularly find 'Brynach' appearing as *Bernac(h)ius*, 'Brieg' as *Brioccius*, 'Dyfrig' as *Dubricius*, 'Magloire' as *Maglorius* and 'Melaine' as *Melanius* (if the latter is indeed Celtic), while most others are treated as consonant-plus-*us* names. On the Irish side, however, the hint of a system seems to emerge, though the -*ius* forms in question are even rarer than on the Brythonic side. The only ones that appear regularly and that derive from Irish forms ending in a consonant are 'Dermitius', 'Lugidius' and 'MacCu(y)rbius', to which we may add 'Echodius' though it does not appear after the usual three titles.[21] What we can perhaps note about these is that the vernacular final consonant in question is in each case phonemically palatal in the original nominative: the underlying early Irish names are 'Díarmait', 'Lugaid', 'Mac Cuirbb' and 'Echaid'. Now the Andersons point out that Adomnán builds Latin oblique cases on Irish nominatives[22] and, somewhat in line with this, we have already seen in the area of declensions that Hiberno-Latin in general seems to avoid attempting to match the latinizing morphology up with that of the form being treated. In short, things are kept simple, but systematic.[23] May one then suggest that, in the matter of 'Dermitius', 'Lugidius', 'MacCu(y)rbius' and 'Echodius', the -*ius* and corresponding oblique sequences are really just further examples of -*us* and the corresponding obliques, the immediately-preceding *i* in fact being an indication of the palatality of the consonant that in turn precedes it, and thus really part of the underlying vernacular name rather than of the latinizing termination? In support of this contention is the fact that in Adomnán's work the -*ius* form *Lugudius* which latinizes 'Lugaid' is systematically distinguished from a consonant-plus-*us* form *Lugaidus*, which represents a different name compounded of 'Lug' and 'Áed' that had a non-palatal final consonant in the vernacular.[24] If we are right about this phenomenon, it could in turn be seen as having a vestigial but logical connection with a convention found in post-apocope ogham inscriptions by which (for example) the palatal nature of the final

21 The name of the saint commemorated at Monasterboice is latinized as case-forms of *Boecius* throughout the late Life of him in the *Collectio Oxoniensis* (L&S no. 469); but see above concerning the influence of the name Boethius in this case.

22 *Adomnan's Life of Columba* (1961), p. 133 (though the associated discussion is not very clear).

23 Registering the same phenomenon in the (much earlier) latinization of mostly Irish names recorded in the post-Roman inscriptions of Britain, Kenneth Jackson considers that it was because the engravers were 'lazy or ignorant' (*Language and History in Early Britain* (Edinburgh, 1953; reprinted Blackrock, 1994), p. 188). In the light of the present considerations Eoin MacNeill may be thought to have have been wiser in his recording of the pattern without comment ('Archaisms in the Ogham Inscriptions', *Proceedings of the Royal Irish Academy*, 39C (1929–31), 33–53 (p. 37)).

24 Andersons, *Adomnan's Life of Columba* (1961), pp. 146 and 147.

consonant in /makʹ/, the genitive of the word for 'son' (modern 'mic'), is indicated by spelling the word with the characters corresponding to *MAQI*, even though the vowel corresponding to the final *-I* had long disappeared in pronunciation.[25] In that case, what our manuscript *-ius* forms show us is Hiberno-Latin authors making the most of the fact that this termination was an acceptably Latin-looking sequence of letters, which could at the same time be exploited so as to reflect the Gaelic phonology of the name more accurately than could otherwise be done. As with the use of glide-vowel symbols in the manuscript writing of the vernacular, such an example of the adaptation of the roman alphabet (and in this case Latin orthographic sequences) to what was the quite different phonemic structure of Old Irish represents a coining of considerable inventiveness.

A final, connected indication of what may be called the cleverness of Hiberno-Latin name formation is the following. In what came to be the fairly standardized spelling system used for the Old Irish vernacular, the letter *e* indicated palatal quality in a preceding consonant just as much as the letter *i* did. One might then wonder whether *-eus* could not be used just as well as *-ius* as a latinizing termination to names ending in a palatal consonant — particularly considering that *-eus* was an extremely common ending in mainstream Latin, both in adjectives like 'arboreus', 'argenteus', 'femineus', 'igneus' and so on, and (with an often-unwritten preceding 'a') in names like Achaeus, Achilleus, Prometheus, Matheus, Timotheus etc. But in fact we very rarely find Gaelic names ending in palatal consonants being latinized this way, and the reason seems to emerge quite clearly. There was a large range of Irish names that in the vernacular ended with the vowel /e/; and as early as Adomnán's time the sequence *-eus* had been systematically appropriated as the best established Latin spelling for rendering this in translation. Although the vowel in question was reduced to a neutral schwa well within the period of our corpus (giving vernacular forms like 'Ailbe', 'Énna', 'Fursa', 'MacNise', 'Mochta' and so on), *-eus* continued to be the spelling used for the latinized versions. The use of *-eus* was not extended to the indication of palatality in a preceding consonant, except in a single instance (within the *Archive*) of the form *Daigeus*, from 'Daig';[26] and *-ius* did not come to be used to latinize Irish names ending in vowels. So, whether deliberately or not, the usages were kept apart; and once again, we find that the result was a gain in precision. Whatever about the consistency with which vernacular names were latinized in Britain and Brittany, I feel this is one more indication that the system that developed for translating forms in the Gaelic-speaking world is one for which we tend to give the early Irish *literati* insufficient credit.

25 A single roman-letter vernacular example of the same phenomenon is to be found in the famous ogham-age Inchagoill inscription; see Eoin MacNeill, 'Archaisms', p. 37.
26 L&S no. 425, the late Codex Salmanticensis Life of St Mochta (p. 400 of Heist's edition).

A Swallowed Onomastic Tale in *Cath Maige Mucrama*?

John T. Koch

UNIVERSITY OF WALES CENTRE FOR ADVANCED WELSH
AND CELTIC STUDIES, ABERYSTWYTH

THE present paper concerns the memorably revolting, but poorly motivated, mouse-swallowing episode of *Cath Maige Mucrama*. At the relevant point in the narrative, the protagonist Lugaid Mac Con has fled
from Ireland. Travelling incognito, he and his retinue have offered their services
to the king of Alba. After learning of Mac Con's exile, the king seeks to discover
which of the Gaels is the band's leader. The text and translation from O Daly's
ITS edition follow.

¶26. 'Maith', or in rí frisin ferthaigis, 'finta cía as toísech fodla 7 ara ṅdéntar
bélaib'. Ni buí and ón acht in rechtaire a óenur. 'Fír', or in rí, 'marbaid dam
dreim de lochdaib'.

¶27. Do-berar im*morro* luch for cuibrend cech f ir díb is sí dergg cona fiṅd, 7
do-berar ara mbélaib. Ocus at-rubrad friu co mair[b]fitis mani estais na lochtha.
Imm(a)[-dergad] dóib. Ro bánta co mór íar sain. Noco tucad cuccu ríam aṅceiss
bud doilgiu leo.

¶28. 'Cinnas atát?' or in rí. 'Ataat ina mbruc(c) 7 a mmíasa 'na fíadnaisi'. 'Is
broc(c) M*u*man dar míasa ón', ar in rí. 'Apa[i]r friu mairbfiti*r* mani essat'.

¶29. 'Nip sén ó timmarnad', or Lug*aid*, la tabairt na lochad inna béolu [ocus] in rí ocó déscin.

¶30. Dos-ṁberat na fir uile la sodain. Buí fer dobbrónach díb no scead la tabairt [n-]erbbaill na llochad dia bélaib. 'Calgg dart brágit', or Lug*aid*, 'iss ithi lochad coa lloss'. Slucid íarum erboll na llochad.

¶31. 'Do-gníat ní airiut', or in rí ón dorus. 'Do-gníim-se erro-som da*no*', or Lug*aid*. 'In tussu in Lug*aid*?' or in rí. 'Iss ed mo ainm', so or Lug*aid*.

¶26. 'Well', said the king to the steward, 'find out who presides over the serving (i.e. before whom it is performed).' There was no one there, that is to say, only the steward. 'So', said the king, 'kill me a batch of mice'.

¶27. Then a mouse, raw and with its pelt still on, is placed on each man's portion and it is put before them. And they were told they would be killed if they did not eat mice. They reddened. After that they became very pale. Never before had there been presented to them a more grievous dilemma.

¶28. 'How are they?' said the king. 'They are troubled, with their dishes before them'. 'That is Munster's dissatisfaction in spite of [full] dishes', said the king. 'Tell them they will be slain if they do not eat'.

¶29. 'No luck to him by whom the command was given', said Lugaid, putting the mouse into his mouth, the king watching him [the while].

¶30. With that all the men put them [in]. There was one wretched man of them who used to vomit while bringing the mouse's tail to his lips. 'A sword across your throat!' said Lugaid. 'A mouse must be eaten [even down] to the tail'. Then he swallows the mouse's tail.

¶31. 'They obey you', said the king from the doorway. 'I obey them too', said Lugaid. 'Are you Lugaid?' said the king. 'That is my name', said Lugaid.[1]

Several years ago, the idea that a covert onomastic tale stood behind this episode fluttered briefly into print, twice.[2] In neither mention was the theory fully expounded. So, the aim of the present contribution is, in part, belatedly to make up this deficit. Beyond that, the earlier published suggestions are noteworthy in two respects. First, they were independent of one another. Second, the ideas, though essentially the same, were deployed in discussions focused on different periods and cultural connections: McCone viewed the episode as symptomatic of biblical/literary inspiration in Early Irish vernacular tales, whereas I saw it as the

1 M. O Daly, *Cath Maige Mucrama*, Irish Texts Society 1 [Roman '50'] (London, 1975), 46–7. In ¶26, I remove O Daly's quotation marks from the second sentence for sense.
2 It would hardly be surprising if the idea had occurred to someone before, though I have been unable to locate it elsewhere in the secondary literature. Cf., e.g., M. E. Dobbs, 'Who Was Lugaid mac Con?', *Journal of the Royal Society of Antiquaries of Ireland* 60 (1930) 165–87.

reflex of developments on the oral, secular, native side and looked to inter-Celtic connections (namely the mouse hanging episode of *Manawydan*[3] and the capture of the *nobilis dux* Lugotorix by Julius Caesar in 54 BC[4]). This difference of interpretation sets matters on a theoretical plane. As the confluence of orality and literacy in the early Celtic literatures, and the comparison of early Irish and Welsh traditional narratives, are areas in which our field has benefited immeasurably from Proinsias Mac Cana's leadership, I hope this small offering will not trigger the gag reflex.

At this point it will be useful to lay the two earlier treatments side by side, together with their immediate contexts.

The key comparison between [The] M[abinogi] and [*De*] B[*ello*] G[*allico*] is that the capture of Lugotorix and the *llygoden* immediately precedes and directly precipitates the capitulation of the individual who caused the disappearance of the people and flocks and the exile of Mandubracios/ Manawydan. In both accounts, the restored realm is presented to Mandubracios/Manawydan and the final condition imposed upon the enemy is that Mandubracios/Manawydan and his people be left in peace by the man who had harmed them.

Lugotorīx may or may not mean 'Mouse-King'. If it does, a better spelling would be *Lucotorix*, which is, in fact, the way Holder listed the name.[5] Ellis Evans, on the other hand, connects it with Welsh *lleu* 'light [, &c.]' and the divine Gaulish name *Lugus*, Welsh *Lleu*, Irish *Lug*.[6] We may compare Gaulish ΛΟΥΚΟΤΙΚΝΟϹ ('Son of Mouse'), *Lucotios*, as against *Lugudunolus*, ogam LUGUDEC, LUGUDECCAS.[7] We should remember that whereas the Celtic word for 'mouse' has an inherent dental suffix -*ot*-, **lugu*- does not and should have *u* after the *g*, not *o*. Here, the important point is that *Lugotorīx* — in either written or spoken form — would have seemed enough as though it contained the word for 'mouse' to inspire a pun or onomastic tale. John Carey has drawn my attention to another Celtic tale which apparently involves a pun on a name in *Lugu*- serving as the basis for a mouse episode: in the Old Irish *Cath Maige Mucrama* the exiled king Lugaid Mac Con is forced to reveal his name when he and his company are compelled to eat mice by their host, the king of Alba.[8]

3 *Pedeir Keinc y Mabinogi*, gol. I. Williams (Caerdydd, 1930) 60–5.
4 *De Bello Gallico* v, 21–2.
5 *Alt-celtischer Sprachschatz*, ii (Leipzig, 1904), p. 303, line 45. The emendation was evidently his own editorial preference and not founded on the manuscripts.
6 *Gaulish Personal Names* [Oxford, 1967] p. 99.
7 For *lucot*- 'mouse' and *lugu*- 'light' names in Old Celtic, see ibid., pp. 218–21.
8 J. T. Koch, 'A Welsh Window on the Iron Age: Manawydan, Mandubracios', CMCS 14 (1987) 17–52 (pp. 30–1).

McCone's proposal comes by way of comparing the biblical and Irish etymological approaches to names, suggesting derivation of the latter from the former.

> In line with this concern [in the Vulgate and Isidore's *Etymologiae*], etymologically significant place-names are usually, and personal names occasionally, rendered by a Latin translation that brings out the connection with the explanatory narrative clearly. A handful of typical examples must suffice here, e.g. "and they came to Marath and could not drink the waters of Mara because they were bitter (*nec poterant bibere aquas de Mara quod essent amarae*), wherefore he also imposed [the] name fitting the place, calling it Mara, that is bitterness (*unde et congruum loco nomen imposuit vocans illud Mara id est amaritudinem*; Ex. 15:23)". . . . After Samson's famous slaughter of the Philistines with the jawbone of an ass (*maxilla asini*) "he cast away the jawbone out of his hand and called the name of the place Ramath-lehi, which is translated 'elevation of the jawbone (*Elevatio Maxillae*)'" (Judges 15:17, cf. 2:15, 1 Sam./Kgs. 7:10–3 etc.). . . .

The author of the medieval Irish saga *Cath Maige Mucrama* (O Daly, 1975) is an example of someone who makes considerable narrative use of etymologies of the names of people and places. Again two or three illustrations will serve here. "Ailill had intercourse with the maiden. While he was at this the woman sucked his ear (*ó*) so that she left neither flesh nor skin on it and so that it never grew on it from that time. So that Ailill Bare-ear (*Ó-lomm*) is his name since" (par. 3). Later on the name [*Mag Mucrama*] is slightly distorted to *Mag Mucríma* and etymologised as 'Plain of Pig-counting' with the help of an elaborate aetiological tale about the difficulty of counting (*rím*) some destructive magical pigs (*muc*) from Hell (par. 34–7). Moreover, although this is not explicitly stated, the striking episode about Lugaid and his followers being forced to eat mice (par. 26–30) seems to have been triggered by the similarity of the hero's name and the Old Irish word for mouse, *luch*, acc. *lochaid*. It thus appears distinctly possible, to say the least, that the etymological machinery so prominent in early Irish narrative literature owes its initial impetus to the Bible.[9]

The underlying version of the mouse episode (according to McCone as well as myself as far as one can judge from the foregoing) is as follows. As in CMM, the exiled band seeks the patronage of a foreign king. As in CMM, their trepidatious leader wishes to conceal their identity and, more particularly, his own. As in CMM, the foreign king aims to discover who the leader is. As in CMM, he knows that the exiles' leader's name is *Lugaid*, or something like that.

---

9 K. R. McCone, *Pagan Past and Christian Present in Early Irish Literature*, Maynooth
   Monographs iii (Maynooth, 1990) 47–8.

As in CMM, he tricks the exiles into revealing which man is Lugaid by feeding them mice (nom. pl. *lochaid*[10] < Celtic *lukotes*). However, unlike what appears on the surface of CMM, the original point of the ruse was not to see who would take charge in a gastronomic crisis, but to force the man who had a prohibition against eating anything that sounded like *Lugaid* to reveal himself. This reconstructed narrative is far more crisply on target than the extant version. After all, there might be any number of memorable traumas that the host king could have inflicted on his mercenaries to coerce a spontaneous display of leadership. There are even any number of disgusting dishes to inflict that particular sort of trauma. Why must it be mice? If the king and storyteller lack such subtle grasp of group dynamics and wish (in a society with onomastic dietary tabus) to reveal who is named *Lugaid*, they can do so directly and unambiguously by finding out who cannot eat *lochaid*. If the hapless gagger continues a character in the more basic episode, that man had perhaps been ordered by Lugaid to consume the tabu dish. In other words, it was not the vomiting that was originally important, nor the chain of command *per se*, but rather showing which man found it necessary to have another eat a mouse for him.

Onomastic dietary tabus do function in early Irish literature as pivotal narrative devices,[11] a famous example being an episode from the 'Death of Cú Chulainn'.

He went on along the road of Midluachair, across Mag Mugna. He saw something: three witches blind in the left eye, before him on the road. They were cooking a lap-dog, with poison and spells, on spits of holly. It was one of Cú Chulainn's *gessi* to pass a cooking-place without visiting it to eat something there. But it was also a *geis* of his to eat the flesh of his namesake. He made haste and sought to go past: he knew that they were not there to do him good.

Then the witch said, 'Pay a visit, Cú Chulainn.'

'I will not,' Cú Chulainn said.

'The food is only a hound [*cú*],' she said. 'If it were a great roast which was here,' she said, 'you would visit; but since there is only a little you will not. He does not deserve the great who will not take the little.'

Then he approached; and the witch gave him the dog's shoulder with the left hand. Cú Chulainn took it from her hand and put it under his left thigh. The hand which took it and the thigh under which he put it were stricken from top to bottom, so that their normal strength did not remain in them.[12]

10 Nom. pl. *lochaid* is attested in Middle Irish at least: see DIL sn. *luch* with a citation to the Irish version of the Alexander Romance.
11 For a recent discussion, see Kelly, *Early Irish Farming* 353.
12 From 'The Death of Cú Chulainn' from the Book of Leinster, trans. J. Carey, in *The Celtic Heroic Age*, ed. Koch with Carey (2nd edition, Malden, Massachusetts, 1995) 126.

At this point, we shall begin to consider whether a more mediaeval and literary approach or a more deeply diachronic and broadly Celtological approach will
get us greater mileage in the specific case of the CMM mouse episode. In other
words, did the earlier episode, as sketched above, more probably arise and then
somehow get redirected within a pre-literary *milieu* or later, as an aspect of
Christian literary activities? McCone's suggested connections to Jerome and
Isidore and mine regarding the Mabinogi and Romano-British history may be
left to the side. There is a fair amount of internal evidence and both sets of
comparisons entail ramifications that fall outside the present scope.

That there are in fact pre-Christian Celtic analogues for the dietary tabus of
the sagas — and that they are not all therefore to be accounted for purely as
literary reflexes of biblical or Isidorean etymology — is demonstrated by
classical references such as Caesar's regarding the Britons' avoidance of the flesh
of the hare, chicken, and goose: *leporem et gallinam et anserem gustare fas non
putant; haec tamen alunt animi voluptatisque causa.*[13] Of course, though suggestive,
such pre-Christian evidence does not in and of itself prove the CMM episode to
be pre-Christian.

From what has been brought out thus far, the mouse episode is seen to be at
least minimally diachronic. That is to say, it is obvious from the passage itself
that the writer of the extant text did not think up the mouse story then (1)
streamline it to omit the onomastic 'punchline', (2) forget that punchline as he
wrote, or (3) think it clear enough to require no explanation. Instead, he
provided a complete and elaborate new motivation for the episode, tied to
themes of hospitality, exile, leadership, and kingly prerogative. He also uses the
story to explain two *seanfhocail*: 'Munster's dissatisfaction in spite of dishes' and

---

13   *De Bello Gallico* v.12, ed. H. J. Edwards, Loeb Classical Library (Cambridge, Massachusetts,
     1917) 250. Pausanias (VII.xvii.10) notes a tabu peculiar to the Galatae of the neighbour-
     hood of Pessinus (south-west of Ancyra and Gordion), which possibly arose from a cultic
     adaptation of, or convergence with, a local myth in Asia Minor.

     ἐνταῦθα ἄλλοι τε τῶν Λυδῶν καὶ αὐτὸς Ἄττης ἀπέθανεν ὑπὸ
     τοῦ ὑός. καί τι ἑπόμενον τούτοις Γαλατῶν δρῶσιν οἱ
     Πεσσινοῦντα ἔχοντες, ὑῶν οὐχ ἁπτόμενοι.

     . . . Then certain Lydians, with Attis himself, were killed by the boar, and it is
     consistent with this that the Gauls who inhabit Pessinus abstain from pork.

     Description of Greece vol 3, trans. W. H. S. Jones, Loeb Classical Library (London, 1933)
     268–9; *Guide to Greece* vol 1, trans. P. Levi (Harmondsworth, 1971) 271–2; see also S.
     Reinach, 'Les survivances du totémisme chez les anciens Celtes', *Revue celtique* 21 (1900)
     269–306, p. 298; H. D. Rankin, *Celts and the Classical World* (London, 1987) 82; cf. S. H.
     O'Grady *apud* G. Murphy, *Duanaire Finn* III, Irish Texts Society xliii (1954) xxxvi n. 1.

'A mouse must be eaten to the tail' (showing one or more authors to be receptive to oral sources). Thus, we can distinguish two stages: an earlier onomastic stage and a later post-onomastic stage, the works of at least two authors or storytellers. That would still leave room for the essence of McCone's interpretation. *Cath Maige Mucrama* is a text, perhaps, of the 9th century. For the etymological onomastic tradition of early Irish literature, McCone invokes literary inspiration from Isidore, which would go back to the 7th century, and primary inspiration from the Bible, which would have been a presence in Ireland from at least the 5th. In fact, if we think of the extant episode as an editorial amplification by a writer who failed to understand — or for some reason rejected — the motives in a more concise earlier text, it would be possible to restore that onomastic version by trimming away the secondary plot roughly as follows.

> [. . .] 'So', said the king, 'kill me a batch of mice [*lochaid*]'. Then a mouse [*luch*] [. . .] is placed on each man's portion and it is put before them. [. . .] They reddened. After that they became very pale. Never before had there been presented to them a more grievous dilemma.
>
> 'How are they?' said the king. 'They are troubled, with their dishes before them'. . . . 'Tell them they will be slain if they do not eat'.
>
> 'No luck to him by whom the command was given', said Lugaid [. . .], the king watching him.
>
> 'Are you Lugaid?' said the king. 'That is my name', said Lugaid.

On the phonetic side, if we assume the pun was between *Lugaid* and *lochaid* 'mice', then there would have been a closer similarity between the Primitive Irish *[Luγuδ′ɪh] < *Lugu-deχs* and *[Luġəd′ɪh] < *lukotes*, than between their Old Irish reflexes. But of course, other paradigmatic forms might be involved where (e.g. the fundamental form, OIr. nom. sg. *luch*) where this would have been less the case.[14] Furthermore, if the linguistic equations of literary dietary-tabu episodes functioned according to the general principles of the mediaeval Irish etymological method (as would seem to be implied by McCone's explanation and use of this example), then the vocalism of the root would have been no obstacle; cf. the *Scithi* : *Scotae* derivation. There is also the question of whether *Lugaid* and *Lugith*, both used for Mac Con in CMM, are actually the same name (gen.

---

14 Primitive Irish *lukus* (Thurneysen, GOI §323), nom. pl. *lochaid* = Middle Welsh *llygot* < Celtic *lukotes*; cf. Welsh *llyg* 'shrew' < *lukūᵗS*.

Luigdech, ogam LUGUDECCAS)[15] or whether the latter should go instead with Ogam LUGUTTI.[16] (More probably the former, as the *Lugith* spelling is limited to O Daly's manuscript N[17], where we also find the spellings *Nuothet, Meith, othchi*, and the like.) None of this can be decisive as to the precise chronological horizon of the near homophony, as the forms in question were all fairly similar in both Old Celtic and Old Irish.

O Daly made a relevant observation about Mac Con's names:

> In all our texts except CMM [i.e. *Scéla Éogain, Scéla Mosauluim*, and *Cath Cinn Abrad*], Mac Con is always so called and the name Lugaid is never applied to him, while in CMM the redactor usually refers to him as Lugaid (37 exx.); six times the form Lugaid Mac Con occurs and Mac Con alone, fifteen times, four of which are in verse.[18]

In the late 7th-century Patrician memoranda of Tírechán, an apparently identical character appears with the name form (gen.) *Maicc Con* (§40).[19] Likewise, in the king list of *Baile Chuind*, which is often regarded as a later 7th-century text,[20] the name is given as *Mac Con maicc aui Lugde Loïgde*.[21] In the Old Irish, possibly 8th-century, *De Síl Chonairi Móir* ('Of The Lineage of Conaire Mór'), he is called *Macc Con machu Luigde* once, and simply *Mac(c) Con* a further six

15 On this name, see D. E. Evans, *Gaulish Personal Names* (Oxford, 1967) 156–8.; D. McManus, *A Guide to Ogam*, Maynooth Monographs 4 (Maynooth, 1991) 86, 89, 103, 116, 117, 125, 177 n. 12, 178 n. 17. L. Joseph proposes the sense 'Worshipper of Lug': IE **dek'-* 'serves' (men to god) 'favour' (god to men), 'Old Irish *tuir*, 'house-post', *Ériu* 33 (1982) 176–7. A different root is suggested by Pokorny, *Indogermanisches etymologisches Wörterbuch*, (Bern & München, 1959–69) 189–90; cf. McManus, *Guide to Ogam* 178, n. 17. Joseph's proposed root could be the base of the verb found in the final repetitive formula of the Chamalières tablet: *Luge dessummiiis Luge dessumiis Luge dessumiis Luχe.*

16 On LUGUTTI, see O. Bergin, '*Varia* 25. *Luchte*', *Ériu* 12 (1938) 231–5; McManus, *Guide to Ogam* 108.

17 Text printed *Cath Maige Mucrama* 94 ff.

18 *Cath Maige Mucrama* 9.

19 Ed. L. Bieler, *Patrician Texts in the Book of Armagh*, Scriptores Latini Hiberniae x (Dublin, 1979) 154.

20 Specifically 675×695; see F. J. Byrne, *Irish Kings and High-Kings* (London, 1973) 91; E. Bhreathnach, *Tara: A Select Bibliography*, Discovery Programme Reports 3 (Dublin, 1995) 50, item B.10. Cf. also Ó Cathasaigh, *Heroic Biography of Cormac mac Airt* 82; 'The Threefold Death in early Irish Sources', *Studia Celtica Japonica* N.S. 6 (1994) 53–75: 69; J. Carey, 'On the Interrelationships of some *Cín Dromma Snechtai* Texts', *Ériu* 46 (1995) 71–92, at 88–9.

21 See G. Murphy, 'On the Dates of Two Sources Used in Thurneysen's *Heldensage*', *Ériu* 16 (1952) 145–56; Byrne, *Irish Kings and High-Kings* 276. The *maicc aui* of the two MSS was emended by Murphy, no doubt correctly, to *moccu*.

times.[22] What this distribution within the earlier texts suggests is that Mac Con was called *Lugaid* first in the prototype of CMM ((2) below), and there so called only because of the presence of the mouse episode that demanded the name *Lugaid*, or something like it. It follows, therefore, that we can now postulate an additional diachronic stage, i.e. a total of three: (1) a stage when the Mac Con character was not yet called *Lugaid*, (2) a later stage when he was given that name so as to motivate the mouse episode, (3) the stage reflected in the extant text in which the mouse episode has lost its onomastic motivation and thus become a more complex narrative.

An interesting question and a significant conclusion follow from the foregoing points. Did some storyteller or author first think up the mouse story as a device for the Mac Con saga and therefore call the protagonist *Lugaid*? Or was there some earlier story in which a hero named *Lugaid*, or something like it, was already part of the mouse episode, and were that name and story then transferred to CMM? It would seem inherently unlikely that anyone would make up a story about the hero's name that required giving him a completely new name to be awkwardly added on to the old one. Furthermore, that primary name *Mac Con* means 'Son of Dog' or 'Son of Wolf' in a way that is even more obvious than the similarity of *Lugaid* to *luch*, &c.[23] So the creator of CMM might just as well (even better one would think) have had the king of Alba feed the exiles dogs, just as the witches gave Cú Chulainn a dog. Therefore, the latter is the more likely alternative, i.e. the mouse episode already existed connected to the revelation of a character with a name like *Lugaid*. This previously existing name and onomastic episode were reworked to create the account of 'Lugaid' Mac Con and the mice.

One might suppose this reworking to be a radical innovation in which the onomastic episode and name were first detached from a tradition relating to a different character and then drawn into the Mac Con saga. But a less radical solution is possible. We see that in the other versions of the saga, Mac Con is called *mac Luigdech* 'son of Lugaid', and as above, the older sources (i.e. *Baile*

---

22 L. Gwynn (ed.), 'De Shíl Chonairi Móir' *Ériu* 6 (1912) 130–43, pp. 134–5. On the date, see E. Bhreathnach, *Tara* 89, item 125.

23 This is the explanation in *Cóir Anmann* ('The Appropriateness of Names') §71; edition and translation: W. Stokes, *Irische Texte* 3 (Leipzig, 1891) 285–444, pp. 322–3; perhaps drawing here on *Lebor Gabála* (LL 1738–40; cf. R. A. S. Macalister edition, vol 5, Irish Texts Society xliv (1956) 44, 66, 92, 100–2). In connection with the present point, we may leave aside, as immaterial to the perceptions of an early Irish audience, O Daly's etymological proposal 'that *Mac Con* has nothing to do with the word *cú* but is a Goidelicisation of the Brittonic Mabon', *Cath Maige Mucrama* 9, n. 84. See further below Appendix.

Chuind and *De Síl Chonairi Móir*) have here an old tribal name, basically *Mac Con moccu Lugde* (and/or *Loígde*). It is likely that it is the latter that preserves the older form of the cognomen and that the patronym *mac Luigdech* represents a reformation of the same, post-dating the obsolescence of the *moccu* names in the 8th century. The gentilic *moccu Lugde* 'of the tribe of Lugde' had once been enough to trigger the mouse tabu. In other words, in the 7th century or earlier, there would have been no need to explain that anyone named *moccu Lugde*, or the like, could not eat mice. Later, when the *moccu* names and associated tribal concepts became obsolete, the episode was revamped by applying the pivotal *Lugaid* directly to the protagonist himself. Then, later still, the idea of the namesake tabu became either obscure or objectionable, and the story was given its surviving expanded form.

The CMM mouse episode is not the only example of an onomastic tale (or for that matter a dietary-tabu onomastic tale) intelligible as such to Celticists today, but having its original point less than obvious in the extant text. Thus the example of 'Tadhg mac Céin and the Badgers' from *Sanas Cormaic*.

> Gaileng .i. gaeleng .i. cacc ar enech .i. Fri Cormac mac Taidc maic Céin as·robrath. Do·rigni side fleid do Thadc .i. dia athair. Cét cech cenéli anmandai occae inge bruicc nammá. Do·cuaid dī Cormac do broccenaig. Ropo mall lais anath fria togail, cota·gart cuice imach for fír n-enech a athar .i. Taidc. Ta·llotarsom in bruicc. Nos·marba iarum Cormac, cét diib. ⁊ tos·aispen oc ind fleid. Ro·gráin cride Taidc frie ⁊ ata·robaid. Ro·fitir iarum a ndo·rigned and ⁊ ro·ainmnigestar a mac hoc nomine .i. Cormac Gaelang.

> *Gaileng*, that is *Gaelang*, that is 'a fouling of honour'. It was applied to Cormac son of Tadhg mac Céin. He made a feast for Tadhg, his father. (There were) a hundred of each kind of animal at it except badgers. Then Cormac came to a badger set. He thought it slow to wait for it to be demolished, so he called them out to him under the protection of the honour of his father Tadhg. The badgers came to him. Then Cormac killed them — a hundred of them — and displayed them at the feast. Tadhg's heart shuddered at it and he refused it. He afterwards found out what had been done and called his son by this name — Cormac Gaelang.[24]

As Mac an Bhaird shows, the Irish name *Tadc* derives from the Celtic *tazgo-* 'badger'. By the Old Irish period, and the time of *Sanas Cormaic* in particular, *brocc*, not *tadc*, was the regular word for 'badger'. So it is not clear, whether the

24 Ed. and trans. A. Mac an Bhaird, 'Tadhg mac Céin and the Badgers', *Ériu* xxxi (1980) 150–5; cf. 'Genelach Síl Cormaic Gaileng', in M. A. O'Brien (ed.), *Corpus Genealogiarum Hiberniae* i (Dublin, 1962) 246.

obsolescent term for 'badger' would have been known to many, only a learned few, or to none at all by the date of the text above. A similar case is Irish *Art*, the name of the father of a different Cormac; as Ó Cathasaigh has written: '. . . the etymology of *Art* (Cormac's father) suggests that Cormac is a Bear-son in origin, for *Art* is the Irish reflex of the IE word for "bear"; it is no longer used for the animal owing to the operation of linguistic avoidance.'[25] Known or not, the basic onomastic premise of the badger story is preserved by explaining *cota·gart cuice imach for fír n-enech a athar .i. Taidc* 'he called [the badgers] out on the honour of his father, i.e. of Tadc'. Clearly the badgers are invoked verbally, using the name *Tadc*.

Now, because *tadc* was no longer the regular word for 'badger', the half-submerged quality of the onomastic tale is not surprising. It is likewise understandable how bear-like qualities in the traditional character of Cormac mac Airt might be vestigial. What is less clear is why CMM had to re-interpret the mouse story. The name *Lugaid Mac Con* would still have had an obvious resemblance to 'Mouse son of Dog' when CMM was written. It seems likely, therefore, that some further factor was at work, a factor that rendered the *Lugaid* : *lochaid* sound-alike problematical or objectionable, rather than merely obscure.

To understand the operation of an onomastic dietary tabu, as in understanding any sort of linguistic avoidance, it is essential to know the language in question, what the tabu words designate. But the prosaic meanings will not by themselves explain to us the sense of danger, *angst*, and potential disgrace that compels the avoidance. For this, we must turn to social and cultural anthropology, where we are at a distinct disadvantage in trying to understand societies of the past. Assuming that the early Irish readership was not being handed an unprecedented plot twist, the episode in 'The Death of Cú Chulainn' shows that taking one's namesake as food was sufficient cause for immediate debility and presaged imminent death. From our present distance, it will be hard to determine when such beliefs were merely strong enough to persist as effective literary devices and how long they remained occasions for real fear. The episode that survives in fact conveys a palpable anxiety in ¶27. It was the worst dilemma that the exiled, battle-hardened *fian* had ever faced: *Noco tucad cuccu ríam anceiss bud doilgiu leo.*

The naming devices in 'The Death of Cú Chulainn' and the Tadc mac Céin tale differ from the CMM mouse episode in two key respects. First, *Cú* and *Tadc* actually mean 'hound' and 'badger' and are not merely homophonous, like *Lugaid*. Second, *Cú* and *Tadc* are both simplexes, whereas *Lugaid* (Ogam gen. LUGU-DECCAS) is a compound. We are thus one step removed from a stronger and more primary version of the anxiety-provoking sound-alike, i.e. the basic member

25 T. Ó Cathasaigh, *The Heroic Biography of Cormac mac Airt* (Dublin, 1977) 82.

of the 'mouse' paradigm, nom. sg. *luch* < Celtic **lukū^tS*, and the name of the central mythological hero Lug[26] < the Celtic theonym *Lugus*. Some important conclusions follow. Even though we might allow some secondary support or multi-causation from Biblical/Isidorean etymology, the cultural power of the episode derives from linguistic associations rooted in Irish folk belief and pre-Christian Celtic religion behind that. In the tales, one of the recurrent properties of Lug is that he is not recognised and that stratagems must be used to reveal him and bring him to his rightful social rôle. The elaborate detailing of skills in the flyting at the gate of Tara in *Cath Maige Tuired* is a key example.[27] In the Fourth Branch of the Mabinogi, Lleu (whose name corresponds to Irish *Lug*) must disguise himself as a cobbler and thus trick Aryanrot into reluctantly naming him.[28] In the Third Branch, the imminent hanging of a mouse — which is a cause for considerable overt anxiety in the narrative — leads to the revelation of a disguised antagonist with the similar name *Llwyt*.

What I am suggesting is that the CMM mouse episode and its peculiar evolution must be understood as minor side effects of a deep-seated and culturally-charged pattern in linguistic folk-life. It has been suggested more than once that the Lugaid Mac Con figure was derived from, and remained in some sense equivalent to, Lug.[29] As noted from *Baile Chuind* and *De Síl Chonairi Móir* the older form of his name was *Mac Con moccu Lugd(a)i*,[30] in which the final term

---

26 Which would have been fully homophonous with 'mouse' in numerous phonetic contexts.

27 ITS vol lii, ed. E. A. Gray (1983) ¶¶54–74, pp. 38–43.

28 It is not improbable that the name *Aryanrot*, which means literally 'silver wheel', arose as a kenning for the moon. This possibility occurred to me when I questioned an elderly native of North Pembrokeshire about her use of the word *rhod* 'wheel'. She said that her usual word was *olwyn*, but she did know the other word, though the only example that came to her mind was the proverb *rhod heno, glaw 'fory*, meaning '[if there is] a wheel [of mist around the moon] tonight, [there will be] rain tomorrow'. Since one of the regular Welsh words for moon is (MW) *lleuat*, one would of course have to use a kenning if the name *Lleu* were under prohibition.

29 A most insightful review of the complex evidence being the work our honorand; see P. Mac Cana, 'Fianaigecht in the Pre-Norman Period', in *The Heroic Process: Form, Function, and Fantasy in Folk Epic*, ed. B. Almqvist, S. Ó Catháin, P. Ó Héalaí (Dun Laoghaire, 1987) 75–99, pp. 77–83; see also G. Murphy, *Duanaire Finn*, Part III (Dublin, 1953) lxxxi ff.; P. Ó Riain, 'Traces of Lug in Early Irish Hagiographical Tradition', ZCP 36 (1977) 138–56.

30 If we confine ourselves to considering the testimony of these two early texts, *Lu(i)gde* would seem to have priority over *Loígde* as Mac Con's tribal name. On *Loígde* and the Munster tribal name *Corcu Loígde*, cf. O Daly, *Cath Maige Mucrama* 11. It is not clear that gen. *Loígde* would go with the pre-apocope ogam LOGIDDEAS, on which see MacManus, *Guide to Ogam* 121. The uncertainty of the proto-form of Old Irish *loíg*, Old Welsh *lo*, Old Cornish *loch*, Middle Cornish *lugh*, Breton *leue* 'calf' is linked to this problem, on which

reflects an adjectival *īo-/īā*-stem, notional Celtic **Luguadīi* 'Lug-like'. The doublets *Lugde* and *Loígde* in the *Baile Chuind* list are remarkable, rendering Mac Con's name conspicuously long. It seems likely that these arose as byforms of the same original, one supporting an ancestral link to Lug and the other to the *Corco Loígde* of Munster (whose foundation legend involves Mac Con's father Lugaid hunting a 'fawn' (*loíg allaid*). (It is also worth noting here the frequent use of *Lughaidh* for the earlier *Lug*, as in e.g. modern folk versions of the Balor story.) It is this underlying oral pattern that explains why an episode that continued to make sense, and had had considerable impact on the tradition, survives in only a roundabout, reworked version. It is possible that, as in many cases of linguistic avoidance, the replacement strategy has been so successful that the original focus was indeed forgotten. But more or less the reverse is also possible, namely that the story remained so belief laden that CMM's author preferred to take a safer approach. A complex authorial attitude is possible, as well. That is, as an Irishman CMM's author was aware of popular beliefs about Lug and his namesakes, but as an educated Christian he worried (personally or officially) over such beliefs as suitable contents for written literature.[31]

In an earlier article, I proposed that in pagan Celtic times the myth and cult of Lugus had been a nexus of linguistic avoidance, involving the theonym itself and exact and near homophones.[32] In particular, I proposed such an explanation to

---

see Jackson *Language and History in Early Britain* (Edinburgh, 1953) 451; P. Schrijver, *Studies in British Celtic Historical Phonology*, Leiden Studies in Indo-European 5 (Amsterdam, 1995) 309-10. Schrijver's suggestion that OW *lo* is a back-formation from **loï* (< **laëgo-*), by way of a notional OW pl. **lo(ï)iöü*, would seem to be invalidated by *nöuïdligi* 'newly calved' in the 'Surexit Memorandum', showing the reflex of Celtic **log-* (i.e. with short, monophthongal *o*). If the base form were OW diphthongal **loï(g̯)*, we would look for **nöuïdluï(g̯)i*. It is possible that analogy or avoidance of the theonym were factors also in the development of this animal name in its various reflexes. The hunt of the *loíg* (*allaid*) by Lugaid in the sovereignty legend of the Corco Loígde, mentioned in the main text, would be another revelant connection.

31 For a parallel development of non-Christian elements in the Ulster Cycle, see J. Carey, 'The Uses of Tradition in *Serglige Con Culainn*', in *Ulidia: Proceedings of the First International Conference on the Ulster Cycle of Tales*, ed. J. P. Mallory and G. Stockman (Belfast, 1994) 77–84, esp. 84.

32 'Further to *tongu do dia toinges mo thuath* &c.', *Études celtiques* 29 (1992) 249–61. On the mythological hero < god Lug < Lugus, see P. Mac Cana, *Celtic Mythology* (1968, rev. ed. 1983, New York) 24–25; A. Tovar, 'The God *Lugus* in Spain', *BBCS* 29.4 (1981) 591–99. The topic of the equivalence of Julius Caesar's Gaulish Mercury and Celtic *Lugus* has been productively, but not necessarily decisively reopened by Bernhard Maier, 'Is Lug to be Identified with Mercury (*Bell. Gall.* vi 17,1)? New Suggestions on an Old Problem', *Ériu* 47 (1996) 127–36. In this article Maier notes that dedications to Belenos are more common than

account for the following three formulae:

(1) *toncnaman toncsiiontio* from the Gaulish tablet of Chamalières,

(2) *tongu do dia toinges mo thuath* 'I swear to god what my tribe swears' or the like, common in the Ulster Cycle,[33]

(3) *tyğhaf tyğhet it* 'I swear (ordain) a destiny on you' (*Culhwch ac Olwen* 50)[34]; *mi a dynghaf dyğhet iöaw*[35].

These I suggested reflected a Common Celtic or Pan-Celtic avoidance of the divine name and near homonym for 'oath', Old Irish *lugae*, Welsh *llw*. The unmarked form of the utterance would have been:

tongu do Lug lugae, (mi a) dyng(h)af lw y Leu, < **tongū (do) Luguei lugiom* 'I swear an oath to the oath-god'.[36]

In the same article, I also suggested that OIr. *toceth, tocad*, Welsh *tyng(h)et* '(a sworn) destiny, fate, &c.' < Celtic **tonketom* had likewise originated in this context. In other words, **tonketom* was coined as a replacement for the unmarked **lugiom* 'oath' to be used specifically in settings of the myth and cult of Lugus where it was necessary to avoid the god's name. As such, **tonketom* immediately took on the specialised meaning of 'divine oath, supernaturally efficacious oath', hence 'sworn destiny'.

Lately, Stefan Schumacher has resifted the evidence for the Welsh formula.[37]

---

those to Lugus. It is worth noting in this connection that the common Welsh name *Llywelyn* probably goes back to **Lugu-belinos*; see K. H. Jackson, *Language and History in Early Britain* (Edinburgh, 1953) §65; P. P. Schrijver, *Studies in British Celtic Historical Phonology* 340. The two gods were perhaps at one time closely associated or even equivalent. On the extent and importance of Lug in Ireland into the literary period, see also T. Ó Cathasaigh, 'The Eponym of Cnogba', *Éigse* 23 (1989) 27–38, pp. 30–3.

33 See further R. Ó hUiginn, 'Tongu do dia toinges mo thuath and related expressions', in *Sages, Saints and Storytellers: Celtic Studies in Honour of Professor James Carney* (ed. D. Ó Corráin, L. Breatnach, K. McCone, Maynooth 1989) 332-41; C. Watkins, 'Some Celtic Phrasal Echoes', in *Celtic Language, Celtic Culture: A Festschrift for Eric P. Hamp* (ed. A. T. E. Matonis, D. F. Melia, Van Nuys 1990) 47-56; 'New Parameters in Historical Linguistics, Philology, and Culture History', *Language* 65.4 (1989) 791-92. Unpublished at the time of this writing is Ó hUiginn's contribution to the Maynooth conference of June 1991.

34 Gol. R. Bromwich, D. S. Evans (Caerdydd 1988).

35 I. Williams (ed.), *Pedeir Keinc y Mabinogi* 79.

36 Cf. the Celtiberian dative sg. LVGVEI which occurs twice in the inscription of Peñalba de Villastar; see A. Tovar, '*Lugus* in Spain', 591–99. That *Lugus* and **lugiom* were perhaps etymologically connected, and not merely near homonyms, was proposed by H. Wagner, 'Studies in the Origins of Early Celtic Civilisation', ZCP 31 (1970) 1–58, pp. 22–25.

37 'Old Irish **tucaid, tocad* and Middle Welsh *tynghaf tynghet* Re-examined', *Ériu* 46 (1995) 49–57.

Providing the examples with altered glosses usefully illustrates that the act of solemnly swearing with reference to the future and that of verbally imposing a destiny are similar enough to be interchangeable in translation. It is hardly surprising that most English speakers need no verb 'destining'. Schumacher excludes the oldest piece of evidence, Gaulish *toncnaman toncsiiontio*, thus eliminating one context in which Celtic **tong-* 'swear' would be regularly devoiced to **tonk-*. Devoicing would likewise occur in the Early Welsh subjunctive and future paradigms, both key environments in the relevant semantic and pragmatic fields. One implication of Schumacher's argument is that Irish *tongu do dia toinges mo thuath*, &c., Welsh *mi a dynghaf tynget ytt*, &c., and Gaulish *toncnaman toncsiiontio* are coincidences, i.e. that they do not contain the same *figura etymologica*. The close connection of Lug/Lleu/Lugus with the three formulae would likewise have to be a coincidence. In the *locus classicus* of the Irish formula, the Ulster cycle, the *dia* who is the object of *do* is likely to be understood as Lug, the central hero's supernatural father (i.e. Cú Chulainn's).[38] In the *locus classicus* of the Welsh formula, the Fourth Branch of the Mabinogi, the second-person object of *y* 'to' (the cognate of Ir. *do*)[39] is Lleu.[40] It is upon Lleu < Lugus that his unwilling mother Aryanrot is swearing the oath or, if one prefers, 'destining' the destiny. The *figura* also recurs as a statement of the bleak fate of Llywarch < **Lugu-markos* 'The Stallion of Lugus', again as the object of the preposition *y* < *do*. The brief Chamalières text culminates in what are now generally taken to be four occurrences of the theonym *Lugus* in the dative — *Luge, Luge, Luge, Luχe*.[41] The avoidance of the usual suppletive verbal noun of *tongaid* 'swears', i.e. OIr. *lugae*, MIr. *luige* 'oath', in the older and more basic forms of the Irish formula would be yet another unmotivated coincidence in Schumacher's argument.

Schumacher concludes: 'In historical linguistics the claims of sound-laws, etymology and morphology must have precedence, and deformation inspired by taboo or the like can only be invoked as a last resort.' This statement has the ring of sound common sense. However, Schumacher gives no reasons or evidence to support the formulation. Linguistics, being a science, sometimes operates according to principles that are not commonsensical; heavy objects do not in fact fall faster

---

38 For an early text showing this relationship, see *Compert Con Culainn*, ed. A. G. van Hamel (Dublin, 1993) §5. For a discussion, see E. A. Gray, 'Lug and Cú Chulainn: King and Warrior, God and Man', *Studia Celtica* 24/5 (1989–90) 38–52.

39 If Welsh *tyngaf* 'I swear' and *tyng(h)af* 'I "destine"' are in origin disrelated, as Schumacher argues, they do nonetheless take the same preposition.

40 I. Williams (gol.), *Pedeir Keinc y Mabinogi* (Caerdydd, 1930) 79, 81, 83.

41 At least this emerged as the consensus at the Continental Celtic Workshop held at Berkeley in October 1998.

than lighter objects. All languages known to me have tabu avoidance,[42] whatever 'claims' and 'precedence' might be assigned to other linguistic processes. In some speech areas it is a great factor; for example, it is likely that we have many more Australian languages than we would otherwise, owing to the productive operation of tabu replacement. Even if we were to allow, for the sake of argument, that all things being equal most linguistic forms crossing our paths will not have tabu avoidance as a factor in their etymologies, it remains the case that in the examples under consideration all things are not equal. We are in specialised and highly marked domains — old formulae involving oaths, gods, fate, and magical prohibitions. In the Ulster Cycle instances, we are close in sense to damning by god's sanction, and in the Mabinogi, to damning by god (Aryanrot) of god (Lleu). Of the three instances of the formula in *Math*, it is the first which is crucial — it must be overcome for the god's identity to be realised: *Mi a dynghaf dyghet iđaw, na chaffo enw yny caffo y genhyf i* 'I swear a destiny on him, that he may not get a name until he gets it from me.'[43] The basic social situation in this is the common one in which a head of household rejects a foundling and hence strives to avoid calling that foundling by any term that could be construed as a name and forbids that anyone else give him a name. The flaw (as unintentional pet owners will understand) is that a common descriptive will come to be felt as a name, despite the wilful prohibition. In short, we are precisely in the usual domains of tabu and euphemistic circumlocution. It is, I think, mistaken to say that linguistic avoidance is the last factor we should consider in interpreting and deriving such utterances.

As Schumacher argues against etymologies based on 'deformation inspired by taboo or the like', it would probably be misleading not to point out that I never claimed that the devoicing of **tong-* to **tonk-* originated as a tabu-inspired violation of sound laws. Rather, it came about by regular voicing assimilation in certain suffixed and/or paradigmatic forms (e.g. *toncsiiontio*). I proposed that that devoiced form then spread, initially in the specialised magical and religious context in which the unmarked word for oath **lugiom* had to be avoided as a near homonym of *Lugus*.

In short, it remains my position that when we seek to understand pivotal formulae and episodes in traditional literatures, diachronic cultural factors *are* linguistic factors and must be taken into account. It is not good historical linguistics if we do not. It may make our lives easier to ignore the complex

---

42 A fact of which I am forcibly made aware almost daily while conveying in Welsh the information that I live in a 'small house'.

43 *Pedeir Keinc y Mabinogi* 79.

evidence for the ancient Celts of mainland Europe, but to do so will not yield more secure etymologies.

Returning to McCone's proposal above, I thoroughly agree that the etymological approaches of Jerome and Isidore go a long way towards accounting for the popularity of explaining place- and personal names in Irish vernacular tales. On the other hand, the mouse episode in CMM is not the best example for making this point. The impact of Christianity is more plausible as an impetus for the elaborate post-onomastic version of the story that survives than it is as the inspiration for the earlier episode. A Celtic theonym has never been far from the surface of literary developments. McCone and myself seem to agree on the basic mechanics of that underlying tale.

APPENDIX: *Mac Con* AND *Maponos?*

For three reasons, unknown to her at the time, O Daly's etymology of *Mac Con* is worth re-opening here. In the introduction to her edition of CMM, she wrote:

> I would suggest that the name Mac Con has nothing to do with the word *cú* but is a Goidelicisation of the Brittonic Mabon [< Gaulish and British *Maponos*], the division into two words being due perhaps to the final stress, a phenomenon which would be foreign to Goidelic.[44]

First, as noted above, it is remarkable that, if the protagonist's name had really always meant 'Son of Dog' or 'Son of Wolf', the dietary tabu episode had been based on a sound-alike involving the gentilic name. Second, the Welsh account of the heroic biography of Lleu (= OIr. *Lug* < Lugus) belongs to a native grouping of tales, the name of which is *Mabinogi*, a word which Eric Hamp has convincingly etymologised as **Maponākiī* 'matter concerning Maponos'.[45] Third, the Gaulish magical inscription from Chamalières juxtaposes an initial invocation of Maponos and a climactic closing with *Luge . . . Luge . . . Luge . . . Luχe* 'to Lugus . . . to Lugus . . . to Lugus . . . to Lugus'.

As brief as O Daly's formulation is, it will be useful to 'flight test' it agnostically, merely to see if it can be ruled out quickly as the linguistic details are fleshed out. One point that she makes ('Mac Con has nothing to do with the word *cú*') is wrong or at best misleading. As shown most clearly by Ó Cathasaigh at several points in *The Heroic Biography of Cormac mac Airt*, Mac Con has lupine and canine associations. However, if we rewrite O Daly's statement as 'the etymology of *Mac Con* had nothing to do with *cú* originally', it is then perhaps salvageable. Irish tradition is filled with so many characters whose names or patronyms contain elements meaning 'dog' and/or

44 *Cath Maige Mucrama* 9.
45 'Mabinogi', *Transactions of the Honourable Society of Cymmrodorion* (1975) 243–9.

'wolf', that once *Maccon had been reanalysed as 'Son of *Cú*', a whole set of established associations would have flowed to it.

As O Daly said explicitly, she had in mind an actual borrowing from Brittonic to Goidelic. Implicitly, the explanation also involves an oral reanalysis as it hinges on the word accent, more specifically an accented Brittonic short vowel that would never have been marked in writing. All that would demand a rather narrow and complex set of circumstances. Necessarily, British would have already fixed its word accent on the penult (whence the Neo-Brittonic ultima). Likewise, Irish would have developed its regular initial stress. Now, we do not know exactly when either variety of fixed accent developed. But when Common Celtic was one language, it had but one common accentual pattern. Therefore, both Common Celtic vocabulary and the older inter-Celtic loans could not possibly show a 'foreign' accent. The older Christian loan-words in Irish not only level the Latin and Brittonic accents, but also shorten, or even syncopate, the formerly stressed long vowels which became unstressed in Irish: e.g. OIr. *sesrae* < Lat. *sextārius*, *eclais* < *eclēsia*, *Notlaic* < **Nātālicia*.[46] Thus, if Brittonic *Mab'on* entered Irish as a foreignly-accented loan translation **Macc'on*, then we have something quite unparalleled and also late, post-dating much of the conversion. We would thus have to do, not with the borrowing of a Gaulish or British god, but with that of a Welsh wondertale figure. Furthermore, by the period in question, the Neo-Brittonic ultima would have had a phonetically long vowel, not a short stressed vowel. Whether that long vowel could have been borrowed as an Irish short stressed vowel is yet another problem. A pre-apocope borrowing of *Map'onos* would have had its accent assimilated to the Irish pattern (i.e. **'Maq^{u}q^{u}onas*) and could hardly have been confused with the four-syllable Primitive Irish **Maq^{u}q^{u}as Cunas* ('Son of Dog') anyway. In light of these considerations, O Daly's etymology looks like a non-starter.

But there is a second possibility, namely written transmission. Let us assume that *Maponos* either had a cognate in Irish or was borrowed early (La Tène Iron Age to pre-Conversion Romano-British period), in either event regularly developing to Primitive Irish **'Maq^{u}q^{u}onas*. Now, in Early Old Irish sources, the reflex of **'Maq^{u}q^{u}onas* would have been regularly written *Maccon*, not yet *Maccan*; cf. *~thēgot* for later *~thíagat* in the Cambrai Homily or *Uloth* for *Ulad* in the Annals of Ulster at 557, 577, 578, 611, and 674. The written form *Maccon* could easily have been miscopied or misunderstood as *Mac Con*. *Maccon* could also have become *Mac Con* by the sort of transference to the vernacular of Biblical/Isidorean etymological methods discussed by McCone in the passage above. If this is what happened, it happened before *c.* 690 when Tírechán wrote the genitive *Maicc Con*. Thus recast, O Daly's etymology is a possibility (a suggestive one in the Celtic contexts discussed presently). But on the strength of the evidence discussed here, it is no more than a possibility.

---

46 See Jackson, *Language and History in Early Britain* 136–7.

Gloses en vieil-irlandais: la glose grammaticale abrégée

Pierre-Yves Lambert

C.N.R.S., E.P.H.E.

DANS UNE ÉTUDE sur les gloses grammaticales brittoniques[1], j'avais attiré l'attention sur des gloses destinées à l'identification de catégories morphologiques latines. Il est apparu clairement que, pour la plupart des conventions suivies par les glossateurs brittoniques, il existait des parallèles dans les corpus de gloses en vieil-irlandais. C'est là une idée dont j'ai bien souvent discuté avec Proinsias Mac Cana, dont les conseils ont été si précieux dans les progrès de ma recherche. Les gloses irlandaises, beaucoup plus abondantes que l'ensemble du corpus brittonique, constituent le point de départ obligé de toute étude sur les gloses celtiques. C'est particulièrement vrai pour la « glose grammaticale abrégée ».

Les « gloses grammaticales » du glossateur peuvent être de trois sortes, ou bien elles dénomment la catégorie morphologique considérée, ou bien elles traduisent mot-à-mot les éléments du syntagme latin, ou bien elles transposent de façon naturelle, mais conventionnelle le syntagme latin (lorsque la langue irlandaise n'a pas d'équivalent littéral). Nous ne nous intéresserons pas au premier type,

---

[1] Pierre-Yves LAMBERT, « Les gloses grammaticales brittoniques », *Études celtiques* XXIV, 1987, 285–308.

généralement en latin (et souvent abrégé: nominatiuus > *nom.*, datiuus > *dā*, etc.). Nous voulons seulement présenter la glose grammaticale de type traduction littérale ou traduction transposée, dans ses variantes abrégées.

L'abrégement de ces gloses de traduction indique sans aucun doute que ce n'est pas le sens lexical des mots latins qui importe, dans ce cas, mais leur construction grammaticale, c'est-à-dire le morphème et sa valeur morpho-syntaxique. Car l'abrégement ne pouvait fonctionner que s'il se fondait sur une traduction établie, conventionnelle, de la forme ou de la construction latine. Nous devrons donc présenter parallèlement des gloses abrégées et des gloses complètes. Enfin, cet abrégement de la glose grammaticale de traduction (qui la réduit généralement au premier mot de la construction irlandaise correspondante), reflète dans une certaine mesure l'intérêt du glossateur, qui se limite à une désinence, ou même à une construction (prédication ou apposition, cas absolu).

I. MORPHOLOGIE NOMINALE

L'identification de cas nominaux comme le génitif ou le datif est relativement fréquente dans les gloses irlandaises.

a) *Génitif*

Le seul exemple d'une glose abrégée pour la traduction du génitif est contestable:

> Ml. 65^{d}17, *indí* gl. passionis
>
> Contexte: non ergo uilescat tibi ob contumiliam passionis quem Tirus illa detissima uenerabitur, approximativement « que tu n'aies donc pas honte pour l'opprobre de la passion, [de celui] que cette très riche ville de Tyr tiendra en vénération »
>
> Comme l'indique la traduction de l'éditeur, « of him who », la glose supplée un antécédent à *quem*, en le rattachant au mot précédent *passionis*. Par conséquent, *indí* est un commentaire explicatif, et n'a aucun rapport avec le cas génitif de *passionis*.

Excursus: Les gloses sur le génitif

Le cas génitif est tout simplement traduit par un génitif. Un sondage dans le début des gloses de Milan montre que les gloses sur le génitif latin comportent très souvent l'article irlandais, sans doute pour mieux marquer les morphèmes de génitif dans la traduction. Dans un cas, on a même deux fois l'article, sans doute par hésitation entre gén. m. et gén. f. sg: Ml. 45^{d}19, sub inquissitionis (scemate), *ind inna-iarfaichtho*. Comme il est habituel, ce type de glose limité à un syntagme peut être encadré par *sechis (nochis)* . . . *són* Ml. 3^{a}6, 24^{b}1 ou simplement suivi de *(s)ón*, avec la valeur « c'est-à-dire » Ml. 40^{d}11, 44^{c}9, mais ces formules s'emploient surtout pour apporter des précisions, des paraphrases qui ne sont pas grammaticales (16^{a}3, 18^{d}23, 23^{c}26, 35^{c}8).

L'article est absent lorsque le génitif est lui-même déterminé par un autre génitif, en particulier les noms verbaux suivis d'un complément objet (16^{a}3, 29^{b}9, 35^{c}8, 35^{d}18, 38^{d}20, 47^{c}13, 49^{a}23; mais cf. 41^{a}11).

Il y a des cas particuliers: une tournure particulière est employée pour indiquer le cas des noms propres invariables ou étrangers (mais aussi, devant *Dæ* gén. de *Dia* « Dieu ») :

> Ml. 23^{b}13, suus (sermo): .i. *indí Chuissi*
> Ml. 29^{d}6, eius (insidias): *indí Saul*
> Ml. 108^{d}1, suae uirtutis: .i. *indí Dæ*
> Sg. 30^{b}14, Thessei: .i. *indí Thessei*

Même traduction pour des syntagmes apposés à un possessif à l'intérieur d'une glose, Ml. 47^{b}16, 48^{a}21, 108^{c}10. On emploie donc le génitif du pronom. *int-í*, au lieu de l'article simple, ce qui revient à substituer un pronom entier à un adjectif déterminant.

J'ai autrefois comparé l'emploi de *innou/inno* dans plusieurs gloses brittoniques, avec la même intention de signaler un génitif latin[2]. L'intérêt de ces gloses brittoniques est précisément de ne faire aucune différence entre le signalement du génitif des noms communs et des noms propres.

Un autre cas particulier est celui où le génitif latin est expliqué par un *génitif de citation*: Liam Breatnach[3] a bien expliqué le fonctionnement de l'expression, utilisant le pronom antécédent neutre *aní (as)*, sur le modèle du latin « id quod est ». Nous trouvons en effet un type de glose (uniquement dans Saint-Gall), où le génitif latin est glosé de la façon suivante:

---

2   Pierre-Yves LAMBERT, « Vieux gallois *nou, nom, inno* », *The Bulletin of the Board of Celtic Studies* XXX, 1982–83, 20–29.
3   Liam BREATNACH, « On the citation of words and use of the neuter article in Old Irish », *Ériu* XLI, 1990, 95–101. Il cite plusieurs exemples du gén. sg. *indí (as)*, cf. ses exemples n° 6, 14.

Sg. 39ᵃ20, *indí as* superior, gl. superioris

Sg. 39ᵃ21, *indí as* inferior gl. inferioris

(Contexte: nam superus et inferus, quamuis uideantur eorum, id est superioris et inferioris, esse possitiua, . . . Keil I 83)

Sg. 55ᵇ6, *indí as* leonis, leena femininum, gl. leonis

Sg. 210ᵇ1, .i. *indí as sui*, gl. sui

(Contexte: Non igitur sui nominatiuus potest constare (Keil II 19))

Il ne s'agit pas vraiment d'indiquer le nominatif (d'ailleurs c'est le génitif qui se maintient après *indí as* dans les deux derniers exemples), mais la construction du mot dans la phrase, comme cela apparaît bien dans le dernier exemple: « Il ne peut donc pas exister un nominatif de *sui* ». De même dans les exemples 39ᵃ20 et 21, *superioris* et *inferioris* représentent en fait des mots grammaticaux (les comparatifs *superior* et *inferior)* qui sont construits au génitif dans la phrase latine, « bien que *superus* et *inferus* paraissent être les positifs de *superior* et *inferior*. . . ».

b) *Datif*

L'identification du datif latin se fait au moyen de deux prépositions différentes, afin de bien distinguer les deux valeurs de cette forme: celui à qui l'on donne (emploi de la prép. irl. *do, du*, « à, pour ») et celui à qui l'on enlève (emploi de la prép. irl. *ar*, « au détriment de »). Cette deuxième sorte de datif, parfois définie comme *datiuus fraudatiuus* chez les glossateurs celtiques[4], est dénommée une fois sous un nom vieil-irlandais, *tobarthaid erdiubartach* « datif qui enlève », gl. prouidentiae, Ml. 122ᵃ16.

Préposition *do* « à, pour »:

Ml. 74ᶜ14, *do* gl. auxiliatori

Contexte: omne secretum curarum mearum tanquam potenti auxiliatori commisi « j'ai confié tous les secrets de mes soucis (à toi), comme à un puissant secours »

Préposition *ar* « au détriment de »:

Sg. 9ᵇ8, *ar* gl. uocalibus (dat. pl.)

---

4 Pierre-Yves LAMBERT, « "Fraudatiuus": une dénomination ancienne du "Datiuus incommodi" dans le monde celtique » *Revue de Philologie*, LVII, 1983, 39–45. — Des manuscrits bretons peuvent aussi employer le terme courant sur le continent, *datiuus priuatiuus* (cf. le ms. d'Orose, Vatican Lat. 296, fᵒ 55ᵛ2, sur: Octauio tribuno plebis obsistenti demit imperium; idem, fᵒ 66ᵛ2, 72ᵛ, etc.).

Contexte: non aliter quam si (aspiratio) antecedens uocalibus auferatur. . . (Prisc. Keil I 19.15), « tout comme l'aspiration qui les précède était enlevée aux voyelles (initiales) »

Ml. 72ª1, *ar–in* gl. dominationi

Contexte: qui me ob notitiam tui iuste dominationi subtraxeris impiorum « toi qui, par la connaissance (que j'ai eue) de toi, m'as soustrait, en toute justice, à la domination des impies »

c) *Ablatif*

Habituellement traduit par la préposition *ó*, *ua*.

Abrégement imparfait dans le cas d'une glose de Saint-Gall:

Sg. 137ᵇ7, *huand neph'* gl. in consonantia

Contexte: Ergo naturae necessitas bipertita (ms. bibertita) est in significatione et in commoditate, id est in consonantia elementorum (Keil I 370; cf. in inconsonantia Karlsruhe) « Par conséquent le besoin de nature est divisé entre la signification et la facilité, c'est-à-dire la consonance des éléments »

Le glossateur a commis un contre-sens en prenant *inconsonantia* pour un seul mot, à l'ablatif. La leçon du ms. de Karlsruhe est une tentative pour réconcilier cette interprétation avec la construction de la phrase. Le glossateur a indiqué clairement son choix en traduisant *in-* comme un préverbe négatif, *neph-*; on trouve la glose complète dans le même corpus:

Sg. 152ᵇ3, *ónd nephchomfogur*, gl. inconsonantia

Contexte: uerba quae uel literarum inconsonantia uel regularum quibusdam rationibus impediantur . . . (Keil I 420)

Avant de quitter la flexion nominale, un regard sur l'expression « être au nominatif », qui en latin se dit avec le nom du cas à l'ablatif:

Sg. 91ᵇ1, *combí dano* filius familiarum nominatiuo

Sg. 99ª3, *ar biid* Iouis *cene* nominatiuo. Cf. encore 106ᵇ6.

On peut se demander si ces ablatifs singuliers n'étaient pas compris comme des datifs en hiberno-latin, puisque la traduction irlandaise est:

Sg. 64ª4, *do ainmnid*, gl. Araris (Arar, quod etiam Araris dicitur) = *do anmnith*, Thes. II 232.12, « pour nominatif » (for a nominative)

Sg. 206^b3, *do foxlaid femin* gl. a qua uel a qui

Cf. la glose fréquente, Sg. 63^b11, *do glúaiss* « for a gloss, pour (une) glose », ou . . . *do anmaim ind eiúin* « comme nom de l'oiseau » Sg. 93^a2.

II. CATÉGORIES VERBALES

a) *Subjonctifs*

On peut citer trois gloses où la conjonction *co*, au-dessus d'un subjonctif latin, semble indiquer sa nature (subordonnée) et, approximativement son sens (conséquence, but):

Ml. 117^a3, *coní*, gl. (ne quid . . .) relinquat

Contexte: hoc illi familiare est, hoc placitum, ne quid inexaminatum relinquat (sur le Ps. 98, 4): « ceci lui est habituel, ceci est sa décision, qu'il ne laisse rien en vie »

Traduction de la négation, mais non du verbe qui devait suivre. Cf. *coní* gl. ne (timens ne. . .), Ml. 22^d12.

Sg. 213^a5, .i. *co*, gl. uterer

Contexte: Sallustius in Iugurthino, 'secundum ea uti debetis uterer' (Keil II 26); texte peu sûr: debetis ou debitis. « pour que j'employasse les dettes de cette façon »

Considéré comme une traduction de *uti*, Contribb. C col. 276.

Sg. 16^a15, *coa* gl. ponamus

Keil I 33: melius ergo nos quoque x solam ponimus, quae locum obtinet cs « nous faisons donc mieux nous aussi en mettant le seul x, qui tient la place de cs »

Problème textuel ici encore: ponemus BK, ponamus L, ponamus G (d'après le *Thesaurus*). La note de l'éditeur du *Thesaurus* est: « *coa* seems to be for *co*, indicating the construction of *ponamus* which is a scribal error for *ponimus* ».

Le subjonctif dans cette phrase a été amené par la fin de la phrase précédente, se terminant par un exemple introduit par *ut*: « ut ἔκστασις ». Cet *ut* a pu être construit comme une conjonction de subordination.

L'éditeur du *Thesaurus* croyait à une glose grammaticale abrégée. Mais il est inhabituel de trouver seulement la première lettre du verbe qui suit la conjonction. Aussi peut-on envisager une autre lecture, *co(n)a* « avec -a- » (allusion au -a- de *ponamus*) — il y a en effet quelques exemples de *co-* prép. « avec » non suivi de nasalisation.

b) *Infinitifs*

Les infinitifs dépendant d'un verbe sont normalement traduits par un verbe conjugué, de forme relative: verbes simples avec désinences relatives, si possible, et dans les autres cas, nasalisation relative (qui est une marque de subordination, équivalent à notre « que » complétif). L'emploi du subjonctif depend du sens de l'infinitif dans la phrase latine.

Ce type de glose n'est pas facile à abréger, la marque grammaticale étant réduite à une désinence et/ou à une nasalisation infixée ou préfixée. On peut citer cependant:

Sg. 66a24, *commais-* gl. aptare

Contexte: mos est aptare. . . Peut-être abrégé pour *comadasaigedar*. (Suggestion de l'éditeur du *Thesaurus*). Cette glose est difficile.

c) *Gérondifs*

Deux conventions s'opposent dans le même manuscrit (Milan), l'une étant beaucoup mieux représentée que l'autre. Il s'agit toujours du gérondif à l'ablatif. Selon la première convention, *dicendo* est traduit par « lorsqu'il dit » abrégé en « lorsque » (*las(s)e*). Selon la deuxième convention, *dicendo* est traduit comme un ablatif, par « du fait qu'il dit », abrégé en « du fait que » (*ondí*).

Premier type:

Ml. 22^{c}2 *lase* gl. dicendo

Contexte: dicendo 'ut scuto' admouit similitudinem . . .
= *lase asmbeir* « lorsqu'il dit », comme l'indique l'éditeur du *Thesaurus*, I 35 note c.

Ml. 29^{c}17 *lase* gl. transeundo

Ml. 46^{c}21 *lase* gl. peccando

Ml. 70^{c}16 *lase* gl. agendo

Ml. 96^{a}12 *lasse* gl. praeordinando

Ml. 107^{c}13 .i. *lasse nad* gl. nulla. . . inflectando

Ml. 121^{c}1 *lase* gl. includendo

Ml. 130^{c}12 *lasse* gl. ammouendo

Ml. 132^{a}11 *lasse* gl.orando

Ml. 139^{d}3 *lase* gl. auxiliando

Cette glose abrégée correspond à une glose complète qui est bien représentée, aussi bien dans Saint-Gall que dans Milan:

Sg. 29^{b}11, *lase asmbiur* « lorsque je dis » gl. dicendo

Ml. 132^{c}1, *lasse nad-n-adraim-se* « lorsque je n'adore pas » gl. non adorando

Les 10 exemples abrégés dans le ms. de Milan sont en rapport avec le nombre de gloses non abrégées: on en compte 36 dans ce même manuscrit[5].

Les Contribb. (s.v. *lase*, L col. 58) suggèrent que ce type de glose exprimerait la valeur instrumental de l'ablatif (*lase* = « par le fait que »). C'est possible. Mais *lasse*, au départ, est simplement la traduction de *cum* + subj. (dès les gloses de Wurzbourg): on peut penser que *lasse* dans la transposition qui nous occupe est la traduction d'une explication latine, « dicendo » > « cum diceret ».

Deuxième type:

Ml. 17^{a}1, *hondi* gl. colendo

Contexte: hoc itaque . . . Heremias . . . exprobrat Iudeis, quod abiecto eius (filii) famulatu idola colendo susceperint « Aussi Jérémie reproche-t-il aux Juifs d'avoir, après avoir rejeté son service, adopté les idoles en leur donnant un culte »

ondí est l'une des conjonctions formées avec *intí*: cf. *isindí* « en ce que », *iarsindí* « après que », *airindí* « à cause que », *dindí* « du fait que » (suivies d'un verbe relatif).

ó est la préposition qui traduit l'ablatif; elle traduit aussi la préposition *ab* + ablatif. Ainsi dans les expressions de citation, Ml. 37^{b}17, ab eo quod . . . inest, *hondí indixnigedar*, cf. *ondí rondgab* PCr.56^{b}1 (ou *ondí as* . . . PCr. 15^{b}1).

óndí conjonction traduisant le gérondif à l'ablatif ne semble pas appartenir à la tradition des gloses grammaticales du vieil-irlandais, mais plutôt à la traduction

5 Ml. 29^{b}10, 40^{d}2, 44^{b}22, 45^{c}2, 50^{b}8, 61^{b}1, 63^{c}3, 63^{d}15, 65^{a}14, 68^{d}1, 80^{a}13, 97^{a}12, 97^{d}14, 100^{d}9, 101^{b}2, 102^{d}5, 104^{b}8, 105^{d}11, 106^{b}8, 114^{c}4, 114^{c}11, 115^{b}12, 115^{b}13, 115^{b}15, 118^{a}11, 119^{a}12, 120^{a}3, 121^{b}17, 123^{b}10, 124^{d}6, 124^{d}7, 125^{c}1, 126^{c}19, 127^{a}17, 127^{a}18, 132^{c}1.

courante. En effet, on ne le retrouve que plus tard, dans des traductions en moyen-irlandais comme les Passions et Homélies du Leabhar Breac.

Parfois l'on trouve aussi le nom verbal après *ó*, particulièrement pour traduire le tour lat. *ab* + gérondif à l'ablatif:

Sg. 27^{b}17 *o thindnacul* gl. a tribuendo

d) *Adjectif verbal*

L'adjectif verbal est correctement traduit par diverses périphrases, incluant généralement la copule (au prés. de l'indic. *is*, ou à l'imparfait du subj. *bed*) et l'adjectif verbal d'obligation:

Sg. 68^{a}5 .i. *cáith bed srethi* « du son qui devrait être jeté », gl. acus substernendum (gallinis parturientibus)

Ml. 105^{b}3 .i. *is remderscaigthi* « il doit être mis en avant », gl. (unus dies . . .) anteferendus est

Sg. 33^{b}10 .i. *is aichthi* « il doit être craint », gl. metuenda (suco taxus), « l'if redoutable par son suc ». Traduction légèrement inexacte, *metuenda* n'étant pas un prédicat principal.

Avec copule négative, *ní* Sg. 27^{a}15, *nit* Ml. 128^{d}1
Copule relative *as:* Ml. 104^{a}5, 127^{b}11, *bes* 126^{c}18, traductions qui sont le mieux adaptées à l'adjectif verbal, la valeur adjective passant dans une relative.

Le gérondif à l'accusatif après *ad* est très souvent traduit, inexactement, comme un adjectif verbal:

Ml. 23^{d}18 *bed diachti* « qui doit être vengé, puni » gl. uindicandum

Contexte: promtos nos ad uindicandum esse tali motu corporis indicamus « par un tel mouvement du corps, nous montrons que nous sommes prêts à nous venger »

Hésitation:

Ml. 24^{a}3 .i. *bed moltai ⁊ do molad* « qui doit être loué » ou « pour louer », gl. ad (p)sallendum Deo: seule la deuxième traduction paraît correcte.

La traduction du premier type est abrégée dans:

Sg. 150b4, .i. *bíid* gl. scribenda

cf. pour la graphie, Sg. 6^{b}22 *bith techtai* gl. habenda

Excursus

Ce que nous avons relevé comme une traduction inexacte du gérondif semble issu d'une confusion entre adjectif verbal et gérondif. C'est ce que montrent les deux gloses suivantes:

Ml. 64^b2, *dúnni bed fortachtigthi* « pour nous qui devons être aidés » gl. ad [ad]iuuandum nos « pour nous aider »

Ml. 76^d4, *damsa bed gabthi* « pour moi qui dois être pris » gl. ad capiendum me « pour me prendre »

La glose Ml. 76^d4 est acceptable, comme traduction littérale, si l'on interprète comme *ad me capiendum*, avec la construction avec adjectif verbal (= ad urbem capiendam). Cette interprétation est plus difficile à appliquer dans le premier exemple, où *adiuuandum* est clairement le gérondif (sans accord avec *nos*).

Il y a plusieurs autres traductions du gérondif et de l'adjectif verbal. La périphrase des grammairiens latins, *laudandus, laude dignus* est transposée directement dans les gloses de Saint-Gall:

Sg. 59^b4, *is huisse a molath* « il est juste de le louer » gl. laudandus. Voir encore Sg. 59^b5–7.

On aurait pu développer à partir de là une glose abrégée *is huisse*, applicable à tous les adjectifs verbaux en *-ndus* au nominatif; cet abrégement n'est pas attesté. Cependant, on comparera le cas du participe futur:

Thes. II.2.28, *doig* gl. gauisurum.

Contexte: S. Augustin *Soliloquia* I v 11, esto plus te ac multo plus quam de istis Deo cognito gauisurum (Migne, *Patrologia Latina* XXXII 875) « qu'il soit (que tu sois?) destiné à se réjouir ... » ?). *doig* = *is doig fáiltigfedar*, « il est probable qu'il se réjouira »

Mais l'adjectif verbal (lorsqu'il n'est pas le prédicat principal, voir plus haut Ml. 105^b3 etc.) reçoit un certain nombre de traductions comparables aux différentes traductions du participe présent ou du participe passé: l'emploi adjectif est rendu par une relative en *as*, ou *bes*, comme on a vu. Pour l'emploi substantivé, cf.:

Ml. 126^c4 *donaibhí bete cheti*, gl. ad canenda, litt. « pour les choses qui doivent être chantées » [dans ce contexte, développement inattendu de l'accord du prédicat au datif pluriel, sous l'influence du latin]

Enfin, la valeur apposée de l'adjectif verbal est traduite, au besoin, par une subordonnée temporelle en *a n-* « quand »:

Ml. 114^{c}12, *ambat bethi* gl. feriendi, litt. « lorsqu'ils doivent être battus »

Traduction employée par erreur en Ml. 81^{b}3 où foetandis est peut-être confondu avec foetandi.

Le gérondif au génitif, dépendant de noms abstraits tels que deuotionem (Ml. 125^{c}3) ou potestatem (126^{c}4) est naturellement traduit comme un infinitif c'est à dire par un verbe avec marques relatives (équivalent de notre subordonnée complétive).

e) *Participes présents substantivés*

On sait que le participe présent latin, qui n'a pas d'équivalent en irlandais ancien, se trouve transposé sous différentes formes selon sa construction dans la phrase[6]: apposé au verbe (c. à d., au sujet du verbe), il est traduit par une subordonnée introduite par *a n-* « quand »; déterminant un autre syntagme, il est traduit par une relative (c. à d. un verbe relatif); s'il est substantivé, il est traduit par une relative précédée d'un pronom antécédent:

Ml. 39^{d}14 beatificantes me statim circumdiderunt me: *an-nu-m-findbadigtis-se* « tandis qu'ils me félicitaient »

Ml. 34^{d}19 a malis eximit instantibus: *intairissitis* « qui se présentaient » (calque de *instare* par **in-to-are-siss-*)

Ml. 41^{d}10 donec . . . persequentem ferre non possint: *inní du-seinned* « celui qui persécutait »

Seul le dernier type se présente de façon abrégée: au lieu du pronom antécédent suivi d'un verbe relatif, on n'a plus que le pronom antécédent.

Ml. 49^{c}11, *indí* gl. lugentis (gén. sg.)

Contexte: lugentis habitus cessat succedente letitia « l'aspect de pleureur se retire, quand la joie lui succède »

indí, abrégé pour *indí choínes* « de celui qui pleure ».

---

6 Déjà signalé dans notre étude, « Les emplois de l'imparfait en irlandais ancien », *Études celtiques* XIV, 1, 1974, 145s. (155–7).

Sg. 212ª9, *innahí* gl. scribentes (acc. pl.)

Contexte: nam sine metris scribentes rarissime hoc inuenias facere . . . (Keil II 24) « car tu trouveras que ceux qui écrivent en prose font cela (postposer une préposition) très rarement . . . »

Abrégé pour *innahí scríbtae,* comme l'indique l'éditeur du *Thesaurus* (II 214, note d).

Sg. 27ᵇ4, *emith lasnahí* gl. tam cum habentibus

Contexte: Praepositionis autem proprium . . . praeponi . . . per compositionem, tam cum habentibus casus quam etiam cum non habentibus casus (Keil I 56) « c'est le propre d'une préposition, d'être placée en tête. . . et en composition, aussi bien avec des mots qui ont une déclinaison qu'avec des mots invariables »

Ici la glose inclut un adverbe *(emith* = tam, quam) et une préposition *(la* = cum). Abrégé pour: *lasnahí techtaite* (cf. Sg. 21ᵇ8).

f) *Participes passés en apposition ou en construction absolue*

Le participe apposé et le participe constituant un ablatif absolu reçoivent la même traduction: ils sont transposés sous forme d'une subordonnée temporelle introduite par *a n-* « quand », avec une forme du verbe « être » conjugué et le participe, ou une forme verbale passive:

Participe apposé:

Ml. 27ᵇ8, *arrumsa assarcaigthe-se* « lorsque j'ai été rempli de joie », gl. dilectatus

Contexte: Exultabo in salutari (Ps. 9.16); Aquila: dilectatus in salute tua

Ablatif absolu:

Ml. 85ᵈ9, *amtis forbristi ind ríg,* gl. principibus oppresís
Ml. 48ª13, *annunadbairtaigfesiu,* « lorsque tu t'opposeras » gl. té . . . auersato

Pour l'ablatif absolu on trouve aussi une traduction littérale:

Ml. 31ᶜ18, *hon gremmaim srithiu* gl. exserto uigore, cf. 31ᶜ21, etc.

Gloses abrégées:

Ablatif absolu:

Ml. 23ª17, *huaitsiu fercach .i. anundá*, gl. irato te « lorsque tu t'es irrité »

La première traduction est littérale, « de toi irrité »; la seconde est abrégée, « quand tu es ». L'abrégement (pour *anunda fercach) était d'autant plus facile que l'adjectif *fercach* avait déjà été exprimé.

Participe apposé :

Ml. 90ᵇ3 (prima manu) .i. *ambat* gl. exaequati

Contexte: ita . . . sustentabit egentes ut exæquati montibus firmitate præsedii infra se inimicos uideant « il soutiendra les hommes dans le besoin au point que, rendus égaux à des montagnes par la force de sa protection, ils verront leur ennemis au-dessous d'eux. . . »

ambat, « quand ils seront », et *anunda* « quand tu es » illustrent un type de glose grammaticale dont on a plusieurs exemples abrégés, aussi, en brittonique: c'est la formule v.gall. *init oid* « quand il était »[7].

Le même type de glose (conjonction de subordination + verbe « être » rajouté) peut se rencontrer dans d'autres cas: ainsi pour une apposition qualifiée par *quasi*,

Ml. 53ᵈ10 .i. *amal robtar* gl. quasi amatores

La glose n'a pas traduit le sens de amatores, mais sa construction. Abrégé pour: *amal robtar carthaig*.

Ml. 73ª8 .i. *annum* gl. liberatus

Contexte: prumpte libenterque gratificatorias tibi immolabo taliter liberatus « librement et volontiers je t'immolerai des victimes d'action de grâce, lorsque j'aurai ainsi été libéré »

Clairement l'abréviation d'une forme verbale passive, *a-nnum-soírfider-se* (hypothèse d'Ascoli citée par l'éditeur du *Thesaurus*, II 248, note b). Traduire: « quand je serai libéré ». Ce type d'abrégement, touchant la fin du groupe verbal, est exceptionnel.

---

7 Outre l'étude citée n. 1 plus haut (p. 81), voir aussi la note sur l'expression irlandaise *fo-deud* dans le ms. du Juvencus, *Ériu* XXXVI, 1985, 189–90.

III. NOMS ET ADJECTIFS APPOSÉS

Il reste à présenter la glose abrégée appliquée à d'autres éléments apposés (adjectifs, noms), et qui utilise la particule épitactique *os*, *ot*, variante *is*, *it*, directement suivie du pronom requis par le sens. Ce type de glose est plus fréquent sous la forme abrégée (16) que sous la forme complète (10); la variante tardive *is*, connue seulement du Ms. de Milan, est plus fréquente dans des gloses abrégées (6) que dans des gloses complètes (3).

Bien sûr quelques adjectifs apposés sont en fait des participes passés (electus Ml. 123ª12, dicta Sg. 77ª8) ou des participes présents (amantes, Ml. 133^d7). Mais que ce soit pour des raisons relatives à leur sémantisme particulier ou à leur traitement dans la tradition scolaire irlandaise, ils sont traités comme les autres adjectifs apposés. De même il n'est pas possible de distinguer une différence entre adjectif apposé et substantif apposé (sauf que le glossateur de Milan n'emploie pas *is*, mais *os*, lorsque c'est un substantif qui est apposé).

Gloses abrégées avec particule de forme *is*, *it*:

Ml. 24ª11, *it-hǽ* gl. diuersi

Ml. 27^b5, *is-me* gl. liber = *os mé soér*

Ml. 77^c1, *is-me* gl. matutinus = *os mé mochtrátaue*

Ml. 100^c4, *it- hǽ* gl. unianimes

Ml. 100^d11, *is-tú* gl. benignus

Ml. 137ª3, *is-tú* gl. memor = *os mé foraithmitech*

Gloses abrégées, avec particule de forme *os*, *ot*:

Ml. 69^c4 *os-hǽ* gl. amicus

Contexte: profeta commonuit. . .neque eius amicitiam magnopere consectentur qui non officia spectet sed munera, donorum magis amicus quam hominum « le prophète les a avertis . . . de ne pas rechercher activement l'amitié de celui qui considère non les devoirs mais les cadeaux, aimant davantage les richesses que les hommes »

Ml. 92ª14 *os-tu a dǽ* gl. arbiter « toi, ô Dieu, étant [. . .] » (une autre glose, Ml. 92ª15, donne le sens complet: *lassaní nonda brithem* « puisque tu es arbitre »)

Ml. 92^b7 *os-m'* gl. securus (abrégement exceptionnellement étendu au pronom *mé*)

Ml. 118ª6 *os-mé* gl. matutinus ultor

Ml. 119^b4 *os-mé* gl. homo

Ml. 122^b14 *os-hé* gl. dissimilis

Ml. 123ª12 *os-hé* gl. electus
Ml. 123b4 *os-hé* gl. captiuus
Sg. 26b1 *os-ní* gl. Latini
Sg. 77ª8 *ot-é* gl. absolute dicta

Pour Sg. 26b1, le contexte: illos adhuc sequimur Latini, comporte une apposition au sujet qui n'est pas une qualification, mais une dénomination. Cela se traduirait en français ou en anglais par une incise après nominatif pendant, avant le verbe: « *Nous*, les Latins, nous les avons suivis jusque ici ». La particule *os*, dans ce cas, est utilisée comme connecteur introduisant un nouveau sujet[8]: *osní* « quant à nous ».

Il est possible que l'on puisse comparer des gloses du ms. de Martianus Capella (*issí, issmi*), mais elles ne s'expliquent que par un calque du vieil-irlandais.

Les gloses en *is* ne peuvent se confondre avec des phrases à copule: car après la copule on emploie de préférence la forme du pronom avec particule personnelle d'insistance. Cf. par ex. dans la traduction du pron. relatif[9], qui = *is mese* Ml. 47ª2. À la 3e personne, où la phrase d'identification présente aussi la séquence *is-hé* (*is-hé Romuil*, Sg. 31ª10, séquence destinée à signaler la fonction prédicative), on constate que le glossateur du ms. de Milan évite la forme *is* lorsque l'élément apposé est un substantif; et que la glose grammaticale du type *is hé Romuil* (avec *is* copule) n'est jamais abrégée. De toute façon, les éléments prédicats ou prédicatifs sont glosés avec l'adjonction d'une copule et pouvaient difficilement être abrégés.

La glose grammaticale abrégée est caractéristique du travail du glossateur, qui est d'abord un professeur de latin: avant de passer à l'exégèse, il doit s'assurer que le sens de la phrase est compris. C'est une aide à la lecture, aussi bien pour lui-même que pour ses élèves. Si l'on abrège une traduction conventionnelle appliquée à une forme ou à un syntagme latin, cela n'est possible qu'à la faveur du caractère normatif, et régulier, de la traduction reçue; l'abrégement, d'ailleurs, renforce lui-même la convention dans son aspect formaliste. Peu importe les mobiles insaisissables et sans doute contingents de l'abrégement ici et là. L'abrégement d'ailleurs se réalise plus ou moins complètement, puisque la négation ou l'article sont parfois épargnés, ou le préverbe vide avec l'infixe qu'il supporte. Ce qui disparaît presque immanquablement, c'est le lexème verbal ou nominal. Cela, d'une part parce que la syntaxe du vieil-irlandais le permet (les particules et conjonctions précèdent le verbe, les prépositions précèdent le nom). Et aussi, parce

8   La même valeur de *os* apparaît dans deux gloses à lat. ipse, *osme* Wb. 11ª14, *ostú* Ml. 47b12.
9   Sur quoi voir notre étude, « La traduction du pronom relatif latin dans les gloses du vieil-irlandais », *Études celtiques* XVIII, 1981, 121–140.

que la glose grammaticale conventionnelle est une paraphrase redondante, plus longue que le texte glosé: les désinences nominales deviennent des prépositions, les désinences verbales des conjonctions de subordination, et l'on rajoute même des éléments explicites là où le latin comporte uniquement un « accord flexionnel » : en utilisant la particule d'épitaxe (= apposition) *os* dessus des adjectifs apposés.

La glose grammaticale sert d'abord à identifier des désinences et des catégories morpho-syntaxiques: ainsi pour le subjonctif présent, parfois difficile à distinguer du futur, ou pour l'ablatif singulier. Certaines formes appellent différents types de gloses: le datif latin est précisé par la prép. *ar* ou *do*, selon qu'il est privatif ou non. Le gérondif à l'ablatif est glosé par *lase* ou *ondí* selon qu'il s'agit d'une circonstance ou d'une cause.

Dans le cas des participes, c'est sans doute le hasard s'il n'y a de gloses abrégées que pour les participes présents substantivés et pour les participes passés apposés; pourquoi pas les participes passés substantivés et les participes présents apposés? En tout cas, il était impossible d'abréger la glose au participe épithète, qui se traduit par un verbe relatif.

Ce qui est sans doute conventionnel, c'est la double traduction des appositions: les *participes* apposés reçoivent la même traduction que les ablatifs absolus, une subordonnée temporelle en *a n-* « quand » avec verbe conjugué. L'ablatif absolu lorsqu'il n'a pas d'élément verbal doit donc être traduit au moyen de la copule. Les *noms et adjectifs* apposés reçoivent une traduction complètement différente, la phrase nominale épitactique introduite par *os*, plus un pronom personnel tonique. La particule *os* aurait pu, à elle seule, suffire à signaler l'apposition, mais le pronom conservé dans la glose abrégée, permettait d'expliciter le support d'apposition. La glose abrégée conserve donc tout ce que la paraphrase irlandaise rajoute au syntagme latin.

Existe-t-il des représentations du dieu Lugh?

Gwenaël Le Duc

UNIVERSITÉ DE HAUTE BRETAGNE, RENNES 2

DANS L'ÉTAT actuel de nos connaissances, nous ne connaîtrions pas de représentations du Dieu Lugh. Cela ne surprend ou n'inquiète personne, dans la mesure où rares sont les statues (gauloises ou gallo-romaines) pourvues d'inscriptions, ou munies d'accessoires ou d'attributs suffisamment explicites pour qu'un rapprochement convainque à fois les archéologues, les linguistes et les historiens des religions, qui hélas ne naviguent que trop rarement dans les mêmes eaux pour des raisons que nous connaissons tous trop bien.

Certes, il faut poser en préliminaire qu'il me semble légitime de tirer parti des textes irlandais médiévaux pour tenter de percer la brume qui entoure la religion gauloise. Refuser tout rapprochement ou comparaison, c'est se mettre des œillères, et renoncer à comprendre. Je suis consterné que certains archéologues renoncent par principe à ce qui est la seule voie légitime d'explication qui nous reste[1].

À l'occasion de la journée belge d'études celtiques organisée à Bruxelles, lors d'une conversation avec mon collègue M. Merdrignac, nous avons été amenés à rapprocher nos fiches, et c'est ce qui m'amène maintenant à émettre une hypothèse où sa contribution n'est pas inférieure à la mienne.

En effet, nous connaissons dans le folklore breton ancien un avatar du dieu Lugh, ce qui est reconnu depuis longtemps[2]. Son nom, *Huccan*, diminutif de *hucc*

---

1   Ce que je regrette de lire par ex. dans J.-L. Brunaux, *Les religions gauloises — Rituels celtiques de la Gaule indépendante*, Paris, éditions Errance, 1996. p. 6, 14.
2   D'Arbois de Jubainville, « Une légende irlandaise en Bretagne », *Revue Celtique*, 7, 1886, 230–233. Cf. Arzel Even (Jean Piette), « Notes sur le Mercure Celtique, II, le démon

« porc », est inconnu ailleurs. Le motif (ou mythème) est probablement d'origine irlandaise, le nom aussi, qui est ailleurs compréhensible en brittonique, et il ne s'agit aucunement d'une erreur de transcription ou de transmission. Simplement, le dieu a été ravalé au rang de démon avant d'être exporté, sans perdre son nom.

Je ne crois pas qu'il s'agisse d'une déchéance, dans la mesure où cet animal est chez les Celtes un animal connu pour sa force et sa violence, un animal guerrier et non un animal méprisé[3].

D'autre part, il existe une dédicace à *Mercurio Mocco*, connue en Gaule[4]. Or, Lugh a bien été assimilé à Mercure, ce qu'il n'est plus besoin de démontrer[5], et l'épiclèse est sémantiquement identique dans les deux cas. Ce ne sont pas les même mots, mais ils nous apparaissent bien comme synonymes. On peut, je crois, refuser de parler de coïncidence simple. Le rapprochement a déjà été noté[6], mais pas prolongé.

Il me paraît donc certain que Lugh a été d'une manière ou d'une autre lié au porc ou au sanglier, que de telles représentations lui sont dédiées ou destinées, à moins que ce ne soit une représentation possible (entre autres sans doute) du dieu.

On pourrait donc à priori non identifier le dieu, car ce serait trop hardi dans l'état de notre documentation, mais reconnaître des traces de son culte dans les nombreuses représentations de porcs ou de sangliers que nous connaissons dans le monde celtique, et dont plusieurs sont de petites œuvres d'art, jamais en tout cas des objets de basse facture[7].

Deux statuettes en particulier[8] méritent notre attention:

Huccan », *Ogam*, 5, 1953, 309–312. Gildas Bernier, *Les chrétientés bretonnes continentales depuis les origines jusqu'au IXe siècle*, CeRAA, E–1982, p. 149. Bernard Merdrignac, *Recherches sur l'hagiographie armoricaince du VIIe au XVe siècle*, Tome 1, p. 118, n. 17. t. II, p. 63 et n. 375. Merdrignac, 'Lug le polytechnicien dans la vie de saint Hervé', dans Xavier Barral i Altet, *et al.*, *Artistes, artisans et production artistique en Bretagne au Moyen-Age*, Rennes, 1983, p. 25–28. Bernard Tanguy, *St. Hervé, Vie et culte*, Treflevenez, Minihi-Lévénez, 1990, p. 97.

3 Guyonvarc'h, *Les fêtes celtiques*, Rennes, p. 54–56.

4 « The Gaulish Mercury occurs with the epithet *Moccus* (Welsh *moch*, 'pigs'), and obviously this refers to a native deity concerned in some capacity with pigs, as hunter perhaps or as divine swineherd » (P. Mac Cana, *Celtic Mythology*, Londres, Hamlyn, 1970, p. 53–55). L'inscription est CIL XIII, 5676. Cf. J. Vendryes, *Lexique étymologique de l'Irlandais ancien*, Paris–Dublin, CNRS/DIAS, 1960, M–68.

5 Ch.-J. Guyonvarc'h, *La société celtique*, Rennes, Ouest-France, p. 108–109. *La civilisation celtique*, 1990, p. 132–133.

6 *Les fêtes celtiques*, p. 56.

7 Par ex. *L'art celtique en Gaule*, ouvrage collectif, sous la direction de Pierre Quoniam, Dieppe, 1983, p. 190–191. Ruth and Vincent Megaw, *Celtic Art from its Beginnings to the Book of Kells*, Londres, Thames and Hudson, no 247–249, p. 161.

8 Je renonce à tenter de dresser une liste des ouvrages où ces statuettes ont été reproduites. On

Le « dieu de Bouray[9] » tout d'abord, qui n'a pu être destiné qu'à une divinité fort notable, personnage représenté accroupi, avec deux jambes où l'on a reconnu des sabots de cerf: pourquoi le cerf, sans doute parce que c'est l'animal noble et majestueux qui vient en premier à l'esprit, et qui d'ailleurs a souvent été représenté, mais il peut tout aussi bien s'agir des extrémités de n'importe quel mammifère périssodactyle. Le seul inconvénient de l'interprétation est qu'elle prête le flanc à l'ironie en français moderne: un dieu « aux pieds de cochon » n'a rien que de malheureux.

Ensuite, le « dieu d'Euffigneix », pour autant qu'on y voie le torse d'un personnage et non un pilier orné d'un sanglier et d'un œil. Le sanglier peut nous indiquer la dénomination possible, qui se substituerait à une inscription impossible pour des raisons religieuses. Quant à cet œil unique sur le flanc, l'interprétation la plus facile est certes d'y voir un œil apotropaïque, mais alors pourquoi n'est-il pas sur le devant, et pourquoi est-il vertical? Je propose, quant à moi, un rapprochement avec la fin du récit de la bataille de Moytirra[10], où Lugh crève de sa fronde l'oeil unique du géant Balor et le tue ainsi. Cet œil serait donc une allusion à un récit mythologique, trophée allusif devenu un des attributs du dieu, si ce n'est simplement une évocation de son aspect solaire et lumineux. Ce qui ne nous permet pas de proposer une version gauloise du mythe.

Si le dieu de Bouray est borgne, hélas, c'est par accident et cela n'a rien à voir avec cet élément.

Certes, l'hypothèse mérite d'être soupesée, sans doute nuancée, il faudra se garder de ne pas mélanger ou amalgamer les éléments de la comparaison, et ne pas faire du comparatisme un syncrétisme: il a existé des différences religeuses entre les Gaulois et les Irlandais, l'assimilation est impossible, mais néanmoins les parentés sont nettes. C'est ainsi qu'il me semble possible de proposer ici un élément de réponse à une question fort irritante. Cela permet au moins de confirmer que le sanglier de Neuvy-en-Sulias fait bien partie d'un dépôt votif, non d'un ensemble simplement décoratif.

---

peut citer, pour la forme au moins, des ouvrages récents: Megaw and Megaw, *Celtic Art*, no 476, p. 171. p. XVIII face à la p. 157. *Les Celtes*, ouvrage collectif, ed. S. Moscati, Milan, Bompiani, p. 505, 507.

9 Bouray-sur-Juine, Essonne.

10 Guyonvarc'h, *Textes mythologiques irlandais*, vol. I, *Ogam-Celticum*, Rennes, 1980, p. 67–69, 100–101. Bernard Sergent, « La mort de Karna et celle de Balor », *Ollodagos*, VIII, 2, 1995, p. 211–237.

Learning Lordship: The Education of Manawydan

Catherine McKenna

QUEENS COLLEGE AND THE GRADUATE CENTER,
CITY UNIVERSITY OF NEW YORK

MANAWYDAN, a figure who appears in the second of the Four Branches of the Mabinogi, is featured so prominently in the third that modern scholars commonly refer to this branch as *Manawydan*, even though it is in fact the only one of the four that does not open with a personal name.[1] The Third Branch opens with an adverbial phrase that links it to the

---

1 The Red Book of Hergest (Jesus College MS. cxi) has *llyma dechreu mabinogi* at the head of the First Branch; *llyma yr eil geinc or mabinogi* at the head of the Second; and *llyma y dryded geinc or mabinogi* and *honn yw y bedwared geinc or mabinogi* in the appropriate places. See John Rhŷs and J. Gwenogvryn Evans, eds., *The Text of the Mabinogion and Other Welsh Tales from the Red Book of Hergest* (Oxford, 1887), pp. 1, 26, 44, 59. But descriptive titles appear to apply to sections of the stories only, as in the case of the claim that *o achaws y carchar hwnnw, y gelwit y kyuarwydyt hwnnw Mabinogi Mynweir a Mynord* at the end of the Third Branch, which has for the most part been taken to refer only to the final episode of the tale, the imprisonment in the Otherworld of Rhiannon and Pryderi. See Sioned Davies, *Crefft y Cyfarwydd* (Caerdydd: Gwasg Prifysgol Cymru, 1995), p. 57. The standard edition of the Four Branches, PKM, employs the titles *Pwyll Pendeuic Dyuet, Branwen uerch Lyr, Manawydan uab Llyr* and *Math uab Mathonwy*. Sir Ifor's usage may be taken as the charter for later editors, translators and critics.

preceding tale: *Guedy daruot y'r seithwyr a dywedyssam ni uchot* . . .   It is Manawydan, however, who is the subject of that sentence: . . .*edrych a wnaeth Manauydan ar y dref yn Llundein.*[2]

And Manawydan is indeed the principal character in the Third Branch, which begins with his receiving the unexpected gift of a very illustrious bride and concludes with his restoration of fertility to the kingdom of Dyfed and of freedom to his wife and son-in-law. Recent scholarship has even proposed that Manawydan is in a sense the most important character in the Four Branches as a whole. Abandoning the emphasis of W. J. Gruffydd and Ifor Williams on Pryderi, later scholars have seen in Manawydan the thematic, moral, and psychological centre of the collection, the figure with whom the author of the Four Branches identified most closely. Proinsias Mac Cana writes that

> as one reads the Four Branches one can hardly avoid the conclusion that the author has created in Manawydan a reflection of his own personality and a vehicle for his own philosophy of life. . . . Vengeance and feud were part of the pattern of medieval life, but Manawydan shows how they may be rejected and circumvented by the exercise of fortitude and prudence.[3]

Brynley Roberts too has praised Manawydan, calling him 'astute, loyal and deep-thinking'.[4] And J. K. Bollard writes that, 'From the very beginning of the enchantment Manawydan takes control of the situation, and he supplies the knowledge, counsel, and craftsmanship by which they are able to survive'.[5]

John T. Koch appears to be the lone dissenting voice. In a densely argued study of the origins of the Third Branch, Koch claims that Manawydan is no 'paragon of Christian patience' but rather 'the complete Un-King'.[6] Manawydan, measured against the standards of kingship set forth in such Celtic texts as the Old Irish *Audacht Morainn*[7] and *Crith Gablach*,[8] is an abject failure; furthermore, the author has so constructed Manawydan's experience and behaviour that a reader versed in Celtic traditions will inevitably perceive him as a kind of anti-hero of the

2   PKM, p. 49.
3   Mac Cana 1992, pp. 47–8.
4   'Characterization in *The Four Branches of the Mabinogi*', in Roberts 1992, 105–113, at p. III.
5   Bollard, p. 175.
6   Koch, p. 36.
7   Ed. Fergus Kelly (Dublin: Dublin Institute for Advanced Studies, 1976).
8   Ed. D.A. Binchy. Mediaeval and Modern Irish Series II (Dublin: Dublin Institute for Advanced Studies, 1941).

paradigmatic Celtic sovereignty myth.[9] '*Manawydan*', he argues, 'can be read as a prolonged exemplary tale of Unrightful Kingship'.[10]

Koch's assessment of the figure of Manawydan is bound up with his argument that the Third Branch represents the survival of traditions concerning a British prince of the first century BC It is not a simple argument, and Koch's observations about the character of Manawydan might be overlooked by a reader absorbed in following and evaluating its individual postulates and its overall import. However, the validity of the observations is independent of the historical argument, and they provide a useful counterweight to the adulation that Manawydan has otherwise enjoyed in the commentary of the last two decades.

Even Koch, though, admits that, 'At the end . . . the redactor would wish us to feel that Manawydan has been vindicated in full for his Job-like patience'.[11] This sympathy he attributes to the formulation of a complete post-heroic ideal which led the author of the Four Branches to celebrate a figure that tradition had originally portrayed as craven and ineffectual, the epitome of 'Unrightful Kingship' — but all the while working within the narrative confines of that very tradition:

> Though clearly siding with Manawydan, he has preserved every episode so that the protagonist has remained in every wise the exact antithesis of the rightful king of the older value system.[12]

From one perspective, Manawydan appears to be a pusillanimous, déclassé tormentor of small animals; from another, he is the astute and long-suffering lord of a land restored to peaceful prosperity. I would argue that Koch's is not the only way to resolve this paradox. Another is to read the Third Branch as a narrative of moral education, to focus on Manawydan as a character in the process of learning and changing, rather than as an *exemplum* of post-heroic Christian virtues. My reading involves a 'synchronic' approach to the text of the Third Branch, rather than the kind of 'diachronic' study that Koch's essay represents.[13] It assumes that the author of the Four Branches was deliberately infusing traditional story materials with his own purposes, values, and meanings. I also accept the now conven-

---

9 Koch, pp. 31–40.
10 Koch, p. 42.
11 Koch, p. 36.
12 Koch, p. 36.
13 A number of recent scholars have pointed to the division of commentaries on the *Mabinogi* into these two categories, and have discussed the different assumptions and strategies of each. Particularly cogent is the review of critical literature by Andrew Welsh, pp. 121–27; another can be found in Mac Cana 1992, pp. 28–38.

tional view that one writer is responsible for the existing text of all four branches, and thus assume at least the possibility of thematic relationships among them.[14]

Some years ago, I suggested that the First Branch of the *Mabinogi* can be read as a story of the development of wisdom and good sense by its protagonist, Pwyll, whose name is in Welsh a common noun meaning 'prudence, judgement, common sense'. I would like to contend here that the Third Branch too is concerned not only with the appropriate exercise of lordship, but also with development of the prudence and self-restraint that must inform that lordship. In developing this theme, the tale of Manawydan echoes certain aspects of the tale of Pwyll, knowingly and tellingly. And like *Pwyll, Manawydan* reflects a sense of the mythical import of some of its material; it depends for the articulation of its meaning upon a fairly complex set of relationships with both the narrative traditions out of which it is built and with the other branches of the *Mabinogi*.

Although the immediate chronological relationship of the Third Branch is with the Second, the reader is likely within moments to be reminded rather of the First, for in the very first lines, Pryderi offers to Manawydan both his mother, Rhiannon, and governance of the seven cantrefs of Dyfed (*medyant y seith cantref [Dyuet]*). Thus the *Mabinogi* returns from the north, where Bendigeidfran held court in Harlech at the start of the Second Branch, to Dyfed, in south-west Wales. At the opening of the first branch, the reader recalls, *Pwyll Pendeuic Dyuet a oed yn arglwyd ar seith cantref Dyuet*, so the movement is a return not only geographically, to the setting of the First Branch, but verbally and textually, to its opening sentence.

The second major chapter, so to speak, of the First Branch concerns the courtship and marriage of Pwyll and the otherworldly horsewoman, Rhiannon. Thus, Pryderi's presentation of Rhiannon as a bride for Manawydan also recalls the First Branch. Moreover, it is with this reintroduction of Rhiannon that the mythic substratum of the *Mabinogi* becomes visible in the Third Branch; the relationship

---

14 These assumptions about single authorship, interrelationship, and fully realised rhetorical intention are shared, for example, by Brynley F. Roberts, who has written that 'It seems generally to have been accepted that individually (or collectively in the case of *The Four Branches*), these tales are the work of single authors' (1988, p. 11), and that

> In the *Four Branches of the Mabinogi* we are aware of a consistent attitude and a thematic unity. The material which these stories use is the most obviously naive and traditional of all the chwedlau, and yet from it the medieval author has produced a work unparalleled in Middle Welsh literature. His moral view of life, tempered by his compassion for human frailty, has taken up the *cyfarwyddyd* which he found and has given it significance beyond that of his own time, not along the way of accepted contemporary literary conventions but along the road of personal conviction shaping a unique narrative form. (1984, p. 228; pp. 102–3 of reprint)

of the story of Manawydan to the setting, plot, and underlying tradition of the First Branch is immediately manifest on multiple levels.

I have previously argued with regard to the First Branch that the author of the *Mabinogi* probably had some sense of the paradigmatic Celtic myth of the sovereignty goddess.[15] His parallel but different deployment of Rhiannon in the Third Branch persuades me more surely than ever that he was far from 'pillaging an antiquity of which he [did] not fully possess the secret', as Matthew Arnold famously put it.[16] Rather, he had some notion of the traditional import of the figure of Rhiannon. He is unlikely to have accepted the ancient sovereignty myth as a sacred narrative in any literal sense. That would not necessarily have prevented him, however, from exploiting its inherent semiotic value.

The tradition of allegorising pagan mythology and poetry, of reading narrative such as Vergil's *Aeneid* and Ovid's *Metamorphoses* in terms of ethics, stretched back as least as far as the sixth century. This practice was essentially an aspect of the art of grammar — the glossing of texts in order to elucidate the underlying meanings that validated the work of pagan poets for the Christian reader. It led to a habit among many medieval writers of investing their stories with secret lessons for those wise enough to discern them, or at least of claiming to have done so. In Marie de France and Chrétien de Troyes, for example, the claim of hidden meaning is explicit.[17] The absence of any such assertion in medieval Welsh narrative is one of the factors that has enabled the ongoing debate between those who read the Four Branches, and some of the other 'native tales', as *cyfarwyddyd*, traditional narrative preserved in writing in order to rescue it from oblivion, and those who regard some or all of them as consciously crafted works of literary fiction. As Brynley Roberts has put it,

> [W]hat is difficult to resolve are questions such as whether these authors may be regarded as *cyfarwyddiaid*, whether the stories are oral traditional tales which have been given written form or whether they were conceived as written compositions which may have taken elements from a number of sources, and what changes may have occurred in the change of medium from spoken to written.[18]

15 McKenna, pp. 45–8.
16 *On The Study of Celtic Literature* (1867), Everyman's Library No. 458 (London: J. M. Dent and New York: E. P. Dutton, 1910), p. 54.
17 On the development of allegorical interpretations of Vergil, see Martin Irivine, *The Making of Textual Culture: 'Grammatica' and Literary Theory, 350–1100* (Cambridge: Cambridge UP, 1994), pp. 118–61.
18 Roberts 1988, p. 11.

However, if it can be admitted that the author may have understood his story to embody a particular meaning, then it is possible as well that he believed that meaning to be encoded in part in the story of Rhiannon as told in the First and Third Branches.

A number of scholars share a sense that the traditional substratum of the Four Branches asserts itself undeniably and irresistibly in the text that we have. Brynley Roberts comments that '[t]hese stories continue to have a peculiar mythic resonance, of which the author is aware and which he uses in his composition, but this is not to say that he is mainly concerned to reproduce traditional narratives'.[19] And Proinsias Mac Cana has written more recently that 'the mythological element pervades all four tales and . . . one cannot properly evaluate them without giving it its due weight'.[20]

The pervasiveness of a paradigmatic Celtic myth in which a goddess chooses for a spouse the rightful king of a territory, thereby validating his claim to the kingship and ensuring the fertility and prosperity of the land, has long since been definitively established by Proinsias Mac Cana and other scholars.[21] The influence of the old myth on the Welsh romances, *Iarlles y Fynnawn (Owein)*, *Peredur vab Evrawc*, and *Gereint vab Erbin* has been noted in particular.[22] Mac Cana has written

> That the sovereignty myth underlies the three romances is beyond question, but it may be asked whether those who composed the extant texts were fully aware of its deeper significance. In general, the indications are that by the eleventh or twelfth century in Wales the knowledge and understanding of native mythology, even among the learned poets, was patchy and unsystematic, but nevertheless, as in a much later period in Ireland, certain basic concepts seem to have survived the social system which had generated them, and of these the myth of the goddess of sovereignty and of the sacred marriage, the *hieros gamos*, was one of the most permanent and productive. . . . When about 1170 Eleanor of Aquitaine had her son Richard installed as Duke of Aquitaine, she arranged that this should take the form of a symbolic marriage between him and St. Valéry, the legendary martyr and patroness of the region. The saint's ring was placed on his finger *in*

19 Roberts 1984, p. 96.
20 Mac Cana 1992, p. 52.
21 Mac Cana 1955–8; Rachel Bromwich, 'Celtic Dynastic Themes and the Bretons Lays', *Études Celtiques* 9 (1960–1), pp. 439–74, and 'The Celtic Inheritance of Medieval Literature', *Modern Language Quarterly* 26 (1965), pp. 203–27; Rhian Andrews, 'Rhai Agweddau ar Sofraniaeth yng Ngherddi'r Gogynfeirdd', *Bulletin of the Board of Celtic Studies* 27 (1976), pp. 23–30.
22 See, for example, Glenys Goetinck, 'Sofraniaeth yn y Tair Rhamant', *Llên Cymru* 6 (1960–1), pp. 138–53; I. C. Lovecy, 'The Celtic Sovereignty Theme and the Structure of *Peredur*', *Studia Celtica* 12–13 (1977–78), pp. 133–46;

solemn token of his indissoluble union with the provinces and vassals of Aquitaine. One does not need to be a Celticist to appreciate the implications of this ritual.[23]

Mac Cana also writes of the strong women in the Four Branches that

> . . . it is more simple to take them for what they are: literary reflexes of the Celtic goddess in some of her many aspects. When Rhiannon comes from the Otherworld and chooses Pwyll for her husband, she reincarnates the goddess of sovereignty who, in taking to her a spouse, thereby ordained him legitimate king of the territory which she personified. Not only does she take the initiative in forming a marriage alliance, but she oversways her lord and her suitor. . . . Her masterful behaviour carries over into her dealings with Manawydan in the third branch, though here the shrewd old protagonist is more her match than the conventional heroic prince.[24]

In the context of such a still potent, even if imperfectly remembered, mythology of sovereignty, the figure of Rhiannon might well have stimulated certain sensibilities in an audience familiar with Welsh tradition, particularly in an audience familiar with her role in the First Branch of the *Mabinogi* as well. Even for a reader, or listener, who was not equipped to recognise in Rhiannon an avatar of the sovereignty goddess with equine affinities, the interplay of the character as she appears in the Third Branch with the Rhiannon of the First Branch would have been evocative of a certain sense of her significance and of the significance of her marriage to Manawydan, of her disappearance, and of her restoration.

In the Third Branch, for example, Rhiannon is given in marriage to Manawydan by her adult son, Pryderi. This accords, of course, with medieval Welsh practice.[25] In addition, however, it reminds us that the goddess cannot be courted and won; she must choose her mate. That is certainly what happens in the First Branch, where Rhiannon informs Pwyll that

> *Riannon, uerch Heueyd Hen, wyf i, a'm rodi y wr o'm hanwod yd ydys. Ac ny mynneis innheu un gwr, a hynny o'th garyat ti. Ac nys mynnaf etwa, onyt ti a'm gwrthyt. Ac e wybot dy attep di am hynny e deuthum i.*[26]

Rhiannon, daughter of Hefeydd the Old am I, and I am being given to a husband against my will. And I have never desired a husband, and that for love of you.

---

23 Mac Cana 1992, pp. 111–12.
24 Mac Cana 1992, pp. 55–6.
25 See *The Welsh Law of Women*, ed. Dafydd Jenkins and Morfydd E. Owen (Cardiff: U WalesP, 1980), p. 19 *et passim*.
26 PKM, p. 12.

And I still don't want one, unless you refuse me. And to know your answer to that have I come.

The Rhiannon of the Third Branch strikes us as very different in some respects, but it remains the case that she is not to be won, like a prize, but must be received as a gift.

It is not Rhiannon herself who chooses Manawydan as her husband, but her son Pryderi:

> Seith cantref Dyuet yr edewit y mi, heb y Pryderi, a Riannon uy mam yssyd yno. Mi a rodaf it honno, a medyant y seith cantref genthi. . . .A chyn bo enwedigaeth y kyuoeth y mi, bit y mwynant y ti a Riannon. . . . Er amser y bu hitheu yn y dewred, ny bu wreic delediwach no hi, ac etwa ny bydy anuodlawn y phryt.[27]

The seven cantrefs of Dyfed were left to me, said Pryderi, and Rhiannon, my mother, is there. I'll give her to you, and possession of the seven cantrefs with her . . . . And though the land is mine in name, you and Rhiannon shall have the enjoyment of it . . . . When she was in her prime, there was no woman more lovely than she, and still you will not be displeased by her form.

Rhiannon is never, apparently, consulted in the matter; she nevertheless retains some of her old spark when Manawydan speaks in her hearing as if she were merely an object in his dealings with Pryderi.[28] John Koch emphasises the differences between the First and Third Branches here: 'Riannon chooses Pwyll for her mate after he proves his valour in Annwvyn, but she is bestowed on Manawydan (after he displays *lleddfdra*) by a powerful man'.[29] It is possible, though, to regard the two episodes as more similar than different, in that each involves the bestowal of Rhiannon upon a husband both surprised and delighted to be so favoured. If the *panache* with which Rhiannon elected Pwyll to be her mate in the First Branch was the ineluctable clue to the presence of a sovereignty goddess, the echo of that episode in the Third Branch brings the goddess back onto the stage.

And yet it is true that the memory of Rhiannon's regal and self-sufficient demeanour in the First Branch evokes at the same time a certain unease with her

27 PKM, pp. 49–50.
28 PKM, p. 50.
29 Koch, pp. 37–8. Charles W. Sullivan III implies that the difference may be one of the elements in the Four Branches that encodes a shift from matriliny to patriliny among the Celts. See 'Inheritance and Lordship in *Math*', in *The Mabinogi: A Book of Essays* (New York and London: Garland, 1996), pp. 347–66, at pp. 361–2; rpt. from *Transactions of the Honourable Society of Cymmrodorion* (1990), pp. 45–63.

position in the Third. The echo signals something gone wrong. She is older, for one thing; Pryderi's words draw attention to this fact. While this makes sense in light of her having become, since the reader first met her, the widowed mother of a son who is now grown and married, her age may also be read as an instance of the theme in which the goddess suffers in her form or condition when without her proper spouse, of the aged hag who is transformed into a beautiful young woman upon sexual acceptance by the rightful king.[30]

What is certain is that Manawydan's marriage to Rhiannon appears initially to be associated with precisely the kind of fertility and abundance that would be expected of the union of the rightful lord with the territorial goddess, but that soon enough he finds himself at the centre of a kind of desert, as might be expected of a failed or bad king. After the wedding feast of Pwyll and Rhiannon, the couple join Pryderi and his wife in a circuit of Dyfed:

> *Ac wrth rudyaw y wlat ny welsynt eiryoet wlat gyuanhedach no hi, na heldir well, nac amlach y mel na'y physcawt no hi.*[31]

And as they wandered the country, they had never seen a more accommodating land than that, nor better hunting grounds, nor a land more ample in its honey or its fish.

But during a second feast, celebrating the return of Pryderi from Oxford, where he has gone to pay homage to Caswallawn, the self-proclaimed king of Britain, all of this changes suddenly and dramatically. The four visit the Gorsedd Arberth, the very spot from which Pwyll first spotted the horsewoman Rhiannon in the First Branch,

> *Ac ual y bydant yn eisted yuelly, llyma dwrwf, a chan ueint y twrwf, llyma gawat o nywl yn dyuot hyt na chanhoed yr un ohonunt wy y gilid. Ac yn ol y nywl llyma yn goleuhau pob lle. A phan edrychyssant y ford y guelynn y preideu, a'r anreitheu, a'r kyuanhed kyn no hynny, ny welynt neb ryw dim, na thy, nac aniueil, na mwc, na than, na dyn, na chyuanhed, eithyr tei y llys yn wac,*

---

30 For further discussion of this theme, see Mac Cana 1955–8, at 7, 84–5; 8, 63–4, and *passim*. For its reflex in the First Branch, see McKenna, 47–8. Since Manawydan already finds that *na welsei eiryoed wreic digonach y thecket a'y thelediwet no hi* ('he had never seen a woman more satisfactory than she in loveliness and charm') before he announces to Pryderi his willingness to accept the match, however, it may be going too far to read her age as an aspect of her privation, at the mythic level.

31 PKM, p. 51

*diffeith, anghyuanhed, heb dyn, heb uil yndunt; eu kedymdeithon e hun wedy eu
colli, heb wybot dim y wrthunt, onyt wyll pedwar.*[32]

And as they were sitting thus, there was a thunderclap, and with the immensity of
the thunderclap, there came a cloud of mist so that none of them could see the
other. And after the mist, there was a brightening everywhere. And when they
looked the way that they would see the flocks and the herds and the dwellings
before that, they saw nothing, neither house, nor animal, nor smoke, nor fire, nor
person, nor dwelling, except the court buildings — empty, deserted, uninhabited,
without person or beast in them; their own companions lost, without their
knowing anything about them, except the four of them.

Proinsias Mac Cana has noted the parallel between the First and Third
Branches in the way that wonders are precipitated by a visit to the Gorsedd
Arberth during a feast.[33] But the descent of the devastating mist stands in stark
contrast to the appearance of Rhiannon: whereas that mystery leads to the designation of Pwyll as the spouse of the goddess and his validation as lord, the desolation that follows the mist appears to reproach Manawydan and Pryderi — their
lordship has led to this. There is more than one echo of the First Branch in this
scene, though. The reader is reminded as well, by the emphasis on the isolation of
the four companions, of Pwyll, hunting from Arberth in Glyn Cuch, and losing
his companions. It is the episode in which Pwyll, having discourteously attempted
to seize the quarry of another hunter, has his first encounter with the Otherworld,
in the form of Arawn king of Annwfn.[34] Both the reiteration of the excursion to
Gorsedd Arberth where wonders are experienced, and the replication of the isolation that accompanies the encounter of Pwyll with Arawn, link this scene of the
Third Branch with the First.

As Andrew Welsh has pointed out, Dyfed is not reduced to a wasteland by
this first enchantment:

it is deserted but not infertile. Even under the enchantment it abounds in game,
fish and wild honey. Only the refinements of civilised life are gone: domestic

---

32 PKM, pp. 51–2.

33 Mac Cana 1992, p. 33.

34 Brynley Roberts (1984) sees *cydymdeithas* 'friendship' as the keyword in Manawydan (p. 99
of rpt.). But the Arawn episode of Pwyll places a similar emphasis on *cydymdeithas*. When
Arawn returns home to discover that Pwyll has not only subdued his old enemy Hafgan, but
has remained chaste with respect to Arawn's wife, he exclaims that Pwyll is *cadarn a ungwr y
gydymdeithas* 'strong and peerless in friendship', for example (PKM, p. 7). For a discussion
of the role of the Arawn episode in the First Branch, see McKenna, pp. 48–51.

herds, dwellings with their hearth fires, the society of people. It is not nature but culture that has failed.[35]

Nevertheless, the change is drastic and dispiriting for Manawydan and his companions. It is ultimately discovered to be part of the vengeance taken by Llwyd son of Cil Coed upon Pryderi and upon Dyfed for the insult inflicted upon Gwawl son of Clud by Pwyll (and Rhiannon) in the First Branch. However, even as the temporary loss of Pryderi in *Pwyll* can be understood as part of an ongoing test of Pwyll's lordship,[36] so too can the enchantment of Dyfed in the Third Branch be read in terms of theme as well as of plot.

In the First Branch, though, there are some fairly clear indications of the ways in which Pwyll is deficient. In his attempted appropriation of Arawn's quarry, he demonstrates *anwybot* and *ansyberwyt* ('ignorance' and 'discourtesy')[37] in the same thoughtless arrogance that will later impel him to send riders in pursuit of the mysterious horsewoman even after it becomes obvious that she is not to be overtaken. *Arhoaf yn llawen. . . ac oed llesach y'r march pei ass archut yr meityn*, she replies when he at last requests her to stop: 'I'll stop gladly, and it would have been better for the horse if you had asked sooner'.[38] An impulsive, rash munificence allows him to be tricked into giving Rhiannon to Gwawl: *ny bu uuscrellach gwr ar y ssynnwyr e hun nog ry uuost ti*, she tells him, 'there was never a man feebler of wit than you have been'.[39]

If the desolation of Dyfed, on the other hand, betokens some failure on Manawydan's part, there is no Arawn to announce what it is, and Rhiannon remains silent. It occurs soon after the return of Pryderi from Oxford, where he has gone to offer homage (*gwrogaeth*) to Caswallawn. John Koch sees one aspect of Manawydan's 'unrightfulness' in his failure to resist the usurpation of the crown of Bendigeidfran by his cousin Caswallawn,[40] although it is of course Pryderi, the ruler in name of Dyfed who submits to Caswallawn, and not Manawydan, to whom he has given the exercise of power (*medyant*) and its enjoyment (*mwynant*)[41]. One way of interpreting Manawydan's position at the moment of the enchantment of Dyfed is to see him as a lord who is enjoying his sovereignty — hunting, fishing, feasting, and marriage to Rhiannon but shirking its responsibilities. He complains about Caswallawn at the beginning of the tale,

35 Welsh, pp. 134–5.
36 For a discussion of this issue, see McKenna, pp. 47–52.
37 PKM, p. 2.
38 PKM, p. 12.
39 PKM, p. 14.
40 Koch, p. 37.
41 PKM, p. 49.

Kyt boet keuynderw y mi y gwr hwnnw, goathrist yw genhyf i guelet neb yn lle Bendigeiduran uy mrawt, ac ny allaf uot yn llawen yn un ty ac ef.[42]

Although he is my cousin, it is distressing to me to see anyone in the place of my brother Bendigeidfran, and I cannot be happy in the same house as he.

Yet he undertakes neither to depose the usurper, nor to acknowledge him formally. It is Pryderi, not Manawydan, who transcends the old heroic ethos with a self-effacing gesture of accommodation of both Caswallawn and Manawydan.

The question of Dyfed's relationship to Caswallawn's kingship does not arise again. However, in the dénouement of the tale, when Manawydan negotiates with Llwyd son of Cil Coed for the liberation of his land, wife, and son-in-law, he demonstrates his ability to engage a powerful opponent successfully but without violence. The courage and cunning with which he does so, however, are not so much qualities that have been operating throughout, invisible to the reader, as they are qualities that have developed in the course of the narrative, qualities that stand in marked contrast to the snivelling about Caswallawn with which the tale opens.

In the immediate aftermath of the enchantment, Manawydan is as helpless to deal with the predicament as are his three companions. No one can think of anything better to do for two years than to continue feasting and hunting as they did before. Although these are regal pastimes, they can be construed, under the circumstances, as irresponsible. They represent the enjoyment of sovereignty (*mwynant y kyuoeth*) that Pryderi offered to Manawydan, without its obligations. In fact, they involve the ongoing depletion of the resources of the land — precisely the sort of behaviour that is associated in many literary and political traditions with bad kingship. In an Irish text generally acknowledged to have its roots in Celtic mythological tradition, *Cath Maige Tuired*, the Fomorian king Bres, who exacts excessive tribute and labour from the Tuatha Dé Danann, is the paradigm of *gáu flathemon*, or what John Koch has called 'Unrightful Kingship'. In another, *Aislinge Meic Conglinne*, like the *Mabinogi* generally dated to the late eleventh or twelfth century,[43] the demon of gluttony that possesses king Cathal mac Finguine threatens to devastate all of Munster, such are Cathal's demands for food.

Ultimately, it is Manawydan who proposes a different response to their situation: *ny bydwn ual hynn. Kyrchwn Loygyr, a cheisswn greft y caffom yn ymborth,*[44] he says to his companions, 'we shall not live like this. Let us go to England, and let us find a craft by which we may support ourselves'. The suggestion is surprising. Manawydan proposes not only that the foursome leave the desolate land,

42 PKM, p. 49.
43 Ed. Kenneth H. Jackson (Dublin: Dublin Institute for Advanced Studies, 1990).
44 PKM, p. 52.

rather than trying to do anything about matters there, but also that they abandon the way of life associated with their noble rank and take on the guise of artisans. At the same time, there is an echo of the First Branch to be heard here: even as Pwyll, in order to redress the ignoble discourtesy that he had shown to Arawn, needed to relinquish his kingdom and travel to Annwfn, so also does Manawydan, confronted with the evidence of his and Pryderi's inadequate lordship, travel out of Dyfed into England.

Arawn explains to Pwyll in great detail what he is to do in Annwfn, and Pwyll redeems himself by following those instructions to the letter. Manawydan, on the other hand, must devise his own agenda. Pwyll returns to Dyfed with the lifelong friendship of Arawn and the title *Pen Annwfn*, and is soon thereafter chosen by Rhiannon as her mate. Manawydan's ventures on the first visit to England, on the other hand, effect no change in his own status or the condition of Dyfed; if anything, the events that take place upon his return suggest that he is still being punished. On the level of plot, of course, his failure to lift the enchantment is the result of his simple failure to discover its source. On a deeper level, however, on which the tale is concerned both thematically and mythically with sovereignty, the failure of the first expedition to England is a failure to develop lordly virtues.

The foursome undertake a series of occupations that seem, on the face of it, to be inappropriate for persons of their rank. While J. K. Bollard wrote accurately that Manawydan 'supplies the knowledge, counsel, and craftsmanship by which they are able to survive',[45] during the desolation of Dyfed, the point of John Koch is equally well taken: that Manawydan supports himself and his companions by sinking 'to the status of . . . a peripatetic craftsman'.[46] Manawydan proposes in turn that the group take to saddlery, shield making, and shoemaking; in each case, it is Manawydan who develops the techniques that allow them to prosper in their craft, effectively driving local artisans out of business. His aptitude for such peaceable and productive work is impressive. In a more broadly Celtic framework, the reader is reminded of the Irish mythological figure of Lug Samildánach, the 'all-arts-together-one', as he appears at the gate of Nuadu's court in *Cath Maige Tuired*,[47] and of his Welsh cognate, Lleu, a central figure in the Fourth Branch of the *Mabinogi*, who also engages in the craft of shoemaking.[48] Yet, as the murderous rage of the local artisans suggests, Manawydan's strategy is an

45 Bollard, p. 175.
46 Koch, p. 37.
47 *Cath Maige Tuired*, pp. 38–43.
48 PKM, pp. 80–1. John Koch observes that 'Manawydan and Lleu are both sovereigns who have been denied their birthright. The craft they practise while thus dispossessed serves as a badge of their thwarted kingly natures: they make the sort of shoes proper to kings'. (p. 33)

inappropriate one for an aristocrat. Rather than fostering prosperity, he causes an economic crisis, albeit not in the kingdom for which he is responsible. As sovereign, he ought, perhaps, ideally to encompass the capacity for all the crafts that his realm needs in order to thrive. His own proper work, however, is to provide his people with protection, wise governance, and the sacral presence that insures fertility — not to make shoes. When he resumes that occupation on the second sojourn in England, Cigfa makes this plain to him: *Arglwyd . . . nyt hoff honno y glanet y wr kynghilet, kyuurd a thydi*, she says, 'Lord . . . I don't think much of the cleanliness of that for a man as able and as noble as you are'.[49] I would disagree with Proinsias Mac Cana's assessment of Cigfa's remark as arising from 'a kind of prim suburban snobbery'[50]. Bourgeois pretension is not an issue for these characters, who are not of the bourgeoisie. They are aristocrats in a hierarchical society, in which there is behaviour that is appropriate and inappropriate to each class. Manawydan himself seems implicitly to recognise this when he insists against Pryderi's counsel that they must not give battle to the angry saddlers of Hereford. *Bei ymladem ni ac wyntwy, clot drwc uydei arnam, ac yn carcharu a wneit*, he warns, 'if we fought with them, we would be of ill repute, and would be imprisoned'.[51] His *clod* — a concept embracing reputation, honour, and fame — was of paramount importance to a nobleman, and Manawydan knew that attacking *taeogau* 'churls' was no way to enhance it.

Later, however, while Manawydan does resist the 'heroic' impulse of Pryderi to kill the unhappy local shield makers, his rationale seems less than kingly. *Caswallawn a glywei hynny, a'e wyr, a rewin uydem* he argues, 'Caswallawn and his men would hear of it, and we would be ruined'.[52] He still lacks the ability to deal with Caswallawn, and in this regard stands in stark contrast to Pwyll, who early in the First Branch establishes a strong and useful fellowship with Arawn. And when he decides upon shoemaking as a third trade, he reasons that *ni byd o galhon gan grydyon nac ymlad a ni nac ymwarauun* 'shoemakers won't have the heart to fight with us or hinder us'.[53] This is hardly the attitude of a man who is rising above the martial ethos of a warrior aristocracy, but rather that of a coward who

49 PKM, p. 58. John Koch argues that

> 'Clean' is neither strong enough nor sufficiently wide in its range of meaning to convey the culturally charged force of *glân*. . . . It hardly needs saying that work that was not *glân* was not appropriate to a king. If we think in terms of the sacral kingship of the ancient Celts, we come near to its exact antithesis. (p. 33)

50 Mac Cana, p. 47.
51 PKM, p. 53.
52 PKM, p. 54.
53 PKM, p. 54.

shirks it by pitting himself against an opponent of lowly status within the context of a society that regards valour as an aristocratic virtue.

As I see it, Manawydan returns to Dyfed stymied. He has not learned to behave in a manner appropriate to his status, and only half knows this. It is the consequence of his failure that not only does Dyfed remain deserted, but that he also loses Rhiannon, the sign and source of his sovereignty, along with Pryderi, the emblem of her fertility. During the course of a hunt, Manawydan and Pryderi come upon a mysterious *caer*, into which their dogs, Pryderi, and finally Rhiannon vanish, after which the entire edifice disappears.[54]

This episode echoes the First Branch again, and in more than one way. Pwyll, too, is given Rhiannon, loses her, and must win her back by outwitting Gwawl at his wedding feast. Pwyll, too, loses Pryderi, his infant son, and with him, in a sense, loses Rhiannon once more, for she cannot reign at his side until the child is recovered and she is exonerated of blame for his death and disappearance. From another perspective, we are reminded, by the hunt that leads Manawydan and Pryderi to the enchanted *caer*, of the hunt that led Pwyll to his encounter with Arawn. The parallelism is underscored by Manawydan's pledge to Cigfa just after the others disappear that he will respect her chastity for the sake of [c]ywirdeb *wrth Pryderi*, 'faith with Pryderi',[55] just as Pwyll remained chaste with respect to Arawn's wife in the First Branch, thus demonstrating his capacity for [c]adw *kywirdeb*, 'keeping faith'.[56] Manawydan, however, remains without the explicit instruction that Pwyll received in how to restore the goodwill of Arawn and to win Rhiannon back from Gwawl.

The second journey to England reiterates, in abbreviated form, the first: Manawydan takes up shoemaking once again, ignoring the censure of Cigfa. The repetition helps to point up the difference, however: on this occasion, when he gives up in the face of hostility from other shoemakers and turns homeward, Manawydan carries with him some wheat, and upon his return to Dyfed he begins to cultivate the soil. Perhaps farming is no more an appropriate occupation for a

54 John Koch offers a detailed reading of the disappearance of Pryderi and Rhiannon in terms of the sovereignty myth:

[T]he hero destined to be king often proves his valour in the chase for a magical white animal in the wilderness . . . .Manawydan holds back . . . as a prelude to losing the personified sovereignty. The paralysing golden bowl, by which Pryderi and Rhiannon are spirited off from Manawydan, can be seen as a reversal of the golden cup with which the personified Sovereignty of Ireland offers liquor to the successive kings of *Baile in Scáil*. (p. 35)

55 PKM, p. 57.
56 PKM, p. 8.

ruler than is shoemaking, but at least he is now devoting himself not only to his own well being, but also to that of the land whose sovereignty he enjoys. The second return, just a bit more than halfway through the text, marks the first real change in Manawydan. He sows, rather than merely garnering the fruits of the land; he engages in essential work, rather than superfluous rivalry with other craftsmen; he concerns himself with the welfare of his realm rather than living from hand to mouth as a vagabond.

Nevertheless, Manawydan's enterprises continue, apparently, to fail. Even as the threat of violence disrupted initial success every time that Manawydan and his companions undertook a craft, so too violence carries off the fruit of his agricultural work. It is at this moment that Manawydan has his first useful insight into his distress and that of Dyfed. *A mi a'e gwnn; y neb a dechreuis uyn diua, yssyd yn y orffen, ac a diuawys y wlad gyt a mi*, he muses, 'I know that it is the one who began my ruin who is completing it, and who has ruined the land along with me'.[57] He has already recognised the malevolent nature of the enchantment. He counsels Pryderi not to venture into the mysterious *caer*. *Ac o gwney uygkynghor i nyt ey idi. A'r neb a dodes hut ar y wlat, a beris bot y gaer yma*, he tells him, 'if you follow my advice, you won't go in. The one who cast the spell on the country caused the *caer* to be here'.[58] Only once up to this point, however, has he employed the verb *gwybod*, 'know'. *Mi a'y gwn*, he says to Pryderi, 'I know it', speaking of the craft of shoemaking.[59] The contrast between the two forms of knowledge accentuates the importance of Manawydan's growing understanding of the enchantment. In place of, or in addition to, the applied knowledge of the craftsman, he is developing the wisdom, the discernment, the *pwyll* that is appropriate to a ruler.

In the First Branch, too, Pwyll ultimately learns to exercise the good judgement that is the hallmark of a rightful sovereign.[60] And he too does so in relation to a threat to the fertility that attends the reign of a true ruler. As I have argued,

> For Pwyll, [the] final achievement of full sovereignty is impeded first by Rhiannon's failure to give birth to a son until nearly three years have passed and then by the mysterious abduction of the boy and the accusation of murder against Rhiannon. Throughout, Pwyll acts in accordance with the wisdom he has

57 PKM, p. 59.
58 PKM, p. 56.
59 PKM, p. 54.
60 In Irish tradition, the importance of good judgement to rightful sovereignty is explicit in *Cath Maige Tuired*, where Bres is lured by the Mac Óc into making a false judgement. He tells the Dagda, *Ispérae iarum an rí de marbad. Isbérae-sa fris, 'Ní fíor flathu deit, a rí óc Fénei, a n-udbere'* 'Then the king will order you to be killed, and you will say to him, "What you say, king of the warriors of the Féni, is not a prince's truth"'. Pp. 30–1.

acquired. He refuses at first to divorce his wife for barrenness because they have been married so short a time, but he promises to submit to the counsel of his men after an allotted period passes. When the child disappears, he refuses again to divorce Rhiannon, but agrees because of the evidence against her that she should be punished.[61]

Fundamental to his defence of Rhiannon is his *gwybod*, knowledge. *Plant a wnn i y uot idi hi. Ac nyt yscaraf a hi*, he insists, 'I know her to have children, and I will not divorce her'.[62]

By the time that he catches one of the mice that prove to be the ravagers of his crop, Manawydan has developed similar wisdom and discernment. He exhibits considerable cunning in his negotiations with the clerk, the priest, and the bishop who approach him as he prepares to hang the mouse. On the level of the plot, he must bargain for the future of Dyfed, seeking not only to undo the enchantment, but to secure a peaceful and prosperous future as well. Forbearance and acumen are the qualities with which he wins restoration of Rhiannon, Pryderi, and the land. On the level of myth, it is those qualities — political, rather than heroic virtues — that achieve his reunion with the goddess of sovereignty. In the world in which the *Mabinogi* was composed, in other words, the sacral king in immobile possession of the *fír flathemon* is a thing of the past. The heir to that mythic position must bear himself in accordance with his status, but also be a wily negotiator.

On four occasions, as he makes elaborate preparations to hang the captured mouse, Manawydan is advised that it is unseemly for a person of his status to have anything to do with such vermin. The first reproach comes from Cigfa, and reminds the reader of her insistence earlier that shoemaking was unclean work for a man of his rank. One effect of the repetition is to underscore the fact that whereas Manawydan had proceeded with his shoemaking despite Cigfa's objection, he does not, in fact, hang the mouse. Cigfa's protest calls attention to what happens next. When the clerk reproaches him for the second time, Manawydan is suspicious, because *neut oed seith mlyned kyn no hynny, yr pan welsei ef na dyn, na mil, eithyr y pedwardyn y buassynt y gyt* 'it had been seven years since he had seen either man or beast except the four who had been together'.[63] From the moment when the clerk first attempts to negotiate the mouse's freedom, Manawydan seems alert to the possibility of a chance to recover Rhiannon, Pryderi, and Dyfed. He not only refrains from hanging the mouse, but bears himself so nobly that he refuses to negotiate with Llwyd ap Cil Coed until he appears in the form of a bishop.

61 McKenna, p. 52.
62 PKM, p. 21.
63 PKM, p. 61.

When that bishop asks Manawydan to 'name his price' (*gwna y guerth*),[64] he must be sure not only to remember every evil that the enchantment has visited upon Dyfed, but also to anticipate future dangers and ward them off. Llwyd underscores the difficulty and importance of Manawydan's task when he says *A dioer, da y medreist . . . .bei na metrut hynny . . . ef a doy am dy benn cwbyl o'r gouut* 'By heaven, you've done well. . .if you hadn't done that .. .all the harm would have been on your head'.[65] Various features of this episode — the setting on the Gorsedd Arberth and the explicit references to the Gwawl and to Pwyll — recall the First Branch once more. These intertextual connections accentuate Manawydan's achievement: whereas Pwyll tricked Gwawl into relinquishing Rhiannon by following her instructions exactly, Manawydan faces Llwyd on the Gorsedd Arberth with only his own wits to guide him in the exchange that will determine the future of Dyfed.

That he succeeds completely is attested by Llwyd's congratulatory comment and by the release of Rhiannon and Pryderi from an imprisonment that recalls once more both their mythic import and their roles in the First Branch. Llwyd tells Manawydan that *Pryderi a uydei ac yrd porth uy llys i am y uynwgyl, a Riannon a uydei a mynweireu yr essynn, wedy bydyn yn kywein gueir, am y mynwgyl hitheu* 'Pryderi had the gate hammers of my court around his neck, and Rhiannon had the collars of the asses, after they had been carrying hay, around her neck'.[66] They have been treated like horses, as was Rhiannon during her penance in the First Branch. Pryderi, too, delivered to Teyrnon's door at the same time that a foal disappears, is associated with horses in the First Branch. The equine affinities of the goddess and her offspring appear to belong to a very early stratum of the sovereignty myth.[67] If the account of Rhiannon's and Pryderi's bizarre suffering in the Otherworld has any rhetorical purpose other than the preservation of tradition, it is surely to remind the reader that they are more than they seem, and that recovering them is an achievement charged with mythic significance.

Manawydan is, after all, the man who achieves for Dyfed 'peace and prosperity, which can only be purchased through the practice of the unheroic and somewhat prosaic virtues of prudence and tolerance'.[68] But he is all the more to be admired

64 PKM, p. 63.
65 PKM, pp. 64–5.
66 PKM, p. 75.
67 See Patrick K. Ford, trans., *The Mabinogi and Other Medieval Welsh Tales* (Berkeley and Los Angeles: U California P, 1977), pp. 5–12, for a full discussion of the equine aspect of the sovereignty goddess and her son.
68 Mac Cana 1992, p. 48.

because he attains to those virtues from ignoble beginnings in passivity, evasiveness, and cowardice. Like Pwyll, he offers the Welsh princes who heard his story a model of effective sovereignty for an age in which shrewdness, circumspection, and accommodation were essential instruments of good governance. He is more sympathetic than Pwyll, however, because he must find his own way to true nobility in a baffling world where the elusive sovereignty goddess gives no instructions.

REFERENCES

Bollard	J. K. Bollard, 'The Structure of the Four Branches of the Mabinogi', in C.W. Sullivan III, ed., *The Mabinogi: A Book of Essays* (New York and London: Garland, 1996), pp. 165–96; rpt from *Transactions of the Honourable Society of Cymmrodorion* 1974–75, pp. 250–76. Page references are to the reprint.
Cath Maige Tuired	Elizabeth Gray, ed., *Cath Maige Tuired: The Second Battle of Mag Tuired.* Irish Texts Society volume LII (London: Irish Texts Society, 1982).
Koch	John T. Koch, 'A Welsh Window on the Iron Age: Manawydan, Mandubracios', *Cambridge Medieval Celtic Studies* 14 (1987), 17–52.
Mac Cana 1955–8	Proinsias Mac Cana, 'Aspects of the Theme of King and Goddess in Early Irish Literature', *Études Celtiques* 7 (1955–6), 76–114, 356–413; 8 (1958), 59–65.
Mac Cana 1992	Proinsias Mac Cana, *The Mabinogi.* 2nd ed. Writers of Wales (Cardiff: University of Wales Press, 1992)
McKenna	Catherine A. McKenna, 'The Theme of Sovereignty in *Pwyll*', *Bulletin of the Board of Celtic Studies* 29 (1980), 35–52; rpt. in C.W. Sullivan, ed., *The Mabinogi: A Book of Essays* (New York and London: Garland, 1996), pp. 303–30. Page references are to the original article.
PKM	Ifor Williams. *Pedeir Keinc y Mabinogi* (Caerdydd: Gwasg Prifysgol Cymru, 1930; 2nd ed. 1951).
Roberts 1984	Brynley F. Roberts, 'From Traditional Tale to Literary Story: Middle Welsh Prose Narratives', in *The Craft of Fiction*, ed. Leigh A. Arrathoon (Rochester: Solaris, 1984), pp. 211–30; rpt. in 'The Four Branches of the Mabinogi', in Roberts, 1992, pp. 95–104. Page references are to the reprint, except as noted.

Roberts 1988   Brynley F. Roberts, 'Oral Tradition and Welsh Literature', *Oral Tradition* 3 (1988), 61–87; rpt. in Roberts, 1992, pp. 1–24. Page references are to the reprint.

Roberts 1992   Brynley F. Roberts, *Studies on Middle Welsh Literature* (Lewiston, Queenston, and Lampeter: Edwin Mellen, 1992).

Welsh   Andrew Welsh, '*Manawydan fab Llŷr:* Wales, England, and the "New Man"', in C.W. Sullivan III, ed., *The Mabinogi: A Book of Essays* (New York and London: Garland, 1996), pp. 121–41; rpt. from *Celtic Languages and Celtic Peoples: Proceedings of the Second North American Conference of Celtic Studies*, ed. Cyril J. Byrne, *et al.* (Halifax: St. Mary's University, 1992), pp. 362–89. Page references are to the reprint.

The Irish Herald[1]

Joseph Falaky Nagy

UNIVERSITY OF CALIFORNIA, LOS ANGELES

THERE are four outstanding passages in the vast body of Irish saints' lives in Latin where the word for herald, *pr(a)eco*, is used. As used in classical Latin, *praeco* means, according to Lewis and Short's Dictionary, 'a crier, herald, in a court of justice, in popular assemblies, at auctions, at public spectacles, games, or processions, etc.'[2] In function the Roman *praeco* is comparable to the Greek *kērux* as the latter appears for example in the context of the Homeric assembly.[3] Furthermore the *praeco* and *kērux* are clearly Indo-European cousins to the ancient Indic oral performer denoted by the term *kārú-* (derived as is *kērux* from a root meaning 'praise loudly').[4] These figures foreshadow the medieval European

---

1 This paper is dedicated to Professor Mac Cana, a scholar who has deftly explored the subtle connections and contrasts among the various terms for performer, poet, and author in medieval Irish literature.

2 Charlton T. Lewis [and Charles Short], *A Latin Dictionary Founded on Andrews' Edition of Freund's Latin Dictionary* (Oxford, 1879), s.v. *praeco*. The Latin word appears to have been borrowed into later medieval Irish as *prechoin* 'crier' (DIL, s.v.). On the uses of *preco* in medieval Latin, see R. E. Latham, *Revised Medieval Latin Word-List from British and Irish Sources* (London, 1965), s.v. *preco*.

3 As in the assembly featured in Book 2 of the Iliad: 'Nine heralds shouting set about putting them in order, to make them cease their clamour and listen to the kings beloved of Zeus' (trans. Richmond Lattimore [Chicago, 1951], p. 78). The Homeric and Hesiodic herald, of whom Hermes was the divine paradigm, was an itinerant artisan whose function overlapped with those of the seer and the poet, notes Gregory Nagy in *Greek Mythology and Poetics* (Ithaca and London, 1990), pp. 3, n. 7; 59–60. See also Robert J. Mondi's 1978 Harvard Ph.D. dissertation 'The Function and Social Position of the ΚΗΡΥΞ in Early Greece.'

4 Pierre Chantraine, *Dictionnaire étymologique de la langue grecque* (Paris, 1970), s.v. κῆρυξ.

herald as described by Constance Bullock-Davies in her book on a royal feast held in London in 1306:

> It is generally accepted that a herald's primary duties were concerned with the tournament, but it is chiefly from literary sources that support for this contention has been derived. Heralds were sent throughout the area, province or country to proclaim when and where a tournament was to be held. At the tournament itself they announced the names of the contestants, described their blazons, gave the signals to commence or cease, called out the combatants in time for their jousts and declared who were the winners. When they were attached to a particular knight, they made it their business to advertise his prowess, to urge him on during tilts or tourneys and, in every way possible, to add to the discomfiture of his opponent.[5]

The word *herald*, I note in passing, is of Germanic origin, originally 'battle-ruler',[6] a figure having among his functions the summoning of troops to battle, similar to the latter-day herald's summoning of knights to the tournament.

Returning to Latin *praeco* or later *preco*, we find that its etymology is uncertain, one surmise being that it contains a reduced form of the verb *praedicare* 'to announce', which, while it is to be distinguished from *praedicere* 'to predict', derives from the same verb stem *dic-* or *dīc-* 'speak'.[7] In post-classical Latin these two verbs are in fact confused. Hence in medieval texts *preco*, in addition to 'crier, announcer, herald,' can mean 'poet' or 'prophet'.[8] We will return to these secondary meanings later in this paper.

Is there an Irish word that is the equivalant of *praeco/kērux/herald*? In one of the Milan glosses the word *praeco* is rendered *erdonál*, 'crier', from *donál* (*do* + *núall*) 'noise, cry' (DIL, s.v. *donál*).[9] Worth mentioning here is *bollsaire*, defined as 'herald' in DIL, probably derived (the entry suggests) from Latin *pulso* as in *pulsator/ius* 'bell-ringer'. *Techt* and *techtaire*, nominal formations of the verb meaning 'go', have the more specific meaning of 'messenger', as does *echlach* (*ech* + *láech*), designating a

---

5 *Menestrellorum Multitudo. Minstrels at a Royal Feast* (Cardiff, 1978), pp. 39–41.
6 *Kluge Etymologisches Wörterbuch*, ed. Elmar Seebold, 23rd ed. (Berlin and New York, 1995), s.v. *Herold*.
7 Cf. A. Ernout and A. Meillet, *Dictionnaire étymologique de la langue latine*, 4th ed. (Paris, 1959), s.v. *praecō*.
8 See Lewis and Short, s.v. *praeco*.
9 Stokes and Strachan 1901, 286: praeconi[bu]s, huaerdonolaib. The word also appears in one of the Triads (ed. Kuno Meyer, Todd Lecture Series, 13 [Dublin, 1906], p. 253: teora sírechta flatha: . . . buiden cen erdonail . . .) and in the sayings attributed to Flann Fína (*Bríathra Flainn Fína maic Ossu*, transcr. Kuno Meyer, in *Anecdota from Irish Manuscripts*, ed. Osborn Bergin and others [Halle and Dublin, 1907–13], 3:14: dligid aurdonal erfocra). On *donál*, see T. F. O'Rahilly's note, *Ériu* 13 (1942), 192–3.

figure whose distinctive features are described in the Book of Leinster *Táin*.[10] And another word whose semantic field overlaps to some extent with those already mentioned is *marcach*.[11] It would be reasonable to assume that one or more of these words lies, in the minds of the authors and their audiences, behind or parallel with *preco* in the hagiographic passages in which the latter word occurs. In fact, we happen to have Middle-Irish counterparts to all four Latin passages, featuring the same episodes, but in none of them do we find any of these Irish words standing in for *preco*. What *do* we find?

Two of these four attestations are to be found in extant versions of a story most plainly narrated in a Latin life of Patrick known by the designation given it in John Colgan's *Trias Thaumaturga*, the *Vita Tertia*. According to its most recent editor, Ludwig Bieler, this life appears to have been composed sometime between the beginning of the ninth and the early twelfth century[12] — the period, in fact, during which most if not all of the saints' lives and other texts I will be citing were composed. The passage in the *Vita Tertia* in which we find this word *preco* runs as follows:

> Patrick came to the region of the men of Munster and a deacon named Mantán made a great feast for him there. While Patrick was preaching the word of God in the area, a *preco* persistently and aggressively begged for food from him. Then the holy man blushed and his spirits sagged. But a certain man by the name of Nessán, now known as Deacon Nessán, gave Patrick a ram, and that was given to the *preco*. Then that *preco* along with his entire family [or retinue] died.[13]

This rather tight-lipped narrative, from what appears to be have been the most popular — or at least the most often copied — Latin Life of the saint in the Middle Ages,[14] is filled out by what we read in a characteristically macaronic section of the Middle-Irish Tripartite Life of Patrick. Note that here Latin *precones*, plural of *preco*, alternates with the Irish *cléir aesa ceirdd* 'band of poets or craftsmen' and *drúith* 'buffoons':

> Patrick then went to the territory of the Uí Fidgeinti, and Lonán, son of Mac Eirgg, organized a feast for him. . . . A man of Patrick's community, Mantán the Deacon,

10 Cecile O'Rahilly, ed., *Táin Bó Cúalnge from the Book of Leinster* (Dublin, 1967), lines 1489–94.
11 See Cecile O'Rahilly's note, *Celtica* 7 (1966), 32.
12 *Four Latin Lives of St. Patrick* (Dublin, 1971), pp. 25–26.
13 Deinde exiit ad regiones uir Mumen, et fecit ibi cenam magnam dechon Matan. Cum autem Patricius illic uerbum Dei predicaret, preco non cessabat grauiter querens ab eo cibum. Tunc sanctus uir erubuit et animus eius afflictus est. Et uir quidam nomine Nesan, qui nunc dicitur dechon Nesan, obtulit ueruecem Patricio, et ille datus est preconi. Tunc preco ille cum sua familia omnes mortui sunt (c. 61 [continental recension], *ibid.*, p. 160).
14 *Ibid.*, p. 13.

assisted [Lonán] the king with the feast. A band of poets came after Patrick seeking food. They would not accept any excuse. Said Patrick, 'Go to Lonán and Mantán the Deacon and ask them to help me'. These, however said [in Latin], '*Praecones* will not bless us for giving them the best part of our feast'. At this Patrick said, 'A youth is coming from the north, to him has the glory been awarded; to Patrick he is coming with a ram on his back'. Just then, a young man arrived, accompanied by his mother who was carrying on her back a cooked ram for the king's feast. Patrick asked him for the ram, for the sake of protecting his, Patrick's, honor. The youth gave it right away, gladly. His mother, fearful of the king, did not approve. Patrick then gave the food to the buffoons, and the earth swallowed them right away. Dercc, son of Scirire of Déis Tuaiscert was their leader. Patrick said that there would be neither king nor prince nor bishop among his [Lonán's?] descendants until Judgment Day. Moreover, he said to Mantán the Deacon that his abode on this earth would not be distinguished, that in fact it would be the dwelling-place of rabble, and that sheep and pigs would trample over its ruins. To Nessán, who had saved his honor, Patrick said, 'You are a leader of people'. He baptized him, ordained him as a deacon, and founded for him the church of Mungarit. To the apologizing mother he said that she would not be buried in the same place as her son. This proved to be true. Her grave is to the west of Mungarit, in a place where the bell in the great church cannot be heard. The graves are close, but they are separated by a wall.[15]

Finally, our third source for this story, the Irish Life of Patrick preserved in the Book of Lismore, refers to Patrick's nemeses in this story as *clíar aesa dána* 'band of poets', *drúith* 'buffoons' and even *cáinti* 'satirists'.[16] It leaves out the figure of Nessán's mother, but adds to the ram on Nessán's back: he is also carrying two

15 Luid íar suidiu cu Úa Fidgente, co ndernai Lonán macc Maicc Eirgg fleid do Patraic i mMulluch Cáe fri Carnd Feradaig andes: 7 boí fer muintiri do Pátraic oc dénum inna fleidi lasin ríg .i. dechon Mantan. Tarraid cléir aesa ceirdd inní Pátraic, do chuinchid bíid. Ní damdatar erchoimded. 'Ergid,' ol Pátraic, 'co Lonán 7 co dechóin Mantán immom chobuir.' Qui dixerunt: 'Non praecones benedicent nobis prinicipium cénae nostrae.' Tunc dixit Pátricius: 'In maccán dothaet antuaid,/is dó ro érnad in buaid:/dochum Cothraigi dodfail/cona moltán fora muin.' Illa uero hóra alius iuuenis cum súa matre gestante arietem coctum in dorso portandum ad cénam regis uenit. Ro gáid Patraic forsin macc in molt do thesorcuin a enich. Dobert in macc fóchétóir la fáilti. Níbu thol día máthir immorro ar húamuin ind ríg. Dobert Pátraic a mbíad donaib druthaib 7 roda sluicc in talam fochétóir. Derc macc Sciriré din Déis Tuaiscirt a toísech. Et asbert Patraic nád bíad rí ná rígdamna ná epscop día chiniud co bráth. Asbert immorro do dechóin Mantán nábad ardd a chongbál i talam, 7 robad ádba daíscarsluaig, 7 darmiregtais caírich 7 mucca tara thaissi. Asbert immorro fri Nessán doresart a enech: 'Pótens es gentis,' et babtizauit eum et ordinauit diacónum, et fúndauit aeclesiam sibi Mungarit. Dixitque matri éxcussanti quod non in loco filii sui sepileretur. Quod uerum est. Atá a fert isin tír fri Mungarit aníar, 7 ní cluinter in clocc asin cathraig móir hisin lucc sin. Péne simul sunt, segregante tantum muro (*Bethu Phátraic*, ed. Kathleen Mulchrone [Dublin, 1939], lines 2379–406).

16 *Lives of the Saints from the Book of Lismore*, ed. Whitley Stokes (Oxford, 1890), lines 479, 481, 490.

different kinds of cheese, *tanag* and three pieces of *faiscre grotha*.[17] 'As the satirists were eating the ram,' this text tells us, 'the earth swallowed them at once, so that they went to the bottom of hell, but the cheeses survived, remaining as standing stones.'[18]

Another attestation of the word *preco* in the Latin Lives of Irish saints occurs in the Life of the sixth-century Munster saint Rúadán of Lothra as it is preserved in both of the major surviving collections of Latin lives of Irish saints. In the Latin text *preco* appears where the Irish Life of Rúadán and the saga text *Aided Diarmata meic Cherbaill* have *maer* 'steward' and *callaire*, the latter a borrowing from Norse meaning 'caller'.[19] All of these terms are used to describe the catalyst in the famous story of the confrontation between Saint Rúadán and the Uí Néill king Diarmait mac Cerbaill — a confrontation that supposedly led to the abandonment of Tara as a royal seat.[20] Diarmait, we are told in these various sources, sends one Bacclám, called a *preco* in the Latin Life, into the territory of the Uí Maini. Inspired, we are told, by the devil, Bacclám demands that the door to the main fort be widened so that he might enter holding his spear horizontally instead of vertically. The building is badly damaged in the process, and in revenge the furious local king and resident of the fort, Áed Gúaire, slays the *preco*. Áed Gúaire then seeks shelter from Diarmait's wrath with Rúadán, who, despite his best saintly efforts, cannot keep Diarmait from seizing the slayer of his *preco*. The confrontation between king and saint comes to a head in the following dialogue as given in the Latin Life:

> (Says Diarmait:) 'Your *paruchia* will be the first to collapse in all of Ireland, and you will lose it.' Rúadán responded, 'Your kingdom will be the first to fall, and none of your descendants will ever reign.' The king responded, 'Your [ecclesiastical] site will be left desolate, and pigs living in it will uproot it with their snouts.' 'Before that,' said Rúadán, 'the city of Tara will have been left desolate for hundreds of years, and it will be without inhabitant for eternity.' The king responded, 'Your body will have a blemish, and one of your parts will perish. Your blind eye will not see the light.' Rúadán said, 'Your body will be destroyed by your enemies, and your members will be brutally scattered.' The king said, 'A most savage boar will dig up your grave with

17 Ibid., line 484.

18 Ibid., lines 490–92: Amal batar iarum na cainti oc ithe in muilt notas-sloicc in talam focedair cu lotar i fudoman ithfrinn, 7 marait fos na faiscre iarna sodh i clocha.

19 *Vitae Sanctorum Hiberniae ex Codice olim Salmanticensi nunc Bruxellensi*, ed. W. W. Heist (Brussels, 1965) p. 163; *Vitae Sanctorum Hiberniae*, ed. Charles Plummer (Oxford, 1910), Vol. 2, p. 245 (*preco*); *Bethada Náem nÉrenn*, ed. Plummer (Oxford, 1922), Vol. 1, p. 321 (*maer*); *Silva Gadelica*, ed. Standish H. O'Grady (London, 1892), Vol. 1, pp. 76–7 (*callaire*); DIL, s.v. *callaire*. These passages were noted by Richard Sharpe, as reported by Patrick Sims-Williams in the latter's 'Gildas and Vernacular Poetry,' *Gildas: New Approaches*, ed. Michael Lapidge and David Dumville (Woodbridge, 1984), 175, n. 42.

20 Plummer, *Vitae*, Vol. 2, pp. 247–49; Heist *Vitae*, pp. 163–65; Plummer, *Bethada*, Vol. 1, pp. 321–26; O'Grady, *Silva Gadelica*, Vol. 1, pp. 75–82.

its tusk.' Rúadán replied, 'The thigh which was not raised before me will not be buried together with the rest of your body; instead, someone will cast it away with a trowel out of a pile of sheepdung.'[21]

Diarmait finally agrees to release his prisoner for a price: Rúadán, or, according to one source, Brendan of Clonfert, supplies the king with a herd of wondrous horses from the sea, which, however, return to the water after Áed Gúaire is freed.[22]

Our fourth encounter with the *preco* in Irish hagiography is in one of the Latin lives of Brendan of Clonfert. This text has a version of the *Navigatio Brendani* worked into it, and it is in one of the episodes of this section that the *preco* appears yet again.[23] Brendan is about to embark on his second voyage out, the first having been declared a failure by his fostermother Ita on account of his having set forth in a boat made from animal skin instead of wood. The departing Brendan is met by a *quidam preconis*, said to be 'performing his duty among the people' (in populo gerens officium). He importunes the saint to take him on board, and Brendan allows him to join the expedition, but only after the saint gives the *preco* an on-the-spot tonsure. Brendan's travels commence immediately, and the second island he travels past on this voyage is populated by man-eating mice, who must be somehow sated if Brendan and company are to land. He convinces the *preco* to offer himself up to the mice in return for the salvation of his soul. The *preco* happily agrees and, after approaching the mice, is consumed down to the bone. 'Expecting the strife to be over,' our text concludes, 'they buried his bones there' (et ibidem finem certaminis expectantes, sepilierunt ossa eius). In the Irish Life of Brendan preserved in the Book of Lismore, Irish *crosán* 'jester, lampooner' is the word used in place of *preco*, and the figure is lauded as a genuine martyr.[24] And, to complete our dossier, we should note that in the *Immram Curaig Úa Corra* (Voyage of the Uí Chorra) text, which clearly owes much to the Brendan legend, the pilgrims accept into their crew a member of a troop

---

21 'Nam in tota Hybernia tua parrochia prima deficiet et recedet a te.' Cui Ruodanus respondit: 'Regnum tuum primum deficiet, et de tuo genere nullus regnabit in eternum.' Rex dixit: 'Tuus locus vacuus erit, et sues, in eo habitantes, naribus subvertent illum.' Ruodanus ait: 'Civitas Temoria multis centenis annis prius vacua erit et sine habitatore in eternum.' Rex respondit: 'Corpus tuum maculam habebit, et de tuis membris unum peribit. Oculus autem tuus cecatus lucem non videbit.' Ruodanus ait: 'Corpus quoque tuum a tuis inimicis iugulabitur, et tua membra per partes turpiter separabuntur.' Rex dixit: 'Aper ferocissimus suo dente tuam piramidem perfodiet.' Ruodanus ait: 'Femor tuum, quod ante me non elevatum est, simul cum tuo corpore non sepelietur, sed vir super drullam illud de stercore ovium proiciet' (Heist, *Vitae*, p. 165).

22 Heist, *Vitae*, p. 165; Plummer, *Vitae*, Vol. 2, pp. 248–9; O'Grady, *Silva Gadelica*, Vol. 1, pp. 67–8, 78

23 Plummer, *Vitae*, Vol. 1, pp. 136–7.

24 Stokes, *Lives of Saints*, pp. 111–2.

of *crosáin*, the leader of which demands that the lampooner-turned-penitent surrender his clothes to his former colleagues. The stripped *crosán* or *fuirseóir* offers his services as an entertainer to the crew in return for their tolerating his nakedness. He is accepted as a member of the crew but dies shortly afterward and is mourned by his mates. A bird approaches and asks them why they are so sad. When they explain, the bird tells them to be of cheer, for he in fact is the soul of the *crosán* on the way to heaven.[25]

In his book *The Irish Trickster*, Alan Harrison, following Charles Plummer,[26] has pointed out that *preco* as used in Hiberno-Latin texts clearly has something to do with the lower orders of poets and entertainers, such as the *crosán* and the *cáinte*, figures whose activities were traditionally condemned by churchmen.[27] In connection with the incidents in the Tripartite Life of Patrick and the Brendan Life presented above, in which the *preco* is contrasted with or even inimical toward the saint, Harrison cites an early Irish penitential that classes the *preco* alongside the *magus*, the *votivus mali*, and the *hereticus*.[28] And so, especially since there seems no good Irish word for 'herald' or 'crier' attested in our medieval texts, it is tempting to view *preco* simply as corresponding to Irish *crosán*. Yet we find an impressively wide range of Irish words that correspond to *precones* in the texts we have examined, all the way from *áes cerda* 'poets' and *maer* 'steward' to the *crosán*, with referents ranging from the distinguished to the lowly. Also to be considered is the sixth-century Gildas's characterization of the sycophantic wordsmiths in the court of Maelgwn as *precones*, as pointed out by Patrick Sims-Williams.[29] The *preco* of the Life of Rúadán, however, is not even characterized as a 'verbal' operator within the story. He carries out his function, we recall, by carrying his spear in a peculiar and troublesome way, not by proclaiming. Clearly, then, *preco* is more than just *crosán*, and more than a translation of any single term, but what is it signifying in the context of these hagiographic episodes?

A possible answer emerges if we take another look at the stories with an eye to what else they have in common, besides the word *preco*. In each instance, a saint or a figure protected by a saint encounters a persistent barrage of communication from someone who is trying to bring about an outcome that would go against the

25 *Immrama*, ed. A. G. Van Hamel (Dublin, 1941), pp. 101–2.
26 Plummer, *Vitae*, Vol. 2, pp. 383–4, s.v. *preco*.
27 Harrison, *The Irish Trickster* (Sheffield, 1989), pp. 41–3.
28 *The Irish Penitentials*, ed. Bieler (Dublin, 1971), pp. 160–1.
29 'Gildas,' p. 175, in reference to *De Excidio Britanniae*, 34.6 (*Gildas, The Ruin of Britain and Other Works*, ed. Michael Winterbottom [London and Chichester, 1978]), 103). In Welsh tradition of a much later period, there is the figure of the *arwyddfardd* 'heraldic bard', on which see Patrick K. Ford's discussion in his edition of *Ystoria Taliesin* (Cardiff, 1992), pp. 103–4, note on line 187.

expectations or desires of the saint or his protégé. The band of poets attempts to force Patrick to share the banquet with him and thus, as his hosts are keenly aware, thwart the whole point of giving him a banquet. Bacclám, the aggressive *preco* of Diarmait the king, penetrates and disfigures Áed Gúaire's fort in an attempt to undermine the latter's royal authority. And the *preco* whom Brendan encounters on the strand talks his way onto the saint's boat. In each case, then, the juggernaut-like persistence of the *preco* pays off — but then the net outcome beyond the immediate outcome turns out to be more ambiguous than the *preco* or perhaps even the saint expected. The poets get the food, but they immediately are shipped off to hell; Áed Gúaire's kingship seems at first undone, but then it is Diarmait's own kingship that suffers a spectacular fall; and the *preco* gets to be a member of Brendan's crew, but only to be dispatched after an island or two.

And yet who has the last laugh? (And the laughter to be heard here is indeed that of a trickster.) The embarrassment to Brendan of travelling with the *preco* is eliminated, but the *preco* is apotheosized in a way never granted to the restless Brendan. Bacclám and Diarmait are relegated to the dungheap of legendary history, but Rúadán will have only one eye with which to view their demise. And, true, the poets barely have the opportunity to enjoy their meal before they are dropped out of the pi*cture, but they exit in good company: namely, that of a king, a deacon, and a mother, all of whom are swept away in a dramatic challenge to established authority and conventional wisdom. Moreover, the persistence of the *preco* pays off in the more-than-routine monumentalization of the episode in which he plays a precipitating role, a monumentalization that signals the beginning of something genuinely new. The poets may be gone, but the cheeses given to them remarkably remain, as signs of the ascendancy of the family of the 'new' deacon Nessán. In the wake of the sacrificial victim's death, Brendan and his fellow crew members can land on an island that is now safe for humans, as well as cherish the unshakeable conviction or even demonstration of the *preco*'s soul having gone on to a eternal heavenly life. And in the case of Diarmait, his dwindling days as king are the dwindling days of the venerable concept of the Tara kingship; after Diarmaid, Tara will remain unoccupied, a permanently emptied sign of this epochal clash between saint and king.

Finally, another element shared among these stories and the *precones* in them is the way in which the outcome of their persistent communication unfolds. Paradoxically, things — the *precones* themselves, their winnings, or those whom they represent — are dispersed and diversified. What remains in place of an original totality is a highly charged metonym. The miraculously petrified cheeses separated from the already consumed ram and the consuming poets; the dismembered corpse of Diarmait, and his lone thigh that turns up in a dung heap; the separated parts that make up Brendan's *preco*, to wit, flesh eaten by mice, bones interred on what is now a habitable island, and celebrated spirit that goes to its eternal reward — these highly charged metonyms are all that remain of what were once inescapable and oppressive totalities. As deconstituted parts of a whole, however, they can be conveniently stored away and reauthorized in their respective hagiographic dossiers.

I would suggest that the term *preco* is applied by our authors and storytellers to the figures we have been examining because in its layered medieval meanings of 'herald, announcer', 'poet', and 'prophet' this Latin word conveys the distinctively medieval Irish concept of memorialization that is on display in all three stories. In these as elsehwere, the dedicated bearer of news, more specifically of an emergent fact, precipitates its emergence, or he becomes the victim of the fact as it emerges. What he articulates, even if it is an account of the past, gains new, living force by virtue of its being so forcefully or persistently articulated, and it takes on the semblance if not the reality of a prophecy about an imminent future. That imminence manifests itself in the dispersal or diversification of the physical being of the newsbringer, a process that provides posterity with the heraldic devices, so to speak, by which to remember and commemorate what happened, and what might happen again so long as the devices continue to signify.

What I have just described is in fact the figure known in Irish as the *sceola* or *sceolang*, the 'survivor' or literally the 'newsbringer', such as Túán mac Cairill, the long-lived and oft- metamorphosed remnant of an ancient invasion of Ireland, who self-consciously utters the following proverbial statement in a text known as the *Imacallam Túáin fri Finnia* (The Dialogue Between Túán and Finnia): Ar ní gnáth orcain cen scéola n-eisi do innisin scel dar n-éisi. Is meisi in fer sin[30] ('For customarily, there is no destruction without a survivor in its wake to tell the news about it. I am that man'). An even more dramatic example of the collapse of anticipation and retrospection in the figure of the *sceola* can be found in the *Táin Bó Cuailnge*, in the role played by Cú Chulainn's mortal (and/or step-)father Súaltaim. The first time he appears, in both Recension I and the Book of Leinster recension, Súaltaim is sent by his son to warn the Ulstermen of the impending invasion.[31] The next time Súaltaim appears, however, the invasion is already well under way, and the strength of the much-perforated Cú Chulainn has waned in the face of repeated attacks. Son once asks father to summon the help of the Ulstermen, but this time

30 Ed. John Carey, 'Scél Túáin meic Chairill,' *Ériu* 35 (1984), 101. On the figure of Túán, see also Carey, 'Suibne Geilt and Túán mac Cairill,' *Éigse* 20 (1984), 93–105.
31 *Táin Bó Cúailnge, Recension I*, ed. Cecile O'Rahilly (Dublin, 1976), line 222; *Táin from the Book of Leinster*, lines 446–49. Whether Súaltaim actually delivers the message, we are not told in our texts. The message Cú Chulainn wants conveyed to the Ulstermen, according to LL, is that they should hide from the invaders — in stark contrast to the message traditionally delivered by, say, the ancient Germanic *herewalda*.

the situation is even more desperate. Súaltaim, Paul Revere-like, delivers the message, but is ignored; indeed, he is held to be in contempt of the conventional channels of Ulster communication and to be merely disturbing the peace. Súaltaim makes them attentive to what he is saying, and respectful toward the role he is playing, only when in his and his horse's agitation his head is accidentally cut off by the rim of his shield — that is, after the violation of the province's boundaries is brought home to Súaltaim and his audience in terms of the integrity of Súaltaim's own body being savagely and suddenly violated. The herald's head continues to talk, however, and the Ulstermen are finally roused out of their stupor by this message that won't go away, by what our texts call Súaltaim's *sírrabad* 'persistent warning'.[32]

A third example of a *sceola* is Donn Bó, as he appears and reappears in the *Cath Almaine* (Battle of Allen) saga. This *airfitid* 'entertainer' joins in the expedition against the Leinstermen. In fact, his participation facilitates the recruitment of the army, which is eager to hear his performance. Yet the night before battle is joined, Donn Bó excuses himself from performing, promising to fulfill his obligation to his audience the next night. The deferred peformance does indeed take place at the end of the following day, but by then it has become a performance piece: the severed head of Donn Bó musically regaling a slain and defeated king on the battlefield, and then entertaining an audience of enemies, the Leinstermen, who, after winning the battle, recovered the performer's head. Anticipation of victory and of an exultant performance has given way to a sobering backward look on defeat, a process reflected in the transformation of Donn Bó into a head that never forgets and a mouth that can still sing.[33]

What is extraordinary about the *sceola* in all of these instances is his ability to be both the subject and the predicate of the narrative 'sentence' that he communicates through his words and through his reformed or reduced person. This is clearly the same defining ubiquity both within the content and even beyond the frame of the story, the same capacity to persist as significant in one form or another, that we saw in connection with the figure of the *preco* as he appears in saints' lives. I propose that we add *sceola* to the range of words and concepts that lie behind the appearances of *preco* that we have examined: a range that includes bearer of news, oral performer, figure of prophecy — and conspicuous survivor.

---

32 O'Rahilly, *Táin, Recension I*, lines 3410–450; *Táin from the Book of Leinster*, lines 3981–4047.
33 *Cath Almaine*, ed. Pádraig Ó Riain (Dublin, 1978), pp. 2–3, 5, 10–13.

Forbairt na nGutaí i nGaeilge Uladh[1]

Dónall P. Ó Baoill

INSTITIÚID TEANGEOLAÍOCHTA ÉIREANN

1.0 RÉAMHRÁ

IS DÓICHE nach bhfuil canúint ar bith sa tír a bhfuil oiread scríofa fúithi de thairbhe foghraíochta de agus atá canúint Ghaeilge Uladh i gcoitinne. Tá cuid de na tuairiscí sin críochnúil agus mion. Clúdaíonn an cur síos atá iontu tréimhse réasúnta fada, an chuid is troime de dhá chéad bliain, má chuireann muid san áireamh go raibh an príomhfhear faisnéise a bhí ag Quiggin (1906) aois an tsean-phinsin nuair a rinne sé taifeadadh air i dtús an chéid seo. Mar an gcéanna le cuid den lucht faisnéise a bhí ag Ó Searcaigh (1925). Rinne seisean an t-ábhar atá ina leabhar a chruinniú nuair a bhí céim mháistreachta ar siúl aige in Ollscoil na Banríona i mBéal Feirste sa bhliain 1915. Cha dtugann sé aois na bhfaisnéiseoirí i gcónaí ach i gcás Ghaeilge Ó Méith agus An Chabháin bhí duine amháin ar a laghad as gach ceantar acu corradh le ceithre scór bliain nuair a d'aithris siad a gcuid Gaeilge dó.

Bíodh sin mar atá, tá faisnéis agus fianaise leathan againn ar fhuaimniú na Gaeilge as seacht gcinn de chontaetha Chúige Uladh ach gur fairsinge go mór ar ndóigh an cur síos atá ar fáil faoi Ghaeilge Dhún na nGall. Foinse eile a chuir an dlaíóg mhullaigh ar a raibh déanta go dtí sin foilsiú Imleabhar 4 d'Atlas Wagner

[1] Tá an t-ábhar atá sa pháipéar seo bunaithe ar léachtaí a thug mé ag Tionól Institiúid an Ard-Léinn i 1987 agus ag an Chomhdháil ar Theangeolaíocht na Gaeilge i Maigh Nuad i mí Aibreán 1996. Is deas liom an deis a bheith agam é a thairiscint i bhfoirm scríofa i bhFéil-scríbhinn in ómós don Ollamh Proinsias Mac Cana ar mhór a shuim riamh in urlabhra agus i gcomhréir Ghaeilge Uladh.

(1969), áit a bhfuil eolas ar réimse mór teanga as sé áit is fiche ar fud Chúige Uladh. Ar ndóigh, mar is eol dúinn ar fad, cha raibh Wagner róthugtha do struchtúr córasach a leagan anuas ar ábhar teanga, rud a fhágann an léitheoir lena chiall féin a bhaint as malairtí foirme agus as éagsúlacht fuaimnithe chomh fada agus a bhaineann le focail aonair de ó chomhthéacs go chéile. Lean a chuid mac léinn agus daoine eile a tháinig faoina anáil den mhodh chéanna oibre sna leabhair agus sna tráchtais a chuir siadsan iad féin ar fáil.

Mar sin féin tá an t-ábhar faoinár mbráid i bhfoirm atá intuigthe agus inúsáide agus is fúinn féin an córas atá le sonrú ann a lorg, a léiriú agus a chur i bhfoirm don té a bhfuil feidhm agus úsáid aige leis. Déanfar gach uile iarracht sna leathanaigh atá romhainn an méid sin a chur i gcrích le súil gur cuidiú é don té a bhfuil suim aige ciall agus brí a bhaint as na forbairtí inmheánacha a tháinig ar Ghaeilge Uladh ó am na SeanGhaeilge anuas go dtí ár linn féin. Téimis ina cheann mar sin.

1.1 AN CÓRAS STAIRIÚIL

Is í an chéad cheist atá le cur againn mar thús díospóireachta — cén bunchóras gutaí a bhí i nGaeilge Uladh go stairiúil? Cha dtig a bheith lánchinnte ar fad de fhreagra na ceiste sin, ach má chuireann muid cúpla rud san áireamh cha bhíonn muid i bhfad ó mharc. Is iad na nithe atá le cur san áireamh, dar liom (a) na hathruithe fuaime a bhfuil cinnteacht ann gur tharla siad agus a chuir athrú éigin ar chóras na ngutaí agus na ndéfhoghar, (b) an córas mar atá sé i láthair na huaire mar scáil ar na hathruithe stairiúla sin, agus (c) an fás agus an fhorbairt inmheánach atá i ndiaidh a theacht (agus atá ar siúl i gcónaí) ar chóras na ngutaí agus na ndéfhoghar sa chanúint.

Má thosaíonn muid leis na gutaí fada is féidir linn de réir a chéile forbairt an chórais a leagan amach. Thig a rá mar thús go bhfuil na bunchontrárthachtaí fóinéimeacha seo a leanas sna fochanúntí trí chéile amach ó Ghleann Ghaibhleann.[2]

iː	uː
eː	ɔː
aː	

2   Is é an chuma atá ar an scéal gur seo mar a bhí go stairiúil chomh maith. Is ceart a rá gur /oː/ a bhíonn i nGaeilge Ghleann Gaibhleann agus nach bhfuil rian ar bith den fhuaim [ɔː] inti. Le Gaeilge Chonnacht a luíonn sí mar sin. Is beag focal a bhfuil /oː/ ann go bunúsach i nGaeilge an Tuaiscirt mar gur as '-abh-', '-obh-', '-odh-', '-ogh-', '-omh-' agus amanna as '-amh-' a d'fhorbair tromlach mór na 'ó'-anna fada atá anois sa chanúint. D'fhéadfadh sé a bheith amhlaidh go raibh malartú idir an défhoghar /ua/, agus /oː/ i mórán focal i ré na SeanGhaeilge féin agus mar atá go fóill i gcuid mhaith ceantar i bhfocail mar *gual/gól*, *scuab/scób* srl.

Léiríonn na samplaí seo a leanas na contrárthachtaí atá i gceist.

/iː/   *bhí, díreach, fíor, mí, pínn* (<pingin), *sí, tír* srl.

/eː/   *bréid, cé?, toil Dé, inné, léim, mé, sé, téid* srl.

/aː/   *ádh, ál, bán, cnámh, lámh, Pápa* srl.
           ard, barr, cairde, carn, mairnéalach, tharlaigh srl.
           allt, allta, gallta (<gallda) srl.
           ábhar (<adhbhar), *ámad* (< adhmad), *Mánas* (< Maghnas),
           Sábha (< Sadhbha) srl.
           blách (< bláthach), *fách* (< fathach), *Ámh* (< Adhamh) srl.

/ɔː/   *beo, cóta, deor, Eoghan, feoil, fóill, lód, ól, ór, rópa, rósta* srl.

/uː/   *cú, cúl, dúil, mún, rún, siúl, súil, údar, Úna, úr* srl.

1.2 CONTRÁRTHACHTAÍ BREISE SNA GUTAÍ TOSAIGH

I dtaca le /iː/de, thig a rá go bhfuil dhá phríomhallafón aige de réir chomhthéacs na gconsan ina bhfaightear é. Sna samplaí atá tugtha ansin thuas is guta tosaigh ard é mar gur in aice le consan caol nó idir dhá chonsan chaola a bhíonn sé. Tá allafón tábhachtach eile aige nuair a bhíonn sé taobh le consa(i)n leathan(a). Bíonn réalú an ghuta sa chás seo lárnaithe agus tarraingthe siar sa bhéal. Bíonn cáilíocht í-úil air i gcónaí agus is féidir é a scríobh mar [ɪː]. Faightear i bhfocail mar iad seo a leanas é: *buí, croí, faoi, rí, snaím* (<snaidhm), *tuí* srl. Is é a bhíonn i dtraidhfil focal ina scríobhtar 'aoi' sna mionchanúintí trí chéile, mar atá: *Aoine, daoibh, Déardaoin, faoi, maoin, naoi, saoi* srl. ach tagair don díospóireacht níos faide ar aghaidh faoi fhuaimniú 'ao'. Is leor a rá anseo go bhfuil canúintí áirithe ann agus gur [ɪː] a bhíonn mar réalú ar 'ao/aoi' an litrithe iontu i ngach focal, féadaim a rá.

1.2.1 AN GUTA LEATHARD NEAMHCHRUINN [ɣː]/[e̱ː]

Ag caint ar /eː/dúinn, caithfear rudaí éagsúla a chur san áireamh. Ar an chéad dul síos, díreach mar a tharlaíonn le /iː/, bíonn allafóin éagsúla aige de réir mar a athraíonn cáilíocht na gconsan atá ina aice. Bíonn fuaimniú níos lárnaí leis in aice le consa(i)n leathan(a). Bíonn cáilíocht é-úil air i gcónaí agus [e̱ː] an comhartha atá agam air. Bíonn leagan níos ísle di ag cainteoirí áirithe agus seans sa chás sin gur [ɛ̱ː] a ba cheart a scríobh. Is mó is cosúil na hallafóin [e̱ː] agus [ɛ̱ː] leis an fhuaim atá sna focail *aon, baol, daor* srl. i nGaeilge na Mumhan. Faightear i bhfocail mar iad seo a leanas sna fochanúintí ar fad iad: *aer, aon, tús an lae, tae* agus i mórchuid na gcanúintí sna focail seo a leanas: *adharc, aghaidh, gael, ladhar, radharc, rogha, slaghdán, togha* srl. Is é a bhíonn i bhfocail mar iad seo thíos fosta de ghnáth: *claidheamh* (C.O. claíomh), *foighde, oidhre, saighead, staighre* srl.[3]

Tá fuaim eile a bhí le fáil ar fud Chúige Uladh agus i mórán ceantar go fóill féin a gcaithfear suntas a thabhairt di ar a cáilíocht. Guta leathard neamhchruinn cúil atá i gceist agam atá beagán chun tosaigh ar [oː] agus is é [ɤː][4] an comhartha atá agam air. Glacaim leis gurb í [ɤː] an fhuaim stairiúil i gCúige Uladh agus nach bhfuil sa dara hallafón [e̱ː]/[ɛː] ach leagan lárnaithe di atá ag druidim i gcónaí i dtreo na ngutaí tosaigh [eː] agus [ɛː]. Go deimhin tá an staid sin sroiste ag cuid de na mionchanúintí mar a léiríonn Wagner (1958, 1959) i gcás Theilinn, Ghleann Cholmcille agus áiteanna eile agus tá a fhios agam go bhfuil an staid sin bainte amach ag cuid mhaith de Ghaeilge pharóiste Ghaoth Dobhair.

Tugaim an stádas stairiúil do [ɤː] mar gheall ar an dáiliú leathan a bhí uirthi mar fhuaim mar is léir ó chuntas na n-údar. Déanaim tagairt go speisialta do Quiggin (1906), Ó Searcaigh (1925) agus do Wagner (1958, 1968). Ní fuaim í seo a bhí sa tSeanGhaeilge ach fuaim a tháinig chun cinn nuair a chaill 'dh/gh' a stádas consanach agus rinneadh guta díobh idir dhá ghuta i lár focail. Is gnách gur i bhfocail ina scríobhtar *adh, agh* a chluintear [ɤː], mar atá: *adharc, aghaidh, cadhan, gadhar, ladhar, radharc, slaghdán* srl. Faightear an fhuaim i roinnt focal ina bhfuil *-ogh-* fosta, mar shampla, *rogha, togha* agus leaganacha a bhunaítear orthu.

Is í an cheist anois ar ndóigh a rá cén stádas fóinéimeach atá ag na fuaimeanna [ɤː]/[e̱ː]/[ɛː] i gcaint na ndaoine sin a bhfuil siad mar ghnáthurlabhra acu. I gcás na bhfocal *gael, ladhar* agus *radharc* abair, d'fhéadfadh duine argóint a dhéanamh nach mbíonn contrárthacht ar bith idir an cineál guta atá iontu agus an cineál a bhíonn idir consan caol agus consan leathan i bhfocail mar *céad, léann, séala* srl., mar go bhfaightear gach cineál acu ina chomhthéacs féin agus gurb iad na consain sa chomhthéacs sin a rialaíonn réalú na ngutaí. I gcomhthéacsanna eile ag tús agus

3   Tá cuma ar an scéal gurb é an próiseas céanna a chuaigh i bhfeidhm ar fhocail ina raibh 'dh/gh' leathan agus orthu sin ina raibh 'dh/gh' caol diomaite de na heisceachtaí atá luaite thíos. Ó tharla gur mar an gcéanna a chuaigh an t-athrú i bhfeidhm ar 'dh' agus 'gh', is léir gur i ndiaidh do 'dh' athrú go 'gh' sa dara céad déag a tháinig an fhuaim úr seo chun cinn. Tá scoilt idir canúintí Dhún na nGall agus Oirthear Uladh i dtaca leis an dá ghné seo a leanas (a) gur défhoghar /ai/ a bhíonn i nGaeilge Dhún na nGall i gcoitinne i bhfocail ina bhfaightear na consain chaola 'd, n, l, s, t' díreach i ndiaidh an 'dh/gh', mar atá: *maighdean, maighistir, saighdiúir, saighneáin* srl. ach gurb é an guta [e̱ː] agus i gcás *maighistir* an guta [ɪː] a bhíos i nGaeilge Thír Eoghain agus i nDeisceart Uladh agus (b) gur [ɯː] a bhíos go minic i bhfocail mar *aghaidh, adharc, ladhar* srl. i dTír Eoghain agus in Oirthear Uladh.

4   Is iad na comharthaí [ö̱ː] agus [ṳ̈ː] atá ag údair eile ar an fhuaim seo ach mheas mé nár mhiste cloí le córas an IPA chomh fada agus is féidir san aiste seo. Sin an fáth a mbainim úsáid as an chomhartha [ɤː]. Níl blas 'é' fada ar fhuaimniú an allafóin seo agus is mó de cháilíocht an 'ó' druidte a bhíonn air agus go deimhin féin níl sé éagosúil ar fad le cáilíocht an [ɯː] ach é a bheith níos ísle sa bhéal.

ag deireadh focail, nuair nach mbíonn consan roimh nó i ndiaidh na bhfuaimeanna [ɤː]/[e̯ː]/[ɛː], tá an scéal níos casta agus níos suimiúla. Is cinnte go bhfuil difríocht shoiléir idir na gutaí sna péirí focal seo a leanas agus dá thoradh sin go gcaithfear stádas fóinéimeach a bhronnadh ar an dá fhuaim. Seo iad:

[e̯ː]/[ɛː]	[ɤː]/[e̯ː]/[ɛː]
é	aghaidh
drochfhéar	drochadharc
éan	aon
Éirinn	oidhre/oighreach
ré (an ghealach)	rogha
a théamh	a thoghadh

Taobh amuigh de chomhthéacs tús/deireadh focail nó san áit annamh ar féidir mionphéire a chruthú trí shéimhiú a chur ar chonsan tosaigh an dá fhocail, is beag suíomh eile ina mbíonn [e̯ː]/[ɛː] agus [ɤː]/[e̯ː]/[ɛː] ag contrárthacht le chéile. Tá teorainn mar sin leis an ualach céille a chuireann an t-idirdhealú foghraíochta seo in iúl. Is dóiche go bhféadfaí a rá, gur sna ceantair sin ina raibh an fhuaim /ɤː/ coitianta go dtí le deireanas agus go fóill féin mar réalú ar an ghuta i bhfocail mar *adharc, cadhan, ladhar* srl., is faide a mhair agus a mhaireann an chontrárthacht atá díreach faoi chaibidil againn.[5]

Tháinig athrú eile ar fhuaimniú an /e̯ː/ stairiúil i gcuid mhaith de chanúintí an chúige a bhfuil impleachtaí an-chinnte leis i dtaca le líon na bhfóinéimeanna de. Is amhlaidh a híslíodh fuaimniú /e̯ː/ i.e. [e̯ː] go [ɛː], ach nach mar an gcéanna a cuireadh an t-athrú i bhfeidhm i ngach áit agus i ngach comhthéacs. Scoilt an t-athrú seo an foclóir ar bhealaí éagsúla sna mionchanúintí. Is é an toradh a bhí air seo gur tugadh stádas fóinéimeach nach raibh aige go dtí sin do [ɛː] sna mionchanúintí sin nár cuireadh an t-athrú i bhfeidhm iontu ach go bollscóideach. Chomh fada agus a thig liom a dhéanamh amach is cosúil gur mar seo a leanas a tháinig an t-athrú chun cinn.

5   Is beag nach ionann na ceantair seo agus na ceantair ina bhfaightear [ɯː]. Bíonn correisceacht ann ach is léir má fhaightear [ɤː] i gceantar gur beag nach féidir a bheith cinnte go mbeidh [ɯː] in urlabhra na gcainteoirí sa cheantar chomh maith.

Má bhí an 'é' stairiúil /eː/ i siolla druidte ina raibh consan liopach/carballach caol roimhe agus consan caol eile ina dhiaidh, tosaíodh ar é a fhuaimniú mar [ɛː] i roinnt mhaith canúintí. D'fhág sin gurb é a bhí le cluinstin feasta i bhfocail mar — *béic, céilí, céim, féile, níos géire, méile, méid, péist* srl. Fágadh an fhuaim stairiúil roimh chonsain dhéadacha/ailbheolacha i siollaí druidte i bhfocail mar iad seo — *bréid, déirce, dréimire, solas na gréine, léigh, léim, séid, téid* srl. Char híslíodh an guta stairiúil ach oiread i gceann ar bith de na canúintí más i siolla oscailte a bhí sé, mar atá sna samplaí seo — *cé?, toil Dé, gé, mé, sé, an té* srl. Sna canúintí inar cuireadh an riail thuas i bhfeidhm go coinsiasach ar ndóigh fágadh an dá allafón [eː] agus [ɛː] comhlánach ar a chéile agus mar bhaill d'aon fhóinéim amháin. Ach scéal eile a tharla sna canúintí sin nár tharla an t-ísliú iontu ach ar bhonn teoranta. Déanfar plé orthu sin go luath ach caithfimid aird a tharraingt i dtús báire ar chomhthéacsanna eile inar cruthaíodh [ɛː] leis an scéal a iomlánú i gceart.

Tá comhthéacs eile inar tharla ísliú ar [eː] ann comh maith. Baineann an t-ísliú sa chás seo le focail a bhfuil an litriú 'ea' i siolla aiceanta iontu, mar atá — *béal, bréag, céad, déag, éad, préachán, séala* srl.[6] Cuirtear an riail i bhfeidhm go hiomlán i gcuid de na canúintí agus go himeallach scáinteach i gcuid eile acu. Fágann sin gur próiseas é seo a bhfuil an-chuid eisceachtaí air ó chanúint go chéile.

Sna canúintí sin nach ndeachaigh ísliú an /eː/ i bhfeidhm ach go himeallach nó ar fhocail ar leith iontu, faightear contrárthachtaí iontu a láidríonn stádas fóinéimeach [ɛː] sa mhéid nach dtig a rá go cinnte feasta cé acu [eː] nó [ɛː] a bheas i bhfocal. Seo samplaí den chontrárthacht a cruthaíodh i gcuid de na beochanúintí nuair nár spréigh an riail tríd an fhoclóir ina iomláine.

[eː]	[ɛː]
méile	*méileach*
déanach	*déan*
bréan	*bréag*
Éabha	*Méabha*

6 Is i ndiaidh na gconsan liopach caol is minice a dhéantar an t-ísliú seo. Lena chois sin caithfear aird a thabhairt ar leaganacha eile de fhocail agus go háirithe an tuiseal ginideach uatha de ainmfhocail atá sa chéad díochlaonadh. Cé gur [ɛː] a bhíonn in *béal, bréag* srl. i mórán ceantar agus ag mórán daoine, is [eː] a bhíonn sa tuiseal ginideach *béil, bréige* srl. Tá cainteoirí eile ann agus is ionann an guta san ainmneach agus sa ghinideach acu rud a fhágann an córas níos rialta ar ndóigh.

1.3 ARDÚ 'á' GO [ɛ:]/[ɛ̞:]

Sa mhullach air seo ar fad tá riail eile i ndiaidh a theacht chun cinn i gcanúintí iar-thuaisceart agus thuaisceart Thír Chonaill i gcoitinne a chuireann tuilleadh eile samplaí den chontrárthacht ar fáil. Is í an riail atá i gceist an t-ardú a dhéantar ar 'á' roimh chonsain chaola agus roimh /d, ɾ, s, t/ leathan. Is cáilíocht [ɛ:] nó [ɛ̞:] a bhíonn ar an ghuta seo de ghnáth. Faightear é i bhfocail mar iad seo a leanas — *áit, báillí, cáis, fáilte, láidir, náire, páiste, bád, bás, cár, lár, scláta, spás* srl. Bíonn sí i bhfocail ina mbíonn an litriú 'eá' sa tsiolla aiceanta iontu, mar atá — *breá, seá, sleán, Seán* srl. Cruthaíonn an t-athrú seo contrárthachtaí mar iad seo thíos i roinnt de na mionchanúintí.

[e:]	[ɛ:]/[ɛ̞:]
sé	*seá*
séan	*Seán*
bréan	*breá*

Is é mín agus réiteach an scéil mar sin go mbraitheann contrárthacht a bheith idir [e:] agus [ɛ:]/[ɛ̞:] ar cé acu a chuaigh rialacha de chineál áirithe i bhfeidhm ar fhoclóir na mionchanúna nó nach ndeachaigh. Lena chois sin tá cuma ar an scéal gur sna mionchanúintí sin nach ndeachaigh an t-ísliú ó [e:] go [ɛ:] i bhfeidhm ach go mírialta iontu a cruthaíodh idirdhealú fóinéimeach idir an dá fhuaim. Tá méid na bhfocal a bhfuil a leithéid de chontrárthacht eatarthu níos líonmhaire sna háiteacha sin ar hardaíodh 'á' go [ɛ:]/[ɛ̞:] iontu. Tugann sin muid go cás an 'á' féin agus an réalú atá anois air i gCúige Uladh.

1.4 AN RÉALÚ ATÁ AR 'á' I NGAEILGE ULADH

Tá réalú réasúnta casta anois ar na fuaimeanna a sheasann do '(e)á' an litrithe ar fud an chúige. I nGleann Ghaibhleann i gContae an Chabháin is léir gur [ɑ:], mar atá ar fud Chonnachta, an réalú is coitianta agus tá an claonadh céanna atá i gConnachta sa chanúint guta níos cruinne ar nós [ɔ:] a dhéanamh as. Tarlaíonn an méid seo gan amhras mar nach bhfuil an fhóinéim /ɔ:/ coitianta i nGleann Ghaibhleann áit a mbíonn /o:/ ina háit.

Tá an scéal cuid mhaith níos casta sa chuid eile den chúige agus i nDún na nGall féin. Cé go bhfuil na fuaimeanna a bhíonn mar réalú ar '(e)á' an litrithe i bhfad níos faide chun tosaigh i gcoitinne ná mar atá i nGaeilge Chonnacht, abair, is léir ach an dáiliú iomlán sioncrónach a chur san áireamh gur guta cúil nó leathchúil a bhí mar réalú ar '(e)á' go stairiúil. Sin an fáth a scríobhaim /ɑ:/ thuas. Is é an guta íseal cúil [ɑ̟ː], a fhuaimnítear beagán chun tosaigh ar [ɑː], an fuaimniú is coitianta sna mionchanúintí trí chéile i bhfocail mar *bán, barr, lámh, Pápa, slán* srl. Cé go bhfuil athrú ag teacht air sin i gcuid de chanúintí (iar)thuaisceart Dhún na nGall sa mhéid is go bhfuil an fhuaim stairiúil an-fhada chun tosaigh sa bhéal agus ardaithe i dtreo [ɛː] fiú amháin, is léir gur nuáil í seo a tháinig isteach le cúpla céad bliain anuas.

Cé go bhfuil mórán éagsúlachta i bhfuaimniú 'á' ó áit go háit agus amanna ó dhuine go chéile, is é an chuma atá ar an scéal nach bhfuil ach aon fhóinéim amháin ag oibriú sa chóras trí chéile.

Is ceart dom i dtús báire cúpla rud a rá faoi úsáid na gcomharthaí foghraíochta le 'á' a léiriú agus go háirithe úsáid [ɑː]. Is dóigh liom nach ionann go díreach an bhrí atá le baint as úsáid na siombaile seo ag údáir éagsúla. Amharc, mar shampla, Ó Searcaigh (1925, 6–8), Wagner (1959, 65–67) agus Stockman agus Wagner i *Lochlann* Vol. 3 (1965, 178–179). Baineann tuilleadh mearbhaill le húsáid [æː] mar atá ag Wagner (1959, 66–67) i gcomparáid le Somerfelt (1921, §29) agus le Ó Searcaigh (1925, §58). Baintear úsáid chomh maith as [ɑ̟ː] in Atlas Wagner (1958, 1969) agus i Stockman agus Wagner (1965). Cuireann an tsiombail seo in iúl gur guta lárnach oscailte íseal atá i gceist. Luaim na nithe sin mar go gcaithfear a bheith níos cúramaí leis na siombailí agus ciall chruinn a chur leo. Cé gur guta oscailte cúil a léiríonn [ɑː] de ghnáth i gcomharthaíocht an IPA, braithim nach guta cúil go hiomlán é i gcanúintí an tuaiscirt mar gur minic é ag malartú le [ä̈ː].[7] Chomh maith leis sin tá réalú na n-allafón éagsúil de 'á' chomh mór sin faoi smacht ag consain áirithe ach nach ionann mar a luíonn an smacht orthu ó chanúint go chéile. Is iad na consain liopacha leathana is mó a imríonn tionchar orthu mar a fheicimid.

Sílim anois go dtig an méid seo a rá faoi fhuaimniú an 'á'-fada i nGaeilge Uladh i gcoitinne.

[ɑ̟ː] nó [ɑː],

Faightear é seo in aice le nó idir consain leathana de ghnáth. Bíonn an guta níos ísle agus níos tarraingthe siar in aice le nó idir consain liopacha. Bhí na fuaimeanna seo le fáil i nGaeilge Oirthear Uladh nuair a mhair sí agus tá siad le cluinstin sa mhórchuid de Thír Chonaill mar is léir ó Atlas Wagner Vol. 1 (1958).[8] Seo samplaí d'fhocail ina bhfaightear na fuaimeanna seo agus níl aon chontrárthacht eatarthu:

7   Is í an tsiombail seo siombail an IPA don ghuta íseal láir. Mar atá ráite cheana féin agam is í an tsiombail [ɑ̟ː] a bhíonn ina Atlas ag Wagner leis an fhuaim seo a chur in iúl.
8   Féadfaidh an léitheoir an scéal a mheas do féin ach amharc ar na léarscáileanna atá ar na leathanaigh seo a leanas d'Atlas Wagner, 1958: lgh. 72, 156, 176, 180, 272, 282 agus 298, áit a léirítear an guta fada sna focail seo, faoi seach: *cál, tábla, adhmad, garrdha, rámha, báidhfear* agus *bás*.

ádh, Ádhamh, bábóg, bád, bán, cál, fás, lámh, mála, Pápa, tálach srl.
ard, barr, bairneach, carn, darna, mairnéalach, thall srl.
allt, (ainmhí) *allta, gallta* (<gallda) srl.
adhmad, Mánas (<Maghnas)*, Sábha* (<Sadhbha) srl.
blách (< bláthach)*, fách* (<fathach) srl.

Cé go mb'fhéidir go bhfaightear na fuaimeanna céanna i gcuid de na focail seo thíos go háirithe sna focail sin a bhfuil consan liopach leathan roimh an ghuta aiceanta iontu, is lárnaí agus is faide chun tosaigh fuaimniú an 'á' iontu i gcoitinne mar gheall ar an chonsan chaol a bhíonn taobh leo. Cuireann an comhartha [a̠ː] thíos 'á' atá tarraingthe siar ó shuíomh ghuta uimhir a 4 de chuid an IPA in iúl agus cuireann an comhartha [ɑ̈ː] guta íseal lárnaithe in iúl. Bíonn anonn agus anall agus malartú ar siúl idir an dá fhuaim seo ó áit go háit, ó dhuine go duine agus ó chomhthéacs go comhthéacs.

[a̠ː] nó [ɑ̈ː]

amháin, báillí, fáinne, Spáinn srl.
Bealtaine, ceardaí, ceárta, is fearr, gearr, Ráth Mealltáin srl.
beách (< beathadhach)*, leách* (< leathach)*, meáchan* (< meadhachán) srl.

Tugadh an léitheoir faoi deara nach mbíonn contrárthacht i gceist idir na hallafóin seo de ghnáth. I gcás an fhocail *fáinne*, mar shampla, tá claonadh láidir ann an guta atá san fhocal a fhuaimniú i bhfad níos faide chun tosaigh sa bhéal nuair a bhíonn séimhiú ar an 'f'. Ní hionann mar sin réalú an 'á' in *fáinne* agus *ar an fháinne,* de ghnáth. Tá cuid den chlaonadh chéanna le feiceáil i bhfuaimniú 'á' i dtús focail i samplaí mar *ádh, adhmad, allt, ard* srl., thar mar a bhíonn in *an t-ádh/adhmad/allt/ ard* srl.

1.4.1 ARDÚ AN GHUTA 'Á' GO [æː]/[ɛ̝ː]

Baineann an t-athrú seo cuid mhaith le canúintí iarthuaisceart agus thuaisceart Dhún na nGall. Ach an oiread le gach rud eile a bhaineann le teanga, char cuireadh riail an ardaithe seo i bhfeidhm go hiomlán críochnúil i gceantair áirithe cé go ndearnadh amhlaidh i gceantair eile. Chan eol dom áit ar bith a bhfuil an riail curtha i bhfeidhm ina hiomláine ann ach sa dúiche sin atá i lár agus i ndeisceart pharóiste Ghaoth Dobhair, an ceantar sin atá taobh istigh de chiorcal trí nó ceathair de mhílte ón Bhun Bheag. Sa cheantar sin i gcoitinne is í an fhuaim [ɛ̝ː] agus amanna [ɛː] féin a bhíonn mar réalú ar an ghuta aiceannta sna focail seo a leanas,

mar atá: *amháin, ard, bád, bábóg, fáinne, is fearr, Máire, mála, barr, adhmad, scáile* srl.
Bíonn an guta níos airde in aice le consain chaola, de ghnáth.

Tá ceantair eile ansin a bhfuil meascán den dá chóras iontu, mar nár cuireadh
riail an ardaithe i bhfeidhm go hiomlán iontu. Orthu sin tá tuaisceart agus oirthear
pharóiste Ghaoth Dobhair, an leath thiar de pharóiste Chloch Chionnaola, an chuid
thuaidh de na Rosa, Árainn Mhór, na Dúnaibh, codanna de Fhánaid agus Gaeilge
Inis Eogain. Má dhéantar scrúdú ar dháiliú na bhfuaimeanna sna ceantair seo,
tiocfaidh duine ar thuigbheáil níos fearr faoin dóigh ar thosaigh an t-athrú seo agus
ar scaip sé. Tá cuma ar an scéal gur roimh chonsain chaola a rinneadh an t-ardú i
dtús báire i bhfocail mar *báillí, Gráinne, náire, sáile* srl. Ina dhiaidh sin cuireadh i
bhfeidhm é roimh chonsain ailbheolacha/dhéadacha leathana mar [d̪ˠ, nˠ, ɾˠ, s̪ˠ,
t̪ˠ]. Seo traidhfil samplaí: *bád, clár, fás, grán, ráta, scláta* srl. Is ar shiollaí oscailte a
chuaigh sé i bhfeidhm ina dhiaidh sin i bhfocail aonsiollacha ar nós *dá, dhá, grá, lá,
mná, (ag) rá, seá, tá* srl. agus i bhfocail mar *bláth, fáth, snáth, tráth* srl. nuair a thit an
'th' ar lár iontu. Ansin ar deireadh cuireadh an riail i bhfeidhm ar an chuid eile de
na consain agus tá a thoradh sin le feiceáil ar chuid mhaith de Ghaeilge pharóiste
Ghaoth Dobhair mar atá luaite cheana féin.

1.5 AN CHONTRÁRTHACHT IDIR /ɔː/ AGUS /oː/

Is dóiche go bhfuil an t-idirdhealú a dhéantar idir an dá chineál 'ó' i nGaeilge
Chúige Uladh ar cheann de na tréithe is suntasaí a bhaineann léi. Is de thairbhe
athruithe stairiúla i gcomhthéacsanna éagsúla a tháinig an chontrárthacht chun cinn.
Coinnigh cuimhne nach raibh an chontrárthacht seo i nGaeilge an Chabháin mar
gur chosúil le Gaeilge Chonnacht í sa mhéid nach raibh ach [oː] inti. Seachas an
[oː] atá sa bhriathar *tóg* agus sa dá fhocal *dólas, sólas* i gcanúintí ar leith, tháinig 'ó'
druidte [oː] chun cinn go stairiúil sa dá shuíomh seo a leanas, (a) roimh chonsain
shrónacha, agus (b) san áit ar ligeadh consan cuimilteach leathan ar nós *bh, gh, mh*
srl. ar lár ag deireadh siolla aiceanta. Dá bhrí sin is í an fhuaim [oː] a bhíonn sna
focail seo a leanas — *Eoin, móin, níos mó, mór, leonta, Nóra, rón, Seonaí, tóin* srl.
agus iontu seo áit ar cailleadh consan — *abhainn, bodhar, cabhair, comhrá,
Domhnach, foghlaim, fómhar* (<*foghmhar*), *Gaoth Dobhair, leabhar, meabhair, tomhas*
srl. Tabhair faoi deara go speisialta an chontrárthacht atá idir an dá ainm *Eoin* agus
Eoghan. Guta oscailte [ɔː] atá sa dara hainm agus guta druidte [oː] sa chéad ainm.
Níl de dhifríocht idir *a Eoin* agus *a Eoghain* mar sin ach cáilíocht an ghuta. Is léir
ón tsampla seo gur i ndiaidh ardú [ɔː] go [oː] a tháinig an riail, a lig an 'gh' in
Eoghan ar lár, chun cinn. Murach sin bheadh an fuaimniú ceannann céanna ar an dá

fhocal.[9] Tá an chontrárthacht seo leitheadach go leor mar gur mór anois an méid focal a bhfaightear [oː] iontu. Seo péirí a léiríonn an scaipeadh mór atá ar an chontrárthacht ar fud an fhoclóra. Tá an fhuaim [ɔː] sna samplaí atá chun tosaigh: *cró/cnó, cófra/comhartha, cóir/cabhair, dódh/lobhadh~loghadh, A Eoghain/A Eoin, ag ól/gabhal, leor/leabhar, óg/tóg, ór/odhar, Róise/tomhais, seol/seó, tóir/tabhair* srl.

1.6 AN GUTA FADA ARD CÚIL [ɯː]

Tréith eile a bhaineann le canúintí Ghaeilge an Tuaiscirt an guta ard neamhchruinn cúil [ɯː] atá le fáil iontu. Cé go bhfuil athruithe móra ag teacht ar úsáid agus ar réalú na fuaime seo sna canúintí atá fágtha againn, is léir gur cuid dhúchasach thábhachtach den chóras i gcoitinne a bhí inti ar fud an chúige agus go fóill féin san áit a maireann sí.

Is í an fhuaim seo an réalú a bhí ar 'ao' an litrithe in Oirthear Uladh agus is í a fhaightear go fóill féin i mórán de mhionchanúintí Dhún na nGall. Tá claonadh láidir mar sin féin sa leath thiar agus theas den chontae an fhuaim [iː] a chur ina háit. Tá an claonadh le fáil fosta in Árainn Mhór, i gcuid mhaith de Ghaoth Dobhair agus sna Dúnaibh.[10] Is cosúil gur sa treo sin atá luí na teanga féin, rud ar ndóigh a dhéanann simpliú mór ar chóras na ngutaí ina iomláine.

Cé gur guta neamhchruinn cúil é seo go stairiúil, tá allafóin éagsúla le cluinstin anois atá níos faide chun tosaigh sa bhéal. Bíonn athrú ann ó áit go háit agus ó dhuine go duine in amanna. Is é an réalú [ɯː] a chluintear in aice le consain bheolacha agus go háirithe más rompu seachas ina ndiaidh a bhíonn an consan. Faightear an fhuaim seo i bhfocail mar iad seo a leanas: *baol, braon, faochóg, fraoch, maol, smaoiteamh* srl. Is í an fhuaim chéanna a bhíonn in aice na gconsan eile ag daoine go leor ach tá claonadh ann an fhuaim a lárnú go [ɨː] i bhfocail mar iad seo: *aon, aol, caol, caora, daor, gaol, gaoth, naoscach, saol, saor, taos* srl.[11] Chomh maith leis sin bíonn na liopaigh níos druidte agus níos teannta le linn [ɨː] a rá ná mar a bhíonn siad nuair a úsáidtear an t-allafón cúil [ɯː]. Is gnách gurb iad na hallafóin chéanna a bhíonn sna bunfhocail a bhíonn i bhfoirmeacha eile de na focail sin, mar shampla, sa tuiseal ginideach nó i gcéimeanna comparáide aidiachtaí, mar atá: *scuaba*

---

9 Dá mba rud é gur cailleadh an 'gh' in *Eoghan* sular tháinig an riail a d'ardaigh [ɔː] go [oː] chun cinn, bheadh duine ag súil gur [oː] a bheadh sa dá fhocal anois. Ach mar a fheiceann muid chan mar sin atá.

10 Tá a fhianaise seo le feiceáil in Atlas Wagner (1958). Is leor amharc ar an réalú atá ar na focail *fraoch* (lth. 159) agus ar *gaoth* (lth. 223) le cruthú a fháil ar an méid seo.

11 Baineann údair eile úsáid as an chomhartha [y] leis an allafón seo a chur in iúl. Chan ionann ar chor ar bith an fhuaim atá i gceist agamsa le [ɨː] agus a mbíonn i gceist ag na húdair seo le [y], dar liom. Braithim gur blas í-úil mar atá sna focail *caoi, naoi, suí* srl. a bhíonn i gceist go minic acu le [y]. Blas ú-úil a bhíonn ar [ɨː] díreach mar a bhíonn ar an allafón [ɯː].

fraoich, ag déanamh aoil, lá na gaoithe, níos caoile/daoire/maoile/saoire srl. Tá cúpla focal ar nós *oíche, choíche* a bhfuil an guta neamhchruinn seo iontu cé nach mbeadh duine ag súil leis sin ón litriú atá orthu. Bíonn sé i bhfocail ina scríobhtar 'aoi' nach ndíorthaítear as bunfhocail ina bhfuil 'ao', mar atá: *aoileach, daoiní, faoileog, scaoil, snaoisín* srl.

Is dóigh liom go dtig glacadh leis gur fóinéim an guta neamhchruinn seo sna mionchanúintí sin a bhfuil sé go forleathan iontu go fóill. Tá péirí den tsórt seo a leanas le fáil áit a mbíonn contrárthacht idir [iː] agus [ɯː]/[ɨː], nó idir [ɯː]/[ɨː] agus [uː] soiléir go leor. Guta neamhchruinn a bhíonn sa chéad fhocal de gach péire acu seo a leanas.

[ɯː]/[ɨː]   *Aodh/í, aoileach/fuílleach, aosta/thíos, baol/buí, gaoth/ag guí* srl.

[ɯː]/[uː]   *aol/úlla, caol/cúl, daor/dúr, gaol/ar gcúl, saor/úr* srl.

1.7 NA GUTAÍ FADA I gCOITINNE

Tugann sin muid go deireadh pléite ar na gutaí fada. Is é an toradh atá ar an phlé ar fad go dtig linn anois na mionchanúintí a rangú de réir na gcóras atá ag feidhmiú iontu. Is iad na mionchanúintí is casta agus is coimeádaí ar fad iad sin a bhfuil na gutaí [ɯː]/[ɨː] agus [ɤː]/[e̝ː]/[ɛː] go fairsing iontu. Tá córas ocht nó naoi nguta i gcuid de na canúintí sin ag brath ar an seasamh fóinéimeach atá ag [ɛː]/[ɛ̞ː] iontu. Ní bhíonn sna canúintí eile ach córas shé nó sheacht nguta mar go bhfuil na gutaí neamhchruinne caillte iontu nó ar bhéal a bheith caillte. Arís eile braitheann uimhir na ngutaí ar an stádas fóinéimeach a thugtar don ghuta [ɛː] agus cé acu atá contrárthacht cheart idir é agus [eː]. Tá an córas is forásaí agus is simplí ó thaobh uimhir na bhfóinéimeanna de i gcodanna de pharóiste Ghaoth Dobhair áit nach bhfuil ach córas shé nguta i bhfeidhm mar atá i Léaráid 3 thíos.[12] Is é an cineál céanna córais atá ag teacht nó i ndiaidh a theacht chun cinn sa leath theas de Dhún na nGall i gcoitinne[13], ach gur guta idir [a̱ː] agus [ɑː], a bhíonn mar réalú ar 'á' sna mionchanúintí sin de ghnáth. Tá coimriú ar an méid sin sna léaráidí seo thíos.

---

12   Is spéisiúil an ní é, ach is beag iarsma de ísliú 'é' i bhfocail mar *béal, Méabha, méileach* srl. atá le fáil sna ceantair sin Ghaoth Dobhair ach i gcorrfhocal fánach, cé go bhfuil ardú 'á' go [ɛː]/[ɛ̞ː] go fada fairsing iontu. Is cinnte go bhfuil baint ag an dá rud lena chéile agus gur chuir próiseas amháin bac ar an phróiseas eile a theacht i bhfeidhm.

13   Tá an méid seo le sonrú i bhfoilseacháin Wagner (1958, 1959, 1968).

Léaráid 1				*Léaráid 2*			*Léaráid 3*	
iː	ɯː	uː		ɪː	uː		iː	uː
eː	ɤː	oː	>>	eː	oː	>>	eː	oː
(ɛː)	aː	ɔː		(ɛː)	aː	ɔː		ɛː	ɔː

2.0 NA GUTAÍ GAIRIDE

Tá córas na ngutaí gairide i nGaeilge Uladh spéisiúil fosta ar a mbealach féin. Tá comhthéacs sa bhreis le cur san áireamh sa chanúint nach mbaineann leis na canúintí eile — is é sin na gutaí fada a giorraíodh go stairiúil i siollaí neamh-aiceanta, rud a chuireann go mór leis na comhthéacsanna ina bhfaightear gutaí gairide. Chomh maith leis sin cuimhnigh gur gutaí gairide a bhíonn roimh na consain fhada *ll*, *m*, *nn* agus *ng* sa chanúint seo. Is minic gairid é roimh *rr* fosta. Ach an oiread leis na hallafóin a bhí ag cuid de na gutaí fada chan eisceacht ar bith na gutaí gairide mar go dtéann timpeallacht na gconsan i bhfeidhm go mór orthu agus dá thairbhe sin go gcluintear cuid mhór gutaí lárnaithe sa chanúint seo. Is é an cás atá le réiteach againne iarracht éigin eagar a chur ar dháiliú na n-allafón sin.

2.1 NA GUTAÍ ARDA TOSAIGH

Tosaímis leis na gutaí arda tosaigh agus déanaimis iarracht fáil amach an bhfuil contrárthacht ar bith idir na leaganacha gaolmhara foghraíochta díobh a fhaightear i bhfocail éagsúla. Tá trí fhuaimniú a gcaithfear díriú isteach orthu mar atá [i], [ɪ] agus [ï]. Is dóigh liom go dtig glacadh leis go mbaineann an chéad dá fhuaim leis an fhóinéim chéanna agus scríobhfar mar /i/ anseo feasta í. Is i gcomhthéacsanna difriúla a tharlaíonn an dá allafón, [i] idir dhá chonsan chaola, ag deireadh for-ainmneacha réamhfhoclacha sa 3ú uatha baininscneach agus mar 'í' a ghiorraítear, agus [ɪ] ag deireadh focail áit a mbíonn consan leathan roimhe, mar réalú ar '-(a)idh/ -(a)igh' agus ar '-(a)ithe' an litrithe agus san áit a ngiorraítear 'í'. Seo a leanas samplaí den dáiliú:

[i] *dinnéar, fiche, ith, nigh, scilling* srl.
  aici, aisti, inti srl.
  aistí, Bilí, brístí, maidí, páistí srl.
  beithígh, cléirigh, coiligh, oifigigh srl.
  instithe, imrithe, oibrithe srl.

[I] *bacaigh, Éireannaigh, fathaigh, madaidh* srl.
   tús an chogaidh, ainm an mhadaidh srl.
   bádaí, fuinneogaí, málaí, préataí srl.
   beannaithe, ceannaithe srl.

2.1.1 SCOILT SAN FHOCLÓIR

Thig an dá allafón thuas a chur faoin aon fhóinéim amháin a gcuirfidh mé an comhartha /i/ léi feasta. Tá guta gairid eile atá le fáil go fairsing i nGaeilge an Tuaiscirt a gcaithfimid tagairt dó anois. Is é [ï] an comhartha is coitianta ag na húdair air agus cloífidh mise leis chomh maith. Is guta é atá níos ísle ná [i] agus é lárnaithe chomh maith. Is mó an lárnú nuair a bhíonn sé idir consan leathan agus consan caol ná idir dhá chonsan chaola. Tá cúpla cúis againn le tagairt don fhuaim seo anois. Sa chéad áit is léir gur lárnaí go mór fuaimniú an 'i' ghairid seo ná an fuaimniú a bhíonn ar a mhacasamhail i gcanúintí eile agus sa dara háit tá cuma ar an scéal go bhfuil mórán de na mionchanúintí ar fhorbair contrárthacht idir [i] agus [ï] iontu.

Tá seans go raibh agus go bhfuil canúintí ann a raibh an dáiliú seo a leanas ar na trí 'i' ghairide iontu áit a bhfaightear i gcomhthéacsanna éagsúla iad agus nach raibh contrárthacht ar bith eatarthu. Allafóin den aon fhoinéim amháin /i/ iad sa chás seo.

[i] roimh chuimiltigh stairiúla 'ch', 'dh', 'gh' agus 'th' i bhfocail aonsiollacha mar *fiche, nigh, ith, suigh* (<*suidh*) srl.[14]
   an 'i' deiridh sna forainmneacha réamhfhoclacha seo: *aici, aisti, inti, roi(m)pi, thairsti* agus *uirthi.*
   'í' fada i siollaí neamhaiceanta i bhfocail mar *brístí, maidí, páistí* srl.
   mar réalú ar '-igh', '-ígh', '-idh' an litrithe, mar atá, *beithígh, cléirigh, coiligh, oifigigh, chun deiridh, tús an gheimhridh* srl.
   mar réalú ar '-ithe' san aidiacht bhriathartha, mar shampla, *cruinnithe, imrithe, oibrithe* srl.

---

14 Bíonn an 'i' gairid a bhíonn i bhfocail den tsórt seo níos airde agus níos faide chun tosaigh ná aon allafón eile de /i/. I dtaca leis na briathra aonsiollacha a chríochnaíonn ar 'igh', is minic a dhéantar 'i' den 'i' ghairid iontu san aimsir Ghnáthláithreach srl. ach chan i gcónaí é. Níl spéis againn sa chuid seo den aiste ar ndóigh ach sna comhthéacsanna ina bhfanann an 'i' gairid.

[1] mar réalú ar '-aigh', '-aidh' agus '-aithe' an litrithe:

bacaigh, Éireannaigh, fathaigh, madaidh srl.

(tús) *an chogaidh,* (ainm an) *mhadaidh* srl.

beannaithe, ceannaithe srl.

mar réalú ar 'í' fada i siollaí neamhaiceanta i bhfocail mar *bádaí, fuinneogaí, málaí, préataí* srl.

[ï] i siollaí aiceanta roimh gach consan caol ach amháin 'ch', 'dh', 'gh' agus 'th' stairiúil i bhfocail mar *fir, im, tinn* srl.

mar réalú ar an litriú 'io' ach amháin roimh chonsain liopacha, mar atá:

biolar, bior, fios, giota, iolar, mion, sioc srl.[15]

mar réalú ar an litriú 'ai/ei/oi/ui' i bhfocail/bhfoirmeacha mar iad seo a leanas:

aire, cait, saint, níos faide/gairbhe srl., *coimheád, coir, goid, cruit, uisce, geimhreadh, greim* srl.

Chan mar sin atá i mionchanúintí eile áit a bhfuil contrárthacht i ndiaidh a theacht chun cinn idir an guta tosaigh [i] agus an guta láir [ï]. Cha léir cén chúis atá leis an scoilt seo ach gur ann di anois, rud a thugann stádas fóinéimeach do na hallafóin stairiúla. Cé nach ionann go hiomlán b'fhéidir an réimse focal a mbíonn fuaim amháin seachas an ceann eile iontu ó chanúint go canúint, bhéarfaidh an dá liosta seo thíos tuairim den scóip atá faoin idirdhealú.

[i]	[ï]
cinn	*cinnte/tinn*
dinnéar	*dinn* (< *ding*)
mire	*fir*
scilling	*sciléid*
Jimí	*d'imigh*

Níl ach sampla ceart amháin agam den chontrárthacht taobh le consan leathan.

15 Is léir gur beag athrú a tháinig ar fhuaimniú na bhfocal seo ó ré na SeanGhaeilge mar a thaispeánann sampla ar nós *iolar.* Deirtear go fóill é ionann is dá mba 'ilar' a bhíthear a scríobh. Cé bith cúis a bhí leis an litir 'o' a chur ann, chan le fuaimniú Chúige Uladh a léiriú é. Bíonn an t-allafón seo níos lárnaí ná tá sé roimh chonsain chaola. Cha bhíonn sé i bhfocail mar *iomaire, iomrá, liom, liopa, scioból, trioblóid* srl. ná sna focail seo *giolla, ionnainn, sionnach* agus *tiocfaidh.*

[I]   [ï]

gairid   níos gairbhe
róthirim   thairim

Is ceart a rá fosta go bhfuil an chontrárthacht féin sa dá ghuta atá sna focail seo a leanas, [ï] sa chéad siolla agus [i]/[I] sa tsiolla deiridh: *aici, aisti, giotaí, imigh, inti, oibrí* srl.

2.2 NA GUTAÍ [e], [e̱] AGUS [ε]

Tá cuma air ón dáiliú atá ar na trí fhuaim seo nach mbíonn contrárthacht ar bith eatarthu agus gur allafóin den fhóinéim amháin iad. Faightear an t-allafón [ε] nuair a thig consan liopach/carballach caol roimhe agus consan caol eile ina dhiaidh. Faightear an dá allafón eile i gcomhthéacsanna eile. Tá canúintí ann agus is beag rian den fhuaim [ε] atá le fáil iontu ar chor ar bith ach amháin i gcorrfhocal fánach. Sílim go dtig a rá fosta i gcoitinne go mbíonn an [e] a bhíonn in aice leis an chonsan [h] níos faide chun tosaigh sa bhéal i ngach uile mhionchanúint ná an [e̱] a bhíonn in aice le consain eile. Bíonn an fhuaim dheiridh seo tarraingthe siar agus lárnaithe agus tugtha de bheith ag imeacht ina [ï] amanna. Seo samplaí dena bhfuil i gceist.

[e] ag *breith, breitheamh,* ag *feitheamh, leithead, neithe, teitheadh* srl.

[e̱] *air, deifre, deireadh, (níos) deise, leis, seisean, teideal* srl.

[ε] *beir, ceist, ceithre, feiceáil, feistithe, geis, Meiriceá, peice* srl.

Mar atá ráite thuas, cé acu dhá allafón nó trí cinn a bhíonn i gcóras mionchanúna, is baill den aon fhuaim shiceolaíoch fhóinéimeach amháin iad. Cuirfidh mé an comhartha /e/ ar an fhóinéim sin.[16] Is annamh an fhuaim i siollaí neamhaiceanta agus nuair a bhíonn is [ε] is minice a chluintear i samplaí mar *aimhréidh, buidéil, coirnéil, sciléid, simléir, ticéid* srl.

2.3 NA GUTAÍ ÍSLE [a̱], [ä] AGUS [ɑ]

Ach an oiread leis na gutaí fada ísle bíonn tionchar an-mhór ag dhá ghné ar fhuaimniú na ngutaí gairide, mar atá (a) béim an ghutha agus (b) cáilíocht na gconsan a bhíonn rompu agus ina ndiaidh. Thig a rá i gcoitinne gur faide chun tosaigh

---

16 Ar ndóigh d'fhéadfaí an comhartha /ε/ a úsáid lán chomh maith.

an fhuaim a bhíonn ar 'a' in aice le consan caol ná mar a bhíonn agus é taobh le consan leathan. Seo a leanas an dáiliú a bhíos ar na hallafóin éagsúla nuair a bhíos an guta faoi bhéim gutha.

[a̲] ~ [ä]   *abar, each, beannacht, ceap, cearr, eallach, feamnach, geab, geal, leac, plean, seachtain, teach* srl.
bhail, caint, cailleadh, maide, paiste, Paiteagó, taibhse srl.

[a]   *abair, ach, amach, balla, blas, cladach, dall, glas, mac, Matha, sac, slat* srl.

Faightear na hallafóin chéanna i siollaí neamhaiceanta áit a scríobhtar '-(e)ach-', '-éa-/-(e)á-' agus go minic fosta san áit a scríobhtar '-eog/-óg' mar go ndéantar guta neamhchruinn astu.[17] Seo roinnt eiseamláirí dá bhfuil i gceist.

[a̲] ~ [ä]   *amaideach, biseach, éisteacht, fuireacht, isteach, misneach, uibheacha* srl.
buidéal, caisleán, coileán, leithscéal, Micheál, oileán srl.
aibhleog, cuinneog, fuinneog, fuiseog, saileog srl.

[a]   *bacach, beannacht, eolach, fearúlacht, mallacht, salach* srl.
amadán, arán, bradán, camán, cnapán, gearrán, meannán, siocán, tobán srl.
bunnóg, ceannóg, dreasóg, feannóg, maróg, ordóg, riabhóg, tortóg srl.

Cé gur cosúil nach mbíonn contrárthacht idir na hallafóin sin thuas de ghnáth, tá cúpla comhthéacs nár mhiste díriú orthu. Tá dhá chomhthéacs faoi leith i gceist (a) i bhfocail a thosaíonn ar ghuta, agus (b) sna canúintí sin nár híslíodh an guta stairiúil /ɛ/ go /a/ iontu, agus sna mionchanúintí ar ardaíodh /a/ go /ɛ/ iontu.

I gcás na bhfocal a thosaíonn ar ghuta tá contrárthacht le feiceáil i roinnt cásanna idir [a̲]/[ä] agus [a], mar a léiríonn na péirí seo thíos.

[a̲]/[ä]	[a]
each	*ach*
abar	*abair*
eangach	*angadh*
eallach	*halla*

---

17 Is coitianta an próiseas seo in Iarthuaisceart/i dTuaisceart Dhún na nGall agus in Oirthear Uladh ná sa leath theas de Dhún na nGall. Gheofar tuilleadh eolais fá chastacht an scéil seo in Ó Dochartaigh (1987).

I dtaca leis an dara grúpa tá cúpla rud le rá. I dtús báire sna canúintí sin ina bhfaightear [ɛ] roimh chonsain áirithe i bhfocail mar *bean, cead, deas, fead, fear, Peadar, peata* srl. iontu, tá an chuma ar an scéal gur comhlánach ar a chéile a bhíonn [ɛ] agus na gutaí ísle [a̱]/[ä] agus [ɑ], mar gur i gcomhthéacsanna difriúla a fhaightear iad. Fágann an méid sin nach bhfuil againn go fóill ach fóinéim amháin /a/.

Chan mar sin do na mionchanúintí inar ardaíodh an guta íseal stairiúil /a/ go [ɛ] iontu[18]. Sa chás deiridh seo cruthaítear contrárthacht fhóinéimeach mar nach ndeachaigh an t-ardú i bhfeidhm ar an fhoclóir ina iomláine. Seo a leanas riar samplaí den chontrárthacht sin as cuid de na mionchanúintí ina bhfaightear an t-ardú.

[ɛ]/[ɛ̜]	[a̱]/[ä]/[ɑ]
cas	*glas*
cath	*Cathal*
lata	*slat*
ladar	*cladach*
leanbh	*plean*
meath [mʲ ɛ̜h]	*meitheal* [mʲ a̱həɫ]
saill	*caill*
tarbh	*dara*

Taobh amuigh de na mionchanúintí a bhfuil contrárthacht den tsórt sin thuas iontu, a bhfuil a bhfurmhór le fáil sa cheantar a shíneann ó Chnoc Fola soir fad an chósta thuaidh, is leor fóinéim amháin /a/ le breith ar na hallafóin ar fad.

3.0 NA GUTAÍ CRUINNE CÚIL

Tá níos mó gutaí cruinne cúil sna canúintí i nGaeilge Uladh i gcoitinne ná mar atá sna canúintí eile ar fud na tíre. Tá cúpla cúis leis seo. Is í an ceann is tábhachtaí orthu go bhfuil an chontrárthacht idir 'o' oscailte /ɔ/ agus 'o' druidte/dúnta /o/, le fáil sna gutaí gairide díreach mar atá i gcóras na ngutaí fada. Chomh maith leis sin tá an giorrú a dhéantar ar na gutaí fada 'ú' agus 'ó' i siollaí neamhaiceanta i ndiaidh cur go mór le líon na gcontrárthachtaí.

---

18 Faightear an t-ardú seo sna canúintí sin inar coinníodh [ɛ] i bhfocail mar *bean, deas, fead, Peadar* srl. Tá cosúlacht an-láidir idir na mionchanúintí seo agus ar tharla i gcanúintí dheisceart na hAlban mar a thuairiscíonn Holmer (1962).

3.1 NA GUTAÍ ARDA

Tá cineálacha éagsúla u-gairid le cluinstin sa chanúint. Bíonn siad go mór faoi smacht ag timpeallacht na gconsan. Is gutaí stairiúla cuid acu nach dtáinig athrú ar bith orthu. Cuid eile acu is as gutaí fada i siollaí neamhaiceanta a d'fhorbair siad. Tá tuilleadh eile a tháinig chun cinn i bhfocail ilsiollacha a chríochnaíonn ar '-(e)adh' agus ar '-(e)amh'. I gcásanna áirithe ardaíodh 'o' stairiúil in aice le consain ar leith ach nár tharla sin i ngach mionchanúint. Tá trí phríomhallafón ann agus dáiliú mar seo a leanas orthu.

[u]   *cruth, dubh, gruth, guth, inniu, prugaí, sruth, tiubh, triuch* srl.
      barúil, canúint, casúr, cosúil, cruthú, duilliúr, galún, míodún, miosúr,
      mothú, séasúr srl.
      briseadh, cailleadh, casadh, milleadh, samhradh srl.
      caitheamh, déanamh, talamh srl.
      leanbh, marbh, searbh, tarbh srl.

[ʊ]   *bog, coinín, frog, iomaire, obair, prugaí, scioból, turtóg* srl.
      boilg, buidéal, boileagóg, coilí, cuidigh, fuinneog, fuiseog, puisín srl.

[ü]   *bain, buille, cuilt, cuir, muiltín* srl.

Is iad sin thuas na hallafóin atá ag an /u/ gairid.[19] Chan fhuil an dá allafón deiridh le fáil i ngach mionchanint ach tá siad i gcuid acu. I mionchanúintí eile is amhlaidh nár hardaíodh /o/ stairiúil go [ʊ], agus is [i] nó [ï] a bhíonn mar réalú ar 'ui' an litrithe iontu. Fágann sin gur ar na fóinéimeanna /o/ agus /i/ a dháiltear na gutaí sa dá aicme dheiridh ansin thuas.

Faightear [ɯ] roimh [h] i gcanúintí an tuaiscirt trí chéile i bhfocail mar *faochóg, gaothach, gaothsán, saothar* srl. agus i roinnt focal eile ar nós *caoradóir, maoilín* srl. ach ó tharla go mbíonn [ɯ:] i gcuid de na bunfhocail mar atá *gaoth, caora, maol* srl. agus i leaganacha mar *ag saothrú*, d'fhéadfaí glacadh leis gur guta fada [ɯ:] go bunúsach atá i gceist.

3.1.1 NA GUTAÍ NEAMHARDA CÚIL

Ach an oiread leis na 'ó'-anna fada, tá dhá chineál 'o' gairid le fáil go coitianta i nGaeilge an Tuaiscirt ach amháin i nGleann Ghaibhleann. Úsáidfear na comharthaí fóinéime /o/ agus /ɔ/ le iad a idirdhealú ó chéile. Thig a rá measaim gurb í an

---

19 Ainneoin sin agus eile, tá dhá fhocal a idirdhealaítear óna chéile i mórán mionchanúintí trí úsáid a bhaint as [u] agus [ʊ]. Is iad sin *dubh* [d̪uw]/[d̪uʍ] agus *domh* [d̪ʊw]/[d̪ʊʍ] rud a thabharfadh go teicniúil cé bith scéal é stádas fóinéimeach don dá ghuta.

fhóinéim oscailte /ɔ/ an ceann is leitheadaí. Tá réimse allafón ag /o/ thar mar atá ag /ɔ/. I dtaca le /o/ de thig dhá allafón ar leith a lua. In aice le [h] cluintear [o] an-druidte agus is leagan gairid é den [o:] a luadh níos luaithe. Tá réimse níos leithne den bhéal faoin dara hallafón a ghluaiseann ó shuíomh leathard go leathíseal. Bíonn sé druidte isteach ón suíomh ina mbíonn [o] agus [ɔ] ach gur annamh a bhíos na liopaí cruinn nuair a bhítear á rá. Is doiligh comhartha cruinn a fháil don fhuaim seo mar nach bhfreastalaíonn na comharthaí atá san IPA i gceart ar an réimse atá fúithi. Bhain Quiggin (1906) agus Wagner (1959, 1969) úsáid as an chomhartha [o̤] ach is le fuaimeanna a mbíonn guth análach leo a úsáidtear [..]san IPA. Is é an comhartha [ʌ] ar bhain Ó Searcaigh (1925) úsáid as, ach arís eile níl an comhartha sin cruinn go leor do fhuaim na Gaeilge (atá le fáil chomh maith i mBéarla na hÉireann). Bíonn fuaim seo na Gaeilge níos faide siar sa bhéal agus níos airde de ghnáth. Is sa raon idir [ə] agus [o̞] a fhaightear é. Bainfidh mé úsáid as an chomhartha [o̞] dó anseo ach tuiscint a bheith ann go seasann sé don réimse fuaimeanna dá bhfuil mé i ndiaidh tagairt. Seo a leanas focail eiseamláireacha a léiríonn an dáiliú atá ar na hallafóin éagsúla.

/o/ [o] *lotha (lofa), mothú, cha/ní ro (< raibh), na bothaigh (< bóithigh)* srl.

[o̞] *bonn, corr, clog, donn, fonn, gob, lom, moll, poll, sompla, ar son, tom* srl.
bulla, bun, cupa, ag cur, furast, muc, pluc, punta, thug srl.
boil (< bail), cuinneog, cuileog, muileann srl.
iomrá, diomaite, giolla, gliomach, liom, liobasta, tiocfaidh, tiomáint srl.

/ɔ/ [ɔ] *boc, coirce, corr, cos, croch, droch-, goradh, gorm, losaid, Oisín, ola, osna, toil, toiseach* srl.
deoch, eochair, feochadán, seo srl.
ballóg, easóg, feannóg, fuinneog srl.

I dtaca leis na mionchanúintí de, tá cuid acu agus is [ɔ] a bhíonn mar réalú ar na deirí '-eog/-óg' iontu cé go bhfuil claonadh i gcoitinne [ɑ] a dhéanamh as. Is treise an claonadh seo in Oirthear Uladh agus sa leath thuaidh de Dhún na nGall.

Is léiriú na péirí seo a leanas ar an stádas fóinéimeach atá ag /o/ agus ag /ɔ/. Allafóin den fhóinéim /o/ atá sna samplaí atá sa chló trom.

corr (edge)	:	*corr* (odd)
moll	:	*mol*
bothaigh (< *bóithigh*)	:	*rothaí*
gur	:	*gorm*
pocán	:	*boc*
bulla	:	*ol(l)a*
culaith	:	*codlaigh*

3.1.2 ARDÚ [ɑ] GO [ɔ]

Caithfidh mé tagairt a dhéanamh anseo don riail a ardaíonn an guta íseal [ɑ] go [ɔ] i gcomhthéacsanna teoranta. Is roimh 'l' singil cúil a fhaightear é de ghnáth agus bíonn sé uaireanta roimh 'll' cúil. Is fíorannamh a chuirtear an riail i bhfeidhm ar an ghuta a bhíonn mar réalú ar 'ea' an litrithe i bhfocail mar *geal, geall, seal* srl. Is cosúil gur allafón den fhóinéim /ɔ/ an fhuaim nua anois, cé go léireodh an éagsúlacht fuaime atá uirthi ó áit go háit go raibh dhá chéim san ardú a tháinig uirthi. Is mar [ɒ]/[ɒ̈] a deir mórán daoine í agus is léir gur sin an chéad chéim san fhorbairt i dtreo an [ɔ] atá ag cainteoirí eile. Seo a leanas eiseamláirí ina ndeachaigh an t-ardú i bhfeidhm. Níltear ag rá go bhfuil na hathruithe sin le fáil i ngach mionchanúint ach gur treith í a bhaineann lena bhfurmór. D'fhéadfaí a rá fosta nach ar na focail chéanna go glan díreach a théann sí i bhfeidhm i ngach áit.

Albain, balbh, dalba, galánta, galar, malairt, salann, talamh srl.
allas, balla, ballán, Ó Gallchóir, mall, mallacht srl.
aiteanach, glas, las, lasóg, maidin srl.

3.2 AN GUTA NEAMHAICEANTA

Is é an guta atá sa dara siolla sna focail *aire, baile, míle, ábhar, mála* srl. atá i gceist anseo againn. Is beag atá le rá faoin ghuta seo mar nach mbíonn contrárthacht ar bith idir na hallafóin atá aige — bíonn [ɪ] nó [ï] taobh le consan caol agus [ə] nó [ɐ] taobh le consan leathan. D'fhéadfaí iad a aicmiú faoi aon fhóinéim amháin, abair /ə/ agus na hallafóin atá luaite aige sna comhthéacsanna cóir.

3.3 NA GUTAÍ GAIRIDE I gCOITINNE

Cuireann sin deireadh leis an phlé atá le déanamh againn ar na gutaí gairide. Tá teorainn leis an ualach céille atá ar iompar ag an idirdhealú idir [a] agus [ɑ] agus idir [ɛ]/[ɛ̞] agus [a]. Is nuáil an t-idirdealú atá i ndiaidh fás idir [i] agus [ï]. Tá coimriú le fáil sna léaráidí seo thíos ar na cineálacha córas atá i mionchanúintí éagsúla. Is dóiche gur as córas éigin mar atá i Léaráid 1 a d'fhás na córais eile.

Léaráid 1			*Léaráid 2*			*Léaráid 3*		
i	u		i	u		i	ï u	
e	o	>>	e	o	>>	e	o	
ə			ə			ə		
ɔ			(ɛ)	ɔ		(ɛ)	ɔ	
a	ɑ		a	ɑ		a	ɑ	

4.0 NA DÉFHOGHAIR

Le scéal na ngutaí a iomlánú caithfidh mé anois cur síos a dhéanamh ar chóras na ndéfhoghar. Tá liosta fada défhoghar ó thaobh na foghraíochta de tugtha ina gcuid leabhar ag cuid de na húdair go háirithe Sommerfelt (1922) agus Ó Searcaigh (1925). I Sommerfelt (1965) deir an t-údar é féin agus é ag iarraidh córas fóinéimeach a chur i bhfeidhm ar chanúint an Toir go gcaithfí glacadh leis nach défhoghair 'chearta' mórán de na défhoghair sin ina raibh [i] nó [u] i ndiaidh guta fada iontu. Deir sé féin:

> Most of the phonetic diphthongs which have been listed in the Dialect of Torr must be interpreted otherwise, mainly as long vowels followed by glides or as vowels in hiatus. Final *i* is in cases phonemically the consonant /γ′/ e.g. /gruaγ′/ 'cheek', gen. /gruaγ′ə/. (Sommerfelt, 1965: 239).

D'fhéadfaí an rud ceannann céanna a rá faoi shamplaí den chinéal chéanna atá ag Ó Searcaigh (1925: 46-59). Sílim go dtig a rá go bhfuil stádas fóinéimeach ag na dé-fhoghair seo a leanas sna canúintí i gcoitinne /ia/, /ua/, /ai/ agus /au/.[20] Tugaim anseo thíos na hallafóin is coitianta a bhíonn ag na défhoghair sin.

---

20 Tá cás ar leith is ceart a phlé i dtaca leis an tsrónáil a bhíonn ar an défhoghar i bhfocail mar *damhsa, ramhar, samhradh* srl. Is í an cheist atá le socrú ar ndóigh an bhfuil nó nach bhfuil contrárthacht eatarthu.

/ia/ [iˑa] ~ [iˑə] *aniar, ariamh, ciall, Dia, fiacha, fial, grian, liath, mias, piachán, pian, sciath, siar* srl.
céanna, féach, scéal

[ia] ~ [iə] *bánliath, drochscéal, Ferdia, seanchliabh* srl.

[ɪa] ~ [ɪə] *carria, gearria* srl.[21]

[iˑɛ̯] *bliain, fiáin, ni fhail (níl)* srl.

/ua/ [uˑa] ~ [uˑə] *anuas, bruach, cluas, cuach, gruama, luath, rua, scuab, slua, suas, tuaim, uascán* srl.

[ua] ~ [uə] *bánrua, leathchluas, seanluach* srl.[21]

[uˑɛ̯] *ar mo chluais, cruaidh, duais, suáilce, suaite, tuaigh, uair, uaisc* srl.

Maidir leis an dá dhéfhoghar /ai/ agus /au/, bíonn an chéad chuid den défhoghar níos cruinne in aice le consain liopacha.

/ai/ [ɑi] ~ [ai] ~ [ə̯i] *aithghiorra, caith, cathaoir, Flaithis, saighdiúir, claí, cluiche, droichead, gnoithe, luigh, reithe, scoith, soitheach*

[ai] ~ [ə̯i] *Condaigh (Contae), d'éalaigh, ag déanamh comhráidh, lucht fostóidh, tiontaigh*

[ɒi] ~ [ɔi] *baoite, bóitheach, ceann na cloiche/loiche, maith, maighdean, maighistir, moithigh*

/au/ [ɑu] ~ [ə̯u] *abhlóir, cabhlach, cabhsa, dabhach, slabhra* srl.

[ɒu] ~ [ə̯u] *babhail, fabhair, modhail* srl.

[au] ~ [ə̯u] *Feabhra, creabhar* srl.

Is é an scéal is troime atá le plé i dtaca le /au/ de cé acu tá an tsrónaíl a fhaightear mar réalú ar '-(e)amh' fóinéimeach nó nach bhfuil. Measaim i gcás na gceantar sin ina bhfuil srónaíl coitianta sa chaint i gcoitinne go bhfuil cás ann stádas fóinéimeach a thabhairt don dá allafón.[22] Seo a leanas péirí focal nach bhfuil de dhifríocht eatarthu i gcomhthéacsanna ionanna ach an tsrónaíl.

---

21 Is sean-chomhfhocail iad seo a bhfuil an phríomhbhéim ar an chéad siolla iontu agus dá bhrí sin cha chuirtear fad ar bith leis an chéad eilimint den défhoghar mar a dhéantar nuair a bhíonn béim láidir air.

22 Is cosúil nach raibh an tsrónaíl chomh suntasach i dTeileann agus i nGleann Cholmcille de réir Wagner (1959). A mhalairt ar fad atá fíor faoi chanúintí iarthuaisceart Dhún na nGall, áit

[ɑu] ~ [ə̯u]	[ãu] ~ [ɔ̃u]
cabhsa	*damhsa*
cabhlaigh	*amhlaidh*
slabhra	*samhradh*

Seo a leanas tuilleadh samplaí ina mbíonn srónaíl láidir ar gach cuid den dé-fhoghar ainneoin nach bhfuil sé marcáilte agam ach ar an chéad cheann.

/ãu/ [ãu] ~ [ɔ̃u]   *amhlaidh, amodha (amú), clamhsán, damhsa, gamhain, ramhar, samhradh, snamh* srl.

[ãu] ~ [ə̯̃u]   *geamhar, neamh, sleamhain* srl.

Sin iad na príomh-dhéfhoghair agus a gcuid allafón. Tá roinnt cásanna eile ann nár mhiste tagairt dóibh anois le críoch a chur leis an chur síos seo ar Ghaeilge Uladh.

4.1 CÁSANNA EILE

Tá roinnt cásanna eile ann a gcaithfimid aird an léitheora a dhíriú orthu anois. Baineann siad leis an réalú a bhíonn ar 'ua' taobh le consain liopacha agus leis na canúintí sin ina bhfuil guta déanta as 'gh' leathan nó as 'ng' iontu.

San áit a raibh 'ua' taobh le consain liopacha rinneadh [ɯ] neamhchruinn den [u] a bhí sa chéad chuid den défhoghar ar fud Chúige Uladh i gcoitinne seachas Gleann Ghaibhleann. Char chruthaigh an t-athrú seo contrárthacht bhreise ach amháin b'fhéidir i gcás an chonsain 'f' mar go dtéann sé ar ceal trí shéimhiú.[23] Seo a leanas comhthéacsanna ina mbíonn contrárthacht foghraíochta.

[ɯə]	[uə]
chan fhuair	*an uair*
san fhuacht	*uachtar*
d'fhuascail	*uascán*

---

a mbíonn srónaíl le fáil go forleathan sa chaint. Is cosúil mar sin gur sna canúintí sin atá an t-idirdhealú atá faoi chaibidil againn.

23 Is léiriú tábhachtach an méid seo go bhféadfadh fuaim, ar 'allafón' go teoiriciúil í, sa mhéid is go dtig a rá go cinnte cén comhthéacs ina bhfaighear í, gníomhú mar 'fhóinéim'. Tá cásanna eile den chineál chéanna sa teanga agus is ábhar staidéir iontu féin iad agus tá sé i gceist agam amach anseo cur síos níos cuimsithí a thabhairt orthu ná mar a bheadh fóirsteanach anseo.

Tá forbairt eile ar an dáiliú seo anois i mórán de chanúintí Dhún na nGall ó na Dúnaibh ó thuaidh go dtí Teileann ó dheas mar go bhfuil [ua ~ uə] athraithe sna mionchanúintí sin go [ɪa ~ ɪə].²⁴ Níl an t-athrú seo le fáil sna canúintí ina bhfaightear [u:] mar réalú ar 'ao' an litrithe iontu. Ní bhíonn sé ach sna canúintí sin arbh é an réalú [i:] a bhíonn ar 'ao' an litrithe iontu i ngach comhthéacs.

Baineann an dara forbairt leis na canúintí sin ina bhfuil rian éigin den [ɣ] stairiúil le fáil iontu go fóill mar go bhfuil claonadh ag an fhuaim seo athrú ina guta ard neamhchruinn agus go dtig léi feidhmiú mar an dara cuid de dhéfhoghar. Athraíodh 'ng' leathan i lár focail sna canúintí seo fosta agus rinneadh [ɣ̃] de.²⁵ Tá an claonadh céanna ag an [ɣ̃] seo agus atá ag an [ɣ] stairiúil athrú ina ghuta ard neamhchruinn [ɯ] nó [ɯ̃]. Mar an gcéanna sna canúintí sin inar [ɪa ~ ɪə], a deirtear in áit [ua ~ uə], is é an défhoghar /ai/ a fhaightear i samplaí mar iad seo thíos.²⁶

[aɣ̃] ~ [aɯ̃] *anglach, ceangal, eangain, iongain, langán, teangaidh* srl.

5.0 CONCLÚID

Is é an rud a léiríonn a bhfuil pléite againn go bhfuil córas na ngutaí fada agus gearra i nGaeilge Uladh i gcoitinne níos forleithne ó thaobh uimhir na bhfóinéimeanna de ná mar atá sna canúintí eile. Tá simpliú áirithe ar siúl sna canúintí sin atá fágtha i nDún na nGall agus baineann an simpliú sin cuid mhaith le seasamh na bhfóinéimeanna /ɯ:/ agus /ɤ:/. De thairbhe na ngutaí gairide de is í an scoilt idir [i] tosaigh agus [ï] lárnach agus an chontrárthacht idir trí ghuta chruinne cúil an rud is suntasaí fúthu. Tá cuid de na canúintí níos coimeádaí ná a chéile agus is iad na canúintí sin a bhfuil na fóinéimeanna /ɯ:/ agus /ɤ:/ iontu na cinn is coimeádaí orthu. Is iontu sin fosta a fhaightear na défhoghair bhreise /ãu/, /ua/ agus /aɯ̃/ a ndearnadh tagairt dóibh thuas.

24 Sa chás seo agus an 'f' á chur ar ceal trí shéimhiú d'fhéadfadh contrárthacht a theacht chun cinn idir /ia/ agus /ɪa/, i bpéirí mar *fiar/fuar, iasc/fuascail* srl., murar ann dó cheana féin.

25 I dtaca leis an 'ng' caol is mar [i] a fhaightear é de ghnáth i bhfocail mar *aingeal, daingean* srl., ach is minic fosta guta láir [e:] mar a bhíonn sna focail *foighid, laghad* srl. a bhíonn mar fhuaimniú leis i dTír Eoghain agus i nDeisceart Uladh.

26 Cé gur [a] atá agam sa chéad chuid den défhoghar anseo thíos is minic [ɑ] agus [ə] ina áit. Má ghlactar leis na défhoghair úra seo mar chuid de chóras na gcanúintí sin ina bhfaightear iad, cuirfidh sé go mór le huimhir na gcontrárthachtaí i measc na ndéfhoghar.

LEABHARLIOSTA

Hamilton, J. N. (1974) *A Phonetic Study of the Irish of Tory Island, Co. Donegal.*, Belfast, Institute of Irish Studies.

Holmer, Nils M. (1962) *The Gaelic of Kintyre*, DIAS, Dublin.

Ó Baoill, D. P. (1996) *An Teanga Bheo — Gaeilge Uladh*, ITÉ, Baile Átha Cliath.

Ó Dochartaigh, C. (1987) *Dialects of Ulster Irish*, Belfast, Institute of Irish Studies.

Ó Searcaigh, S. (1925) *Foghraidheacht Ghaedhilge an Tuaiscirt*, Brún agus Ó Nualláin, Teor., Béal Feirste, Baile Átha Cliath, Corcaigh agus Port Láirge.

Quiggin, E. C. (1906) *A Dialect of Donegal*, Cambridge, CUP.

Sommerfelt, (1922) *The Dialect of Torr, Co. Donegal.* Christiania, Jacob Dybwad.

_____, (1965) *The phonemic structure of the dialect of Torr, Co. Donegal, Lochlann*, vol. 3, 237–254, Oslo University Press, Oslo

Stockman, G. and Wagner, H. (1965) *Contributions to a Study of Tyrone Irish, Lochlann*, vol. 3, 43–236, Oslo University Press, Oslo.

Wagner, H. (1958, 1969) *Linguistic Atlas and Survey of Irish Dialects*, vols. 1 & 4, DIAS, Dublin.

_____, (1959) *Gaeilge Theilinn*, Institiúid Ard-Léinn Bhaile Átha Cliath.

Searmanas Cois Teallaigh Choigilt na Tine

Séamas Ó Catháin

AN COLÁISTE OLLSCOILE, BAILE ÁTHA CLIATH

I

'CENN desna paidreacha is lia cóip' an gradam a bhronnann an tAthair Piaras de Hindeberg ar 'Phaidir Choigilt na Tine' ina thráchtas *Paidreacha na nDaoine*.[1] Bhí an breithiúnas seo bunaithe ar an chnuasach shé leagan agus fiche a thiomsaigh sé den phaidir bheag seo ó fhoinsí éagsúla — leabhair, irisí agus lámhscríbhinní Choimisiún Béaloideasa Éireann agus anuas air sin leagan amháin a bhailigh sé féin, de réir cosúlachta. Ó cheantracha Gaeltachta nó Breac-Ghaeltachta ar fad iad seo agus is i nGaeilge atá siad. Sa bhliain 1889 a foilsíodh an leagan is sine acu seo agus baineann fuílleach na leaganacha seo leis an tréimhse uaidh sin anuas go dtí deireadh na dtriochaidí sa chéad seo. Paidir aonair seachas paidir pháirteach í agus mar is intuigthe ón teideal a bhaistear go coitianta uirthi — 'Paidir (nó 'Paidear') Choigilt na Tine' — is paidir ócáideach chomh maith í. Tá leaganacha éagsúla den phaidir seo (ceithre cinn acu ó Chúige Connacht agus ceann amháin ó Chúige Mumhan) ag Dubhghlas de hÍde in *Abhráin Diadha Chúige Connacht*, áit a bhfuil an cur síos seo a leanas aige uirthi mar phaidir:

---

1 Tráchtas PhD d'Ollscoil na hÉireann 1942 (gan foilsiú), 36. Tá plé ag údar an tráchtais seo ar ábhar an tráchtais le fáil in 'Paidreacha na nDaoine', *Irisleabhar Muighe Nuadhat* 1956. 35–41.

Is beag nach fíor le rá é, nach raibh gníomh sonnradhach no speisialta ar bith d'a dtigeadh le bheith deunta ag an Éireannach ar feadh an laé nach raibh focal no dó de phaidir aige roimhe, anuas go dti seal gearr ó shoin. Bhí gníomh sonnradhach de'n tsórt so le deunamh aige h-uile oidhche nuair chuireadh sé cuid de'n teine do bhí ar an dteaghlach i dtaisge, ag folughadh splainnc no dó go doimhin faoi an ngríosach agus faoi an luaithre, 'd'á gcoigil,' mar dubhairt sé i riocht go mbeidheadh pór na teineadh beó aige arís ar maidin. Budh é sin gníomh dheireannach an laé aige; do tháinig an oidhche agus dorchadas na h-oidhche leis an ngníomh sin. Is dóigh nach gan phaidir bhig do ghnidheadh sé é, agus tá an phaidir seo le fághail ann s gach uile áit i n-Éirinn ann a bhfuil an Ghaedheilg beó fós, agus i n-Albainn[2] mar an gcéadna. Ag so mar sgríobh mo chara Eóin Mac Néill í ó bheul Mhártain Uí Fhualáin i n-Inis Meadhon:

Coinglighim an teine seo
Mar choingligheas Críost cáidh,
Muire i mullach an tighe
Agus Bríghid ann a lár.
An t-ochtar ainglidhe is tréine
I gcathair na ngrás
A' cúmhdach an tighe seo
'S a dhaoine thabhairt slán.[3]

(*Tíopa 1* ag de Hindeberg)

2 Féach, mar shampla, A. Carmichael, *Carmina Gadelica. Hymns and Incantations*, Edinburgh & London (1940), III, 324–7. Go bhfios domh, tá ar a laghad cúig leagan den phaidir seo (a bailíodh idir 1951 agus 1970) i mbailiúcháin Sgoil Eòlais na h-Alba in Ollscoil Dhún Éideann. B'fhiú go maith na leaganacha Albanacha ar fad a chur i gcomórtas leis na leaganacha Éireannacha den phaidir, rud nach bhfuil seans agam a dhéanamh anseo.

3 D. Hyde [An Craoibhín Aoibhinn], *Abhráin Diadha Chúige Connacht or The Religious Songs of Connacht. A Collection of Poems, Stories, Prayers, Satires, Ranns, Charms etc.*, Cuid II, London & Dublin [1906], 44, 46. Is dóiche gurab é seo an leagan a bhailigh 'MAC-LÉIGHINN' (i.e. Eoin Mac Néill) agus a foilsíodh in *Irisleabhar na Gaedhilge*, Uimh 33, Iml. IV (1889) faoin teideal 'Some ancient Gaelic prayers, &c. (written by MAC-LÉIGHINN) from natives of Inismaan, Arann Islands'. Luaitear 'Martin Folan' i.e. 'Mártan Ó Fualáin' leis. D'fhoilsigh S. O'Sullivan aistriúchán Béarla den leagan seo in *The Folklore of Ireland*, London (1974), 139 agus in *Irish Folk Custom and Belief*, Dublin [1967], 18 [S. Ó Súilleabháin], áit a bhfuil an bunleagan Gaeilge le fáil chomh maith. Tá aistriúchán Béarla de leaganacha eile den phaidir seo le fáil in R. MacCrócaigh, *Prayers of the Gael*, London & Edinburgh 1914, p. 35, agus in G.A. Hayes McCoy, 'Smooring', *The Terminal* 2 (1935), 3–4.

Tugann de hÍde leagan Árainneach eile den phaidir a bhailigh Mac Néill ó 'Bhrigid MacDonagh' ('Brighid Ní Dhonnacha' mar a thugann sé uirthi). Tá difríocht shuntasach idir an leagan seo agus leagan Mhártain Uí Fhualáin thuas:

Coiglighim an teine seo
Le crann clanna Pádraig,
Aingle Dé dá'r ndúiseacht
'S nár fhuasglaid an námhaid.
Ocht n-each faoi an teach
Teach nach luigheann ceó air,
Nach n-imtheochaidh aon mharbh as
'S nach ngointear duine beó ann.

(*Tíopa 2a* ag de Hindeberg)

Foilsíodh roinnt mhaith leaganacha éagsúla eile ó shin i leith — ar na samplaí is deireanaí ar fad tá na trí cinn atá ag an Athair Diarmuid Ó Laoghaire in *Ár bPaidreacha Dúchais*,[4] an dá leagan ó Iorras i gcontae Mhaigh Eo (a d'fhoilsigh Caitlín Uí Sheighin agus mé féin)[5] agus an leagan (mar aon le haistriúchán Béarla) a d'fhoilsigh Seán Ó Súilleabháin (leagan Eoin Mhic Néill ó Inis Meáin).[6] Bailíodh mórán mór eile leaganacha chomh maith ón traidisiún bheo, rud a fhágann go bhfuil faoin am seo corradh le dhá scór go leith leagan sa bhreis faoi lámh againn nach raibh tarraingt ag an Athair de Hindeberg orthu agus é i mbun a shaothair, beagán beag os cionn leathchéad bliain ó shin. Ó tharla gur earra inbhailithe go fóill féin an phaidir seo, d'fhéadfaí cur leis an díolaim sin go réidh

4   *Ár bPaidreacha Dúchais, Cnuasach de phaidreacha agus de bheannachtaí ár sinsear*, Baile Átha Cliath 1975. Rinne P. Ó Fiannachta ceann acu seo a athfhoilsiú (Uimh. 245, l. 76) in *Saltair. Urnaithe Dúchais. Prayers from the Irish Tradition*, Dublin 1988, 21 (leagan é seo a foilsíodh den chéad uair in Searloit Ni Dhéisighe, *Paidreacha na ndaoine*, Baile Átha Cliath 1924). San leabhrán urnaí is deireanaí den chineál seo — S. Redmond S.J., *Prayers of Two Peoples. Traditional Scottish and Irish Verse Prayers*, [Dublin 1996] — níl tásc nó tuairisc le fáil ar Phaidir Choigilt na Tine agus ní raibh ach oiread sa bhailiúchán a rinne an tAthair T. S. Mac Cionaith i nGleann Ghaibhleann, contae an Chábháin, sa bhliain 1921, *Night Prayers (Rosary, Litany). Prayers after Mass etc. in Irish*. Leabhairíní Bhreifne 1, Cavan 1921, bíodh is gur bailíodh trí leagan de Phaidir Choigilt na Tine sa cheantar sin i ndiaidh an ama sin: seans go dtaispeánann an fhaillí seo nár measadh aon úsáid a bheith sa phaidir feasta ó tharla an cleachtas féin a bheith imithe nó ag imeacht as faisean.

5   S. Ó Catháin agus C. Uí Sheighin (eag.), *A Mhuintir Dhú Chaocháin, Labhraígí Feasta !*, Indreabhán 1987 (leath. 75) agus leis na heagarthóirí céanna, *Le Gradam is Le Spraoi*, Indreabhán 1996 (leath. 52).

6   Féach Nóta 3 thuas.

gan trácht ar chor ar bith ar an mhéid leaganacha eile sa bhreis air sin ar ais arís nach dtángthas go fóill orthu i gcnuasach Roinn Bhéaloideas Éireann.[7]

Is minice ina dhiaidh sin agus uile gan againn sna bunfhoinsí ach focla na paidre go lom gan aon chur síos *à la* de hÍde ar an chomhthéacs ina ndeirtí í nó ar gheaitsí nó iompar an té a déarfadh í ach oiread. Tugann ráitis mhaola mar — 'Said at raking the fire at night before retiring'[8] nó, 'An phaidir a deirtear aig coigilt na teinneadh roimh dul a chodladh'[9] nó, 'Tá eólas ag na daoine uile annsin [Coillte Mách, contae Mhaigh Eo] air'[10] — le fios gur gnás a chleachtaítí go forleathan tráth den tsaol é agus gur traidisiún é a raibh cur amach ag an phobal air, amhail is go mb'fhéidir gur síleadh go raibh an méid sin uilig chomh hintuigthe sin ar mhodh ar bith agus nárbh fhiú mórán dua a chaitheamh le tuilleadh mínithe nó tráchtaireachta a sholáthar faoi. Is fíor-thaitneamhach agus is ríthábhachtach iad tagairtí mar na cinn seo a leanas i gcomhthéacs an ghanntanais mhí-ámharaigh seo:

Choiglídís an tine ansan nuair a bhídís ag dul a chodladh. Dá mbeadh *range* agat ní fhéadfá an tine a choigilt in aon chor istoíche. Bhíodh mórán den luaith-ghríosach acu sa tinteán — carn di. Chaithfeá an luaith a bheith agat chun an tine a choigilt. Bheadh sé dearg mar do bheadh sméaróidí beaga den tine tríd: thabharfá luaithghríosach ansan air. Is minic a bheadh poll in aice na tine i gcomhair na luatha. Thabharfá poll na luatha air. Bheadh cuid den luaith fágtha ansan chun an tine a choigilt leis. Ghlanfá láthair na tine ar dtúis agus thógfá amach na sméaróidí ar an dtinteán. Chuirfeá isteach ansan arís iad leis an ursal. Ba cheart cúpla fód móna, nó na caoráin a chuir isteach leis. Thógfaidís sin tine agus bheidís dearg agat ar maidin nuair a bheadh an tine á adú arís agat. Nuair a bheidís go léir socair istigh agat thiocfá leis an sluasaid agus chuirfeá an luaithghríosach anuas orthu. Choimeádfadh sé an tine ina bheatha istigh agus san am gcéanna ní leogfadh sé dó dó amach. Bheadh an tine go maith aibí istigh ann nuair a éireofá ar maidin. Déarfainn gur mar sin a dheineadh gach aoinne é.[11]

7   Is dóigh liom go bhféadfaí teacht ar go leor leaganacha breise den phaidir seo sa chnuasach lámhscríbhinní ar a dtugtar Lámhscríbhinní na Scol agus sna taifid fuaime i mbailiúchán Roinn Bhéaloideas Éireann, An Coláiste Ollscoile, Baile Átha Cliath, an áit a bhfuil bailiúcháin an Choimisiúin agus bailiúcháin eile béaloidis ar caomhnú.

8   É. Ó Tuathail, *Sgéalta Mhuintir Luinigh. Munterloney Folk-Tales*, Dublin 1933, 186.

9   D. Ó Fotharta. *Siamsa an Gheimhridh*, Baile Átha Cliath 1892, 139.

10 *Record of the League of St. Columba. St. Patrick's College, Maynooth* (1902-1903), 107.

11 CBÉ 841: 389. Seán Ó Cróinin, a bhailigh ó Phádraig Ó Murchadha, Béal Átha an Ghaorthaidh, contae Chorcaigh, 1942. Seasann CBÉ do Chnuasach Béaloideas Éireann .i. príomhbhailiúchán lámhscríbhinní Roinn Bhéaloideas Éireann agus seasann na figiúirí ar dhá thaobh an idirstaid d'uimhir an imleabhair agus d'uimhir an leathanaigh (nó na leathanaigh) ar a bhfuil an t-ábhar araon. Tá litriú na sleachta as lámhscríbhinní CBÉ leasaithe agam de

Thagadh oícheanta áirithe go bhfágtaí an tine gan coigilt: trí oíche tar éis bháis
duine, Oíche Shamhna agus Oíche Nollag. I gcomhair na marbh a dhéantaí é sin;
chreid[id]ís go dtugaidís cuairt ar an dtigh na hoícheanta san. Is leis an luaith a
dhéantaí an tine do choigilt. Sula gcaithfí aon chuid den luaith ar na sméaróidí
dearga deirtí paidir choigilte na tine. Thugtaí suas do Dhia agus do Mhuire
Bheannaithe an tigh agus a mbíodh ann go lá. D'fhanadh mo mháthair chríonna
ar an dtinteán nó go mbíodh an duine déanach fágtha an tinteán. Ní thabharfadh
sí coigilt na tine d'éinne ach di féin. Agus deireadh sí an phaidir, agus, dar ndóigh,
is aici a bhí a raibh de sheana-phaidreacha in Éirinn.[12]

Tá tábhacht nach beag le cuntais den chineál seo a léiríonn mionsonraí na nós-
mhaireachta a bhain leis an ghnás seo — an chaoi cheart leis an choigilt a
dhéanamh agus an téarmaíocht a théann léi, an cosc ar choigilt oícheanta áirithe,
agus na hoícheanta eile, cá huair go pointeáilte a déarfaí an phaidir agus cé
déarfadh í, mar shampla. San am go mbíthí ag dul don nós seo ar thinteáin na
hÉireann ba mhinice bean an tí i mbun dioscaireachta nó ag cur deis ar bhalcaisí
éadaigh ag am luí ná éinne eile sa teach agus dealraíonn sé gur uirthise a d'fhágtaí
cúram seo na tine go hiondúil. I seilbh na mban is mó a bhí stóras na
seanphaidreacha dúchais de réir cosúlachta agus is ó mhná go cinnte is mó a
bailíodh an phaidir seo againne. Ach, ó am go ham agus ag brath ar an líon tí,
tharlódh sé ar a mhalairt de chaoi:

Ní raghadh Seán chuig codlata roimh Mháire go dtí go mbeadh adú na tine age
féinig mar do bhí paidearacha beaga speisialta 'ge do dheireadh sé nuair a bhíodh
sé ag coigilt na tine.[13]

Soláthraíonn cuntas pearsanta ó pheann an Athar Benedict léargas ar leith ar
chomhthéacs an tsearmanais chois teallaigh agus cuireann dhá shampla eile den
phaidir a théann leis ar fáil dúinn chomh maith:

[Cuireann an tuairisg sin i dtuisgint dúinn cén chaoi a dtáinig ár bpaidreacha
dúthchais anuas chugainn.] Níor sgríobhadh iad ná níor foillsigheadh i n-aon
leabhar Urnaighthe iad. Sé an chaoi a dtáiniceadar anuas ó bhéal go béal, mar a
chuala an fear sin agá n-a shean-athair iad, agus mar a chluineadh páistí eile iad
agá n-aithreacha nó agá n-a máithreacha cois teallaigh nó ag colbha na leapthan

---

réir an ghnáthnóis normálaithe .i. foirmeacha gramadaigh a fhágáil gan athrú ach an
caighdeán a oibriú ar an chuid eile den téacs chomh fada agus is féidir.
12 CBÉ 1513:12-3. Micheál Ó Gaoithín, Baile Bhiocáire, Dún Chaoin, contae Chiarraí, a scríobh
sa bhliain 1957.
13 CBÉ 243: 445. Baile Icín, Dún Chaoin, contae Chiarraí.

iad. Tá rian an bhéaloideasa sin orthu mar Phaidreacha, nídh nach iongantas. Is
minic athrú beag orthu ó cheanntar go ceanntar agus ó theach go teach féin. . . .
An fhaid a bhíos na Paidreacha sin dá rádh dóibh féin ar an leapthain ag muintir
an tighe, chluinfeá paidir bhreágh eile dá mbeitheá i bhfus ins an gcistinigh, áit a
rabhas féin go tráthamhail oidhche amháin idir dhá Nollaig tá cupla bliain ó
shoin ann i dteach thiar i gCois Fhairrge. Comh luath agus a bhí an Paidrín
Páirteach ráidhte againn an oidhche sin, chuaidh gach duine suas a chodladh cé's
móite de bhean a' tighe a raibh rudaí beaga le déanamh aici.

D'fhanas féin i mo shuidhe cois na teineadh ag aithléagh[amh] a raibh
sgríobhtha ó mhaidin agam de chainnt na gcómharsan agus de leaganacha suan-
tasacha agus d'fhoclaí nach gcualas cheana. D'éirigheas i gcionn tamaillín agus do
lasas mo choinneal ag bráth ar dhul siar a chodladh. 'Tá sé chomh maith agam an
teine a choigilt mar sin, a Athair,' arsa bean a' tighe, 'má tá tusa réidh.' Rug sí ar
an tlú. An fhaid a bhí sí ag socrú na bhfód timcheall na gríosaighe agus ag cur na
luaithe orthu, bhí paidir dá rádh go beag aici, agus nuair a bhí an choigilt déanta
aici, ghearr sí an Chroich Cheasta ar an teallach leis an tlú.

Bhí barúil mhaith agam gurbh í Paidir Choigilt na Teineadh a bhí dá rádh aici,
mar bhí a fhios agam cheana a leithéid sin de phaidir a bheith ann. Ach ní raibh
an phaidir sin cloiste agam roimhe sin ón mbéal beo, agus is mór idir an focal nó
an phaidir a bheith léighte agat agus an focal nó an phaidir sin a chloisteál ins an
gcainnt bheo.

'A Úna [Úna Thaidhg, Salathóna],' adeirimse, 'cén phaidir í sin a bhí dá rádh
agat anois díreach agus tú ag coigilt na teineadh.' 'Cheal nach gcuala tú cheana í?'
ar sise, 'sin í an phaidir adeirtear le linn choigilt na teineadh. Pé ar bith cé a
choigleochas í, déarfaidh sé an phaidir sin.' Agus dubhairt sí ós árd dom annsin
an phaidir bhreágh seo:

> Coiglighim an teine seo mar a choigligheas Críost cách,
> Muire i dhá cheann an tighe agus Brighid ina lár,
> A bhfuil de Naoimh a's d'aingealaibh i gCathair na ngrást
> A' cúmhdach an tighe seo agus ár ndaoine go lá.

> (*Tíopa* 1 ag de Hindeberg)

'Ag mo Mhamó a bhíodh an phaidir sin,' ar sise annsin, 'deirim 'c[h]uile oidhche í
ag coigilt na te[i]neadh dom, agus cupla uair nó trí féin, b'fhéidir. Agus an
Chroich Chéasta a chur ar an teallach leis an tlú.'

Tá an urnaighe bheag sin chomh coitchianta i ngach cheanntar den Ghaedheal-
tacht agus nach lia teach féin ná malairt leagain di. Gideadh is beag nach mar a
chéile gach aon leagan díobh amach ón leagan seo [ó Shiobhán Ní Laoghaire,
Baile Mhúirne, contae Chorcaigh]

Coiglighim an teine seo leis na fearta a thug Pádraig dúinn,
na hAingil ghá chlúdach, a's nár mhúsglaidh ár námhaid í,
Nár dhóightear ár dtig a's nár mharbhuightear ár bhfir,
Claidheamh Chríost ar an ndorus go dtiocfaidh solus an lae
amáirigh.[14]

(*Tíopa 2b* ag de Hindeberg)

Mar aon le tuilleadh den saintéarmaíocht, léirítear réimse ar leith de mheoin an phobail i leith chúinsí tromchúiseacha de chineál eile ar fad sna cuntais seo thíos:

Ní mhaith leo an tine a ligeant in éag fadó. Ní mhaith leo í a choigilt istoíche gan síol na tine a fhágaint inti. Ba mhaith leo an tine a choimeád beo mar b'fhéidir gur mó duine go gcuirfí purgadóireacht ar an dtinteán air.[15]

Mo sheana-mháthair a chuala á rá san, nár cheart duit aon luaith a chuir i mbarra na tine — gan aon luaith a chuir ina barr nuair a bheifeá á coigilt istoíche — agus gan aon chuid den luaith a fhágaint timpeall an tinteáin — an tinteán a stobháil nuair a bheifeá ag dul a chodladh.

Do chuala-sa go raibh tigh [ann] agus ar feadh trí bliana tar éis iad a phósadh. Lánú óg ab ea iad agus dheineadar tigh nua sharar phósadar agus is ann isteach a chuadar tar éis pósta dhóibh. Agus ar feadh trí bliana tar éis pósta dhóibh chloiseadh sí — an bhean óg — port feadaíl bheag thuas aige an dtine nach aon oíche tar éis dul a chodladh dhóibh — thíos in íochtar an tí a chodlaídís. Bhíodh an port feadaíl thuas agus in imeall na tine nach aon oíche. Níor chuir sé aon eagla uirthi. Ach dúirt sí go gcinníodh sí an tinteán go breá glan agus níor choigil sí barra na tine riamh. Is dócha gur anam bocht éicinteach a bhain leis an dtigh a bhíodh ann agus go mbíodh áthas air an tine a bheith dearg roimis agus an tinteán a bheith go deas glan.[16]

[Ba cheart] an tinteán a scuabadh go breá glaen ansan nuair a bheifeá ag dul a chodladh agus roinnt de sméaróidí beo a fhágaint leo féinig amuigh, i dtaobh amuigh dhen choigilt agus an ursal a chur ar leith na láimhe deise, mar do bheifeá ag braith go dtiocfadh na 'daoine maithe' isteach chun iad féinig a théamh nuair a bheadh na daoine imithe a chodladh.[17]

14 An tAth Benedict O.C., 'Guidhimís', *Knock Shrine Annual/Irisleabhar Cnuic Mhuire* 1965, 23–4.

15 CBÉ 778: 101. Seosamh Ó Dálaigh a bhailigh ó Bríd Bean Uí Dhálaigh, Cam Uí Neól, Cill Maolcéadair, contae Chiarraí, 1941.

16 CBÉ 1421: 80-1. Tadhg Ó Murchadha a bhailigh ó Shiobhán Ní Shéaghdha, Fearann na hAbhann, Paróiste na Dromad, contae Chiarraí, 1955.

17 CBÉ 43: 99. Pádraig Ó Suibhne, Béal Átha an Ghaorthaidh, contae Chorcaigh a bhailigh, 1931.

II

Ba é an modh oibre a bhí ag de Hindeberg, agus é ag cur síos ar an phaidir seo, téarmaíocht agus foclaíocht iomlaoideach na leaganacha a scrúdú go mion, na malartacha faoina gcrot chanúnach a chur i gcomparáid lena chéile, struchtúr imlíneach na paidre a rianú, agus dáileadh na paidre ó cheann ceann na tíre a thaispeáint dá réir sin ina dhiaidh sin. Bhí oiread samplaí faoi réir ag de Hindeberg agus a chuir ar a chumas anailís chuimsitheach go leor a dhéanamh uirthi. Tríd is tríd, treisíonn an raidhse leaganacha breise a tháinig chun solais ó shin (a mhéadaíonn faoi thrí nach mór a bhfuil de leaganacha den phaidir seo againn ar fad) leis an chur amach atá aige ar na cúrsaí seo agus is féidir dá bharr sin glacadh le roinnt mhaith den scagadh bunúsach a rinne sé. Anailís easnamhach agus mhíshásúil ar mhórán bealaí ina dhiaidh sin í agus theastódh, dar liom, go gcuirfí le bunobair thaighde sin de Hindeberg a) maidir le scóp na dtíopanna a fhairsingiú agus b) maidir leis an phlé buntosach a rinne sé faoi nádúr agus brí na paidre a neartú agus a dhoimhniú.

Déanann de Hindeberg amach go bhfuil dhá bhuntíopa den phaidir seo i gceist — 'leagan 1' agus 'leagan 2' (a bhfuil, dar leis, dhá fho-leagan de ann, mar atá, 2a agus 2b) agus léirítear samplaí díofa seo thuas. Baineann formhór mór na samplaí a bhí ag de Hindeberg le *Tíopa 1* ('leagan 1') .i. an chéad phaidir thuas. Aontaím le leagan amach dhá bhuntíopa de Hindeberg ach dhéanfainnse dhá chuid de *Thíopa 1* agus trí chuid de *Thíopa 2*. Mar seo, más ea, a bheadh siad agamsa:

Tíopa 1a

Coiglighim an teine seo
Mar a choigligheas Críost cách,
Muire i dhá cheann an tighe
Agus Brighid ina lár.
A bhfuil de naoimh a's d'aingealaibh
I gCathair na ngrást
A' cúmhdach an tighe seo
Agus ár ndaoine go lá.[18]

Tíopa 1b

Coiglimse an tine seo
Mar a choigleas cách
Bríd ina bun
Agus Muire ina barr
Is naoi n-aingle fichid
As Flaitheas na nGrást
Go raibh ag gardáil an tí
Is a dhaoine go lá.[19]

---

18 An tAthair Benedict, *op.cit.*, 24. Tá dhá chuid déanta agam de línte na ceathrúna san sampla seo agus sna samplaí eile anseo thíos chun gur féidir iad a chur i gcomórtas le chéile go héasca. Is minic a scríobhtar mar sin iad chomh maith sna bunfhoinsí.

19 Ó Catháin agus Uí Sheighin, *op.cit.* 1987, 75.

Tíopa 2a

Coiglighim an teine seo
Leis na fearta a thug Pádraig dúinn,
Na hAingil ghá chlúdach,
A's nár mhúsglaidh ár námhaid í,
Nár dhóightear ár dtig
A's nár mharbhuightear ár bhfir,
Claidheamh Chríost ar an ndorus
Go dtiocfaidh solus an lae amáirigh.[20]

Tíopa 2b

Coigilim an tine seo
Leis na fearta fuair Pádraig
Na haingil 'á cúnlacht
Nár spiúnaig aon namhaid í !
Go ndine Dia díon dár dtig
Da bhfuil ann istigh, dá bhfuil as amuh !
Claídheamh Chríost ar an ndorus
Go dtí solus an lae amáirigh ![21]

Tíopa 2c

Coiglimse an tine seo
Le cranna Pádraic
Aîgheal Dé dar ndúsgadh,
A's nar dhúisighe sé ár námhaid
A loch an áidh, a' gcluin tú sin
Air an loch nach luigheanns ceo ?
Nár fhágadh marbh an toigh seo
A's nar ghontar duine beó ionn.[22]

San am i láthair, tá 25 leagan de *Thíopa 1a*, 29 leagan de *Thíopa 1b*, 6 leagan de *Thíopa 2a*, 2 leagan de *Thíopa 2b* agus 6 leagan de *Thíopa 2c* againn mar aon le 4 leagan eile atá meascaithe agus nach bhfeileann do thíopa amháin nó do thíopa eile thar a chéile nó gur leaganacha truaillithe iad. Maidir le dáileadh na dtíopanna ó chontae go contae agus ó chúige go cúige, is mar seo atá an cás:

---

20 An tAthair Benedict, *op.cit.*, 124.
21 *Béaloideas* 3 (1932), 234.
22 Ó Tuathail, *op.cit.*, 134–5.

Tíopa 1a: Ciarraí (8), Corcaigh (7), Port Láirge (2), An Clár (1), Gaillimh (6) agus Dún na nGall (1)

Tíopa 1b: Gaillimh (14), Maigh Eo (7), [Connacht (1)], Dún na nGall (4), An Cábhán (3)

Tíopa 2a: Corcaigh (6)

Tíopa 2b: An Clár (1), Corcaigh (1)

Tíopa 2c: Gaillimh (3), Lú (1), Tír Eoghain (1), Dún na nGall (1)

Ilchineálach (4)

Níl d'áiméar agam anseo mionchuntas a thabhairt ar na tíopanna seo frí chéile ach ní miste na pointí seo a leanas a lua go hachomair. Leagann *Tíopa 1a* béim ar chosaint an tí ('Muire i dhá cheann an tighe/Agus Brighid ina lár') agus leagann *Tíopa 1b* béim ar thimpeallú agus ar shrianadh na tine ('Bríd ina bun/Agus Muire ina barr'). Déanann 51 de na 54 leaganacha faoi *Thíopa 1a* agus faoi *Thíopa 1b* 'Bríd' a lua go sonrach sa dá chomhthéacs áirithe seo. Is ar chosaint an tí, más ea, seachas ar shrianadh na tine a dhírítear aird i bformhór na leaganacha Muimhneacha agus i gcuid mhaith de na leaganacha Gaillimheacha: d'fhéadfaí a rá, ar ndóigh, gur ionann an cás é slánú an tí agus smachtú na tine i ndeireadh na dála. Rud eile de, is í an fhoclaíocht '. . . mar a choiglíonn Críost cách' (seachas '. . . mar a choiglíonn Críost') is fearr leis na leaganacha Muimhneacha de *Thíopa 1a* a úsáid agus is amhlaidh gur mar sin atá i gcás an chuid is mó de na leaganacha Gaillimheacha de *Thíopaí 1a* agus *1b*. Ní hamhlaidh atá sa sampla de *Thíopa 1b* thuas agus ní hamhlaidh atá in aon leagan eile de *Thíopa 1b* seachas na leaganacha Gaillimheacha úd.[23]

Iarrann leaganacha *Thíopaí 2a* agus *2b* cosaint na tine ('Nár spiúnaig aon namhaid í!') agus cosaint an tí ('Nár dhóightear ár dtig') agus an líon tí ('A's nár mharbhuightear ár bhfir') agus níl de dhifríocht eatarthu dáiríribh ach an bealach rúndiamhrach ina ndéantar an achainí dheiridh acu sin — 'Da bhfuil ann istigh, da bhfuil as amuh!' (*Tíopa 2b*) — a lorg. Paidir Mhuimhneach amach is amach í idir *Thíopa 2a* agus *Thíopa 2b* nach raibh fáil ró-fhairsing uirthi.

---

[23] 'Críost *cáidh*' atá ag Eoin Mac Néill sa leagan a bhailigh sé in Inis Meáin (féach Nóta 2 thuas) agus leanann Ó Súilleabháin go dílis é (féach Nóta 2 thuas). Tá 'Críost *cáthach*' ag Ó Fotharta (*op.cit.*, 139), 'Críost *lách*' ag Hyde (*op.cit.*, 50) agus 'i n-ainm Chríost *lághaigh*' i leagan 'Conallach' amháin (*Béaloideas* 6 [1936], 50, leagan a bhfuil drochamhras áirid orm faoi); tá 'Críost *cách*' ag Áine Ní Dhíoraí, sa leagan atá aici in *Na Cruacha. Scéalta agus Seanchas*, Baile Átha Cliath 1985, 184, leagan neamh-Chonallach eile, dar liom.

As contae Chorcaigh na leaganacha de *Thíopa 2a* ar fad (sé cinn acu) agus is as contae an Chláir agus contae Chorcaigh araon an dá leagan de *Thíopa 2b* atá againn. De réir cosúlachta, níl fáil ar an dá thíopa seo i gCiarraí nó i bPort Láirge, dhá chontae ina bhfuil *Tíopa 1a* in uachtar. I gCorcaigh, déantar faoi thrí *Tíopa 1a* agus *Tíopa 2a* a cheangal le chéile in aon phaidir amháin agus spéisiúil go leor, sa dá leagan mar seo atá againn ó Bhaile Mhac Óda, is é 'Paidir an Tromluí' a bhaistear uirthi mar phaidir sa dá chás. Luann seacht gcinn de na naoi leaganacha den dá thíopa seo 'Pádraig'; ní luaitear 'Bríd' maith nó olc in aon cheann acu.

Tá na leaganacha de *Thíopa 2c* mórán ar aon dul le *Tíopa 2a* agus le *Tíopa 2b* ach amháin an mhír dhúfhoclach rí-spéisiúil seo a leanas:

'*A loch an áidh, a' gcluin tú sin air an loch nach luígheanns ceo?*' (as leagan Thír Eoghain thuas).[24] '*Ocht n-each faoi 'n teach againn a's teach a luigheann ceó air*' atá sa leagan Gaillimheach atá ag Dubhghlas de hÍde[25] agus '*Teach neamhdha an teach seo, teach ná luíonn ceo air*' atá i leagan Gaillimheach eile;[26] '*Teach geal an teach seo níos gile ná an ceo*' atá sa leagan atá againn ó na Cruacha i nDún na nGall[27] agus is *Lucht na n-aingeal [nó 'Loit naomhtha'] fa'n toigh seo lucht nach luigheann orra féur no fód*' atá ag An Athair Lorcán Ó Muireadhaigh ó Óméith.[28] 'Pádraig' amháin a luaitear i dtrí cinn acu seo, 'Bríd is Pádraig' a luaitear i gceann acu agus luaitear 'Muire mháthair' i gceann eile acu.

'Mar is soiléir as na téaxanna, cumhdach tighe a iarrann an phaidir seo' a mhaíonn an tAthair de Hindeberg agus is ea go deimhin. Ach is léir ón réamh-scrúdú seo ar an ábhar seo go bhfuil go lánchinnte tuilleadh mór eile ann, an té a thuigfeadh é!

24 Ó Tuathail, *op.cit.* 'The meaning of the third line is obscure. *Loch an áidh* was translated "lake of luck" ' (*op.cit.*, 186).
25 Hyde, *op.cit.*, 48 (nóta).
26 CBÉ 72: 161. An Lochán Beag, Indreabhán.
27 CBÉ 104:93. Maighréad Ní Ghiobúin ó Mhaighréad Ní Ghallchobhair, Mín na Sróna, Na Cruacha 1934.
28 L. Murray, 'Omeath', *Journal of the Louth Archaeological Society* III, No. 3 (1914), 227.

Bréagfhoirmeacha, *tét* agus *tét cliss*, i *dTochmharc Eimhire*

Tomás Ó Concheanainn

DEILGNE, CO. CHILL MHANTÁIN

1. **tét /*téit*

Is éard atá i dTochmharc Eimhire scéal grá Chú Chulainn agus Eimhire, maille le tuairisc ar an oiliúint a fuair Cú Chulainn ar ghrádha gaisce faoi bhanghaiscíoch arbh ainm di Scáthach. Is ceann de réamhscéalta na Tána é agus is i dtéacsanna Meán-Ghaeilge faoin teideal *Tochmarc Emire* (TE) a tháinig sé anuas chugainn. Tá trí théacs iomlána den scéal caomhnaithe sna trí lámhscríbhinn seo: Royal Irish Academy (RIA), D iv 2 (D feasta);[1] RIA, 23 N 10 (N feasta);[2] British Library, Harley 5280 (Hl feasta).[3] Is é an leagan céanna atá iontu sin agus atá sa lámhscríbhinn stairiúil ar a dtugtar Leabhar na hUidhre (LU), ach go bhfuil cuid mhór de théacs na lámhscríbhinne seo caillte i dhá bhearna inmheánacha.[4] Tá leagan eile, atá curtha i stíl choimrithe, ach nach maireann ach an dara leath de, ar

1 Féach *Catalogue of Irish Manuscripts in the Royal Irish Academy* (Baile Átha Cliath (BÁC) 1926–70), uimh. 1223.
2 Féach R. I. Best, *Facsimiles in Collotype of Irish Manuscripts VI: MS. 23 N 10 (formerly Betham 145) in the Library of the Royal Irish Academy* (BÁC 1954); féach freisin *RIA Cat.*, uimh. 967.
3 Féach Robin Flower, *Catalogue of Irish Manuscripts in the British Library [formerly British Museum]*, II (Londain 1926; athchló 1992), 298–323.
4 Féach R. I. Best agus Osborn Bergin (eag.) *Lebor na hUidre: The Book of Dun Cow* (BÁC 1929; an tríú hathchló, le roinnt ceartuithe, 1992), lgh 307–19.

caomhnadh in Oxford. Bodleian Library, Rawlinson B 512 (R feasta).[5]

San alt seo ní bhactar le scaoileadh na nod a thaispeáint sna sleachta as na téacsanna sin, ach i gcúpla áit a bhfuil difríocht chinnte idir na lámhscríbhinní.

In D, N, agus Hl tá na foirmeacha *tet* agus *teit* tugtha mar ainmfhocail neamhcháilithe (TE §§75, 77) agus freisin san fhrása *tet* (*teit*) *cliss* (§§75, 76). Chomh maith le *tet*/*teit*, tá againn freisin in Hl: *ted* (§75), *tetd* agus *teid* (§77).[6] Mheasfaí ar an gcéad amharc gur 'téad, rópa' is brí le *tet* 7rl sa scéal seo, ach tá a fhios againn anois nach bhfuil sna foirmeacha sin ach litriú iomraill ar *tsét* 7rl, is é sin, foirmeacha 'foghraíochta' an fhocail *sét* 'casán' sa tabharthach i gcuideachta an ailt faoi réir réamhfhocail; mar shampla, is as *forsin tséit* 'ar an gcasán' a tháinig an fhoirm *forsin tét* (*téit*).[7] Bhí an fhoirm chaolaithe *séit* le fáil freisin sa tabharthach sa tseanteanga.[8]

Ba é Kuno Meyer a mhínigh an scéal seo ar dtús, gur litriú iomraill ar *tsét* 7rl atá sna foirmeacha *tét* 7rl i dTochmharc Eimhire, nuair a chuir sé eagar ar théacs R. Ach cheana féin bhí leide tugtha aige faoi sin san aistriúchán a chuir sé ar an leagan iomlán den scéal san *Archaeological Review*, agus gur aistrigh sé *tet* 7rl mar 'path' agus 'road'.[9] Is casán thar ghleann aistreánach a bhí le trasnú ag Cú Chulainn atá sa *sét* (*sed* Hl §67). Is as an dá théacs, LU (bearnach) agus Hl, a bhain Meyer leas le haghaidh an aistriúcháin sin san *Arch. Rev.*; agus is é an t-aistriúchán sin, le beagán leasuithe stíle air, atá tugtha ag Cross agus Slover.[10]

De bhrí gur *tet* 7rl atá le fáil in D agus R, ar ón gcúigiú haois déag iad, agus in N agus Hl ón séú haois déag, is léir gur *tét* (*téit*) a bhí curtha síos mar litriú ar *tsét* (*tséit*) i seantéacs éigin de Thochmharc Eimhire. Tharlódh sé gur i gcuid

5 Kuno Meyer, 'The oldest version of Tochmarc Emire', *Revue Celtique* 11 (1890) 433–57; tagairtí agam anseo do línte an téacsa sin mar atá tugtha ag Meyer. I dtaobh na lámhscríbhinne a bhfuil an téacs seo inti féach R. I. Best, 'Notes on Rawlinson B. 512', *Zeitschrift für celtische Philologie* 17 (1928), 389–402.
6 Níl an síneadh fada (gan bacadh leis an stríoc a bhíonn os cionn *i*) le fáil sna lámhscríbhinní i gceann ar bith de na ceithre théacs D, Hl, N agus R.
7 Go stairiúil is le deireadh an ailt a bhaineann *t-* san fhoirm seo *t[s]ét*/ *t[s]éit*. Tá an teagasc a bhaineann le *t-* roimh *sh-* sa chineál seo forbartha curtha síos go hachomair in *Stair na Gaeilge*, eag. K. McCone *et al.* (Maigh Nuad 1994) 360 (An Ghaeilge Chlasaiceach), 605 (Gaeilge Chonnacht).
8 Tá fianaise ar an bhfoirm sin sa tuiseal tabharthach le fáil in aon ionad amháin i ngluaiseanna Würzburg, *dind seit* [= *dint séit*, Wb. 24ᵃ17; cf. *Dictionary of the Irish Language* (RIA 1913–76; luaite mar *DIL* feasta) S 200 s.v. I *sét*.
9 K. Meyer, 'The wooing of Emer', *The Archaeological Review* I (1888), 68 seq.
10 Tom Peete Cross agus Clark Harris Slover (eag.), *Ancient Irish Tales* (Londain 1937; athchló BÁC 1969) 153–71.

atá caillte anois den mhéid a bhreac an scríobhaí úd 'H' ('An tIdirshliochtaí') de théacs LU a bhí an litriú *tét* (*téit*) tugtha sa scéal seo ar dtús.

2. THURNEYSEN AG DUL AMÚ AR AN BHFOIRM *tét* (*téit*)

Sa chuimriú atá déanta ag Thurneysen ar Thochmharc Eimhire in *Heldensage* is *Seil* ('téad, rópa') a thugann sé mar aistriú ar *tet* (*teit*) gach áit dá bhfuil an tagairt sin aige, mar shampla, i dtaobh an chonair thar an ngleann gáifeach a bhí le trasnú ag Cú Chulainn ar a bhealach chuig dún Scáthaí mar a d'inis óganach áirithe (Eochu Boirche) dó:

> Weiter sagt er ihm, er werde zu einer grossen Schlucht kommen, über die nur ein dünnes Seil führe; das sei der Weg zu Scāthach.[11]

Seo tús an radhairc scáfair a bhí roimh Chú Chulainn amach:

(i) Sa leagan iomlán [§65]

Asbert int oclaech friss beos bai glenn mor ara chind 7 oenteit coel tairis . . . (D 77(83)ra14)[12]

Aspert in t-oclach fris ueos. Bai glend mar ara chinn 7 aenteit cail tairis . . . (N 124.22)

Aspert an t-oclaech fris iarum bai gleunn maur ar a cinn 7 æntet coel ar a cinn tairiss . . . (Hl §65)[13]

Seo mar a aistríonn Meyer an giota sin:

> The youth had also told him there was a large glen before him, and a single narrow path through it . . .[14]

(ii) I leagan R

Oentet atá in R 57, ach go ndéanann Meyer coigeartú ar an bhfoirm sin:

11 Rudolf Thurneysen, *Die irische Helden- und Königsage bis zum siebzehnten Jahrhundert* (Halle 1921) 389; cf. 391 (*ter*).
12 'Tochmarc Emire' in eagar i bhfoirm ársaithe ag A. G. van Hamel, *Compert Con Culainn and Other Stories* (BÁC 1933) 16–68.
13 Téacs Hl curtha in eagar ag K. Meyer, 'Tochmarc Emire la Coinculaind', *Zeitschrift für celtische Philologie 3* (1900), 229–63. Leanaim an téacs seo mar atá sé tugtha ag Meyer.
14 *Arch. Rev.* 298.

Asbert fris bui glend mar ar a chind. Oent[ṡ]et coel tairiss . . . (R 57)[15]

He told him there was a large glen before him. One narrow path across it . . .[16]

Is léir as an méid sin thuas nár thug Thurneysen, san *Heldensage,* aon aird ar an leasú téacsach a rinne Meyer in R, ná ar an aistriúchán atá tugtha aige ina eagrán den téacs sin, ná fós ar an aistriúchán ar an téacs iomlán a d'fhoilsigh sé san *Arch. Rev.* D'fhéadfadh sé gur thuig scríobhaithe go mba 'casán' ba bhrí leis an bhfoirm nua seo, *tét/téit* (go neamhspleách ar *sét*); ach ní féidir glacadh le *teit* in *oenteit* 7rl sna sleachta sin thuas mar fhianaise air sin.[17]

Níl sé éasca a dhéanamh amach ar samhlaíodh freisin do scríobhaithe deireanacha Thochmharc Eimhire gur téad chrochta, ag ríochan thar an ngleann aistreánach úd, a bhí sa *tét/téit,* mar go measfaí go mbeadh siúl ar théad thar an ngleann sin ina chonstaic mhór d'aon dream a bheadh ag triall ionsaí ar dhún Scáthaí (§65).[18]

3. AN FHOIRM *sét*

Níl ach aon chás amháin sa scéal, idir an téacs iomlán (D, N, Hl) agus an téacs neamhiomlán de leagan R, a bhfuil an fhoirm *sét* in úsáid go soiléir ann mar fhoirm nach bhféadfadh aon mhíthuiscint a bheith fúithi, áit ar 'casán' is brí léi:

(i) Sa leagan iomlán [§67]

Luid Cú Chulainn forsin *sét* (LS .s.) sin tarsin mag ndobuil. (D (77)83ra24)

Luit Cú Chulainn forsan *sét* (LS .s.) sin tarsan magh ndobuil. (N 124.31)

Lvid Cú Chulainn didiu in sed sein darsa maug ndophail. (Hl §67)

Then Cuchulind went on that road across the plain of Ill-luck.[19]

---

15 Chuidigh an dul coitianta, séimhiú ar *s-* i ndiaidh an ailt sa tabharthach (thuas n. 7), trí analach, le séimhiú a chur ar *s-* i bhfoirmeacha mar *oent[ṡ]ét.*

16 Is é an t-aistriúchán a rinne Meyer ar R a thuctar le gach sliocht as an téacs sin.

17 Ní féidir a rá go raibh an bhrí 'casán' le baint aon uair as an bhfocal *tét/téit* go simplí (seachas *t[ṡ]ét*), mar a thuigfí, b'fhéidir, as *DIL* T 160, s.v. 3 *tét*: '(? *cf. sét*) *road, way:* tet .i. slige, RC xx 412.12 (ACC). o tharrastair . . . int en con nemcumscaighthe for in tet., YBL 165ᵃ27 (*cf.* conair, 25).'

18 Maidir le *triall* ('act of journeying') sa chiall 'act of attempting; endeavour, purpose' anseo féach *DIL* T, s.v., 304 (b); *triall indsaighi* 305. 11.

19 *Arch. Rev.* 298.

As na trí théacs iomlána is in Hl amháin atá an fhoirm cheart *set* (LS *sed*) in úsáid san áinsíoch gan an réamhfhocal *tar* roimhe (*Luid Cú Chulainn didiu in sed sein*);[20] cf. 'CūChulainn geht diesen Weg . . .', *Heldensage* 389). Is mar gheall ar gan aon réamhfhocal a bheith roimh an alt sa dul cainte seo a coinníodh foirm an áinsígh ag an bpointe céanna in D agus N, *forsin/forsan sét*, is é sin le rá nár tháinig foirm an tabhartaigh (*forsint sét > forsin tét*) chun cinn, mar atá in áiteanna eile sa téacs.

D'fhéadfadh sé gurb as na samplaí sin in Hl agus R a b'fhearr a thuig Meyer gurb é an focal *sét* atá taobh thiar de na foirmeacha **tét* 7rl sa scéal seo.

(ii) I leagan R

Luid dono in set sinnisin R 60 ('He then went that way').[21] Deimhníonn an leagan sin agus leagan Hl *sed* (= *sét*) le chéile gurb é an múnla *luid Cú Chulainn in sét sin* (agus nach *luid Cú Chulainn forsin tsét sin*) an leagan bunúsach anseo.

4. **tét (téd/téit) cliss*

Taispeánann an leagan *tét cliss* atá in áit *tét* i gcúpla áit i dTochmharc Eimhire go raibh an fhoirm *tét* daingnithe in aigne scríobhaithe an téacsa seo mar bhunfhoirm agus an chiall 'téad, rópa' léi. B'fhéidir, áfach, gurb iad na foirmeacha *oentét* 7rl (thuas, Roinn 2) ba mhó ba chúis leis an dearcadh sin.

Nuair a thagaimid go dtí an chéad tagairt eile don *sét* sa leagan iomlán den scéal, mar atá, *tét (téd/téit) cliss*, is léir go raibh radharc caillte ar bhunfhoirm an fhocail (*sét*), abair ag scríobhaí téacsa idirmheánaigh éigin ónar chin D, N, Hl, agus R. Sna ceithre shliocht seo leanas (TE §75) is í foirm an tabhartaigh atá ann, *forsin/for an/ tét/téd/téit* (*<tsét/ tséit*), cé gur gluaiseacht agus nach cónaí atá á chur in úil:

(i) Sa leagan iomlán [§75]

Lotur dano tri mic Essi Enchindi .i. Ciri 7 Biri 7 Blaicne, tri milid aili do Aife 7 forfuarsat (*sic*) comlonn for da mac Scathaige. Doloturside forsin tet clis . . . Luid didiu Cú Chulainn fria da macsi 7 nusleblaing forsin tet . . . (D 77(83)va20)

---

20 Maidir le húsáid an áinsígh sa tseanteanga i ndiaidh briathair ghluaiseachta féach *DIL* T 130, II (a) agus (b).

21 *sinnisin:* foirm threise mhírialta den fhorainm taispeántach.

Lotur dono tri mic Essi Encindi .i. Cir ⁊ Bir ⁊ Blaicne tri mili aile do Aife ⁊
forfuacarsat comlonn for da mac Scathaige. Doloturside forsin teit chlis . . . (N
12.32) Luit didiu Cú Chulainn fria da macsin ⁊ nusleblaing forsan teit . . . (N
25.2)²²

Lotar div tri mic Esse Enchinne ⁊ (*recte* .i.) Ciri ⁊ Biri ⁊ Bailcne (*sic*) tri milid
aili di Aiffe ⁊ forfvacarsad comlonn for dá mac Scatqui. Dolotar side for an ted
cliss . . . Lvid div Cuchulaind fria a da macsi ⁊ nusleublaing for an tet . . . (Hl
§75)

Then went the three sons of Esse Enchinde, viz. Cire and Bire and Blaicne, three
other warriors of Aife, and began combat against the two sons of Scathach. They
went on the path of feats . . . Then Cuchulind went up to her two sons, and
sprang on the path . . .²³

(ii) I leagan R

Seo an chuid chomhfhreagrach as R mar atá sí curtha síos agus aistrithe ag Meyer:

Luid didiu arabarach a thriur chetna ar chend tri mac Eissæ Enchende .i. Ciri ⁊
Biri ⁊ Bailcne, tri milith aili Aiffe. Focherded didiu Scathach osnaid cech lái ⁊ ni
fedeth cid nombith, co m-bo hiaram notheged-som forsan t[ŝ]ét. (R 105)

On the morrow the same three went against the three sons of Eiss Enchend, viz.
Ciri and Biri and Bailcne, three other warriors of Aiffe's. Now, Scathach would
utter a sigh every day and knew not what would come (of it). Then he would go
on the path.

Ansin tharla comhrac idir Cú Chulainn agus Aoife (§76):

Dolotur forsin tet clis Cú Chulainn ⁊ Aifi ⁊ fersat comlann fair. (D 77(83)va32)

Do lotur forsin teit chlis Cú Chulainn ⁊ Aife ⁊ fersa[t] comlann fair. (N 25.6)

Dilotur didiu for in tet cliss Cvchulaind ⁊ Aiffi ⁊ fersaid cumleng fair. (Hl §76)

Cuchulind and Aife went on the path of feats, and began combat there.²⁴

22 Tá ord na mbileoga in N mícheart anois. Ag an bpointe seo léimeann an téacs ó bhun lgh
    12 go dtí barr lgh 25.
23 *Arch. Rev.* 301. Is botún ag Meyer an ginideach 'Esse Enchinde' a choinneáil san aistriúchán
    seo (a foilsíodh in 1888), ach dhá bhliain níos déanaí ina eagrán de R (1900) tugann sé an
    dul ceart; féach faoi (ii) sa Roinn seo.
24 *Arch. Rev.* 302.

Mar atá amhlaidh i gcás an tsuímh as §65 atá luaite thuas creideann Thurneysen gur in airde ar théad rite a chuaigh Cú Chulainn agus Aoife anseo le comhrac aonair a dhéanamh:

Auf dem Seil springen Aife und CūChulainn gegeneinander an . . .[25]

Is í an chiall chéanna sin, téad rite chrochta, a bhain van Hamel as an bhfocal anseo, mar is léir as an nGluais ('Glossary') atá curtha aige leis an mbailiúchán téacsanna a bhfuil eagrán criticiúil ársaithe de Thochmharc Eimhire ina measc:

tét, téit, f., *a string, cord, rope*. Tét cliss *the rope of tricks*, the rope upon which the heroes performed their tricks.

Mar sin, ach an oiread le Thurneysen níor thug a dheisceabal van Hamel, sa téacs criticiúil atá bunaithe aigesean ar D, aon aird ar an gcoigeartú ná ar an aistriúchán a rinne Meyer ar an bhfoirm *tet* 7rl sa scéal seo.

(ii) I leagan R

Níl an leagan *tét cliss* le fáil in R, rud a thaispeáineann gur as cóip eile de Thochmharc Eimhire a rinneadh an téacs sin, is é sin, as cóip níos sine ná an sinsear idirmheánach a bhí ag D, N agus Hl:

co m-bo hiaram notheged-som forsan t[ṡ]ét. . . Fersat iarom cuimleng forsan t[ṡ]ét, Cuculaind 7 Aiffe. (R 108–15)

Then he would go on the path . . . Then they fought upon the path, Cuchulind and Aiffe.

5. AN GINIDEACH AIDIACHTACH *cliss*

Is dóigh gur chuidigh an téarma eile úd *tétchless*, ainm ceann éigin de chleasa Chú Chulainn, leis an míthuiscint ar an bhfoirm *tét cliss* a thabhairt isteach i dTochmharc Eimhire; ach ní mhíneodh sin amháin an ginideach *cliss* anseo. Tá an ginideach aidiachtach seo curtha síos le haon focal amháin eile sa téacs, an focal *cliab*. Tagraíonn seo don chliabh a raibh Scáthach ina luí ann thuas i gcrann mór iúir (*isin iburdos mór* §70) agus í ag teagasc a beirt mhac (§71):

---

25 *Heldensage* 391.

(i) Sa leagan iomlán [§71]

Luid iarom Cú Chulainn co hairm a mbaí Scáthach. Dobeir a da c[h]ois for da bord in c[h]leib c[h]lis 7 nochtais a c[h]laidem[26] 7 do berar a rinn fo c[h]omair a craide 7 atbert bás uasut ol se. (D 77(83)rb27)

Luith iarom Cú Chulainn co hairm a mbaoi Scathach. Do ber a da cois for da bord in chleib chliss 7 nochtaiss a chloidhem 7 do bretha a rinn fo comair a croide 7 atbert bás u[a]sat olse. (N 11.34)

Lvid ierum *Cuchulaind* co hairmb i mboi Scatoig. Dobir a di coiss for da mbordaib in clep cliss 7 nochtaiss in cloideb 7 dobretha a rinn fo comair a cride 7 ispert bas hvassut ol se. (Hl §71)

Then Cu Chulainn went to the place where Scathach was. He placed his two feet on the two edges of the basket of the *cless*, and bared his sword, and put its point to her heart, saying, 'Death over thee!', said he.[27]

Ní bheadh aon chiall lena shamhlú gurb é ucht (cliabh nó cliabhrach) Scáthaí is brí le *cliab cliss* anseo, mar a chreid Thurneysen:

Als Scāthach in einer Eibe auf dem Rücken liegend ihre zwei Söhne Cuar und Cat lehrt, springt er ihr auf die Brust und zückt das Schwert gegen sie.[28]

Fágann seo fós sa dorchadas sinn faoi bhrí an ghinidigh aidiachta in *cliab cliss*. Is léir gur cliabh nó cliabhán a b'fhéidir a ardú suas san aer atá i gceist. Tá an *cliab cliss* a bhí ag Scáthach luaite freisin i bhFoghlaim Chú Chulainn (*Foghlaim Con Culainn*), scéal a bhfuil gaol ó thaobh ábhair aige le cuid de Thochmharc Eimhire: *is amhlaidh théid Sgáthach d'agallmha na ndee 7 clíabh clis fuithe* ('Tis thus that Scáthach goes to have speech with the gods, with a feat-basket beneath her').[29] Chuirfeadh sin in úil, measaim, gur cliabh draíochta a bhí ann, mar a thugtar le fios sa míniú coinníollach 'magic (?)' atá curtha síos, s.v. *cles*, in *DIL* C 231.72, leis an tagairt sin.

26 'a chl*aideb* ém' atá ag van Hamel anseo. Cé gur bhain mí-thapa éigin de scríobhaí an téacsa (D) is léir gur mar 'a chl*aidem*' is cóir an méid sin a chur síos.
27 *Arch. Rev.* 300.
28 *Heldensage* 390.
29 Whitley Stokes (eag.), 'The training of Cúchulainn', *Revue Celtique* 29 (1908) 111–52 (132). Tá an sliocht seo luaite s.v. *cles* in *DIL* C 231.71–2, agus míniú coinníollach' 'magic (?)', tugtha ar *clis* ansin. Tá eagrán nua den téacs seo, *Oileamain* (nó *Foglaim*) *Con Culainn*, á réiteach ag an Ollamh Ruairí Ó hUiginn.

6. TÉACS DIOPLÓMAITIÚIL

Is in §77 den leagan iomlán de Thochmharc Eimhire agus sa chuid atá ag freagairt dó in R 133–7 is soiléire atá sé le tuiscint gur [. . .] *tšét* /*tšéit* 'casán' (a bhfuil cuid de ag imeacht ar bharr aille ar bhruach na farraige) agus nach 'téad, rópa' a bhí i gceist sa scéal seo ar dtús. Tá sé le tabhairt faoi deara, áfach, nár chuir Meyer an coigeartú *t[š]et* (*t[š]eit*) i bhfeidhm san eagar a chuir sé ar théacs Hl (thuas, n. 14) ós téacs dioplómaitiúil a bhí sé a chur ar fáil ansin; sin nó ghlac sé le *tét* (*téit*) mar fhoirm dhleathach a chiallaigh 'casán'.

(i) Sa leagan iomlán [§77]

Atonintai iarsin Cú Chulainn aitherruch coa muintir fesin ⁊ is ed tainic forsin teit chetna. Co foirnic sentuinn tuathcaeich forsin teit. Atbertsi frisium ar forchaine arna beth fora cind forsin teit. Atbertsom nach boi ocai leth do coised acht isind alt mara boi foi. Atchisi fris in conair do lecen di. Do leicsium dano don teit acht giuil a ladar airi nama. A ndo-luidsi uasa fornessa a ordain do chor don teit dia chor fon alt. (D 77(83)vb6)

Atonintai iar sin Cú Chulainn aitherrach coa muintir feisin ⁊ is ed forsin teit *cétnai* co foirnic sentuinn tuathcaeich forsin teit. Atbertsi frisium ar fercaire ⟨arná⟩ beth fora cinn forsin teit. Atbertsom frissium ar forcaine ⟨arna⟩ beith for a cinn forsin teit. Atbertsom nach boi occai leth do coised acht isint alt mara boi fai. Atchisi fris in conair do lecan di. Do lecsium don teit acht giuil a ladar aire nama. A ndo luitsi uassa fornessa a ordain do cur do teit dia cor fon alt. (N 25.22)

Ataninntai Cvcvlainn coa muindtir n-iarum fessne ⁊ issed tanic for an tét *cétnoi*. Co farnoic sentvinn tuathcæich for a cinn for an teid. Atbertsom frissom ara forchaine ar na beth for a cinn iersan teid. Aspertsom nad mbvi occo conar diroisevd acht fon ald mor[a] roboí foi. Aidchisi fris an conair do legivd ndii. Dolec seum din tet acht giuil a ladair aire namaa. A ndolvid si vassae fornessæ a ordain di cor den tetd dia chor foan ald. (Hl §77)

Thereupon Cuchulind returned back again to his own people, and came along the same road. He met an old woman on the road who was blind of her left eye. She asked him to beware and not be on the road before her. He said there was no room for a footing for him, save on the cliff of the sea which was beneath him. She besought him to leave the road to her. Then he left the road, except that his toes clung to it. When she passed over him she hit his great toe to throw him off the path down the cliff.[30]

30 *Arch. Rev.* 302.

Seo mar a thugann Thurneysen tuairisc ar an eachtra sin:

> Als er von Aife heimkehrt und sich auf dem Seil befindet, kommt von der andern Seite ein altes, links blindes Weib und bittet ihn auszuweichen. Da das unmöglich ist, lässt er sich vom Seil nieder und hält sich nur mit der Gabel (seiner Zehen) daran fest.[31]

(ii) I leagan R

Seo mar leanas atá an chuid chomhfhreagrach as R curtha in eagar agus aistrithe ag Meyer:

> Atonintoi iarom. Teit aitherrach. Tofornic sentainde caich tuathchaich ar a chind forsint [ṡ]et. Asbert fris ar ferchaire arna beith ar a chind. Nacha boi dochoissed isintd all moro. Tolleic sis dint [ṡ]et 7 giuil a ladair aire namma. A n-doluid si hvaise, fornessa a orddain arancorath foan alla. (R 133)

> He then returned. He went back again. On the path before him he met an old blind woman, blind of her left eye. She said to him to beware and not be in her way. There was no footing on the cliff of the sea. He let himself down from the path, and only his toes clung to it. When she passed over them she hit his great toe to throw him down the cliff.

Ó nach bhfuil an leagan *tét cliss* le fáil in R (gan ann ach an focal neamhcháilithe *tét*) is léir gur scríobhaí téacsa éigin a bhí idir LU (an bhunfhoinse) agus sinsear coitianta na dtéacsanna deireanacha (D, N agus Hl) a chuir an téarma *tét cliss* isteach mar gur bhain sé an chiall 'téad, rópa' as *tét* (< *tṡét*) sa chás áirithe seo.

7. AN tSEANFHOIRM DHLEATHACH ÚD *tétchless*

(i) I dTáin Bó Cuailnge

Ní fios céard a bhí ar intinn ag údair na Rúraíochta leis an tseanfhoirm úd *tétchless*, ceann de na cleasa gaiscidh a bhí ag Cú Chulainn agus atá ráite i dTochmharc Eimhire a d'fhoghlaim sé ó Scáthach. Tá an *tétchless* ar na cleasa gaiscidh atá Cú Chulainn a chleachtadh roimh eachtra áirithe le linn Tháin Bó Cuailnge. Seo tús na tuairisce sin mar atá sé i dtéacs Leabhar na hUidhre den Táin:

---

31 *Heldensage* 391–2.

LU 5969–74

In t-ubullchless 7 faeborcless 7 fáencless 7 cless cletenach 7 tétcless 7 corpchless 7 cless caitt 7 ích n-erred 7 cor ndeled . . .

The ball-feat, the blade-feat, the feat with horizontally-held shield, the javelin-feat, the rope-feat, the feat with the body, the cat-feat, the hero's salmon-leap, the cast of a wand . . . [32]

(ii) Iasacht as an Táin i dTochmharc Eimhire

Is léir gur as an tuairisc sin ar na cleasa a tháinig an leagan atá tugtha (go bearnach anois) i ndeireadh Thochmharc Eimhire in LU:

LU 10340–5

‹. . .› cles ‹. . .› erred 7 cor ndeled ‹. . .›

Is gcuid a bhreac scríobhaí H (agus atá ar iarraidh anois) a bhí an mhír sin ar fad tugtha in LU. Seo mar atá an tuairisc ar chleasa Chú Chulainn curtha síos sa chéad lámhscríbhhinn thuasluaite (D iv 2) den téacs iomlán:

[§78] uballcless 7 toranncless 7 foebarcless 7 foencless 7 cless cleitinech 7 tetcless 7 corpcless 7 cless cait 7 ich n-erred 7 cor ndeled . . . . (D 77(83)vb22–4)

Maidir leis an *tétchless* thuasluaite mheabhraigh an Dr John Carey dom go bhfuil tagairt do chleasa a dhéanadh na gaiscígh in airde ar théada sa Chraobhruaidh in Eamhain Mhacha le fáil i dtosach Thochmharc Eimhire (§4):

No clistís errid Ulod for súanemnaib tarsnu on dorus diarailiu isin tig i nEmain, *LU* 10138–9.

The warriors (*lit.* chariot-fighters) of Ulster performed on ropes stretched across from door to door in the house at Emain.

Dála an scríobhaí aineoil sa mheánaois a chum an fhoirm *tét cliss* i dTochmharc Eimhire tháinig van Hamel faoi anáil na foirme dleathaí *tétchless* nuair a mhínigh sé (mar a luadh thuas) *tét cliss* mar seo: 'the rope of tricks, the rope upon which the heroes performed their tricks'.[33]

---

32 Cecile O'Rahilly, *Táin Bó Cúailgne: Recension I* (1976) 173.
33 Tá mo buíochas ag dul freisin do Ruairí Ó hUiginn faoi dhréacht den alt seo a léamh agus roinnt leasuithe a mholadh dhom.

An Greann i Saothar An Athar Peadar Ua Laoghaire

Brian Ó Cuív

INSTITIÚID ARD-LÉINN BHAILE ÁTHA CLIATH

Is DÓCHA ná raibh scríbhneóir Gaeilge riamh ba thorthúla i mbun pinn ná an tAthair Peadar Ua Laoghaire. Ní beag mar chruthúnas ar an méid sin an clár-liosta don chuid sin dá shaothar a cuireadh i gcló atá mar 'Supplement' le *Celtica* 2 (1952–54). Agus cuínímís go bhfuil saothair eile a dhin sé nár foillsíodh riamh, mar shompla an t-aistriú a dhin sé ar an SeanTiomna idir 1913 agus 1916.[1] Ní hamháin gur rug sé an chraobh leis ar a thorthúlacht, ach chomh maith san ar ilghnéitheacht na nithe a scríobh sé.

Daoine go raibh aithne mhaith acu ar an Athair Peadar do bhraitheadar go raibh féith an ghrinn go láidir ann. Cuirim i gcás sa réamhrá ó pheann Torna atá sa leabhar *An tAthair Peadar Ó Laoghaire agus a Shaothar* a scríobh an tSiúr M. Uinseann fén ainm chleite 'Maol Muire' agus a foillsíodh sa bhliain 1939 tá an méid seo:

---

1 Féach B. Ó Cuív, 'An t-Athair Peadar Ua Laoghaire's translation of the Old Testament', ZCP 49/50, 643–52.

Fear sultmhar ab eadh é. Ba ghnáth leis bheith go hoscailte ina mheon agus gealgháiriteach i gcuideachtain, go mór mór nuair a bheadh cuideachta le Gaedhilg timcheall air. Do bhí féith láidir den ghreann ann, féith nádúrtha gan aonphioc den cheilg ná den olc ann. Dá bhrígh sin ba thaitneamhach ar fad an chuideachta é. Níorbh annamh an tinneas ar chuid againn ón gháire ag éisteacht leis. Tabharfar fé ndeara an tréith chéadna 'na scríbhinní.

In ainneoin na tuairisce sin ag Torna ní foláir a rá go raibh taobh eile ag an Athair Peadar, taobh ná raibh chomh suáilceach san, isé sin go bhféadfadh sé bheith suarach neamaiteach ar uairibh. Tá an tréith sin ann léirithe go maith ag an Athair Shán Ó Cuív san aiste 'Caradas nár Mhair: Peadar Ua Laoghaire agus Eóin Mac Néill' a cuireadh i gcló sa leabhar *The Scholar Revolutionary* (Shannon 1973). Ach fágaimís an taobh dorcha san i leataoibh, mar is ar thaobh an ghrinn atá an aiste seo agam dírithe.

Uaireanta chímid i saothar an Athar Peadair greann atá díreach neamhchasta. Is mar sin, is dóigh liom, atá sé i mórchuid desna scéalta beaga atá i gcló in *Ag Séideadh agus ag Ithe* agus *Ár nDóthain Araon*. Ach uaireanta eile tuigimíd go bhfuil tuairim fé leith á léiriú aige fé scáth an ghrinn. Sompla de seo a ritheann liom tá sé sa chaibidil ar 'Éagcóir agus díoghaltas agus smachtdlighthe' (Caibidil XXV) i *Mo Sgéal Féin* ina bhfuil cur síos aige ar an slí a cheap sé chun airgead a dhéanamh suas dos na fearaibh a bhí sa phríosún sa Ráth mar gheall ar sheasamh leis an Land League. Sid í an tuairisc atá aige.

Shocaruigheas ar shaghas *raffle* a dhéanamh, agus sidiad na duaiseana a bhí ar thicéad an *raffle*.

'A splendid Bengal tiger called "Resources of Civilisation." Warranted sound in wind and limb.'

'A huge African elephant called "Passive Resistance." '

'An Egyptian mummy called "Rackrent", said to be as old as the days of Moses.'

'A magnificent puck goat called "Peel", alias "Fix Bayonets".'

'With many other highly interesting and valuable prizes.'

Do díoladh na ticéadaí go tiugh. Chonaic an sagart paróiste ceann acu. Bhí sé ar buile. Tháinig sé chúgham agus ticéad acu 'n-a láimh aige.

'Is tusa chuir amach iad so, a Athair,' ar seisean.

'Is mé gan amhras,' arsa mise, 'ná feicean tú m'ainim thíos ortha?'

'Agus cad chuige iad?' ar seisean.

'Chun airgid a dhéanamh,' arsa mise.

'Agus cad chuige an t-airgead?' ar seisean.

'Neósfad-sa san duit go cruinn,' arsa mise, 'ó chuiris an cheist chúgham. Chun é chur ag triall ar na fearaibh ó'n sráid seo atá istigh sa phríosún ag *Buckshot*.'

Bhí fearg i nglór gach duine againn an fhaid a bhíomair ag caint.

Níor bh'fhada 'n-a dhiaigh san gur chuir an t-Easbog mise soir go Cill Úird i n-inead an tsagairt paróiste a bhí ann, mar bhí an duine bocht ró chríona agus bhí ag dul d'á chiall, agus ní raibh sé oireamhnach chun na h-oibre.

Tamall gairid ó shin agus mé ag dul trí shaothar i bhfoirm láimhscríbhinne ó pheann an Athar Peadair a tharla bheith im sheilbh thánag ar an eachtra atá á chur i láthair agam anso. Is dóigh liom gur maith an tsolaoid é ar ghreann an tsagairt ina bhfuil iarracht den íoróin. Tá beagán caighdeánaithe déanta agam ar an litriú atá sa láimhscríbhinn.

Glaoidh chúm amáireach

Bhí duine breóite i dtigh i Maghchromtha fiche éigin blian ó shin. Bhí sé ag dul in olcas. Do cuireadh fios ar an ndochtúir agus ar an sagart. Do chuir an sagart an olla air. Ansan tháinig an dochtúir i bhfianaise na leapan agus do rug sé ar chuislinn ar an nduine breóite. Do bhreithnigh sé an chuisle.

'Humhth', ar seisean. 'Cuir amach do theanga', ar seisean.

Do chuir an duine breóite a theanga amach agus isí a bhí go breá bog leathan agus screamh dorcha uirthi chomh ramhar, ba dhóich leat, le bonn do bhróige.

'Humhth', ars an dochtúir nuair a chonnaic sé an teanga agus an screamh a bhí uirthi.

Bhí an bhean fhriotháilte 'na seasamh ag cosaibh na leapan.

'Cad é an deoch is ceart a thabhairt dó, a dhochtúir?' ars an bhean fhriotháilte.

'Cad é an deoch atá agat á thabhairt dó?' ars an dochtúir.

'Tá meadhg dhá bhainne agam á thabhairt dó, a dhochtúir', ars an bhean fhriotháilte.

'Meadhg dhá bhainne!' ars an dochtúir, 'á chur 'on ghorta ataoin tú!' ar seisean.

'B'fhéidir gur mhaith an rud braon fíona 'thabhairt dó, a dhochtúir', ars an bhean fhriotháilte.

'Braon fíona!' ars an dochtúir. 'A bhean', ar seisean, 'bheadh sé chomh maith agat nimh a thabhairt dó agus é 'chur as an saol gan a thuille rínis!'

'B'fhéidir, a dhochtúir', ars an bhean fhriotháilte, 'gur mhaith an rud breac-bhainne 'thabhairt dó.'

'Breac-bhainne!' ars an dochtúir. 'Ar airigh aoinne riamh a leithéid! Breac-bhainne do dhuine chomh lag!'

'Tá fuiscí maith le fáil sa tsráid seo, a dhochtúir. B'fhéidir gur mhaith an rud braon biotáil 'thabhairt dó, braon fónta', ars an bhean fhriotháilte.

'Ochón!' ars an dochtúir. 'Ná fuil eólas ar do ghnó agat ach mar sin?'

'Agus cad a thabharfaidh mé dhó?' ars an bhean fhriotháilte, agus fearg ag teacht uirthi.

Do stad an dochtúir agus dhin sé a mhachtnamh, machtnamh fada rín, agus chuir sé 'Humhth' as anois agus airís. Fé dheire do labhair sé. 'Glaoidh chúm amáireach', ar seisean, agus d'imigh sé.

Nuair a bhí sé amuich ar an sráid do bhuail garsún uime, garsún a bhí ag foghlaim Laidne i scoil Laidne a bhí sa tsráid.

'A dhochtúir', arsan garsún. 'Táim ceapaithe ar Ghaelainn a dh'fhoghluim. Tá Gaelainn mhaith agatsa agus táim á chuíneamh le tamall gur tú is fearr fhéadfadh a dh'insint dom cá bhfuil an Ghaelainn is fearr le fáil. Dá dtugainn fé í a dh'fhoghlaim ba mhaith liom an saghas is fearr di a dh'fhoghlaim. An gcomhairleófá dhom Gaelainn na Mumhan a dh'fhoghlaim, ó sí is cóngaraí?'

'Faire, faire! a mhic ó', arsan dochtúir, 'ná din a leithéid. Gaelainn na Mumhan! Airiú níl inti sin ar fad ach drabhaíol! Ní caint cheart in aonchor í, gan trácht ar Ghaelainn cheart, Féach ar an abairt seo: "an fear a mhairbh Seán." Ca bhfios d'aoinne ón abairt sin cibé 'cu do maraíodh, Seán nu an fear? Caint liobarnach neamhchruinn isea Gaelainn na Mumhan. Ná bí ag cáilliúint aimsire lé.'

'Agus, ar nóin, a dhochtúir', arsan garsún, 'dá mb'é an fear a bheadh marbh cad é an bac a bheadh orm a rá "an fear gur mhairbh Seán é", nú dá mb'é Seán a bheadh marbh d'fhéadfainn a rá "an fear a dhin marú ar Sheán" nú "an fear a dhin marú Sheáin".'

'Mar sin féin', arsan dochtúir, 'ní fhicimse aon tslacht ar na habairtibh sin. Dá mbeinn ad chás ní bheinn am bodhradh féin le Gaelainn na Mumhan.'

'Is dócha, a dhochtúir, go bhfuil sé chomh maith agam aghaidh a thabhairt ar Ghaelainn Chúige Connacht má sea', arsan garsún.

'Ná din in aonchor', arsan dochtúir. 'Sin í Gaelainn is gráinne dhíobh go léir; "coisméic" a thugaid siad ar "chiscéim", agus "sturabúta" a thugaid siad ar an leitin! "Sturabúta" a thugaimse ar an saghas Gaelainne atá acu ansúd thiar.'

'Más mar sin é, a dhochtúir', arsan garsún, 'is dócha go gcaithfead aghaidh a thabhairt ó thuaidh ar Chúige Uladh.'

'Ach, a mhic ó', arsan dochtúir, 'ní bheadh ansan duit ach dul ó thigh an diabhail go tigh an deamhain! Níl sa Ghaelainn atá acu san ach madaraíol cainte. B'fhearr liom bheith ag éisteacht le madairíníbh ag sceamhaíol ná bheith ag éisteacht leó ag caint.'

'Agus, a dhochtúir, ní dócha go gcomhairleófá dom Gaelainn na Laighneach a dh'fhoghlaim', arsan garsún.

'Ní chomhairleóinn go deimhin mar níl aon Ghaelainn in aonchor acu san', arsan dochtúir.

'Agus cad a dhéanfad, a dhochtúir, nú cá bhfaghad Gaelainn le foghlaim?' arsan garsún.

'Foghlaim an Ghaelainn uasal', arsan dochtúir, 'an Ghaelainn ar a dtugtar "classical Irish". Siní an Ghaelainn is ceart duit a dh'fhoghlaim.'

'Tá go maith, a dhochtúir', arsan garsún, 'ach cá bhfuil sí sin le fáil? Tá Laidin uasal againn, "classical Latin", i leabhraibh na Laidne, agus tá Gréigis uasal againn le fáil i leabhraibh na nGréag. Ach bhí gach teanga acu san ag fás ar feadh míle blian sar ar huaislíodh í. Bhí an Laidin ag fás ar feadh breis agus míle blian san Iodáil, i mbéalaibh na nEtruscach ar dtúis, agus ansan i mbéalaibh na Rómhánach. I gcaitheamh na haimsire sin bhí sí dá meilt agus dá líomhadh, dá cíoradh agus dá slámadh, i mbéalaibh daoine, agus i leabhraibh, i ngnóthaíbh stáit agus i ngnóthaíbh comharsanachta, i ngnóthaíbh síochána agus i ngnóthaíbh cogaidh, ins gach sórd aighnis dá n-éiríodh idir chomharsanaibh nú idir phobalaibh go dtí go dtáinig Cicero agus go raibh sí ag rith 'na caise amach as a bhéal agus í go bríomhar agus go slim agus go snasta agus go huasal. Bhí an fás céanna déanta ag an nGréigis, ar an gcuma gcéanna, nuair a bhí na Gréagaigh ag éisteacht lé agus í ag teacht 'na sruth uasal a béal Dhemostenes.'

'Féach, a dhochtúir, níor uaislíodh riamh, agus ní uaisleófar choíche, aon tsaghas cainte ach ar an gcuma 'nar huaislíodh an Laidion agus an Ghréigis, 'sé sin, í bheith i mbéalaibh náisiúin ar feadh míle blian agus gnóthaí uile an náisiúin sin a bheith dá ndéanamh tríthi, agus inti, agus aisti; gan aon chaint eile dá labhairt go coitchian ag an náisiún san ach í. Ní féidir caint uasal a thabhairt ar an saol ar aon chuma eile. Dá mbeadh an Ghaelainn dá labhairt ag muintir na hÉireann, anso in Éirinn, le míle blian, agus gnóthaí stáit agus gnóthaí comharsanachta, gnóthaí cogaidh agus gnóthaí síochána, an uile shaghas gnóthaí dá mbaineann le náisiún, dá ndéanamh trí Ghaelainn agus i nGaelainn, agus as Gaelainn, bheadh Gaelainn uasal anois againn anso in Éirinn.'

'Cogar, a dhochtúir, an amhlaidh a mheasfása a chur 'na luí ormsa gur féidir, tar éis an mhíle blian atá imithe uainn gan mhaith, gur féidir d'aon fhear beo, go mór mór dá mba ná beadh aige ach beagáinín Gaelainne, suí 'na chathaoir agus an Ghaelainn a bheadh againn de thoradh an mhíle blian úd do scríobh dhúinn anois, amach as a cheann féinig! Ní raibh duine buile riamh i nGleann na nGealt a chreidfeadh a leithéid! Inis dom, a dhochtúir, cá bfuil an "classical Irish" le fáil agus foghlamód í.'

'Glaoidh chúm amáireach', arsan dochtúir, agus d'imigh sé.

Ní gá dhom a rá nach dóigh liom go n-aontódh an tAthair Peadar leis an ndochtúir i dtaobh Gaelainn na Mumhan.

Finnio and Winniau:
A Return to the Subject

Pádraig Ó Riain

NATIONAL UNIVERSITY OF IRELAND, CORK

O NLY once in his many publications, as far as I am aware, does Proinsias Mac Cana touch on the subject of St Finnian, patron among other important churches of Movilla in County Down, and of Clonard in County Meath, correspondent of Gildas and, most notably, author of one of the earliest surviving documents of the Irish Church, the *Penitentialis Vinniani*. This was in the course of an influential article on the prehistory of *Immram Brain*, where he cited Finnian's meeting with Tuán mac Cairill as another example of the basic theme found in *Imacallam Choluim Chille ocus ind Óclaig*.[1] There is, of course, nothing remarkable about this apparent lack of concern with the saint; only rarely do the traditions surrounding Finnian touch upon the themes that have attracted Professor Mac Cana's wide-ranging scholarly interests. There are, however, some questions thrown up by the saint's record that merge with lines of enquiry otherwise pursued by him, thus justifying, I would suggest, the inclusion in this volume of an article on Finnian. And not the least of these questions is the one essentially at issue here, namely the character of the relations between Ireland and south-western Britain in the defining period of Christianity in both areas, between the writings of St Patrick in the fifth century and the letters of Columbanus dating to about 600. This is a period of more than a hundred years; yet, as L. Bieler pointed out in a brief survey of the Irish sources,[2] it lacks almost

---

1 P. Mac Cana, 'On the "Prehistory" of *Immram Brain*', in *Ériu* 26 (1975) 33–52 (41).
2 L. Bieler, 'Christianity in Ireland during the Fifth and Sixth Centuries: a Survey and Evaluation of the Sources', in *The Irish Ecclesiastical Record* 101 (1964) 162–7 (162).

entirely in contemporary written evidence. Indeed, so meagre is the documentation from the period on both sides of the Irish Sea that any general conclusions concerning it necessarily turn on such details as the problem of Finnian's name and the implications this has for his ethnic background. Just as Professor Mac Cana's exploration of the background to the Mongán mac Fiachna tales allows inferences concerning literary links between Ireland and Britain above and beyond the immediate context,[3] so also the evidence bearing on Finnian's name and origins has considerable implications for the more general question of the character of the so-called Irish Sea Province in the sixth century.[4]

Since 1978, when L. Fleuriot revived a theory originally put forward by H. Bradshaw that Finnian was a Briton or even a Breton, the saint's alleged Britishness has been endorsed by several other scholars, including R. Sharpe, J. Stevenson, and W. Davies.[5] The most persistent proponent of the theory since Fleuriot, however, has been D. Dumville with two articles bearing on the subject, the second of which, recently published in a collection of essays on County Down, responds to criticism I made in 1984 and again in 1994 of both Fleuriot's and Dumville's own treatment of the evidence.[6] Far from accepting, however, that, as recently put by J. F. Eska[7], my use of the onomastic evidence turns on its head the argument that the saint was a Briton, Dumville concluded his recent article by stating that it is perverse to suppose that the saint was other than British. Since this implies for Dumville's own view the support of incontrovertible evidence, it is appropriate that the basis of his confidence in the validity of Fleuriot's theory be once more tested.

The debate to date has shown that the case for a British Finnian rests on two factors. One is the Brittonic character of the hypocoristic or pet form of his name,

3 P. Mac Cana, 'Mongán Mac Fiachna and *Immram Brain*', in *Ériu* 23 (1972) 102–42 (104–7).
4 For this term, see D. Moore, ed., *The Irish Sea Province in Archaeology and History* (Cardiff, 1970).
5 L. Fleuriot, 'Le "saint" breton Winniau et le pénitentiel dit "de Finnian"', *Études Celtiques* 15 (1976–8) 607–17; R. Sharpe, 'Gildas as a Father of the Church', in M. Lapidge, D. Dumville, ed., *Gildas: New Approaches* (Woodbridge, 1984) 191–206 (198–202); J. Stevenson, 'The Beginnings of Literacy in Ireland', in *Proceedings of the Royal Irish Academy* 89 C (1989) 127–65 (157); W. Davies, 'The Myth of the Celtic Church', in N. Edwards, A. Lane, ed. *The Early Church in Wales and the West* (Oxford, 1992) 12–21 (20),
6 D. Dumville, 'Gildas and Uinniau', in M. Lapidge, D. Dumville, ed., *Gildas: New Approaches* (Woodbridge, 1984) 207–14. Idem. 'St. Finnian of Movilla: Briton, Gael, Ghost?', in L. Proudfoot, ed., *Down: History and Society* (Dublin, 1997) 71–84. P. Ó Riain, 'Finnian or Winniau?', in P. Ní Chatháin, M. Richter, ed., *Irland und Europa: Ireland and Europe* (Stuttgart, 1984) 52–7. Idem. 'Finnio and Winniau: a Question of Priority', in R. Bielmeier, R. Stempel, ed., *Indogermanica et Caucasica* (Berlin, New York, 1994) 407–14.
7 Eska makes the comment in a review of the volume containing my 1994 article in *Studia Celtica* 30 (1996) 326.

viz., in its earliest attestations, Latin *Vennianus* (*Venneanus*), *Uinnia(u)us*, Irish *Finnio*;[8] the other, of which more later in this article, is what Sharpe has termed historical probability.[9] The Brittonic origins of the Irish form of the pet name are not in dispute; the *-io* ending, which is very rare in Irish, is based on *-iaw* (*-iau*), the regular Brittonic reflex of Celtic *-iauos.[10] Fleuriot's use of this onomastic evidence revealed, however, at least two critical weaknesses. First, he failed to advert to the existence of not one but several saints hypocoristically known as *Finnio*, which is the earliest attested Irish form of the name. Secondly, he made no attempt to address the problem created by the fact that these saints were usually also known by other, fully Irish, names, such as *Findbarr* or *Bairrfhind*.[11] To have chosen only one saint of the name, therefore — in Fleuriot's case Finnian or *Finnio* of Clonard — was not only to ignore the need to explain the fully Irish cognate names, it was also tantamount to saying that all other saints so named must likewise have originated, albeit separately, as Britons or Bretons.

Having been made aware of these difficulties with Fleuriot's arguments, Dumville directed his attention to their resolution in his 1984 article, beginning with the question of the many ostensibly distinct British saints named Finnian or *Finnio* active in Ireland in the sixth century. A solution to this problem had in fact been put forward by me in an earlier article on the cult of St Finbarr of Cork, where I had contended that all saints of the name attached to churches in Ireland and Britain were localisations of a single original cult.[12] Wherever Finnio's original church may have been, and this remains a contentious issue,[13] my view of his singular origins seems to have gained acceptance, at least from those who, since Fleuriot, have touched on the question of his identity.[14] And since Dumville also acknowledged the force of my argument, this straightway eliminated the need to address the possible existence of several distinct British saints of the name in Ireland.[15]

The second problem left unaddressed by Fleuriot, the fact that the pet form *Finnio* formed part of a thoroughly Irish series of related full and also hypocoristic names, such as *Findbarr*, *Finnu*, *Bairrfhind*, *Barrae*, has proved to be more intractable. Although failing to support his argument with other similar examples,

8 For the early attested forms, see Ó Riain, 'Finnio and Winniau', 408–9.
9 Sharpe, 'Gildas as a Father of the Church', 198.
10 R. Thurneysen, *A Grammar of Old Irish*, § 275. K. Jackson, *Language and History in Early Britain* (Edinburgh, 1953) 369.
11 P. Ó Riain, 'Finnian or Winniau?', 52.
12 P. Ó Riain, 'St. Finnbarr: A Study in a Cult', *Journal of the Cork Historical and Archaeological Society* 82 (1977) 63–82.
13 Cf. Dumville, 'St. Finnian of Movilla', 76–8.
14 Cf. Sharpe, 'Gildas as a Father of the Church', 198.
15 Dumville, 'Gildas and Uinniau', 212.

Dumville contended that the saint had acquired the fully Irish additional names by a process of assimilation to his Gaelic context some time in the second half of the seventh century.[16] In practice, this means that the saint would first have established himself in Ireland either in person or, as Dumville seems now more inclined to believe, in the form of a cult,[17] under the Brittonic pet form of his name. Then, well after his death sometime in the sixth century, the saint would have come to be known also as *Findbarr*, which in turn would have made possible the application to him of a series of other names derived either from *Findbarr* itself or from its cognate and interchangeable form *Bairrfhind*.

My 1994 article challenged the validity of this attempt to rescue the onomastic component of Fleuriot's theory on two main grounds.[18] The first of these is the inherent improbability of pet forms generating full names, rather than vice-versa, which is underlined by the fact that no other example of the proposed process is known. As Dumville very properly insists, we are dealing with a period notoriously lacking in sources. It is of paramount importance, therefore, that inferences drawn from later sources bearing on the period at least conform to otherwise demonstrable patterns. There is no lack of examples of full names generating hypocoristics, including several of a Brittonic character, such as the many examples of saints' names ending in *-óc* (< Brittonic *-ǫc*, OW *-auc* cf. Goidelic *-ach/-ech*). When explaining the opposite procedure, therefore, it is scarcely adequate to appeal to the 'strongly self-interrogatory' character of the record as a whole, and to suggest, as Dumville does in his recent article, that if only the British-based hypocoristic were known, viz. *Finnio*, there would have been a 'desire to retrieve full names' for it, viz. *Findbarr, Bairrfhind*.[19] This argument can only bear up to examination when the record can be shown to have produced other similar examples. In the meantime, however, it may be noted that names of numerous early Irish saints survive in hypocoristic form only, with no evidence whatsoever of a desire to retrieve their full forms. *Abbán* (probably from *Ailbe*), *Buite* (from *Báeth/Baíthín*), *Cainnech* (from *Colum*), *Fursu/Fuirse* (from ?), *Gemmán* (from ?), *Gobbán/Goppóc* (from full name based on *goba* 'smith'), *Lallóc* (from ?), *Mella* (from ?), *Mocholla* (from *Colum*), *Mochonna* (from *Colum*), *Mochumma* (from *Colum*), *Teille* (from *Ailill*), *Tomma/ Tommán/Tommíne* (from ?), represent a

---

16 Dumville, 'Gildas and Uinniau', 210. Dumville does not specifically place the assimilation in the second half, but this is implicit in his argument. Such a date, at the latest, is needed because of the occurrence together of the full form *Findbarrus* and hypocoristic *Finnio* in Adamnán's Life of Columba.

17 Dumville, 'St Finnian of Movilla', 78, 81, 84 (n. 81).

18 Ó Riain, 'Finnio and Winniau'.

19 Dumville, 'St Finnian of Movilla', 76–7.

few only of the numerous saints whose records are bereft of the non-hypocoristic forms of their names. By contrast, the single comparandum cited by Dumville, the unfounded allegation in the *Salmanticensis* collection of saints' Lives that Finnian of Clonard's baptismal name was *Finluch*, would seem to be irrelevant.[20] As is clear from the context, it is an invention devised to explain the circumstances of the saint's baptism. And, more importantly, as the hagiographer himself implies through his reference to the more common name *Finnianus*, it was otherwise never — or never became — attached to the saint.

My second objection to the onomastic part of Dumville's argument lay in the seventh-century date he proposed for the process.[21] Little is known of the influences at work on the spread of cults in Ireland. What little evidence there is, however, indicates that the proposed assimilation of the saint to an Irish context would need to have taken place either during, or very close to, his lifetime, rather than about a century after his death. When the cult's existence first becomes observable, it is already present in at least two churches, Clonard and Movilla, each using a distinct *moccu*-formula to lay claim to the saint.[22] The use of this formula shows that by 700 the cult had already fragmented. Moreover, when it begins to be more fully documented about 830 in the form of numerous entries in the Tallaght martyrologies, its fragmentation is already complete. Not only were churches throughout Ireland by then attached to the saint, there was also a rich array of possible variations in the form of his name. The extent of its spread, the evident existence of several local versions of it and the rich variety in the forms of its saint's name, are all factors that point to a remote diffusion of the cult. But, if this diffusion is to be dated much earlier than 700, which seems a reasonable enough inference in view of the evidence for its early localisations at Clonard and at Movilla, then Dumville's theory becomes unworkable, at least from the chronological point of view. Should the spread of the saint's cult have been earlier than his supposed assimilation to an Irish context, as Dumville's argument implies, then one would have to contemplate a situation in which the process either came about independently at each of the saint's churches or occurred successively, one church following the example of the other. Neither alternative is plausible. In the one case, one might as well argue that the several saints named *Finnio* were independently British, each succumbing in turn to the need for additional fully Irish versions of his name. In the other, the question would arise as to where the change

20 Heist, ed., *Vitae Sanctorum Hiberniae*, 96. As Dumville points out, he owed this example to my 1977 article on 'St. Finnbarr', where I had described it as 'guesswork'.
21 Ó Riain, 'Finnio and Winniau', 410.
22 At Movilla the saint became known as *Finnio moccu Fiatach*; at Clonard he was called *Finnio moccu (Tel)duib*. The use of *moccu* is generally taken to indicate the period before 700.

is likely first to have taken place. Clonard, which Dumville, following Fleuriot, is now inclined to regard as the saint's more likely original Irish church,[23] would scarcely be entitled to figure among the list of possible originating churches; of all versions of the saint, the Clonard one shows least variation in the range of his names.

These implications hinge, however, on acceptance of the argument that the pattern of associations of sixth-century or earlier saints with churches was more or less complete, at the latest by about 650. This argument has been rejected by Dumville as undemonstrable, on the basis that the saints' Lives of the second half of the seventh century, which are our only available roughly contemporary sources, provide no more than patchy coverage of the country.[24] But it is precisely the concordance discernible between those churches mentioned in seventh-century hagiography and the surviving hagiotoponomy that justifies the inference in the first place. Cogitosus alludes hardly at all to names of people and places, so that his description of Brigit's *paruchia* as being spread throughout Ireland, from sea to sea, however justified by the hagiotoponymic evidence, cannot be sustained from his own text for the period in question.[25] As K. McCone has pointed out, however, in his examination of the saint's early dossier, the detailed journeys undertaken by Brigit according to her slightly later *Vita Prima* represent 'no mere travelogue. . . . but are intended to have contemporary reference to Brigidine *paruchia* and spheres of influence'.[26] And, just as examination has shown that those areas visited by Brigit are later documented centres of her cult, so also those passages of Adamnán's Life of Columba that bring the saint, for example, to Munster or to south Connacht are still echoed by local hagiotoponomy. As I have shown elsewhere,[27] names of local churches in these areas reveal numerous associations with a saint named Colum. This is not to say that changes in local patterns of association with fifth or sixth-century saints were not later brought about. For example, in the course of expansion of Armagh influence in Munster in the early ninth century, several new centres of the cult of St Patrick were established. As a rule, such changes were due to the *paruchia* activities of major churches. Other than Clonard, however, whose abbots are shown to have been active outside their own immediate area by the ninth-century annals and by other sources,[28] there is

---

23 Dumville, 'St Finnian of Movilla', 80.
24 Dumville rightly points out that this cannot be held to apply to such sainted groups as the anchorites of the late eighth and early ninth century. In their regard, however, it should be pointed out that the churches named after them were as a rule newly–founded.
25 *Acta Sanctorum* February 1 (1658) 135–41
26 K. McCone, 'Brigit in the Seventh Century: a Saint with Three Lives', in *Peritia* 1 (1982) 107–45 (122).
27 P. Ó Riain, *The Making of a Saint: Finbarr of Cork 600–1200* (London, 1997) 26–7.
28 K. Hughes, 'The Cult of St Finnian of Clonard from the Eighth to the Eleventh Century',

no church associated with Finnian that might have encouraged greatly the later spread of his cult.[29] But, as already stated, of all Finnian's churches, Clonard seems to have had least interest in popularising variations in the saint's name.

In fact, what evidence there is, sparse as it may be, would suggest that, during its initial period of expansion, Finnian's cult was promoted not by any church of his own but by Iona. At least, the cult appears often to have travelled in conjunction with that of Colum Cille. The evidence for this is again not contemporary; it begins with the martyrologies of the early ninth century, where there is a profusion of feasts shared by the two saints, and culminates in the distribution of churches associated with them which, remarkably often, lie in close proximity to one another.[30] But, despite its non-contemporary character, the link this evidence implies between the spread of both cults carries force, for at least two reasons. First, the evidence reveals a recurrent pattern which, given the dearth of contemporary sources, necessarily enhances its quality. Secondly, the interpretation of the evidence proposed here finds support in related external sources. Since Delehaye, for example, it has been recognised that the sharing of feasts is often due to an association between saints on the ground.[31] Assuming, therefore, that Colum's cult had already wandered to the extent reflected by his journeys and other associations in Adamnán's late seventh-century account, including connexions with Munster, both north and south,[32] it is proper to suppose that Finnian's cult was by then also already established countrywide.

The lines of argument pursued by Dumville, then, in his support of Fleuriot's theory are clearly open to serious objection. The onomastic component of the case for a British Finnian essentially derives from a single Brittonic-based form, viz. the hypocoristic *Finnio*, as against a whole array of fully Irish names, viz. *Findbarr*, *Bairrfhind* etc.[33] Despite the paucity of evidence, however, the advocates of the case

Irish Historical Studies 9 (1954–5) 13–27.

29 There is, for example, no evidence to show that Cork ever had much of a *paruchia*. The claims on churches it was making in the late twelfth century were inspired by a desire to absorb the neighbouring dioceses of Cloyne and Ross.

30 Ó Riain, *The Making of a Saint*, 22.

31 H. Delehaye, *Cinq leçons sur la méthode hagiographique* (Brussels, 1934) 55.

32 For the connexion with south Munster, see Ó Riain, *The Making of a Saint*, 24.

33 In his contribution to the present volume (above 15ff., pp. 18–19), Thomas Charles-Edwards suggests that I may not have given sufficient consideration to the implications of a British counterpart of the full Irish name *Findbarr* preserved in an Ogam inscription from Wales as *Vendubari*, which, he states, would have required little change to make it purely Irish. The point made by me, however, in 'Finnian or Winniau' (pp. 55–6), was that, unlike the Irish record, nowhere in the Welsh or more generally British record of the saint is a full form of the name brought together with, or equated with, the hypocoristic form. If both forms of the name had been borrowed into Irish, as seems to be suggested, then some evidence

are now prepared to use a British form of the saint's name in their own writings and, more worryingly, to cite Adamnán's usage as a precedent for this. In the earliest surviving manuscript of Adamnán's Life of Columba, copied soon after 700 by the biographer's successor, Dorbéne, the Brittonic-based Latin *Vinniavo* (dat.) is used alongside the Goidelic-based Latin *Findbarrum* (acc.) to refer to the saint.[34] This is one of several examples of Irish sources where the Brittonic-based form is preferred. For Dumville, however, who is joined by Stevenson and Sharpe, it is more than this. It is nothing less than an example of the use in Irish sources of a purely British form *Uinniau*, complete 'with the original diphthong of the Neo-Brittonic hypocoristic termination -*iau*'.[35] This form, which reflects a minor adjustment of the name *Winniau*, used for the saint by Fleuriot throughout his article. Although attested solely in British or Breton sources,[36] it is now being used with increasing frequency as an alternative name for *Finnio* or the more conventional Finnian. It is used as such by Dumville for the whole of the second half of the article under discussion. It is also the form of the name preferred by Sharpe, on the grounds that Adamnán 'calls him St Uinniau'.[37] Stevenson follows suit, likewise naming Adamnán as her authority.[38] Yet, despite the united opinion of these scholars, it has to be said categorically that neither Adamnán nor any other Irish writer used an actual British form *Uinniau*. The form used in Irish sources is the regular, received Latin name *Uinnia(u)us (Vinniavus)*, which is also found later with initial *F- Finniaui* (gen.).[39] This is the form of the name found in the attribution of the *Penitentialis*, where it alternates with *Vinnianus*,[40] and another variant, *Vennianus*, is found in the manuscript tradition of Columbanus's letter to Pope Gregory.[41] The Latin ending may be based ultimately on a Brittonic form containing the suffix -*iaw*, as Thurneysen supposed,[42] but following A. Harvey's study of Dorbéne's spelling habits, even this is no longer certain. Harvey showed that Dorbéne used -*u-/-v-* as a hiatus-filler between stem with vocalic auslaut and

---

should have survived in the British record of their use together in connection with the saint.

34 A. O. and M. O. Anderson,. *Adomnan's Life of Columba* (Edinburgh, 1961) 324–6(53ab). Dumville's reference to pp. 94–5 of the same source in his 'St Finnian of Movilla', 82 (n. 27) is to be corrected accordingly.

35 Dumville, 'St Finnian of Movilla', 74–5.

36 Fleuriot, 'Le "saint" Breton', 611.

37 R. Sharpe, *Adomnán of Iona: Life of St Columba* (London, 1995) 317.

38 J. Stevenson, 'The Beginnings of Literacy in Ireland', 156–7. Stevenson cites Dumville also as her guide in this matter.

39 Best, Lawlor, *The Martyrology of Tallaght*, 20 (March 2), 74 (Sept. 27).

40 L. Bieler, *The Irish Penitentials* (Dublin, 1963) 15, 94.

41 G. S. M. Walker, ed., *Sancti Columbani Opera* (Dublin, 1957) 8.

42 Thurneysen, *Grammar*, § 275.

ending, as, for example, in his spelling of the supposedly also British-based *Fergnoi* as *Virgnovi*.[43] Moreover, although there treating *Finnio* (nom.) as opposed to *Vinniavo* (dat.) as an example of hypercorrection stemming from the use of -*v*- as a hiatus-filler, Harvey would now have no formal objection to the proposal that the latter form be also viewed as a case of orthographic hiatus-filling.[44] In that case, Adamnán's *Vinniavo* would not in itself be indicative of a remote Brittonic diphthong -*au*-. Whichever may apply, however, neither Thurneysen's explanation nor that of Harvey would support the conclusion that Adamnán actually knew the British form, complete with diphthong, presenting it to his readers in Latin guise. The only non-Latin form known to Adamnán was the Irish *Finnio*, which, at the beginning of the third part of the Life of Columba, is actually given a separate Latin declension, with accusative *Finnionem*.[45]

As already stated, *Uinniauus* alternates with *Vinnianus* in the earliest attested examples of the name, which proves that the former name was in any case not the only received Latin form in circulation. Dumville takes no cognisance of this in the onomastic section of his argument. Instead, he passes over the early attestations of *Vennianus*/*Vinnianus* in order to focus on an example in the Annals of Ulster under the year 579, which is preserved in manuscripts of the fifteenth and sixteenth centuries. Moreover, with a view to restoring the original sixth-century entry, he explains the manuscript form *Uinniani* (gen.) as an unnatural late formation, unaffected by one sound change in Irish — viz. the replacement of initial *u*- by *f*- about 600 (which is clearly not reflected in *Uinniani*), but affected by the ninth-century change from -*nd*- to -*nn*-. Combining these developments with the effects of the realisation of Old Irish -*éne* as Latin -*ian*-,[46] Dumville then arrives at the conclusion that the spelling '*Uinnianus* is . . . purely graphic, representing an untidy . . . response over a long period of time to changes in the sound-system of the Irish language'. Despite its early attestation, therefore — indeed, it is among the variants listed by Thurneysen to prove the continued use of *u* for *f* down to the end of the sixth century — Dumville is here suggesting that *Uinnianus* is a late construct. What's more, he drives a wedge between it and its variant *Uinniauus* by positing as its original underlying form the allegedly sixth-century Irish name *Uindéne, later *Findén*.[47]

43 A. Harvey, 'Retrieving the Pronunciation of Early Insular Celtic Scribes: the Case of Dorbbéne', *Celtica* 22 (1991) 48–63.
44 Ibid., 61n. Harvey's present view was conveyed in a note dated 3.11.1997, in response to a query on my part.
45 Anderson and Anderson, *Adamnán's Life of Columba*, 470 (106b).
46 Dumville, 'St Finnian of Movilla', 73–4..
47 Ibid., 74.

Unfortunately for this argument, there is, as far as I am aware, no early example of the allegedly corresponding Irish *Findén*[48]. Where this form survives, as *Findén, Finnén*, in association with the saint, it is usually in late sources where it is substituted for *Finnian* and indeed appears to be a back-formation from it.[49] But, if there is no example in the early hagiological literature of the equation *Findén/Uinnianus/Finnian*, then Dumville's restored Irish form must be ruled out, as must his contention that *Uinnianus* is a late construct. Having regard to its early attestation, it is far more likely that the form either originally arose from a scribal tendency to confuse the minims of *u* and *n*, *Uinnianus* being misread for *Uinniauus*, as suggested by the Andersons,[50] or, as probably also in the case of *Cummianus*, that it came about separately through imitation of such regular Latin forms as *Marianus*.

So much for the chronological and onomastic evidence bearing on the case for a British *Finnio* or Finnian. If the objections presented here are at all valid, then, in terms of the onomastic argument, we are back where we began, with the long recognised presence of Brittonic influence on the formation of one variant form of the Irish saint's name, viz. *Finnio*. This is not, however, the end of the story, at least as far as the possibility of the saint's external origins is concerned. As I have shown in my 1994 article, there is indeed evidence to suggest that the saint may originally have come from outside the Irish mainland.[51] His mention in the Martyrology of Óengus, for example, includes a reference to his bringing of law *tar sál* 'from oversea'.[52] Also, the wide diffusion of his cult in south-western Britain, where, unlike the situation in Ireland and in northern Britain, it appears to have ranked higher in importance than that of Columba, may mean that there was a greater affinity to the saint in this area than to his better known pupil.[53] It is important also to note, however, that this apparent affinity was confined to that part of Britain where there is independent evidence of Irish settlement in the sixth century. An unusually close connexion with this area would also best explain the saint's association with Gildas who appears to have lived and worked on the

---

48 Pace Thurneysen, *Grammar* §275.

49 For examples of the use of *Findén* for *Finnia(n)*, see P. Ó Riain, *Corpus Genealogiarum Sanctorum Hiberniae* (Dublin, 1985) §§ 136, 402, 423, 662.140–1, 703.18; W. Stokes, *Félire Oengusso Céli Dé: The Martyrology of Oengus the Culdee* (London, 1905) 94; *Irisleabhar Maighe Nuadhad* 22 (1926) 3; *Irish Texts* 2 (1931) 69, §3; Best, Lawlor, *The Martyrology of Tallaght*, 43 (May 17).

50 Anderson and Anderson, *Adomnan's Life of Columba*, 69.

51 Ó Riain, 'Finnio and Winniau', 411. Cf. idem, *The Making of a Saint*, 9–10.

52 Stokes, *Félire Oengusso Céli Dé*, 193.

53 See P. Ó Riain, 'The Saints of Cardiganshire', in J. L. Davies, D. P. Kirby, ed., *Cardiganshire County History*, 1 (Cardiff, 1994) 378–96.

periphery of the Irish settlement there.

This is arguably the nub of the whole problem. If Finnian was born into an area of Irish settlement in Britain, he could have come by his British pet name in the most natural way possible, from Brittonic-speaking neighbours. His case could then be added to the small but growing corpus of evidence to show that in the fifth and sixth centuries the strongly Goidelic atmosphere which, according to E. G. Bowen, helped to form local Welsh Christianity, was also exercising a considerable influence on Ireland itself.[54] Indeed, the saint could then be said to have personified this influence.

This brings us to the second factor underlying the notion that Finnian was just as British as Gildas, the somewhat intangible concept labelled 'historical probability'.[55] As elaborated by Sharpe, this concept works along the following lines. Knowing, as we do, that Gildas influenced both Finnian and Columbanus, and accepting Fleuriot's arguments for the British origins of the former, 'we may infer that the mainspring of developments in the Celtic Churches during the sixth century was a movement from western Britain'.[56] What Sharpe has in mind with the Celtic Churches are the *ecclesiae occidentis* referred to by Columbanus in his first recorded letter. He takes these to embrace not only the Irish but also the British Churches, and he regards the ethos of both as the legacy of Gildas.[57] What Sharpe fails to take into account here is the role then being played by northern Britain, through the most important of the *ecclesiae occidentis*, Iona, in setting the agenda of the Irish Church. As is clear from Adamnán's *Vita Columbae*, by 700 Iona's interests and influence extended throughout Ireland, as far south indeed as the most southern part of Munster.[58] What is more, the long standing consensus among scholars has been that it was *via* Iona that the main intellectual, literary, artistic and spiritual influences from without reached Ireland, with Columbanus's church of Bangor acting, as Proinsias Mac Cana has put it,[59] 'as the focal point of this commerce'. And if this be the case, then is it not historically very probable that, just as Iona's role was played out against a background of Irish settlement in northern Britain, so also the intellectual contacts between Ireland and south-western Britain would have been mediated principally by products of Irish schoolrooms there?

54 E. G. Bowen, *The Settlements of the Celtic Saints in Wales* (Cardiff, 1954) 19, 30–2, 43. J. Carey's recent article on 'A Túath Dé Miscellany', *The Bulletin of the Board of Celtic Studies* 39 (1992) 24–45, adds a new dimension to the history of the influence excercised by the Irish settlers, showing that it also extended to British vernacular culture.
55 Sharpe, 'Gildas as a Father of the Church', 198.
56 Ibid., 200.
57 Ibid., 201–2.
58 Ó Riain, *The Making of a Saint*, 24.
59 Mac Cana, 'Mongán Mac Fiachna', 105.

In his plenary paper to the seventh International Congress of Celtic Studies, M. Lapidge demonstrated how Welsh Latin learning in the ninth and tenth centuries was permeated by those orthographical features often regarded as Irish and that many aspects of Welsh scholarship have affinities with 'Hiberno-Latin' exegesis.[60] Having concluded, however, that these symptoms reflected traditions centuries old, stretching back to before Gregory the Great and Gildas, Lapidge chose to ignore the implications of the clear evidence of the presence of Irish masters in Gwynedd of the ninth century, to which he himself alluded. Shying away from what he termed the most economical explanation of his findings, which would have involved positing numerous Irish masters in sixth-century Wales instructing the Welsh how to spell (or misspell!) and transmitting some of the more curious exegetical texts from their own libraries,[61] he opted instead to follow T. J. Brown, whose views on the subject have been shown by W. O'Sullivan to be open to serious objection,[62] and Dumville, whose views, as I hope to have shown here, are similarly questionable, in assuming that those features of Welsh Latin learning traditionally regarded as Irish were of British origin.[63] But, since then Thomas Charles-Edwards has shown that the Irish of western Britain, although deliberately promoting Irish as an expression of their own cultural legitimacy, at the same time showed a keen appreciation of the continuing high status of Latin,[64] thus implying that the schools of grammar and rhetoric needed to sustain this status would have been maintained in some form by local Irish rulers. Pace Lapidge, therefore, the inscriptional evidence for Latin learning in western Britain in the fifth and sixth centuries would seem almost to presuppose the existence of local Irish masters of Latin. And, there being at least some evidence to show that Gildas himself may have been taught to misspell his name by an Irish master,[65] it is all the more regrettable that Lapidge did not opt for the more economical way of explaining his important findings.

60 M. Lapidge, 'Latin Learning in Dark Age Wales: Some Prolegomena', D. E. Evans, J. G. Griffith, E. M. Jope, ed., *Proceedings of the Seventh International Congress of Celtic Studies* (Oxford, 1986) 91–107 (102).
61 Ibid.
62 For W. O'Sullivan's criticism of Brown's approach, see his 'Insular Calligraphy: Current State and Problems', *Peritia* 4 (1985) 346–59 (351–3).
63 Lapidge, 'Latin Learning in Dark Age Wales', 102.
64 T. Charles-Edwards, 'Language and Society among the Insular Celts AD 400–1000', in M. J. Green, ed., *The Celtic World* (London and New York, 1996) 703–3 (723). C. Thomas, *'And Shall these Mute Stones Speak?' Post-Roman Inscriptions in Western Britain* (Cardiff, 1994) 4, has shown that he holds the same view.
65 See P. Ó Riain, 'Gildas: a Solution to his Enigmatic Name', in C. Laurent, H. Davis, ed., *Irlande et Bretagne: vingt siècles d'histoire* (Rennes, 1994) 32–9.

To discuss in detail the many other points of contact between Welsh and Irish learning that might be cited in support of the view that a mediating role, such as that embodied by Finnian, was played by the Irish communities of south-western Britain would go beyond the scope of this paper. It may be nonetheless appropriate briefly to pass in review here what is known of contacts of this kind, leaving aside altogether the extensive evidence of trade between this part of Britain and Ireland in the fifth and sixth centuries which provides a natural framework for the interchange of other influences.[66]

(a) The best known witness to the vibrancy of Irish culture in south-western Britain in the sixth century is that region's collection of Ogam-inscribed stones. Some forty Ogam inscriptions have been discovered in Wales and six in Cornwall.[67] The distribution of the inscriptions agrees closely with the extent of Irish settlement, and in south-west Wales, where most of the Ogams have been found, Irish continued to be spoken into the seventh century. Here also a dynasty of Irish kings is known to have ruled over several centuries. As is now generally conceded, Ogam is based on the Latin alphabet, and one of many theories explaining its origins, that put forward by K. Jackson,[68] traces the inventor to among the Irish of Britain, whence, having learned his Latin, he returned to live in Ireland with his kindred, where he then composed this simplified script. Although on the face of it at odds with McManus's statement that there is not a single piece of evidence to support the argument that Ogam was introduced to Ireland from outside,[69] as with the proposed location of Finnian's place of birth among the Irish of Britain, Jackson's argument would in fact conform with the notion of an Irish origin for the Ogam alphabet. As Charles-Edwards has put it, South Wales is the most likely place of origin of Ogam simply because it is the part of Roman Britain in which there was the most extensive contact between Irish and Latin.[70]

(b) As in Ireland, the period before about 650 may be regarded as defining in relation to the distribution of cults of saints in Wales.[71] If we except E. G.

66 See, for example, N. Edwards, *The Archaeology of Early Medieval Ireland* (London, 1990). Cf. D. Dumville, 'Some British Aspects of the Earliest Irish Christianity', in P. Ní Chatháin, M. Richter, ed. *Irland und Europa: Ireland and Europe* (Stuttgart, 1984) 16–24 (21).
67 K. Jackson, *Language and History in Early Britain* (Edinburgh, 1953) 153–4.
68 Ibid., 156–7.
69 D. McManus, *A Guide to Ogam* (Maynooth, 1991) 20. In his 'Early Literacy in Ireland: The Evidence from Ogam', *Cambridge Medieval Celtic Studies* 14 (1987) 1–15 (5), A. Harvey has also distanced himself from Jackson's theory, as has Thomas, *'And Shall these Mute Stones Speak?'*, 13.
70 T. Charles-Edwards, 'Language and Society', 722n.
71 Despite his tendency to interpret the sources as evidence of the movement of people rather than of cults, this belief underlies E. G. Bowen's approach to the Celtic saints in Wales. Cf.

Bowen, up to now few commentators have chosen to emphasise the Goidelic character of early Christianity in Wales.[72] Moreover, the kind of evidence traditionally cited in support of this character has mainly been onomastic — for example, the use of Irish-influenced *Illtud* for more regular Welsh *Elltud*. As I have contended in two articles, however, there is also evidence to show that the distribution of saints' cults in Wales mirrored the extent of Irish settlement in the region.[73] Both articles focused, it is true, on the cult of Finnian in Wales, but, as already stated, the manner in which the spread of this cult corresponds to the area of Irish settlement is itself a strong argument for the saint's essential Irishness.

(c) Native Welsh saints are also typified by the emphatically Irish character of the earliest part of their records. This documentation is late by Irish standards, beginning with the martyrologies of the early ninth century where the feastdays of David, Beuno and Deiniol are recorded.[74] Despite its comparative lateness, however, the documentation may still be seen as reflecting close relations between the Irish and Welsh churches dating, at the latest, to the ninth century. As such, its evidence ties in neatly with the ninth-century exchanges between Welsh and Irish ecclesiastics illustrated by the Bamberg cryptogram,[75] and by the considerable knowledge of Welsh displayed by the author of Cormac's Glossary.[76] These intellectual exchanges provide glimpses of what, in the historical and geographical circumstances, can scarcely have been less than both ongoing and longstanding close contacts between Welsh and Irish

---

also for Wales, Ó Riain, 'The Saints of Cardiganshire', 381; for Cornish evidence to show that the modern pattern of association with early Christian saints was largely already in place by about 900, see B. L. Olson, O. J. Padel, 'A Tenth-Century List of Cornish Parochial Saints', *Cambridge Medieval Celtic Studies* 12 (1986) 33–71; this points towards an early distribution of dedications.

72 For Bowen see note 55 above. Cf. idem, 'The Cult of St. Brigit', *Studia Celtica* 8/9 (1973/74) 33–47 (43/4).

73 P. Ó Riain, 'The Irish Element in Welsh Hagiographical Tradition', in D. Ó Corráin, ed., *Irish Antiquity* (Cork, 1981) 292–303; idem, 'The Saints of Cardiganshire'. Pace S. Victory, *The Celtic Church in Wales* (London, 1977) 10, who contended that dedications to Irish saints were few, these now often masquerade as Welsh.

74 The feasts of the three Welsh saints are recorded in the Martyrology of Tallaght, composed about 830; March 1 (David), April 21 (Bugno, early spelling of Beuno), and September 11 (Deiniol).

75 J. F. Kenney, *The Sources for the Early History of Ireland: Ecclesiastical* (New York, 1929) 556. Cf. N. K. Chadwick, 'Early Culture and Learning in North Wales', in idem et al., ed., *Studies in the Early British Church* (Cambridge, 1958) 29–120 (93–110).

76 Charles-Edwards, 'Language and Society', 710–1. P. Russell, 'The Sounds of Silence: the Growth of Cormac's Glossary', *Cambridge Meadieval Celtic Studies* 15 (1988), subscribes to the traditional date of this text of about 900.

ecclesiastics. From the early eighth century, as Lapidge has pointed out,[77] we know of a Welsh bishop of Irish race named Sedulius. And, if the evidence concerning the correspondence between Gildas and Finnian is to be our guide, then the Irish and Welsh churches were visibly exchanging information as early as the sixth century. In this connexion, it also bears remembering that the two main foci of David's cult in Wales, in Pembrokeshire and in Cardiganshire, were within the compass of Irish settlement there.

(d) By far the most outstanding potential example of the mediating role of the Irish diaspora is the record of Gildas, one of Britain's most notable saints and scholars of the sixth century, and author, among other works, of *De Excidio Britanniae* (the Ruin of Britain). Whether or not Gildas was taught to write his name by an Irish master, as I hold,[78] it is an established fact that his writings appear mainly to have been first received by the Irish. This certainly applies to his penitential, and also to the fragments of his correspondence.[79] Indeed, if M. Winterbottom is correct, his *De Excidio* may have had Columbanus as its earliest known reader.[80] Those who advocate sixth-century British influence on the Irish Church rightly emphasise Gildas's role. The point being made here, however, is that Gildas's influence must have been greatly facilitated, if not entirely mediated, by what appears to have been his own working milieu, on the periphery of the area of Irish settlement in Wales. Needless to say, a proximity of this kind could also easily have led to Gildas's correspondence with Finnian. Lapidge, followed by Herren, attributed Gildas's Latin learning to his attendance of classical schools, and accordingly moved backwards about fifty years the traditional chronology of his life.[81] In the light of the history of the reception of his writings, however, it must seem more likely that his education also lay in the hands of Irish masters, as is in fact claimed in his eleventh-century biography.[82]

77 Lapidge, 'Latin Learning in Dark Age Wales', 92. The bishop attended an episcopal synod convened by Pope Gregory II. Cf. A. W. Haddan, W. Stubbs, *Councils and Ecclesiastical Documents relating to Great Britain and Ireland* 2 (1878) 7.
78 Ó Riain, 'Gildas: a Solution to his Enigmatic Name'.
79 The texts accompanying Gildas's penitential in both manuscripts containing it are otherwise mainly Irish in character; see L. Bieler, *The Irish Penitentials* (Dublin, 1963) 3, 12–3. For the transmission of the Fragments, see R. Sharpe, 'Gildas as a Father of the Church', in M. Lapidge, D. Dumville, ed., *Gildas: New Approaches* (Woodbridge, 1984) 191–206 (194–6).
80 M. Winterbottom, 'Columbanus and Gildas', *Vigiliae Christianae* 30 (1976) 310–17.
81 M. Lapidge, 'Gildas's Education and the Latin Culture of Sub-Roman Britain', in idem, D. Dumville, ed. *Gildas: New Approaches* (Woodbridge, 1984) 27–50. M. Herren, 'Gildas and Early British Monasticism', in A. Bammesberger, A. Wollmann, ed., *Britain 400–600: Language and History* (Heidelberg, 1990) 65–78.
82 H. Williams, 'Two Lives of Gildas', *Cymmrodorion Record Series* 3 (1899) 17.

(e) Whereas Fleuriot was prepared to concede that Finnian had spent his final
   years in Ireland,[83] Dumville would now go so far as to suggest that the saint
   may never have been there.[84] This is the equivalent of stating that, despite the
   thoroughly Irish character of his record, Finnian is conceivably to be placed on
   the same basic level vis-à-vis the Irish Church as, for example, Gildas and
   David. The quite distinct nature of the Irish reception of Gildas and David,
   however, when compared to that of Finnian, undermines this thesis. Neither of
   the two genuinely British saints could be said to have lagged behind Finnian in
   his involvement with the Irish of Britain. Yet, despite claims to the contrary in
   later Lives, neither saint ever founded a church or became the subject of an
   early cult in Ireland. This immediately sets Finnian apart, and shows that much
   more than the evidence of the hypocoristic form of his name is needed to
   prove that the saint was as British as Gildas and David.

To sum up, then. The purpose of this article has been to challenge once more
the argument for an essentially British Finnian, initiated by Fleuriot and continued
by Dumville, which rests principally on the British-based pet name of the saint,
and which flies in the face of most other parts of the saint's record, onomastic and
otherwise. What this renewed challenge sets out to achieve in the first instance is to
defend the view that early Irish Christianity was profoundly influenced from
Britain. As presented by an ever increasing number of disciples of Léon Fleuriot,
this view invariably supposes the influences to have come from British masters. As
I hope to have shown here, however, the associations of Finnian's name, together
with other evidence, would seem to indicate that British influence on the formation of Christianity in Ireland in the sixth century was to a great extent exercised
through masters produced by the transmarine Irish of the south-western part of
the island of Britain. As already stated, the initial Christian encounter with the
Irish settlements in northern Britain, through Iona, led to a change in the direction
of Christianity in Ireland itself, as is indicated, for example, by the extraordinary
spread of Columba's cult. But, as we also know, Finnian was Columba's master
and, through his teaching, he too must have influenced the process that led to this
enrichment of Irish Christianity. The probability that Finnian's own background
lay among the transmarine Irish might then be viewed as evidence of the involvement not only of northern but also of south-western Britain in that reinvigoration
of Irish Christianity in the sixth century that set the scene for Ireland's role, in
Bieler's words,[85] as harbinger of the Middle Ages.

83 Fleuriot, 'Le "saint" Breton Winniau', 613.
84 Dumville, 'St Finnian of Movilla', 78, 81 (and note 81).
85 L. Bieler, Ireland: Harbinger of the Middle Ages (London, 1963).

Grammatica, grammatic, Augustine, and the *Táin*

Erich Poppe

PHILIPPS-UNIVERSITÄT MARBURG

THE intellectual and ideological framework within which the medieval Irish *literati* operated, has always been one of Proinsias Mac Cana's central scholarly concerns. In the following I propose to explore one tiny segment of this learned tradition, taking two Old Irish glosses on Augustine's *Soliloquia* as my starting point.

In his recent study *The making of textual culture. 'Grammatica' and literary theory, 350–1100*, Martine Irvine has made a strong case for *grammatica* as the central discipline concerned with literacy, language, interpretation, and literature in late classical and medieval societies. In his view, '*grammatica* had an essentially constitutive function, making a certain kind of literacy and literary culture possible *per se*.'[1] Within the context of medieval Ireland, textual genres participating in *grammatica* are the glosses, the so-called exegetical grammars, and the metrical tracts. I have suggested elsewhere that *Auraicept na nÉces* — an important and fascinating tract which Proinsias Mac Cana fittingly characterized as 'a fairly typical product of Latino-Gaelic learning'[2] — is the vernacular exponent of the

---

1 Martine Irvine, *The making of textual culture. 'Grammatica' and literary theory, 350–1100* (Cambridge 1994), xiv.
2 Proinsias Mac Cana, 'The rise of the later schools of *filidheacht*', *Ériu* 25 (1974), 126–46, p. 136.

otherwise Hiberno-Latin exegetical grammars.[3] Morgan Thomas Davies has applied Irvine's model to medieval Irish glosses and commentaries, and primarily to the commentary on the *Amra Choluimb Chille*:

> the hermeneutic revealed in the commentary to *Amra Coluim Cille*, as well as in the glosses to other vernacular texts, is in a fundamental continuum with the approach to interpretation taught through the study of *grammatica* in schools throughout early medieval Europe, and at a much earlier date in Ireland than the tenth century.[4]

Meta-theoretical discussions of the scope of *grammatica* in the vernacular are — to my knowledge — more or less non-existent, but are found in Hiberno-Latin exegetical grammars, for example in Donatus Ortigraphus with quotations from Isidore and Victorinus.[5] In vernacular texts the issue is probably addressed in the introduction to the legal tract *Cóic conara fugill* and in the so-called 'Caldron of Poesy'. In *Cóic conara fugill* 'fid 7 deach, reim 7 forbaidh, alt 7 indsci 7 etargairi' ('letter and syllable, declension and accent, juncture and gender and distinction') are described as the seven categories which constitute every legal text,[6] in the 'Caldron of Poesy' the *Coire Goiriath* is said to distribute knowledge 'i moth, i toth, i tráeth, i n-arnin, i forsail, i ndínin- dísail' ('of masculine, feminine and neuter, of the signs for double letters, long vowels and short vowels'), or in the words of its editor Liam Breatnach, of 'knowledge of grammar, writing and metrics, which is of course a necessary prerequisite for any learned person'.[7]

Perhaps not surprisingly, given the lack of interest in a theoretical discussion of the issue, a comprehensive term for the discipline *grammatica*/grammar is rare in the vernacular. It occurs as a loan in the two forms *grammatic* (uninflected *i*-stem) and *gram(m)atach* (feminine a-stem).[8] The first form appears to be attested only in

3   Erich Poppe, 'Die mittelalterliche irische Abhandlung *Auraicept na nÉces* und ihr geistes-geschichtlicher Standort', in K. D. Dutz and H.-J. Niederehe (eds), *Theorie und Rekonstruktion* (Münster 1996), 55–74.

4   Morgan Thomas Davies, 'Protocols of reading in early Irish literature: Notes on some notes to *Orgain Denna Ríg* and *Amra Coluim Cille*', *Cambrian Medieval Celtic Studies* 32 (1996), 1–23, pp. 19–20.

5   Donatus Ortigraphus, *Ars Grammatica*, ed. by John Chittenden (Turnhout 1982 = CCCM XL D), p. 4.

6   Rudolf Thurneysen, *Cóic conara fugill. Die fünf Wege zum Urteil. Ein altirischer Rechtstext* (Berlin 1925 [1926] = Abhandlungen der Preussischen Akademie der Wissenschaften. 1925. Phil.-hist. Klasse, 7; repr. in Rudolf Thurneysen, *Gesammelte Werke*, vol. 3, ed. by P. de Bernardo Stempel and R. Ködderitzsch (Tübingen 1995), 3–87), p. 26.

7   Liam Breatnach, 'The Caldron of Poesy', *Ériu* 32 (1981), 45–93, pp. 63 and 48.

8   Compare Patricia Kelly, 'Variation in early Irish linguistic terminology', in A. Ahlqvist and

the Old Irish glosses on Augustine's *Soliloquia* in MS Karlsruhe Augiensis CXCV, written in the first half of the ninth century in Ireland — or by Irish scribes in Western Francia[9] — in the following two instances:

isecen doneuch fosisedar dán inna grammatic continola innahuili doilbthi. (*Thes.* II.6)

it is necessary for everyone who is interested in the art of *grammatica*, to collect all inventions.[10]

glossing Augustine, *Soliloquia* II.xi.19:[11]
Est autem grammatica uocis articulatae custos et moderatrix disciplina: cuius professionis necessitate cogitur humanae linguae omnia etiam figmenta colligere, quae memoriae litterísque mandata sunt.

the discipline *grammatica* is the guardian of ordered speech and its governor; in its pursuit it has to collect even all inventions of human language which have been transmitted by memory or writing.

nígrammatic tantum astoisc do deimnigud as uera disciplina per dialecticam acht it na huili besgna ata fira per dialecticam. (*Thes.* II.7)

it is not *grammatica* alone which is shown *per dialecticam* to be *uera disciplina*, but all disciplines are shown to be true *per dialecticam*.

glossing Augustine, *Soliloquia* II.xi.21:
Grammatica igitur eadem arte creata est, ut disciplina uera[12] esset, quae abs te superius a falsitate defensa: quod non de una grammatica mihi licet concludere, sed prorsus de omnibus disciplinís.

Grammatica has thus been made a true discipline from the same art which you defended above against the accusation of falsehood [viz. dialectics], and I would

---

V. Čapková (eds), *Dán do oide. Essays in memory of Conn R. Ó Cléirigh* (Dublin 1997), 243–46, pp. 242–44.

9 Compare Johanne Authenrieth, 'Irische Handschriftenüberlieferung auf der Reichenau', in H. Löwe (ed.), *Die Iren und Europa im früheren Mittelalter* (Stuttgart 1982), 903–15, p. 905.

10 *Doilbthe* is the participle of *dolbaid*, used in the Old Irish glosses to translate the verb *fingo* in its various meanings. Compare Ml 61^b13 *doilbthib* 'invented' glossing *fictis uerbís*, Ml 61^b18 *innandoilbthe* 'of the inventions' glossing *uota fictorum*, Ml 54^c12 *nodolbtais gnimu* 'they used to feign deeds' glossing *calumniam commouebant actionis*, and Wb 4^c26 *dondí rodndolbi* 'to him who has formed' glossing *ei qui sé finxit*.

11 The edition used here is Augustinus, *Opera. Sct. I Pars IV. Soliloquiorum libri duo. De inmortalitate animae. De quanitate animae*, ed. by W. Hörmann (Wien, 1986 = CSEL, 89). I wish to thank Monika Rener for her help with the English versions of the Latin quotations.

12 I follow here the Latin text printed in *Thes.* II.7, Hörmann's edition has the variant 'ut disciplina et ut vera esset' instead.

like to draw this conclusion not only about *grammatica*, but about all other disciplines.[13]

The first passage supplies a good justification of a learned interest in the whole range of texts produced in a textual culture without regard for their intrinsic truth, and it is perhaps not insignificant that the Irish glossator selected this particular passage for a translation.

It is clear that the semantic range of Ir. *grammatic* — a loan translation of Augustine's *grammatica* — in the two glosses is not confined to modern 'grammar', but covers the wider and more inclusive late classical and medieval concept.[14] It is relevant in this context that Paul Edward Dutton and Anneli Luhtala have pointed out that Augustine's definition of *grammatica* from the *Soliloquia*, as 'articulatae uocis custos et moderatrix disciplina', was inserted by an Irish scribe into a (ninth or tenth century) manuscript of Eriugena's *Periphyseon*, viz. Rheims, Bibliothèque Municipale 875.[15]

The variant form *gramadach* occurs in *Auraicept na nÉces*, and here its semantic range is more difficult to define: *gramadach* is said to be one constituent of philosophy, besides dialectics and *rím* (see below):

acht do uilideataid na feallsamnachta eter gramadaigh 7 dileachtaigh 7 rim, amal atbert in fili:

> Foglaim, feallsamnacht is fas,
> Legeand, gramadach, is gluas,
> Litirdheacht leir ocus rim
> Is beg a mbrig for nimh thuas.[16]

but to all of philosophy, including grammar, dialectics, and *rím* (lit. 'counting'), as the poet said: 'Learning and philosophy are futile / Reading, *grammatica* and gloss / Diligent booklearning and *rím* / Their value is small in heaven above'.

---

13 The reference is to the discussion in Augustine, *Soliloquia* II.xi.19–20 on the relationship between *grammatica* and dialectics.

14 For a discussion of Augustine's concept of *grammatica* see Irvine, *Making of textual culture*, pp. 169–89.

15 Paul Edward Dutton and Anneli Luhtala, 'Eriugena in Priscianum', *Mediaeval Studies* 56 (1994), 153–63, p. 155, and compare Eriugena, *Periphyseon (De Diuisione Naturae) Liber Primus*, ed. by. I. P. Sheldon-Williams with the collaboration of L. Bieler (Dublin 1978 = SLH 7), p. 110.32–3.

16 George Calder, *Auraicept na n-Éces. The scholars' primer* (Edinburgh 1917), p. 6; for the text of the complete poem compare Kuno Meyer, 'Ein Gedicht aus Additional 30,512', *Zeitschrift für celtische Philologie* 9 (1913), 470, und Kuno Meyer, 'Mitteilungen aus irischen Handschriften', *Zeitschrift für celtische Philologie* 12 (1918), 358–397, p. 385.

The opposition of *grammatica* and dialectics is an important issue in Augustine's *Soliloquia* which was also noticed by Irish glossators (see above), but the problem in this passage is the conceptual range of *rím*, literally 'counting': Calder suggests a meaning 'metrics', and this may be implied in the stanza's enumeration of learned activities which are all centered around grammatical skills. In the medieval concept of *grammatica* metrics would be one of its constituents, rather than a separate discipline — but a similar dichotomy between the teaching of linguistic structures and metrics respectively appears to be implied in the description of the contents of the first year of a poet's training in the second *Mittelirische Verslehre*[17] and in the structure of the Welsh *Gramadegau'r Penceirddiaid*, with its first section on basic grammatical concepts with Welsh examples.[18] *DIL*, however, suggests a meaning 'computation' for *rím*,[19] and this may suit the prose passage — note that in the seventh-century Hiberno-Latin tract *De ratione conputandi*, *grammatica* and *numerus* 'computus'[20] are given as disciplines of equal rank, albeit with positive connotations, in a paraphrase of Augustine's definition of the 'quattuor necessaria [. . .] in ecclesia dei':

> Canon diuinus, in quo narratur et praedicatur uita futura; historia, in qua narrantur gesta rerum; numerus, in quo facta futurorum et solempnitates diuine enumerantur; grammatica, in qua scientia uerborum intellegitur.[21]

---

17 'Is hi tra cetus foglaím na cetbliadna .i. coeca ogum im certoghum 7 airacept na neicsiné cona broluch 7 cona reímendaib 7 fiche drécht 7 se diana' (Rudolf Thurneysen, 'Mittelirische Verslehren', in Wh. Stokes and E. Windisch (eds), *Irische Texte mit Übersetzungen und Wörterbuch*, 3. Ser., 1. Heft (Leipzig 1891), 1–182 (repr. in Rudolf Thurneysen, *Gesammelte Schriften*, vol. 2, ed. by P. de Bernardo Stempel and R. Ködderitzsch (Tübingen, 1991), 340–521), p. 32) ('to begin with, this is the teaching of the first year: fifty *ogam* including *certogam*, *Airacept na nÉicsíne* with its introduction and its inflexions, twenty divisions (?), and six *dán-metres*').

18 Compare G. J. Williams and E. J. Jones, *Gramadegau'r Penceirddiaid* (Caerdydd 1934) for the texts, and R. Geraint Gruffydd, 'Wales's second grammarian: Dafydd Ddu of Hiraddug', *Proceedings of the British Academy* 90 (1996), 1–28, and Paul Russell, '"Gwr gwynn y law": Figures of speech in *Gramadegau'r Penceirddiaid* and Latin grammarians', *Cambrian Medieval Celtic Studies* 32 (1996), 95–104.

19 I wish to thank John Carey for reminding me of this alternative.

20 Compare Maura Walsh and Dáibhí Ó Cróinín (eds), *Cummian's letter De controversia paschali and De ratione conputandi* (Toronto, 1988), p. 118: '"conpos" uel "conpotus" uel "numerus" et "rima" apud Latinos' — the similarity between Latin *rima* and Irish *rím* would certainly have been noticed by medieval Irish etymologists.

21 Walsh and Ó Cróinín, *Cummian's letter*, p. 117 — there are some interesting differences between the text and the Augustinian source quoted by Walsh and Ó Cróinín, p. 117, with regard to the use of terms for the four disciplines and the definition of *grammatica*.

Canon divinus — in which the eternal life is narrated and anounced, *historia* — in which past events are narrated, *numerus* — which lists future liturgical dates, *grammatica* — in which the understanding of words is taught.

In the *Amra Choluimb Chille* and its commentary the form *grammatach* is used,

atgaill grammataig greic .i. ocus ro foighlainn grammataich dano amal Grécu.[22]

he learned Greek grammar, i.e. and he also learned grammar like the Greeks.

but the conceptual range of the term, '*grammatica*' or 'linguistic structure', is not clear from the limited context.

Doilbthi as the Irish rendering of Latin *figmenta* calls to mind one of the most important items of explicit literary criticism from medieval Ireland, the Latin colophon to *Táin Bó Cúalnge* in the Book of Leinster:

Sed ego qui scripsi hanc historiam aut uerius fabulam quibusdam fidem in hac historia aut fabula non accommodo. Quaedam enim ibi sunt praestrigia demonum, quaedam autem figmenta poetica, quaedam similia uero, quaedam non, quaedam ad delectationem stultorum.[23]

But I who have written this *historia*, or rather this *fabula*, do not trust certain things in this *historia* or *fabula*. For some things there are delusions of demons, others poetic inventions, some resemble the truth, others do not, some are for the delectation of fools.

The opposition *historia* versus *fabula* is reminiscent of Isidore, *Etymologiae* i.40–41,[24] but the passage also partakes in a critical tradition ranging from Macrobius to twelfth-century schools of thinking.[25]

22 Whitley Stokes, 'The Bodleian Amra Choluim Chille', *Revue celtique* 20 (1899), 30–55, 132–83, 248–89, 400–37, p. 404.
23 Cecile O'Rahilly (ed. and transl.), *Táin Bó Cúalnge from the Book of Leinster* (Dublin, 1967), p. 136.
24 Compare Irvine, *Making of textual culture*, pp. 234–41.
25 Compare A. J. Minnis and A. B. Scott with David Walker, *Medieval literary theory and criticism c. 1100–c. 1375. The commentary tradition* (Oxford 1991). Another important point of reference within the Christian critical tradition is of course Servius: 'fabula est dicta res contra naturam, sive facta sive non facta, ut de Pasiphae, historia est quicquid secundum naturam dicitur, sive factum sive non factum, ut de Phaedra' (Georg Thilo and Hermann Hagen (eds), *Servii Grammatici qui feruntur in Vergilii Carmina Commentarii*, vol. 1 (Lipsiae, 1881, reprint Hildesheim, 1961), p. 89.

In the sentence immediately preceding his definition of *grammatica* quoted above, Augustine gives the following definition of *fabula*, and in this definition the notion of *delectatio* also plays a central role:

> est fabula compositum ad utilitatem delectationemve mendacium. (Augustine, *Soliloquia* II.xi.19)

> *fabula* is a deception created for utility and delectation.

Figmenta in Augustine's definition of *grammatica* therefore takes up this notion of *fabula*, and their study, of *fabulae* and *figmenta* respectively, is thus seen as the duty of the grammarian, in the wide, late classical sense of the word. The collocation *figmenta poetica* and, more often, its formal variant *figmenta poetarum* are well attested — often with negative connotations — in Augustine's *De civitate Dei*,[26] which was known to and used by medieval Irish scholars.[27] A collocation which describes *daemones* as performers of *praestigiae*, and which is thus curiously reminiscent of the Book of Leinster's *praestrigia demonum*, occurs in *De civitate Dei*, xviii.18, 'Neque enim daemonibus iudicio Dei permissis huius modi praestigiae difficiles esse potuerunt' ('for delusions of this sort cannot have been difficult for demons who were permitted to perform them by God's judgement'). Furthermore, *figmenta poetarum* is an important and common *topos* in late classical and medieval literary theory where the term refers to the problem of a text's truth value and is often directly applied to texts of the pagan period or to pagan myths.[28]

Cecile O'Rahilly suggested, if I interpret her correctly, that *praestrigia* in the Book of Leinster is a mistake for *praestigia*, but the fact that the same form occurs in the seventh-century Hiberno-Latin tract *De ordine creaturarum* and in the

26 Compare Augustinus, *De civitate Dei*, 2 vols, (Turnhout, 1955 = CCSL 47, 48), ii.14, iv.17, vi.7, viii.18, ix.1, with more neutral connotations ii.8, iv.26, xix.12. *Figmenta* on its own is used in one other instance in the *Soliloquia*, II.vi.11: 'Iam vero animantium opera sunt in picturis et huiuscemodi quibusque figmentis; in quo genere includi etiam illa possunt, si tamen fiunt, quae daemones faciunt' ('but the works of humans are in paintings and such-like inventions, in which, if they should indeed come about, could be included those which demons produce').

27 Compare Próinséas Ní Chatháin, 'Early Ireland and western Christendom: The Bible and the mission', in P. Ní Chatháin and M. Richter (eds), *Irland und die Christenheit. Bibel- studien und Mission* (Stuttgart, 1987), 473–504, pp. 503–4, and Martin McNamara, 'Some aspects of early medieval Irish eschatology', in P. Ní Chatháin and M. Richter (eds), *Irland und Europa im früheren Mittelalter. Bildung und Kultur* (Stuttgart, 1996), 42–75, pp. 67–9.

28 Compare Ludwig Gompf, 'Figmenta poetarum', in A. Önnerfors et al. (eds), *Literatur und Sprache im europäischen Mittelalter. Festschrift für Karl Langosch zum 70. Geburtstag* (Darmstadt, 1973), 53–62.

perhaps tenth-century theological treatise *Scéla na Esérgi* 'Tidings of the ressurrection', would seem to indicate that this variant — which already seems to have been freely used in classical Latin — is the more common form in the Irish context — which is also etymologically less opaque (< *praestringo*).

> praestrigia atque oracula fingentes.[29]
>
> concocting apparitions and oracles.

> Ind esergi coitchenn tra bias tall il-lo brátha, ni hinund 7 ind esergi dianid ainm isind augtartas praestrigia .i. esergi fuathaigthi, amal in pitóndacht.[30]
>
> Now the general resurrection which shall be beyond on the Day of Judgement is not the same as the resurrection which in the authority is called *praestrigia* ['delusion'], that is, an apparitional resurrection, like the pythonism.[31]

Martin McNamara, in his discussion of *Scéla na Esérgi*'s doctrine on the resurrection, has drawn attention to its partial dependence on Augustine's *De civitate Dei*.[32]

I do not wish to claim that the colophon to *Táin Bó Cúalnge* in the Book of Leinster draws explicity on Augustine. All I want to argue here is that the concept of *grammatica* was a constitutive and integral part of the intellectual framework in which the medieval Irish *literati* operated, and that the literary theories implied in the colophon result from the application of the textual analysis which *grammatica* teaches. Augustine was one author who played a part in the transmission of this approach to Ireland, as is reflected in the Irish glossators' interest in the relevant passages of his *Soliloquia*. With the editors' suggestion in mind, to select a subject which I would like to discuss with him, I offer these notes to Proinsias.

29 Quoted John Carey, 'The uses of tradition in *Serglige Con Culainn*', in J. P. Mallory and G. Stockman (eds), *Ulidia. Proceedings of the first international conference on the Ulster cycle of tales* (Belfast: 1994), 77–84, p. 79.
30 Whitley Stokes, 'Tidings of the resurrection', *Revue celtique* 25 (1904), 232–59, p. 250.
31 Pythonism: occult power derived from the possession by a prophetic or oracular spirit.
32 McNamara, 'Some aspects', p. 69.

Syntactica

Karl Horst Schmidt

SPRACHWISSENSCHAFTLICHES INSTITUT, BONN

UNSER JUBILAR hat *Celtica* 15 (1983) 55–59 "Three Syntactic Notes" geschrieben, die seine Kompetenz auf dem Gebiete inselkeltischer — d.h. vornehmlich irischer und kymrischer — Syntax unterstreichen.

1. *la* with v.n. to denote concomitant action: Typus: *'Is lond in fer so', ol Mani la sóud úad* '"What a bad-tempered fellow!" said Maine turning away from him' (55) = kymr. *efe a ddaeth atynt, gan rodio ar y mor* 'he cometh unto them, walking upon the sea' Mark. 6.48 (56). Der Typus wird folgendermaßen definiert: a) für das Irische: "where the preposition *la* is used with a verbal noun to convey the idea of concomitant or contemporaneous action" (55); b) für das Kymrische: "that the Welsh use of *gan* in this type of sentence is fairly close to the use of *la* in the Irish instances ... However, there is one notable difference: in all these latter instances the main sentence or phrase to which the *la* phrase is subordinated is in direct speech. Whether this holds true for all other instances of the construction in Irish remains to be seen" (57).

Die "syntaktische Gleichung" zeigt Übereinstimmung in der *inneren Form* der inselkeltischen Sprachen. Schwerer zu bestimmen ist das Alter des Syntagmas, das sozusagen als gemeinsame Neuerung durch Sprachkontakt ausgebildet wurde; nach den Feststellungen von P. Mac Cana 1983 bleibt die Zahl der Belege begrenzt. Hinzuweisen ist auf folgende Punkte:

a) Bei der Präposition *la* handelt es sich um eine auf das Goidelische beschränkte Neubildung[1]; kymr. *gan* verfügt dagegen als präfigiertes Element (Präfix, Präverb) über eine ältere keltische Etymologie: altir. *cét-*, akymr. *cant*, kymr. *can, gan*, korn. *cans, gans*, abret. *cant-*: griech. κατά[2]; vgl. besonders kymr. *canfod* = altir. *cétbaid*. Im Falle höheren Alters des Syntagmas war demnach davon auszugehen, daß das kymrische Äquivalent *gan* formal den älteren Status bewahrt hat, während altirisch *la* der späteren Substitution für älteres *$k\d{m}ta$- > *cét-* entspricht. Andererseits könnte im Falle jüngeren Alters des Syntagmas die altirische Wendung mit *la* einen *terminus post quem* geben für die goidelische Neuschöpfung *la*.

b) Motiv für das Aufkommen der präpositionalen Periphrase ist der Verlust des Partizip Praesens Aktiv in den inselkeltischen Sprachen[3]. Dies zeigt sich bereits an den griech./lat. Vorlagen für das Bibelzitat Mark. 6.48, die mit dem Partizipium konstruiert sind: ἔρχεται πρὸς αὐτοὺς περιπατῶν ἐπὶ τῆς θαλάττης / *venit ad eos ambulans super mare*.

Andererseits findet sich in der altarmenischen Bibelübersetzung von Mark. 6.48 eine typologische Parallele zur Umschreibung des Partizips in der kymrischen Wiedergabe von Mark. 6.48: *gáy ar nosa gnalov i veray covun* — mit *gnalov*, dem Infinitiv/Verbalnomen von *gnam*, Aorist *gnac'i* 'ich gehe, ἔρχομαι, πορεύομαι' im Instrumental[4] und *gay* ἔρχεται als finiter Verbalform. Der Beleg macht deutlich, daß im Altarmenischen die gleichen Voraussetzungen, d.h. das Fehlen des Part.Präs. Aktiv, zu einer vergleichbaren Umschreibung des Part.Präs. Aktiv durch das Verbalnomen geführt haben.

Eine ganz andere Lösung begegnet in der ältesten altgeorgischen Bibelübersetzung der Šat'berd-Redaktionen aus den Jahren 897, 936 und 973[5], wo in dem gleichen Bibelzitat Mark. 6.48 die Hypotaxe parataktisch aufgelöst erscheint: DE *movida* (finites Verbum im Aorist) *mata iesu da vidoda* (finites Verbum im Imperfekt) *zɣuasa zeda* "es kam (*movida*) zu ihnen Jesus und wandelte (*vidoda*) auf dem Meer (*zɣuasa zeda*)" = C *movida mata, vidoda zɣuasa zeda*[6].

---

1 Vgl. N. Müller, Die Präposition *la* im Altirischen, ZCP 45 (1992) 102-131.
2 Lewis/Pedersen, *A Concise Comparative Celtic Grammar* 48; Vendryes, *LEIA C* (1987) 83f.
3 Vgl. Vf., Zur Entwicklung indogermanischer Partizipien im Keltischen. *Linguistique Balkanique* 31 (1988) 25-29.
4 Vgl. R. Stempel, *Die infiniten Verbalformen des Altarmenischen* (Frankfurt a. M./Bern/New York 1983) 19.
5 A. Šanize, *Kartuli otxtavis ori ʒveli redakcia sami šat'berduli xelnac'eris mixedvit* (897, 936 da 973 c'c') (Tbilisi 1945): 897 = Adišis otxtavi (Evangelium von Adiši) = C, 936 = ʒruč'is otxtavi (Evangelium von ʒruč'i) = D, 973 = P'arxlis otxtavi (Evangelium von P'arxli) = E. D und E gehen auf eine gemeinsame Vorlage zurück.
6 Vgl. Vf., Zur Wiedergabe aktiver griechischer Partizipialkonstruktionen in den altarmenischen und altgeorgischen Bibelübersetzungen. In: R. Schulz/M. Görg, *Lingua restituta*

c) Inwieweit es sich, wie zu vermuten, bei der von dem Jubilar festgestellten kontextuellen Einschränkung der irischen *la*-Konstruktionen auf Subordination zu direkter Rede um eine spätere sekundäre Entwicklung handelt, bedarf der weiteren Untersuchung.

2. *fri* 'of, about, concerning' (57–58): kymr. *wrth*. Die als *note 2* besprochene Beobachtung unseres Jubilars geht aus von der funktionalen Studie, die J. E. Caerwyn Williams, On the uses of Old Irish *fri* and its cognates, *Celtica* 3 (1956) 126–148 vorgelegt hatte. Diesem Material beigefügt wird die Glosse *ní fris ru-chét* 'it is not with reference to it that it was sung' Ml 64ª13, zu der der Jubilar feststellt: Die Konstruktion "comes close to the MW instances of verbs of asking, hearing, knowing, etc. with *wrth* 'concerning, about'". Subtile Beobachtungen dieser Art setzen die souveräne Kenntnis älterer irischer und kymrischer Texte voraus, ein Merkmal, das die Arbeiten von P. Mac Cana stets in unvergleichlicher Weise ausgezeichnet hat. Die kontrastive/konfrontative Grammatik der Präpositional- phrasen in den inselkeltischen Sprachen bleibt als Frucht solcher wertvollen Beobachtungen noch zu schreiben.

3. *Labraid Lúath Lám ar Claideb* (58–59)[7] enthält mit der Trennung von *Lúath Lám ar Claideb* durch den Jubilar die Korrektur älterer Schreibungen, wie z.B. *Lúathlám ar Claideb* durch Myles Dillon, *Serglige Con Culainn* (Dublin 1953; reprint 1975) 91. P. Mac Cana definiert *Celtica* 7 (1966) 91–115 den zugrundeliegenden Typus des komplexen Attributes folgendermaßen: "The thing or quality denoted by the second noun (B) pertains to or is part of the person or object denoted by the first noun (A), the latter being represented by the poss. pronoun; thus for example *dyn budr ei wedd*, "a man of filthy appearance"' (91).

Bei der Herausarbeitung dieses Typus diskutiert P. Mac Cana eine Reihe von Varianten, darunter besonders:

a) Attraktion des Adjektivs an das vorangehende Nomen, z.B. y *uorwyn* uwyaf y mawred *a uu yn teir ynys prydein*, WM 470.5 'the maiden of most majesty that was ever in the three islands of Britain', wo die Lenierung von *uwyaf* (anstelle des parenthetisch konstruierten *mwyaf y mawred* durch Attraktion an das feminine y *uorwyn* bewirkt ist, im Prinzip vergleichbar der Schreibung *Lúathlám:* In beiden Fällen wird das komplexe Attribut — *Lúath Lám ar Claideb* bzw. *mwyaf y mawred* grammatisch nicht mehr verstanden.

b) 'a variant of our basic syntax in which the poss. pron. is replaced by the article. This usage which is quite frequent in the Bible and later literature generally

---

orientalis. Festgabe für Julius Aßfalg (Wiesbaden 1990) 298–302.

7 Vgl. hierzu Vf., *ZCP* 41 (1986) 304.

occurs with the word *golwg*, as in *gwraig lân yr olwg*, Gen. XII.11' (1966: 111). Das Zitat, dem in der Septuaginta-Übersetzung γυνὴ εὐπρόσωπος entspricht, wird von dem Jubilar mit dem irischen Typus in Verbindung gebracht, 'where the pred. of the subordinate clause is an adjective, in fact leaves the genitive unexpressed, as in *intí as énirt hiress* "he whose faith is weak", Wb 10ᶜ1' (1966: 112)[8].

Konstruktionen dieses Typus haben vor 50 Jahren eine zusammenfassende Bearbeitung erfahren durch G. Deeters, Komplexe Attribute und Possessivkomposita, *IF* 60 (1949) 47–62, der u.a. den türkischen Beleg *dam-ı̇ qı̇rmı̇zı̇ ev* 'Haus mit rotem Dach', wörtlich 'sein Dach rot Haus' zitiert (1949: 48). Die zahlreichen typologischen Parallelen aus dem außerkeltischen und außerindogermanischen Bereich unterstreichen die Erkenntnis, daß die Wurzeln der vergleichbaren keltischen Syntagmata sehr alt sind und außerhalb des Bereiches des keltischen Relativsatzes gesucht werden müssen.

---

8 Vgl. dazu Thurneysen, *Grammar* 321; Pedersen, *Vergl. Gramm.* II 225f.

A Turkish-Celtic Problem in Chrétien de Troyes: The Name *Cligés*

Patrick Sims-Williams

DEPARTMENT OF WELSH, UNIVERSITY OF WALES, ABERYSTWYTH

CHRÉTIEN DE TROYES's *Cligés* is rarely of direct concern to Celtic scholars. In the words of Lucie Polak,

> It is his only romance not to make use of Celtic mythical material and in spite of the fact that the hero and his father visit Arthur's court and that the hero is actually Arthur's grand-nephew, it cannot meaningfully be called an Arthurian romance.[1]

I agree with this. The only aspect of Chrétien's romance with which I shall be concerned is the hero's name. I shall also be considering a much later appearance of this name — not that in the thirteenth-century *Marques de Rome*, which is widely thought to derive from Chrétien's romance,[2] but that in the Middle English *Sir Cleges*, a short romance which shares no more than its title with Chrétien's. The character Cligés in the *Roman d'Yder* and the rather similarly named knight Gliglois in the *Roman de Gliglois* will also be discussed.

Did Chrétien simply invent the strange name *Cligés* out of nothing or did he base it on some real name? I shall assume that it is not a simple invention because, generally speaking, made-up names for characters in romances, including Chrétien's, either contain transparently meaningful elements or at least are expres-

---

1 Lucie Polak, *Chrétien de Troyes: Cligés* (London, 1982), p. 9. Line references are to the edition by Claude Luttrell and Stewart Gregory, *Chrétien de Troyes: Cligés* (Cambridge, 1993).
2 Polak, p. 88.

sive in themselves; and Old French *Cligés* is neither meaningful nor expressive, at least to my ears.

The father of Chrétien's hero is Alexandre, eldest son of the emperor of Constantinople and Greece. Attracted by the fame of Arthur, he comes to Britain, lands at Southampton, and seeks out King Arthur at Winchester. Before long he falls in love with Arthur's niece, and eventually marries her. Arthur makes him crowned king of the best kingdom in Wales ('le meillor reiaume de Gales', vv. 1454–55 and 2351). The happy pair have a son and heir, the hero of the 'estoire'. We would expect them to baptize him with a Byzantine or a British name, or perhaps one acceptable in both lands. They name him Cligés (v. 2364).

For many years there was no remotely plausible answer to Foerster's exclamation: 'if only one knew whence the name Cligés derived!'.[3] More recently, a number of scholars, starting on the Byzantine track, have suggested independently that Cligés's prototype was the contemporary Seljuk sultan of Iconium (Konya) in Turkey, Kilidj Arslan II, who reigned 1156–92. Kilidj Arslan defeated Manuel, the emperor of Constantinople in 1176, just as Cligés defeats his usurping uncle Alis, emperor of Constantinople, and, according to some sources, in 1173 Kilidj had attempted to win the hand of the daughter of the Emperor of Germany (Frederick Barbarossa), as Chrétien's Cligés does, but successfully and in different circumstances, by the end of the romance, in marrying Fénice.

The names *Kilidj Arslan* and *Cligés* were first equated in 1961 by Henry and Renée Kahane,[4] and again in 1962 by Günter Reichenkron;[5] then in 1972 Endra v. Ivánka proposed the identification again,[6] evidently being unaware of the earlier publications.[7] The identification was sympathetically received by some,[8] but certain doubts were voiced in a review of the Kahanes' article by Raffaele de

3   *Kristian von Troyes: Cligés*, ed. Wendelin Foerster, rev. Alfons Hilka (Halle (Saale), 1921), p. xxxiv: 'Wenn man nur wüsste, woher der Name Cligés stammt!'

4   'L'énigme du nom de *Cligès*', *Romania*, 82 (1961), 113–21. (Variation between the grave and the acute accent on *Cligés* is *sic!*)

5   'Chretienstudien, I. Teil: Zur Namensform *Cligès*', *Saggi e ricerche in memoria di Ettore li Gotti*, III, *Bollettino del Centro di Studi Filologici e Linguistici Siciliani*, 8 (1962), 72–82. This study has not received due credit. On the historical background see further Paul Magdalino, *The Empire of Manuel I Komnenos, 1143–1180* (Cambridge, 1993).

6   'Fragen eines Byzantinisten an Germanisten und Romanisten (Wolfdietrich und *Cligès*)', *Germanische-Romanische Monatsschrift*, 53 = N.F. 22 (1972), 433–35.

7   Cf. Erich Köhler, ibid., 54 = N.F. 23 (1973), 238.

8   Polak, pp. 10–11; Krijne Ciggar, 'Encore une fois Chrétien de Troyes et la "matière byzantine": la révolution des femmes au palais de Constantinople', *Cahiers de civilisation médiévale*, 38 (1995) 267–74 (pp. 267–8).

Cesare.[9] While noting the 'vaga omofonia' of the names, he wondered quite why Chrétien would have wanted to turn a pagan Seljuk sultan into a Christian Byzantine prince. He also noted that a short Byzantine form *Κλι(τ)ζης, with a Greek -ης suffix, which was posited by the Kahanes (and also, with some less likely alternatives by Reichenkron), is unattested.

The name Kilidj Arslan is made up of the Turkish elements kılıc (or qılıc) 'sword' and arslan 'lion' (the latter is familiar from Aslan in C. S. Lewis's Narnia novels). The sultan of Iconium is rarely (or never?) named in Western sources, but Byzantine Greek writers, syncopating the first vowel of his name (a schwa sound [ə]), transcribed the first element in his name as Κλιτζ-, which recalls the first syllable of Cliges. (In Old French the medial g was pronounced [dʒ].) In Greek sources the name is given in full as Κλιτζιεσθλὰν, Κλιτζασθλαν, and (with a Greek termination) Κλιτζασθλάνην (acc.). The simple name Κηλήτζ representing Kılıc does not appear in Greek sources until the turn of the twelfth to the thirteenth century,[10] and this is far from the posited form *Κλι(τ)ζης.

Without wishing to rule out the Seljuk etymology for Cligés's name, I would like to suggest a Welsh one; Chrétien may have fixed on this particular name because he could pass it off as both Oriental and Celtic, like his hero. My candidate is the Welsh personal name pronounced [*gləwïs], spelt Glywys in Middle and Modern Welsh, but Gliguis, *Gligues, *Gliguois, etc. (as well as Gliuis, etc.) in the Old Welsh spelling which obtained up to and for much of the twelfth century.[11] In this name the medial g was not pronounced at all like that in Old French Cligés, but formed part of the graph -gu- which represented the semi-vowel [w], later spelt -w-.[12] What I am proposing, then, is not an oral borrowing from Welsh into French, but a written borrowing, during the process of which the value of the symbols would be liable to be misunderstood.[13] Misunderstandings

9 In Studi francesci, 16 (1962), 120.
10 Reichenkron, p. 80
11 cf. Ifor Williams, 'The Ogmore Castle Inscription', Archaeologia Cambrensis, 87 (1932), 232–38 (p. 236). For spellings of this name see Kenneth Jackson, Language and History in Early Britain (Edinburgh, 1953), pp. 189 and 386; P. C. Bartrum, Early Welsh Genealogical Tracts (Cardiff, 1966), p. 190; and Ifor Williams and Rachel Bromwich, Armes Prydein (Dublin, 1972), p. xv. *Gligues and *Gliguois are possible but unattested; for ue instead of ui in Old Welsh compare gueleri in Geiriadur Prifysgol Cymru, s.v. gwyleri, and for oi see Jackson, Language and History, p. 330.
12 See Patrick Sims-Williams, 'The Emergence of Old Welsh, Cornish and Breton Orthography, 600–800: The Evidence of Archaic Old Welsh', Bulletin of the Board of Celtic Studies, 38 (1991), 20–86 (pp. 27 and 72 and references).
13 Examples involving transmission into Old English and Old Irish include Rigwatlan in the Anglo-Saxon Chronicle s.a. 1063 (cf. Jackson, Language and History, p. 393, n. 1), and Pangur

due to written transmission between Brittonic Celtic and French were quite common. For example, the Welsh name *Branwen* [*branweɴ], would be spelled *Branguen(n)* in Old Welsh, with silent *g*, yet the *g* duly appears in the Tristan romances (*Brangain, Brangein, Brangien, Branguain, Brangve(i)n*, etc.), where it would have been pronounced (mostly as a 'hard' [g], not as a 'soft' [dʒ] as in *Cligés*).[14]

The difference in the initial consonants of *Cligés* and *Glywys* is no great problem from a Celtic point of view, since initial *c-* and *g-* alternate regularly in Welsh by the initial mutation known as lenition, and in certain circumstances the first consonant of a name might change from *G-* to *C-* by a kind of back-forma-tion or hypercorrection, which may be why *Clemens* seems to have been an acceptable Latinization of *Glywys* in medieval Wales.[15] It is not impossible, therefore, that the name could have been transmitted in written form with a *C-*. Yet we must also reckon with the possibilities of simple miscopying by Chrétien or a predecessor of C for G, of mismatch between two phonemic systems (French *Guiot* > German *Kyot* being a well-known example), and of neutralization of the voiced/voiceless distinction before /l/; a parallel in French romance is *Clamorgan* for *Glamorgan* in the early-thirteenth-century *Meriadeuc, ou, Li Chevaliers as deus espees*.[16] It may be significant that Merthyr *Glywys*, Glamorgan appears on modern

---

in a ninth-century Old Irish poem (Patrick Sims-Williams, 'The Evidence for Vernacular Irish Literary Influence on Early Mediaeval Welsh Literature', in *Ireland in Early Mediaeval Europe: Studies in memory of Kathleen Hughes*, edited by Dorothy Whitelock, Rosamond McKitterick, and David Dumville (Cambridge, 1982), 235–57 (p. 241)). See also n. 19 and n. 31 below.

14 Louis-Fernand Flutre, *Table des noms propres avec toutes leurs variantes figurant dans les romans du moyen âge écrits en français ou en provençal* (Poitiers, 1962), p. 34. See further Patrick Sims-Williams, 'Did Itinerant Breton *Conteurs* Transmit the *Matière de Bretagne*?' *Romania*, t. 116 (1998), 72–111 (pp. 77–78).

15 Cf. Bartrum, *Tracts*, p. 177. In *Bonedd y Saint*, §39, Glywys ap Solor, father of St Petroc, appears as 'Clemens/Climens tywyssauc o Gernyw' ('Klemais, Iarll Kerniw' in *Achau'r Saint*, §48); see ibid., pp. 60, 71, and 143 (who suggests simple corruption), and he is also 'Klemens' in 'Pedigrees of the Tribal Patriarchs', ed. P. C. Bartrum, *National Library of Wales Journal*, 13 (1963–64), 93–146, §70. For Clemens, Clemuis, etc. as a personal name in the Book of Llandaf see: *The Text of the Book of Lan Dâv*, ed. J. Gwenogvryn Evans and John Rhŷs (Oxford, 1893), p. 392, and Sims-Williams, 'Emergence', p. 53 (cf. John T. Koch, 'The Conversion and the Transition from Primitive to Old Irish *c.* 367–*c.* 637', *Emania*, 13 (1995), 39–50 (p. 50, n. 5)).

16 Flutre, p. 224. D. Ellis Evans, *Gaulish Personal Names* (Oxford, 1967), p. 400, notes 'very many instances of the interchange of *c* and *g* in Continental forms', one of which is the Gaulish place-name *Glanum/Clanum* (dép. Aude). Cf. *Plenmeller* in Northumberland (with *Pl-* attested since 1256) : Welsh *blaen moelfre*, on which Eilert Ekwall, *The Concise Oxford Dictionary of English Place-Names*, fourth edition (Oxford, 1960), p. 368, comments: 'The

maps in the anglicized form *Clevis*.[17] In view of the above-mentioned equation of *Glywys* and *Clemens* it is probably no coincidence that places called *Clementislond* and *Clemenstoun* are attested near Merthyr Glywys in the fifteenth and sixteenth centuries (see below).[18]

Another possibility is that Chrétien himself altered the initial consonant of the Welsh name in order to assimilate it to the Seljuk name Κλιτζασθλαν. A hint that the name was current with a *G-* in French is provided by the thirteenth-century Arthurian romance *Gliglois*. The hero's name *Gliglois* (-*z*) or *Glyglois* (-*z*) comes very close to a hypothetical Old Welsh **Gliguois* or **Glyguois*, and could be due to a misreading; alternatively the second /l/ could be due to a corruption of *Gligois* (a form which actually occurs, presumably in error, at v. 977).[19] I am

---

substitution of Engl. *P-* for Welsh *B-* is not without analogies'. On *c* and *g*, see also John T. Koch, '*Cothairche, Esposito's Theory, and Neo-Celtic Lenition', in ed. Alfred Bammesberger and Alfred Wollmann (Heidelberg, 1990), 179–202 (p. 199); J. F. Eska, 'On Voicing Crossover in Gaulish Plosives' (forthcoming).

17 In Newton Nottage, Grid Reference SS8377; Merthyr Glywys is so identified in: *Book of Llan Dâv*, p. 412 ('Clivis' is the modern form cited); R. J. Thomas, *Enwau Afonydd a Nentydd Cymru* (Cardiff, 1938), p. 145; William Rees, *South Wales and the Border in the Fourteenth Century* (Cardiff, 1932), SE Sheet; and by implication in Melville Richards, *Welsh Administrative and Territorial Units* (Cardiff, 1969), p. 156, s.n. 'Merthyr Glywys *ch* Newton Nottage'. Richards distinguishes Merthyr Glywys from Merthyr Mawr (SS8877), whereas they are tentatively identified by Wendy Davies, *An Early Welsh Microcosm: Studies in the Llandaff Charters* (London, 1978), pp. 99, n. 1, and 121. She takes *Mawr* as the adjective 'great', whereas it is really from a personal name *Myfor*; see Gwynedd O. Pierce, *The Place-Names of Dinas Powys Hundred* (Cardiff, 1968), p. 134. In *Book of Lan Dâv*, p. 225 (charter 224), *Merthir Gliuis* appears in the bounds of Merthyr Mawr (*Merthir Miuor*), and seems therefore to be a distinct place.

18 Now Clement (SS8578) and Clemen(t)stone (SS9273). These are two of only three Clemens/Clement place-names recorded by B. G. Charles, *Non-Celtic Place-Names in Wales* (London, 1938), pp. 31, 145, 147, and 293. (The third is Treglemais (*Trefclemens* 1326, *Clementiston* 1332) in Pembrokeshire; see idem, *The Place-Names of Pembrokeshire*, 2 vols (Aberystwyth, 1992), I, 230 (cf. Parc-Clement, ibid., pp. 376–77)).

19 *Gliglois: A French Arthurian Romance of the Thirteenth Century*, ed. Charles H. Livingston (Cambridge, MA, 1932), pp. 176–77; on pp. 22–23 it is noted that Gaston Paris saw a reference to this hero in the allusion to 'Clipois' (rhyming with *liegois* and coupled with 'Cliget') in *Richars li Biaus* (c. 1275). Paris compared the name *Giglain/Guinglain* in *Le Bel Inconnu* and the German *Wigalois* (ibid., p. 25). *Wigalois* is interpreted as a form of Breton *Wingualoe/Winwaloe* (Gwénolé) by Léon Fleuriot, 'Les lais bretons', in *Histoire littéraire et culturelle de la Bretagne*, 3 vols, ed. Jean Balcou and Yves Le Gallo, I, *Héritage celtique et captation française*, ed. Léon Fleuriot and Auguste-Pierre Ségalen (Paris, 1987), 131–38 (p. 134). Presumably this would then be another example of misunderstood medial *g*; but compare Fleuriot's analysis of the name of the German romance hero *Wigamur* as *wig-* 'combat' + *amur/amor* 'sort, fortune succès' (ibid., 136–37), and see Hendricus Sparnaay,

not suggesting that the author of *Gliglois* himself drew on Welsh sources,[20] but that he adopted, or adapted, the name of his hero from a pre-existing French work that had done so (such as the lost *lai* of *Glygis* dicussed below).

The etymology of the name *Glywys* is debated. Ifor Williams and R. J. Thomas derive it from Welsh *glyw* 'lord', although a possible older etymology deriving it from *Glevensis*, 'man of Gloucester' (Romano-British *Glevum*), is still current.[21] The only well-known bearer of the name was the eponym of the early south-east Welsh kingdom of Glywysing, who was supposed to have flourished in about the fifth or sixth century. Glywysing and its kings are mentioned in the ninth century in the *Historia Brittonum*, §41 (*Gleguissing*), and in Asser's *Life of Alfred*, §80 (*Gleguising*), and in the eighth- and ninth-century charters preserved in doctored form in the early-twelfth-century Book of Llandaf. Asser distinguishes Glywysing and Gwent but in the charters, grants by kings of 'Glywysing' cover modern Glamorgan and Monmouthshire, presumably because they had established some sort of overlordship in Gwent.[22] Roughly speaking, Glywysing was the predecessor of *Morgannwg* or *Gwlad Morgan* ('Morgan's Land'), that is, Glamorgan, which takes its name from a later king Morgan.[23] Glamorgan/ Glywysing was, for

---

'Hartmann von Aue and his Successors', in *Arthurian Literature in the Middle Ages*, ed. Roger Sherman Loomis (Oxford, 1959), 430–42 (pp. 439 and 441).

20 'It is certain that he has not drawn upon the Celtic tradition, that there is no folk-tale motif, and that there was no legend of Gliglois' (Livingston, p. 33). Gliglois comes from 'Almaigne', presumably Germany (see Flutre, p. 193), although confusion with *Albaine* (Scotland) has been suggested in other romances; see Ernst Brugger, 'Almain and Ermonie as Tristan's Home, II. Almain', *Modern Philology*, 26 (1928–29), 1–12; *The Romance of Yder*, ed. and trans. Alison Adams (Cambridge, 1983), pp. 19 and 253.

21 Williams, 'Ogmore Castle Inscription', p. 236; Thomas, *Enwau Afonydd*, p. 145; cf. *The Description of Pembrokeshire by George Owen*, Part IV, ed. Henry Owen (London, 1936), p. 607 (where it is said to be 'once a fairly common name in S.-E. Wales'); Bartrum, *Tracts*, p. 143; G. O. Pierce, 'The Evidence of Place-Names', in *Glamorgan County History*, II, *Early Glamorgan*, ed. H. N. Savory (Cardiff 1984), 456–92 (p. 490, n. 85); *Culhwch ac Olwen: Testun Syr Idris Foster*, ed. Rachel Bromwich and D. Simon Evans (Cardiff, 1988), p. xlviii, n. 91; Patrick Sims-Williams, *Religion and Literature in Western England, 600–800* (Cambridge, 1990), p. 24; Thomas Charles-Edwards, 'Language and Society among the Insular Celts A D 400–1000', in *The Celtic World*, ed. Miranda J. Green (London, 1995) 703–36 (p. 705, n. 9). An instance in north Wales is a Clwyd farm-name Glyn Liws (*Glyn Glewys* in 1334; *Glyn Gliwys* c. 1550): Bedwyr Lewis Jones, *Yn ei Elfen* (Capel Garmon, 1992), p. 62; J. Gwenogvryn Evans, *Report on Manuscripts in the Welsh Language*, I (London, 1898), p. 981.

22 Cf. J. E. Lloyd, *A History of* Wales, third edition, 2 vols (London, 1939), I, 273, n. 254; Davies, *Microcosm*, p. 91; Sims-Williams, *Religion and Literature*, p. 46. (I accept the authenticity of Asser.)

23 On the history of the area see further J. K. Knight, 'Sources for the Early History of

the Normans, the wealthiest kingdom in Wales, just like the unnamed Welsh kingdom which Arthur grants to Cligés's father, Alexandre, in Chrétien's poem.

Up to 1081 Glamorgan had its own native Welsh king, Caradog *rex Gulatmorganensium*, who apparently held his kingdom from the king, William the Conqueror.[24] On Caradog's death in 1081, William marched through south Wales to St Davids, probably establishing the mint and castle at Cardiff (the largest in Wales) *en route*, as well as castles at Caerleon and elsewhere.[25] In about 1093, William II set up his favourite Robert fitz Hamo between the rivers Ogmore and Usk, in southern Glamorgan and in Gwynllŵg (the adjacent lordship); fitz Hamo's chief castle was Cardiff, where the Norman knights of the shire-fee (the whole lowland zone) owed him service at his court.[26] About 1120, Glamorgan passed by marriage to Henry I's natural son, Robert, earl of Gloucester (d. 1147), who enlarged the lordship and defended it against the successful attacks of King Caradog's grandsons Morgan and Iorwerth, with whom he was obliged to come to an accommodation. As late as the 1150s, the brothers were holding lands from Henry II — the 'honour of Caerleon' (an evocatively Arthurian name) — and Morgan (d. 1158) was styling himself *rex*. He was last native 'king' in Glamorgan.[27] Lesser Welsh lords continued to hold lands in the area, even as close to Cardiff as the manor of *Beganston* ('Bychan's *tun*'), near Brynwell, just across the river Ely from Cardiff; and those in the uplands, though owing allegiance to the lord of Cardiff, made periodic raids on his castle, as in 1158 and 1183/84.[28] Nevertheless, the lordship of Glamorgan remained one of the most secure and fertile Norman colonies in Wales. Arthur's gift to Cligés's father of the

Morgannwg', in *Glamorgan County History*, II, 365–409; Philip Jenkins, 'Regions and Cantrefs in Early Medieval Glamorgan', *Cambridge Medieval Celtic Studies*, 15 (Summer 1988), 31–50.

24 David Crouch, 'The Slow Death of Kingship in Glamorgan, 1067–1158', *Morgannwg*, 29 (1985), 20–41 (pp. 24 and 30), citing the *Life* of St Gwynllyw, §15, in *Vitae Sanctorum Britanniae et Genealogiae*, ed. and trans. A. W. Wade-Evans (Cardiff, 1944), pp. 188–90; the *Life* also calls him *regulus*. See also J. Beverley Smith, 'The Kingdom of Morgannwg and the Norman Conquest of Glamorgan', in *Glamorgan County History*, III, *The Middle Ages*, ed. T. B. Pugh (Cardiff, 1971), 1–43 (p. 7).

25 Crouch, pp. 25 and 27–28.

26 ibid., pp. 28–29; J. Beverley Smith, 'The Lordship of Glamorgan', *Morgannwg*, 2 (1958), 9–37 (pp. 15–16).

27 Crouch, pp. 32–36. On the significance of Caerleon here see John Gillingham, 'The Context and Purposes of Geoffrey of Monmouth's *History of the Kings of Britain*', *Anglo-Norman Studies*, 13 (1990), 99–118 (pp. 114–15 and 118).

28 Crouch, p. 31; Smith, 'Lordship', pp. 23–24. Beganston is marked by Rees, *South Wales and the Border*, SE Sheet. Brynwell is at ST1474; cf. John Newman, *Glamorgan*, The Buildings of Wales (Harmondsworth, 1995), p. 371. For Cardiff castle, see ibid., pp. 196–97 and pl. 32.

'best realm in Wales' as his kingdom makes sense against this background, if we take it that Glywysing/Glamorgan is implied.

Another resemblance between Glywys and Cligés is that in twelfth-century Welsh legend Glywys was reputed to be a descendant of Constantine the Great; thus he had a remote connection with Constantinople, although his father was said to be a Solor, not an Alexander.[29] One might not expect Glamorgan saints to be mixed up with Byzantium, but the twelfth-century *Life* of St Cyngar, possibly by Caradog of Llancarfan, claims that Cyngar was born to the Emperor of Constantinople and was known to the Welsh as St Dogwy, the patron of Llandough, Glamorgan.[30]

A stronger link between Cligés and the Glywysing area is provided by the late-twelfth- or early-thirteenth-century romance of *Yder*. The author of *Yder* no doubt knew Chrétien's works; however, he undoubtedly drew on earlier sources, some going back to the period of the Modena archivolt of *c.* 1120–40, and his knight Cligés (-*ez*) is 'probably not to be identified with the Cligés who originates in Chrétien's *Cligés*', being 'an insolent and brutal knight'.[31] Yder son of Nuc himself comes from 'Alemaigne' (as does Gliglois in *Gliglois*, curiously[32]), but most of the action of *Yder* takes place 'round the Severn estuary'.[33] In particular, the

29 Bartrum, *Tracts*, pp. 24 and 132; *Vita S. Cadoci*, §45, ed. Wade-Evans, *Vitae Sanctorum Britanniae*, pp. 116–19.
30 Knight, 'Sources', pp. 390–91.
31 *Yder*, ed. Adams, pp. 18 and 257; Alexandre Micha, 'Miscellaneous French Romances in Verse', in *Arthurian Literature in the Middle Ages*, ed. Loomis, 358–92 (pp. 375–76). On Modena, see Jacques Stiennon and Rita Lejeune, 'La légende arthurienne dans la sculpture de la cathédrale de Modène', *CCM*, 6 (1963), 281–96; Sims-Williams, 'Breton *conteurs*'. Its name *Winlogee* is explained by Léon Fleuriot as '*Winloge(n)* . . . une transcription approximative du nom breton armoricain *Winloguen*, prononcé Wenlowen, composé des deux éléments *win-*, "blanc, heureux, béni" et *lowen-*, "gai, joyeux"' (review of Jean Markale, *Le roi Arthur et la société celtique*, in *Romania*, 98 (1977), 410–12 (p. 411); cf. Claude Evans, 'Women's Names in Early Brittany', in *Proceedings of the First North American Congress of Celtic Studies*, ed. Gordon MacLennan (Ottawa, 1988), 545–53 (pp. 547, 549, and 552): *Uuen-louuen*). Flutre, p. 100, suggests 'celt. *Winwaloe*, nom masculin' (cf. n. 19 above).
32 See above, n. 20. Brugger, pp. 2–3, argues that Scotland is meant. Yder's birthplace is *Cardoil* (Carlisle).
33 Adams, p. 19. Compare the interpolation in William of Malmesbury's *De Antiquitate Glastonie Ecclesie*, ed. John Scott, *The Early History of Glastonbury* (Woodbridge, 1981), §34, where Ider son of Nuth is associated with Arthur's court at Caerleon and with *mons Ranarum* alias Brent Knoll (cf. John of Glastonbury in *The Chronicle of Glastonbury Abbey*, ed. and trans. James P. Carley and David Townsend (Woodbridge, 1985), pp. 74–75 and 284, n. 116). Did the Glastonbury monks misunderstand *Bryn Buga* (Usk) as *Bryn Broga* (W. *broga* 'frog')? If Ider's father was identified with the famous north British hero Nudd Hael son of Senyllt, Ider would have been supposed to be the nephew of Dingad son of

knight Cligés is a vassal (*tenant*, v. 4281) of Queen Guenloïe (the *Winlogee* of the Modena relief), whose court is at 'Carvain', that is, Caerwent (< *Venta Silurum*, the city which also gave its name to Gwent), one of the earliest Norman outposts in Wales. Cligés's fief is confiscated by the queen, but restored fourfold at the end of the poem (v. 6735). Here again we may see an echo of Glywys, the eponym of Glywysing. If Cligés's name began with *G-* in the source used by the author of *Yder*, the prestige of Chrétien's works would be enough to warrant changing it to *C-*.

Glywys's earliest associations are with western Glamorgan. No grants by him appear in the Book of Llandaf (perhaps he was just too early), but what purports to be one of the earliest charters in the book (no. 76b) is a grant of Bishopston, Gower, 'in the reign of Merchwyn ap Glywys' (*regnante Merchguino filio Gliuis*), who was presumably his son. Glywys (assuming it is the same Glywys) seems to have enjoyed a religious cult, like other early medieval kings.[34] A local parallel is Tewdrig, ancestor of the next dynasty of kings of Glywysing, who gave his name to Merthyr Tewdrig (Matharn, Gwent), after a heroic and saintly stand against the Saxons at Tintern.[35] Rather similarly, Glywys gave his name to another *merthyr* ('church' < *martyrium*), for the bounds of Merthyr Mawr, an estate near the river Ogmore in a tenth-century charter in the Book of Llandaf, include *Merthir Gliuis*, the *martyrium* of Glywys.[36] An eleventh-century stone at Merthyr Mawr was erected for the soul of Saint *Gliussi* (gen.) and others, and another eleventh-century stone nearby at Ogmore grants land 'to God and to *Gliguis*' and others.[37] Here Glywys is clearly the patron saint of some church or religious community.[38]

Senyllt, and Dingad was king of Bryn Buga, according to the *Life* of St Llawddog (*Tracts*, ed. Bartrum, p. 31).

34 Cf. David Rollason, 'The Cult of Murdered Royal Saints in Anglo-Saxon England', *Anglo-Saxon England*, 11 (1982), 1–22. There is no reason to regard Glywys as a martyr, however, since *merthyr* 'church' and *merthyr* 'martyr' were distinct, though no doubt liable to confusion; see Pierce, *Dinas Powys Hundred*, p. 134. The identity of the culted Glywys and the eponym of Glywysing is doubted by Williams, 'Ogmore Castle Inscription', p. 236.

35 *Book of Llan Dâv*, pp. 141–42 (no. 141); Richards, *Units*, p. 156; Sims-Williams, *Religion and Literature*, p. 52. For a translation of the Tewdrig story see Walter de Gray Birch, *Memorials of Llandaff* (Neath, 1912), pp. 96–97.

36 See above, n. 17. The name is ambiguous, since it may mean either a church erected by Glywys or one at which he was venerated. The latter interpretation is supported by the Merthyr Tewdrig parallel.

37 V. E. Nash-Williams, *The Early Christian Monuments of* Wales (Cardiff, 1950), nos. 239 and 255; Royal Commission on Ancient and Historical Monuments in Wales, *An Inventory of the Ancient Monuments in Glamorgan*, I, Part iii (Cardiff, 1976), pp. 55–57.

38 cf. Davies, *Microcosm*, p. 140.

The above-mentioned *Clementislond* and *Clemenstoun* may have been dependent estates.

The main *literary* source for Glywys is the *Life* of St Cadog, his alleged grandson and patron saint of Llancarfan, Glamorgan. This was composed by Lifris of Llancarfan *c.* 1100, and is preserved in a MS of *c.* 1200 from Monmouth (London, British Library, Cotton Vespasian A.xiv), which contains a collection of Welsh Latin saints' Lives probably originally assembled at Gloucester Abbey.[39] A revised version of the *Life* of Cadog, which does not include the passage about Glywys,[40] was made by Caradog of Llancarfan, the 'contemporary' whom Geoffrey of Monmouth warns off the Arthurian period at the end of his *Historia Regum Britanniae.*[41] Caradog, or one of his pupils, may also have composed the Vespasian collection's *Life* of St Gwynllyw, Glywys's alleged great-grandson; and the *Life* of St Tatheus of Caerwent in the same collection seems to be by the same author, writing probably in the 1130s.[42] When these hagiographers were at work, Glywysing was coming under the rule of the Normans, among them Robert of Gloucester, one of the dedicatees of Geoffrey of Monmouth's *Historia.* Lifris's *Life* of St Cadog is generally regarded as a response to the Norman political and ecclesiastical conquest of south-east Wales — in particular, to the subordination to Gloucester Abbey first of St Gwynllyw's church at Newport in 1093,[43] and then of St Cadog's church at Llancarfan *c.* 1095.[44] Similarly, J. K. Knight has argued that the *Life* of St Gwynllyw reflects a long running dispute between Gloucester Abbey and Robert of Gloucester, a dispute not settled until 1156. He sees it as covert propaganda against Robert on behalf Gloucester Abbey:

39 *Vitae Sanctorum Britanniae*, ed. and trans. Wade-Evans, pp. 24–141. See Kathleen Hughes, *Celtic Britain in the Early Middle Ages* (Woodbridge, 1980), pp. 53–66.

40 The Vespasian text of Lifris's *Life* is partly interpolated from Caradog's *Life*, but this does not affect the passages in question here. On the relationship between the two see Wendy Davies, 'Property Rights and Property Claims in Welsh "Vitae" of the Eleventh Century', in *Hagiographie, cultures et sociétés IVe–XIIe siècles*, Études augustiennes (Paris, 1981), 515–33 (pp. 528–30).

41 cf. Christopher N. L. Brooke, *The Church and the Welsh Border in the Central Middle Ages* (Woodbridge, 1986), pp. 41, n. 98, and 43.

42 *Vitae Sanctorum Britanniae*, ed. and trans. Wade-Evans, pp. 172–93 and 270–87. Cf. Brooke, p. 39, n. 93; Jeremy K. Knight, 'St. Tatheus of Caerwent: An Analysis of the Vespasian Life', *Monmouthshire Antiquary*, 3 (1970–78), 29–36. Knight, 'Sources', p. 392, dates the *Life* of Gwynllyw 1130×1136 and that of Tatheus 'soon afterwards'.

43 Brooke, p. 52.

44 ibid., pp. 60, n. 38, 64–65, 73, and 89. Davies, 'Property Rights', argues that lay depredations were a long-standing native problem, so that the Norman context is not necessarily implied. Cf. Crouch, pp. 21–22; John Reuben Davies, 'Church, Property, and Conflict in Wales, AD 600–1100', *Welsh History Review*, 18 (1997), 387–406.

The Earl of Gloucester was too powerful a man to be threatened too harshly with divine retribution, but it is made clear that the rights of the church of Gwynllyw had been respected by an impressive list of lords and kings and whilst the saint was quite capable of defending his property by supernatural means, it was quietly hinted that when the Earl learnt the true facts of the case, he might well be willing to right the wrong that the saint had suffered at his hands.[45]

The work of these and other Welsh hagiographers illustrates the sort of Welsh literary material that must have come to the attention of the Norman marcher lords and the clerics in their entourages. It is highly significant for the development of Arthurian romance that Arthur plays a part in them.[46]

Lifris begins his *Vita Cadoci* with an account of Glywys:

> Formerly within certain borders of the Britannic country, which was called Dyfed, there reigned a certain regulus, Glywys (*Gliuguis*) by name, from whom throughout all the days of his life the whole monarchy of that district took the name of Glywysing (*Gleuguissig*). He is said to have begotten ten children, of whom the first-born was called Gwynllyw, from whose name too after the death of his father that country which he ruled is called Gwynllŵg to the present day.[47]

By a fiction paralleled elsewhere, each of Glywys's sons (apart from Petroc who becomes a saint in Bodmin, Cornwall) gives his name to a district of Glywysing.[48]

---

45 Knight, 'St. Tatheus', p. 35.

46 cf. Brooke, pp. 82–83; note also that Arthur and Caradog Fraichfras appear in the *Life* of St Padarn (*Vitae Sanctorum Britanniae*, ed. Wade-Evans, pp. 252–69), and that Llanbadarn was granted to Gloucester *c.* IIII (Brooke, pp. 55–56). This *Life* has been dated *c.* 1120 (see R. Geraint Gruffydd, 'Why Cors Fochno?', *Transactions of the Honourable Society of Cymmrodorion*, 1995, n.s. 2 (1996), 5–19 (pp. 12–13)). Caradog also figures in the *Life* of St Tatheus (§5).

47 Gwynllŵg lay between the Usk and the Rhymni.

48 Cf. Patrick Sims-Williams, 'Some Functions of Origin Stories in Early Medieval Wales', in *History and Heroic Tale*, edited by Tore Nyberg, Iørn Piø, Preben Meulengracht Sørensen, and Aage Trommer (Odense, 1985), 97–131 (pp. 102–3); Charles-Edwards, 'Language and Society', pp. 709–10. A useful map is given by Jenkins, p. 32. Glywys is called 'Glywys Cornubiensis' and 'Glewys Kerniw' in *Cognatio Brychan*, §15, and *Plant Brychan*, §3a (ed. Bartrum, *Tracts*, pp. 18 and 82), and he is called 'Glywis Earle of Cornewall', in *Nicholas Roscarrock's Lives of the Saints: Cornwall and Devon*, ed. Nicholas Orme (Exeter, 1992), p. 77. This may be an inference from Petroc's Cornishness, or does it result from an equation with the Cornish saint Gluvias? On Gluvias see Gilbert H. Doble, *The Saints of Cornwall*, III (Truro, 1964), pp. 15–19. Dr O. J. Padel tells me that he thinks the equation of Gluvias and Glywys possible, and has given me the following forms: Glyviacus 1291, Gluviacus 1318, Glywyatus 1334, Gliwyath 1342, Glewyas 1565. See now Nicholas Orme, *English Church Dedications with a Survey of Cornwall and Devon* (Exeter, 1996), p. 84.

King Gwynllyw falls in love with Gwladus, daughter of Brychan of Brycheiniog, and carries her off from Talgarth by force, pursued by Brychan and his host. As they pass the border between Brycheiniog and Gwynllŵg, they are seen by 'three vigorous heroes' (*tres heroes strenui*), namely Arthur and his two *equites* Cei and Bedwyr (*Bedguir*), who are sitting on a hill playing the game of *alea* (doubtless reflecting *gwyddbwyll* in the vernacular). Arthur, placed in a bad light, as usual in Welsh saints' Lives, is filled with lust for the girl and thinks to carry her off for himself; he is rebuked by Cei and Bedwyr, whose rebuke reflects the helpful, Robin Hood-like character of the Arthurian band in non-hagiographical works like *Culhwch and Olwen*: 'Far be it that so great a crime should be perpetrated by thee', say they to Arthur, 'for we are wont to aid the needy and distressed'.[49] One might think that they would now rescue the girl; instead, having ascertained that Gwynllyw has now crossed the border into his own kingdom, they drive back Brychan's host, allowing Gwynllyw to carry her home and marry her! But this is providential, as in due season she gives birth to St Cadog. Moreover, we learn from the *Life* of Gwynllyw, that Gwynllyw and his wife Gwladus themselves became saints. This *Life* also begins by mentioning Glywys (*Gliuusus*) as the 'most noble king of the Southern Britons' (§1). We see, then, that although no Welsh narrative about Glywys himself survives, he and his family appeared in tales in the twelfth century; in fact the *Life* of Gwynllyw, §11, tells us that Gwynllyw was the subject of a vernacular praise poem.

While it is interesting that the family of Glywys is involved with Arthur and his warriors, I must note that according to Lifris it is Gwynllyw who is Arthur's contemporary. This places his father Glywys a generation earlier than Arthur, unlike Chrétien's Cligés (and Gliglois in *Gliglois* and Cligés in *Yder*). Obviously this is one of various gaps between the Glywys of the Welsh hagiographers and Chrétien's Cligés. Can the credibility gap in my argument be bridged? Is there any evidence for a source that might be an intermediary between the South Welsh marches and Champagne?

In Shrewsbury School MS 7, a manuscript from Chester, Neil Ker discovered a late-thirteenth-century list in French of sixty-seven narrative lays.[50] Some can be

49 Cf. Brynley F. Roberts, '*Culhwch ac Olwen*, the Triads, Saints' Lives', in *The Arthur of the Welsh*, ed. Rachel Bromwich, A. O. H. Jarman, and Brynley F. Roberts (Cardiff, 1991), 73–95 (pp. 74 and 83).

50 Georgine E. Brereton, 'A Thirteenth-Century List of French Lays and Other Narrative Poems', *Modern Language Review*, 45 (1950), 40–45; N. R. Ker and A. J. Piper, *Medieval Manuscripts in British Libraries*, IV, *Paisley — York* (Oxford, 1992), 297. It seems clear that the titles are those of lays rather than romances. The list must be the result of a process of

identified with extant lays by Marie de France and others, but many are not extant. Several of these have Welsh subjects; this is understandable, for Chester was, after all, near the border, and already in Marie de France's *Lais* there is a distinct south Welsh emphasis, particularly in *Yonec* and *Milun*, with references to Caerleon and Caerwent, allusions resting on local knowledge according to the late Constance Bullock-Davies, who compared, for instance, Marie's statement in *Yonec* that Caerwent used to be reached by ships with a passage in the *Life* of St Tatheus, §3, from which that might have been (wrongly) inferred.[51] The anonymous *Lai de l'espine* even claims that the true originals of the lays were still preserved in writing at St Aaron's church in Caerleon![52] In the list from Chester, Caerleon appears as *Karleyn*, *Rey Mabun* is the Welsh character Mabon (see below), *Veyn le fiz Urien* is Owein vab Urien, *Luelan lychlez* [= le chevaliers?] is a Llywelyn, and *Van delmer* is probably [Bendigeid-] Vran vab Llyr marini ('[Blessed] Brân son of Sea'). There are some interesting eponymous characters. *Glou degloucestes'* (no. 17) is clearly the eponym of Gloucester (Gloyw of Caer Loyw in Welsh tradition). *Le eir deleycests'* (no. 38) must be Geoffrey of Monmouth's Leir of Leicester (*Caer Lŷr* in Welsh). The next item after this, *Lay deuent* (no. 39), is probably not a lay about the wind, but a lay either about the kingdom of Gwent (centered on Caerwent/ *Venta Silurum*) or about its pseudo-eponym Wentus who appears as St Malo's father in the ninth-century Breton Latin *Life* of that saint.[53] Now the lay preceding these two eponymous items is entitled *Glygis* (no. 37). In the context, it is very tempting to equate *Glygis* with *Gliguis* eponym of Glywysing, and to see the form *Glygis* as an intermediary between the Old Welsh form *Gliguis* and the French forms *Gliglois/Glyglois* (in *Gliglois*) and *Cligés* (in Chrétien and *Yder*). Could we hypothesize that Chrétien knew, or knew of, this French narrative lay of *Glygis*, and seized on the name of this south-east Welsh character for his own hero, whose father was king of the best kingdom in Wales?

While the French *Lai de Glygis* does not survive, I should like to suggest that a Middle English version or adaptation of it is extant in the shape of the short tail-rhyme romance of *Sir Cleges* or *Clegys*.[54] (The C- rather than G- may again be

compilation, as there are traces of an underlying alphabetical arrangement. I have been preparing an edition of it for many years.

51 Constance Bullock-Davies, 'The Love-Messenger in "Milun"', *Nottingham Mediaeval Studies*, 16 (1972), 20–27; also Glyn S. Burgess, *The Lais of Marie de France: Text and Context* (Manchester, 1987), pp. 21–27.

52 ibid., p. 24.

53 *Tracts*, ed. Bartrum, pp. 23 and 131.

54 Edited as *Sir Cleges* from the Edinburgh manuscript by Walter Hoyt French and Charles

due to the direct or indirect influence of Chrétien.) Like another tail-rhyme romance based on a French *lai* — *Sir Launfal*, which is based on Marie de France's *Lai de Lanval* — *Sir Cleges* does not specifically state that it is a lay or translated from French.[55] On the other hand, its length and structure is that of a *lai*, and the beginning and end respectively resemble those of the French *Lai de Lanval* and *Lai du Cor*.[56] The south-east Welsh setting is clear and significant. Uther Pendragon, Arthur's father, has a poor but loyal knight Sir Cleges, who lives 'beside Cardiff' (*be Kardyfe syde*, v. 87)—one thinks of minor Welsh lords such as the Bychans of *Beganston*, mentioned earlier, just across the Ely from Cardiff. The unusual choice of Uther as monarch is significant, since Glywys was similarly one generation earlier than Arthur in Lifris's *Life* of St Cadog, as noted above. The link between Uther and Cardiff in *Sir Cleges* is reminiscent of the early Welsh Arthurian poem 'Pa gur?', in which 'Mabon son of Mydron, Uthr Pendragon's servant' is listed as one of 'the vultures of Eléï', apparently the now less than romantic river Ely (OW *Eléï*).[57] Sir Cleges's wife is called Clarys (< Old French *Claris(se)*[58]), which in meaning, and to some extent form, recalls *Gwawr* ('dawn'), the name of Glywys's wife in Welsh sources.[59] Chrétien's Cligés, of course, marries *Fenice*, whose name 'phoenix' reflects the theme of Resurrection in

Brockway Hale, *Middle English Metrical Romances*, 2 vols (New York, 1930), II, 877–95 (the edition I shall cite). *Sir Clegys* is the form in the Oxford manuscript edited by G. H. McKnight, *Middle English Humorous Tales in Verse* (Boston, 1913), pp. 38–59. The name *Clegis/Clegys* is uncommon in Middle English romances; see Robert W. Ackerman, *An Index of the Arthurian Names in Middle English* (Stanford, 1952), pp. 60–61, who notes the variant *Clegius* in *The Anturs of Arthur at the Tarnewathelan*, edited by John Robson, *Three Early English Metrical Romances*, Camden Society (London, 1842), p. 4, st. VIII: 'Syr Cador, Syr Clegius, Syr Costantyne, Syr Cay'.

55 *Sir Launfal*, ed. French and Hale, I, 345–80.

56 *Les Lais de Marie de France*, ed. Jean Rychner (Paris, 1966), pp. 72–73; *Lai du Corn*, ed. Philip Bennett, *Mantel et Cor: deux lais du XIIe siècle* (Exeter, 1975), p. 59. As noted by McKnight, pp. lxiii–lxv, the beginning of *Sir Cleges* also like *Sir Amadace* (*Metrical Romances*, ed. Robson, pp. xxvi and 27; cf. *A Manual of the Writings in Middle English*, ed. J. Burke Severs, I (New Haven, 1967), pp. 169–70), but that is acephalous and we do not know if it was a *lai*.

57 Patrick Sims-Williams, 'The Early Welsh Arthurian Poems', in *Arthur of the Welsh*, ed. Bromwich and others, 33–71 (pp. 38–40). For a later Welsh allusion to Cardiff see Roger Middleton, '*Chwedl Geraint ab Erbin*', ibid., 147–57 (pp. 150–51).

58 Flutre, p. 49.

59 Bartrum, *Tracts*, pp. 20 and 49 (PK §5 and JC §47) — *Guaul* in *Vita S. Cadoci*, §47 (ibid., p. 25).

Chrétien's poem; but it is noteworthy that on her first appearance in his poem he stresses her 'grant clarté' (v. 2730), which lights up the hall like the sun.[60]

The plot of *Sir Cleges* is made up of international motifs, so it is impossible to say whether or not it is based on Welsh narrative.[61] Sir Cleges and his wife expend all their wealth in throwing Christmas feasts and in giving to the poor. They bear their poverty with saintly fortitude, and while Sir Cleges is praying under a cherry-tree in his garden one Christmas, he is blessed by the miraculous growth of cherries on it. This miracle is paralleled in Celtic hagiography,[62] as elsewhere. Whether or not there is a Welsh source here, it is significant that Sir Cleges and his wife move in a saintly atmosphere, like Glywys and his family. (Religion was not necessarily out of place in a *lai*; witness the end of Marie de France's *Eliduc*.) The second part of *Sir Cleges* is more rumbustious. Cleges and his eldest son (Gwynllyw perhaps?) walk to Cardiff castle to present the cherries to the king. Cleges goes in disguise. Before he can be admitted to the king's presence, he has to promise a third of any future reward in turn to the porter, usher, and steward of Cardiff castle. Uther Pendragon is delighted with the cherries; he sends them by a sort of Interflora to a lady from Cornwall (Arthur's future mother, no doubt). Needless to say, he grants Sir Cleges the traditional 'rash boon'. Sir Cleges demands twelve blows, and deals out four apiece to steward, usher, and porter. Meanwhile the king is listening to a harper singing a *gest* about Sir Cleges (a *lai?*),[63] and this puts him in mind of his former knight. Sir Cleges reveals his identity, and the tale ends with Uther Pendragon rewarding Cleges by granting him the castle of Cardiff with all its appurtenances. Compare the end of *Yder* where Queen Guenloïe of Caerwent reinstates Cligés and restores his lands fourfold.

---

60 Polak, pp. 65, 67, and 75–76. Admittedly, 'the description of beauty in terms of radiance seems to have been conventional' (ibid., p. 76). Gliglois's beloved is called Beauty (*Biauté*).

61 See McKnight, *Humorous Tales*, pp. lxiv–lxxiii and 89–91, for full notes on folklore parallels; also *Manual of Writings in Middle English*, I, 170–71 and 330. On 'blows shared' see further F. R. Whitesell, '*Iwein* 836: Den halben Schaden', *Journal of English and Germanic Philology*, 52 (1953), 549–54.

62 C. Grant Loomis, 'Sir Cleges and Unseasonable Growth in Hagiology', *Modern Language Notes*, 53 (1938), 591–94; Kenneth Hurlstone Jackson, 'The Sources for the Life of St Kentigern', in *Studies in the Early British Church*, ed. Nora K. Chadwick (Cambridge, 1958), 273–357 (pp. 325–26 and 355–56); John Shaw, 'Scottish Gaelic Traditions of the *Cliar Sheanchain*', in *Celtic Languages and Celtic Peoples: Proceedings of the Second North American Congress of Celtic Studies*, ed. Cyril J. Byrne, Margaret Harry, and Pádraig Ó Siadhail (Halifax, 1992), 141–58 (pp. 146 and 155).

63 Compare the lay of *Sir Orfeo*, vv. 523–39, ed. French and Hale, I, 339.

The story of *Sir Cleges* looks very much like a explanation, cast in a modern feudal guise, of how Glywys came to be lord of Glywysing in the generation before Arthur. In reality, the old Roman site of Cardiff seems to have been unimportant until the castle was founded *c.* 1081,[64] when it became the caput of the Norman lordship of Glamorgan. Besides the ensuing conflict with the native Welsh dynasty, there was friction between the castle and borough and the adjacent episcopal community of Llandaf. This was resolved by a treaty with Robert of Gloucester in 1126.[65] The church of Llandaf also sought to resist Robert of Gloucester's encroachments by forging an ancient privilege of St Teilo, shielding the church from the depredations of the unnamed 'king of Morgannwg', which would presumably have been read as a coded reference to Robert.[66] Such encoding of contemporary conditions was normal in twelfth-century Welsh ecclesiastical writings about the past, as we have seen, and it spilled over into Geoffrey of Monmouth's *Historia*, as Christopher Brooke and John Gillingham have shown.[67] Is it too fanciful to suppose that sometimes it also influenced the vernacular French literature of the marches? The emphasis in *Sir Cleges* is on the well-worked minstrel theme of generosity. But perhaps the underlying message of the *lai* of *Glygis* was that in the good old days Glamorgan (then called Glywysing) had been ruled from Cardiff castle not by Robert of Gloucester and his ilk but by a generous Welsh lord, Glywys; and that Glywys had been both a pious man of religion and the bane of the avaricious entourage that surrounded the king of Britain when he came to hold court in Cardiff castle.

I would suggest, at least, that Chrétien knew of the lost French lay of *Glygis* or Glywys, and that he drew on it when he was looking for a suitable name for the son of the Byzantine prince to whom Arthur had given the best realm in Wales. If the name *Glygis* or *Cligés* also sounded rather like the name of a topical sultan, Κλιτζασθλαν, that would have been all the better for his purposes.

64 See above; also Knight, 'Sources', p. 404; D. G. Walker, 'Cardiff', in *Boroughs of Mediaeval Wales*, ed. R. A. Griffiths (Cardiff, 1978), pp. 103–28.

65 *Book of Llan Dâv*, pp. 27–29.

66 ibid., pp. 118–21; cf. Wendy Davies, 'Braint Teilo', *Bulletin of the Board of Celtic Studies*, 26 (1974–76), 123–37.

67 Brooke, pp. 16–49 and 95–106; Gillingham, 'Context and Purposes'. But cf. the note of caution in Brooke, p. 102; also Patrick Sims-Williams, 'Historical Need and Literary Narrative: A Caveat from Ninth-Century Wales', *Welsh History Review*, 17 (1994–95), 1–40.

More on Modified Narrative Repetition in *Fled Bricrenn*

Edgar M. Slotkin

UNIVERSITY OF CINCINNATI

IN A FRUITFUL ARTICLE in 1969 Proinsias Mac Cana defined one of the most basic issues for students of Irish literature as 'the interaction of [the oral and the written] modes [of transmission] which constitutes the great problem — and in some ways the peculiar interest — of Irish literary history'.[1] This program remains true today in that the whole sweep of Irish written and oral literature offers a unique opportunity to study the interaction of writing and oral tradition on the creation of a corpus of literary work over centuries. Professor Mac Cana himself has made many contributions to this study over the years. In this short tribute, I would like to go back to an interesting article he published in *Ériu* 27, 'An Instance of Modified Narrative Repetition in *Fled Bricrenn*.' In this piece he examined the 'Giant in the Mist' episode from 'Bricriu's Feast,' demonstrating that it had a tripartite structure, as each of the three heroes in turn encounters the giant, and that each of the three encounters employed similar language which 'contrived to modify the recurring verbal pattern without

---

1   Proinsias Mac Cana, 'Irish Literary Tradition' in Brian Ó Cuív, ed., *A View of the Irish Language* (Dublin: The Stationary Office, 1969), p. 35.

obscuring it. [The redactor] does this very simply by echoing each phrase of the passage while varying one or more of its constituent elements.'[2] Professor Mac Cana then lists twelve examples of such variation from the rather brief narrative episode from LU. He concludes: 'This kind of extended elaboration clearly presupposes a written text and part of the interest of the passage in *Fled Bricrenn* is that it exemplifies the adaption to the written medium of devices that remain characteristic of oral narrative.'[3]

In *Ériu* 29 I published an article in which I attempted to show that the 'Giant in the Mist' episode in LU had been removed by the interpolator H from its genuine position in the narrative (following the events in Cruachan) and placed earlier in the sequence of events. Moreover, I suggested that H had considerably shortened the episode in order to fit it into his interpolated pages; the text as found in the other manuscripts, the Leiden Codex Vossianus, Trinity College MS H.3.17 and British Library MS Egerton 93, preserves both the original order and a longer text which probably conformed to Mael Muire's original LU text before H had rewritten it.[4] From this perspective, Professor Mac Cana's proposition that the LU version of H represents a literary reworking of traditional material would seem, indeed, to be an accurate assessment. The question that interests me here is, what do we find when we examine the text common to the three other manuscripts and probably inherent in Mael Muire's original as well?

What follows is an edited text derived basically from Egerton 93 together with the parallel text from LU-H. I list variant readings only when my text varies significantly from Eg and I have silently added marks of length and expansion of abbreviations. There is substantial verbal agreement among the three manuscripts in any case. A comparison with the text from LU, however, will reveal the major differences: H's narrative text is much terser; and the description of the giant in the other texts is much longer. I have also arranged the texts in columns to show such verbal correspondences which exist between them, evidence of H's work of condensation. I have also arranged the descriptive passages in such a way as to highlight their inherently metrical form, roughly following the rhythm of cadenced heptasyllabic verse.

2   Proinsias Mac Cana, 'An Instance of Modified Narrative Repetition in *Fled Bricrenn*', *Ériu* 27 (1977): 170.
3   Mac Cana, 1977, 172.
4   Actually, the Trinity College MS breaks off two-thirds of the way through the passage; see Edgar M. Slotkin, 'The Structure of *Fled Bricrenn* Before and After the *Lebor na hUidre* Interpolations,' *Ériu* 29 (1978): 64–77.

Eg. 93

La sodain ro gabait a eich do
Lóegaire, ⁊ ro hinled a charpat ⁊ ro
leblaing ind. Brethais in t-ara brot
forsin n-echraid oc techt⁶ amach fó chetóir
co táncatar dar Mag Dá Gabul fri hUltu,
dar Bernai⁷ na Foraire, dar Áth Carpait
Fergusa, dar Áth na Mórrígna, do
Cháerthiund Cluana Dá Dam, hi Clithar
Fidbaide, hi Commur Cethrisliged⁸, dar
sligtib Dúine Delga, dar Mag Sligech
siar hi Sliab⁹ mBreg mbláthsolus. Is ann
sin atracht duibnéll trom tiug doborda
duibchiach dorcha doeólais for Lóegaire.
Is ann is-bert fria araid:

'Toirind¹⁰ an carpat,' olse, '⁊ scuir na
na eochu co ro dígla in ceó don-fáinic.'
Do-gníther samlaid. Ro chuir in gilla
na heochu hi férgort bói hi comfocus dó
⁊ ro gab 'ca forairi ⁊ 'ca forcoimét iar sin.

Ní cian boí and co n-acca in scáilfer¹¹
mór¹² ina dochom; is é

mullachtlethan bélremor bolcshúilech
gránna grendétenach¹³ grúgánach
adétig dúr dosmailgech.
Ba duibithir gual cech n-alt ⁊ cech n-ága¹⁴

LU–H, ll. 8507–8550⁵

La sodain ro inled a charpat do Lóegaire
⁊ ro leblaing ind ⁊ imreid dar Mag Dá

Gabul, dar Bernaid na Forairi, dar Áth
Carpait Fergusa, dar Áth na Mórrígna, do
Cháerthiund Clúana Da Dam, hi Clithar
Fidbaidi, hi Commur Cetharsliged, sech
Dun Delca, dar Mag Slicech siar hi Sléib
Breg. Ro gab tromcheó doborda dorcha
doeolais dó and sin connarb inríata dó in
chonar. 'Anam sund,' for Lóegaire fria
araid, 'coro dígla in ceó dind.'

Tairbling Lóegaire asa charput. Ro
chuir in gilla na eocho hi fergort boí hi
comfocus dó.

A mboí and in gilla co n-acca in
scáilfer mór ina dochom. Nirbo segunda
a tuarascbáil sé
mullachlethan bélremur bolcsuilech
grendetanach granna grucánach
dosmailgech docraid adetig.
Sé tailc talchar tinsensach;

5 H's interpolation actually begins somewhat before the giant episode.
6 hoctecht L; ag toigecht Eg
7 berren Eg
8 ceitrisligte Eg
9 a sliab Eg, L
10 dond rind sis Eg
11 in scal Eg
12 *add* chuicce Eg
13 grinde tanch Eg
14 naige Eg

de ó mullach co bonn[15]. Ba samalta
fri herball fiadech
in mong gaísidech[16] gréliath;
con-suiged tar a formna siar sechtair.
Súili duibliatha lindacha lais.
Ba méitigthir
clár fithchille[17]
cech dét glasbuide
boí a cechtar[18] a dá drant. Ba samalta
co rachad long
fo[19] lánshéolaib
tar a chráesgin oslaicthi.
Srón cham chuasach leis.
Medón fethech[20] brec i ngalar aicci.
No scerdfidte salannméich[21]
do thulaib a lurgan fiar fochamm[22].
Oircne mellacha grebancha foi[23].
Sliasta sacacha sithchamma leis[24],
sé adbronnach lethanshluaistech,
sé glúnmár tónchóir glaisingnech[25].
Ba héccruta[26] écsamail in fer sin.
Ba dub teimnide[27];
ba brogda bachlachda;
ba fuachda forgránda;

sé sotal sucach séitfidach;
sé rengmar rigtrén rochalma;

sé borb brogda bachlachda.
Mael dub demsidi fair;

15 talmoin *for* bonn Eg
16 gaeisitech Eg
17 fichille Eg
18 anegar Eg
19 for Eg
20 *om.* fethech Eg
21 Nosceirt fidte salnnmeich Eg
22 bfiar bfocamm Eg
23 lais *for* foi Eg
24 aicce *for* leis Eg
25 glasrignech Eg
26 heccrata Eg
27 teimnige Eg; teimni*dhe* L,T

ba hansuairc anáebda
a²⁸ thuaruscbail ind f[h]ir sin. Is é
immorro²⁹ ba móom di feraib domuin
cona matán magluirce³⁰ fadbuide
draigin droch dénmoige
co forcraid for deglán
a duirn dó fri glenn a dá gualann.
Aroile arait múscraide brechlachtna imme
cona himlib iarnidib;
si imt[h]rom fri himthecht,
si aduar fri hanad,
si³¹ éitig fri hairechtus,
áithe óenbruit³² na haraiti³³ sin ro boí immon
mbachlach.

   Iar sin iarfoigis³⁴ in t-aithech do araid³⁵
Lóegaire Buadaig can dó 7 cúich a t[h]igerna.
   'Ní ansa,' ol in t-ara: 'Lóegaire Buadach mac
Connbuide maic Iliach mo t[h]igerna-sa.'
   'Is gilla daigfir ón,' ol in scál 7 is amlaid
at-bert anní sin 7 ro tógaib a matán magluirci
7 do-breth béim dó ó c[h]luais co caraid.
Cnetais³⁶ 7 iachtais³⁷ 7 égmis in gilla iar
facbáil in mórimnid 7 ind écomlainn³⁸.

arit odor immi inar co folph a thona in
sodain senbrisca a salcha má chossa.

Mátan maglorci móri fria ais amal mol
mulind.

   'Cóichet na heich sé, a gilli,'
for sé la fegad co andíaraid fair.
   'Eich Lóegaire Buadaig,' for in
gilla.
   'Fír,' for sé, 'maith in fer asa
eich.' Is amlaid ro raid sin la
turcbail a mátan fair 7 do-bretha
béim dón gillu o adbrond co hó.
Égis in gilla.

---

28 *om.* Eg
29 *om.* Eg
30 matluirge Eg, *et passim.*
31 *om.* Eg
32 aenbroit Eg; aonbruit L; aonbrait T
33 hároiti Eg
34 iarfoidis Eg
35 arad Eg
36 Cnetaig Eg
37 *add* in tarraid la sodain Eg
38 *om.* 7 egmis . . . écomlainn Eg

'Fé amae,' or Lóegaire ac cloistin iachta ind arad.[39]

La sodain[40] atracht Lóegaire fo chétóir cona armgaisced do fóirithin in arad. Imma-comráinic dó 7 don scál; ní raibe bá do sodain do Lóegaire. Tógbaid in scál a matán magluirci 7 do-breth béim dó o c[h]luais co caraid cor tuitset a airm uad cen comus. Techis Lóegaire iarsin fo méla 7 fo mebail co riacht Emain Macha iar fácbáil a ech 7 a arad 7 a armgaiscid.

Nirbo chian iar sin co toracht[41] Conall Cernach iarsin sligid cétnoi[42] 7 cusin maigin i tuarcaib in dubcheó druídechta for Lóegaire reme[43]. Atraigis in ceó cétna for Conall connar-cungain[44] nem no talmain[45]. Tairlingis iarsin 7 tairntir a c[h]arpat, 7 scuiris in t-ara na heochu isin férgort cétna feib ro-scuirit[46] eich Lóegairi.

Nirbo chian don araid co n-aca in fer cétna cuici[47] 7 iarfaigis dó, 'cia occa mbissi aile[48],' ol sé.

Doroich Lóegaire fua.

'Cid dia mbá don gillu,' [for] Lóegaire.

'Hi cinta ind fergoirt do milliud,' for in t-aithech.

'[Is m]é féin ticfa,' for Lóegaire.

Immacomsinitar dóib dano. Techid Lóegaire íar tain co ránic Emain Macha iar facbail a ech 7 a gilli 7 a armgascid.

Nirbo chian iar tain co toracht Conall Cernach in sligid cétna co ránic in magin in ro artraig in ceó druidechta do Lóegaire. Artraigid dano in dubnel cétna dorcha doborda for Conall Cernach connar cungain nem no talmain. Tairblingis Conall iar tain 7 scurid in gilla na eochu isind fergort chétna.

Nirbo chían dó iar sudi co faca in scál cétna chuci. Iarfaigis dó cia diambo cheli.

39 *om. sentence* Eg
40 *om.* La sodain Eg; Attra*cht* fo c*et*oir inti l. Eg
41 co ria*cht* Eg
42 *om.* cétnoi Eg
43 roime Eg
44 cumaing Eg
45 *add* do faicsin Eg
46 roscuirid Eg, L, rosg*uir*it T
47 chuige Eg
48 *om.* aile Eg

'Oc Conall Cernach[49] mac Amorgin,' ol in t-ara.

'Maith in fer,' ol in scál la tócbáil in matán magluirci boí[50] ina láim ⁊ la tabairt béme dó[51] co riacht[52] in t-ara.

At-cluin Conall sin[53] ⁊ éirgis fo c[h]étoir ⁊ imma-comráinic[54] dó ⁊ don scál. Ni bo ferr son dó[55] dano; for-uaisligther Conall feib ro Lóegaire ⁊ teichid co riacht Emain Macha iar fágbáil a arm ⁊ a ech ⁊ a arad.

Do-luid immorro Cú Chulaind ina charput iar niamad ⁊ iar slemoin-chírad a fhuilt iar sin sligid chétna do etergléod a imresna ⁊[56] errid Ulad[57] immon curadmír conus tarraid in dubcheó drúidechta cétna feib tarraid in lucht remi[58] coro lín in coibéis ndímain tarraid eter nem ⁊ talmain. Tairlingis Cú Chulaind isin maigin sin[59] ⁊ scuiris[60] Láeg na hechu isin férgort cétna[61].

Nirbo chian boí ann co n-acca in fer cendgarb corpremor chuice cona matán magluirci ina láim amal ticed reme[62].

'Am celisea Conaill Cernaig,' for sé.

'Maith in fer,' for in scál la tócbáil a lámi co tarat beim dó ó hó cóa fodbrond. Iachtais in gilla.

Tic Conall fo sodain. Imma-comarnaic dó ⁊ don scál. Tresi cluchi ind athig. Techis Conall ón mud chétna amal ro theich Lóegaire iar fácbáil a armgaiscid ⁊ a ara ⁊ a ech co ránic Emain Macha.

Dolluid Cú Chulaind iar sin forsin tsligid chétna co ránic in n-inad cétna conos tarraid in dubcheó cétna feib tarraid in lucht remi. Tarblingis Cú Chulaind ⁊ berid Láeg na eocho sin fertgort.

Nirbo chian dó co n-acca in fer cétna chuci ⁊ immafoacht de coich diambo cheli.

49 *om.* Cernach Eg,T
50 roboi Eg
51 ndo Eg, nde L
52 corro ia*cht* Eg
53 *om.* sin Eg
54 immacomairnicc *om.* dó Eg
55 *om.* dó
56 aimrisnae *om.* ⁊ Eg
57 aile *for* Ulad Eg
58 cétna *for* remi
59 cétna *for* sin Eg
60 cuires Eg, chuiris L, sc*u*ris T
61 *om.* cétna Eg
62 roime Eg,T; remhe L; T ends here, in fact.

'Cia tussa, a gilla?' olse co handiarraid.

'Ni mé fuil cin tigerna,' ar Lóeg: 'Cú Chulaind mac Subaltaim.'

'Maith ón an cách fil ann[63],' ol in scál ⁊ tócbaid fair in matán[64] magluirci ⁊ do-breth béim dó ó chluais co caraid. Garthis Láeg.

At-etha[65] Cú Chulaind a gaisced ⁊ fo-cerd cor n-iach n-erred de dochum in scáil ⁊ do fóirithin Láoig. Dercais cách a c[h]éle díb. Ba féig immorro ⁊ ba forgránna in fégad ⁊ in fritháilem do-bert cách díb for a c[h]éle[66], Cú Chulainn ⁊ in scál. Imma-comtuairg dóib, ⁊ do-berid[67] Cú Chulaind dá béim im cech n-áen béim dó-sum, .i. tathbéim ⁊ béim co comus, coro foruaislig Cú Chulaind a bruth ⁊ a bríg in scáil; coro-dílsig na hechu ⁊ in araid ⁊ co ruc Cú Chulaind eochu ⁊ aradae in lochta aile uaid[68], .i. Conall ⁊ Lóegaire, fon cuma cétna. Do-luid Cú Chulaind remi[69] do Emain Macha[70] i ndiaid in lochta aili ⁊ do-breth a n-eochu ⁊ a n-arada dóib.[71]

'Celi do Choin Chulaind,' for sé.

'Maith in fer,' for in scál la fuirmed in mátan fair. Iachtais Láeg.

Tic Cú Chulaind fo sodain ⁊ immá-comarnaic dó ⁊ don scál; ⁊ nos tuarcend cách araili díb. Traitar in scál coro dilsig na eocho ⁊ in n-araid ⁊ co ruc eocho ⁊ aradu ⁊ armgaisced a coceli leis co ránic Emain Macha cona morchoscur ⁊ dorat dia fíadnaib féin íat.

The following translation is that of the edited text only. Readers wishing a translation of H's abbreviated text in LU can refer to Professor Mac Cana's article, pages 169–170.

With that his horses were caught for Lóegaire, and he had his chariot yoked and he leaped aboard. The charioteer brought the goad to bear on the steeds

---

63 Maith cach on *om.* fil ann Eg
64 mathan Eg
65 atethai Eg
66 ceile *add* dib .i. Eg
67 dobeir- Eg
68 aile *om.* uaid Eg
69 *om.* remi Eg
70 *om.* Macha Eg
71 Strictly speaking, the passage continues on from this point with Cú Chulainn's arrival back at Emain, but at this point further contact with the giant is concluded.

coming out immediately so that they came across Mag Dá Gabul toward Ulster, over Berna na Foraire, over Áth Carpait Fergusa, over Áth na Mórrígna to Cáerthann Clúana Dá Dam into Clithar Fidbaide, into Commur Cetharsliged, over the roads of Dún Delga, over Mag Sligech westwards into the bright, blooming uplands of Brega. It is there a heavy, dense, thick, black, misty, dark, impenetrable black cloud arose around Lóegaire.

Then he said to his charioteer, 'Lower the chariot,' he said, 'and unyoke the horses until the mist that has come may clear away.'

It is done thus. The lad put the horses in the field which was near to him and took to guarding them and watching over them after that.

He was not there long until he saw the big giant coming towards him; and[72] he was broadheaded, thick-mouthed, boss-eyed, ugly, bristle-faced, wrinkled, repulsive, severe, bushy-browed. Every joint and every member of him from crown to sole were as black as coal. The bristly fur-grey hair was like the tail of a wild horse; he arranged it backwards out across his shoulders. He had black-grey, watery eyes. Every greenish yellow tooth in each of his two jaws was as big as a fidchell board. It seemed as if a ship under full sail might go across the maw of his open mouth. He had a crooked, concave nose; a belly flourishing with the spots of disease. A sackful of salt could have been stripped from his bent and very bowed shins. He had knobby, white hairy calves. He had long, crooked, sack-like thighs. And he was gnarled-jointed, broad, shovel-like; and big-headed, straight-assed, grey-clawed. That man was deformed, outlandish. The appearance of that man was black, dark-hued, strong, uncouth, sharp, fearsome, unpleasant, unattractive. He was, moreover, the biggest man in the world with his knotty, ill-wrought blackthorn cudgel of destruction with an excess of two of his handfuls against the valley of his two shoulders. He had a certain speckled, dun soiled mantle about him with its borders made of iron; very heavy for travelling, very cold when stopping, unseemly for an assembly, but with the lightness of one cloak of that mantle which was about the churl.

Then the boor inquired of Lóegaire Buadach's charioteer who he was and who was his lord.

'Not hard,' said the charioteer, 'Lóegaire Buadach mac Connbuide maic Iliach is my lord.'

'That is the gilly of a good man,' said the giant, and having said that, he took his cudgel and he gave a blow to him from his ear to his haunch. The gilly groaned and shouted and screamed after getting that great suffering and oppression.

'Alas,' said Lóegaire at hearing the cry of the charioteer.

72 The translation of some of the giant's description still remains speculative.

Then Lóegaire arose at once with his arms to help the charioteer. He met up with him and with the giant; there was no profit from that for Lóegaire. The giant raised his cudgel and he gave him a blow from ear to haunch so that his weapons fell uncontrollably from him. Lóegaire fled then in shame and disgrace until he reached Emain Macha having left his horses and his charioteer and his arms.

Not long after that Conall Cernach arrived along the same road and came to the spot where the black magical mist arose on Lóegaire before. The same mist appeared to Conall Cernach so that he could not distinguish heaven or earth. He alighted then and his chariot was unyoked, and the charioteer unyoked the horses into just the same field that Lóegaire's horses were unyoked into.

It seemed not long to the charioteer until he saw the same man approaching him, and he inquired of him, 'Whose man are you, then?' he said.

'Conall Cernach mac Amorgin's,' the charioteer said.

'A fine man indeed,' said the giant, raising the cudgel in his hand and giving a blow to him that struck the charioteer.

Conall heard that and rose up at once and met up with him and the giant. That was not better for him though; Conall was overcome as Lóegaire had been overcome, and he [Conall] fled until he reached Emain Macha after leaving his weapons and his horses and his charioteer.

As for Cú Chulainn, however, he came in his chariot along the same road after adorning himself and after his hair was combed smooth to decide his feuds with the warriors of the Ulstermen about the champion's portion until the same black mist overtook him as it overtook the ones before him and it filled the same amount of space of the journey between heaven and earth. Cú Chulainn alighted into that spot, and Láeg unyoked the horses in the same field.

He was not there long until he saw the same rough-headed, big bodied man approaching him with his cudgel in his hand as he had come before that.

'Who are you, gilly?' he said angrily.

'I am not without a lord,' said Láeg: 'Cú Chulainn mac Subaltaim.'

'The man who is there is good,' said the giant and lifted the cudgel and he gave a blow to him from ear to haunch. Láeg cried out.

Cú Chulainn seized his weapons and he leaped a hero's salmon leap to the giant and to help Láeg. Each one stared at the other. And it was keen and fearsome the scrutiny and the anticipation each one gave to the other, Cú Chulainn and the giant. They smote each other, and Cú Chulainn gave two blows for every one blow of the latter's, i.e. a return blow and a powerful blow, and Cú Chulainn overpowered the fury and the power of the giant; and he gave up the horses and the charioteers, and Cú Chulainn took the horses and charioteers of the other people from him, i.e. Conall and Lóegaire, similarly. Cú Chulainn came from him to Emain Macha after the other people and he gave their horses and their charioteers to them.

Long ago Axel Olrik identified a number of characteristics of *Sage* narration which are relevant here. By *Sage* Olrik meant 'myths, songs, heroic sagas, and local legends.'[73] He called these characteristics 'laws,' although they are rather only large-scale tendencies and applicable only to Indo-European folk narratives. Among these 'laws' is the Law of Repetition ('*das Gesetz der Wiederholung*') which 'is almost always tied to the number three.'[74] This tendency, according to Olrik, leads to a more general Law of Three, what the Russian folklorist Vladimir Propp called 'trebling,'[75] in which triple replication happens on a variety of levels. While repetition in general is a feature of all literature,[76] indeed all aesthetic productions, trebling seems most apparent in folk literature. Heda Jason writes, 'the repetition of elements in the [oral] narrative . . . happens on all levels: (a) on the level of texture a certain number of synonyms and parallelisms are used; (b) among the common features of the narrative structure are the appearance of a certain number of heroes, who may be parallels or opposites (such as the three sons of the king, of whom only the youngest succeeds in overcoming the dragon); and (c) episodes are repeated a certain number of times in various combinations.'[77] All three levels manifest themselves in *Fled Bricrenn* which on the face of it appears to be a fully realized early Irish saga with the most features of oral composition accruing to it.[78] Its structure is modeled on trebling with the three heroes in a kind of quest or contest, the youngest among them the clear winner.[79]

However, the patterning in terms of three produces content which is generally not trebled or, as such, repeated. When three characters are brought into the same plot complex, the first episode is generally expounded in full but the second is generally much briefer since we already know much of the information from episode one. The third episode must necessarily differ from the other two by

73 Axel Olrik, 'Epic Laws of Folk Narrative' in Alan Dundes, ed., *The Study of Folklore* (Englewood Cliffs: Prentice Hall, 1965), 129.

74 Olrik, 133.

75 V. Propp, *Morphology of the Folktale*, 2nd ed., Austin: University of Texas Press, 1968.

76 See especially Madeléine Frédéric, *La Repetition: Etude linguistique et rhétorique*, Tübingen: Max Niemeyer, 1985.

77 Heda Jason, 'Content Analysis of Oral Literature: A Discussion' in Heda Jason and Dimitri Segal, eds., *Patterns in Oral Literature*, (The Hague and Paris: Mouton Publishers, 1977) 286.

78 See Edgar M. Slotkin, *Evidence for Oral Composition in Early Irish Saga*, Harvard Diss., 1977 for a great variety of more such features.

79 Although not particularly emphasized in *Fled Bricrenn*, elsewhere in the Ulster Cycle Cú Chulainn's youth *is* emphasized; he is the youngest hero — another folk trait.

having a positive outcome for the real hero. This is certainly what we find in the 'Giant in the Mist' episode in *Fled Bricrenn*: Lóegaire's encounter not only includes the catalogue of place-names detailing his route, reduced to the *sliged cétna* 'the same road' of the other characters, but the long description of the giant. It is interesting that while the Conall episode omits any descriptive detail, the Cú Chulainn episode — somewhat against expectation — does introduce two alliterative compound adjectives when the giant appears. These are not verbal repetitions in that the compounds do not occur in the more formal description in the Lóegaire episode, but they are thematic repetitions rather as if the narrator, having a charioteer see the approaching giant, could not resist introducing them though they contribute nothing new to the narrative or the meaning of the narrative. This sort of compulsive thematic association is much more typical of oral narrative than written literature.[80] In any case, the Conall Cernach episode is much reduced since only the bare bones of the giant's victory are required by the story. The Cú Chulainn episode, however, is somewhat longer with a tad more attention paid to the actual combat which Cú Chulainn wins. Hence, the elements that are *not* repeated are nevertheless a function of treble repetition within the narrative framework of the story, and as such follow the 'laws' of oral narrative.

In his original article Professor Mac Cana listed twelve instances where 'the redactor has contrived to modify the recurring verbal pattern without obscuring it.'[81] It will be useful to examine these listed twelve in the passage above:

(i) Nirbo chian iarsin *co toracht* Conall Cernach iarsin sligid cétnoi II > *Do-luid* immorro Cú Chulainn ina charput . . . . iarsin sligid chétna III (Following Mac Cana, I italicize the most notable variants.) This is precisely the same as LU.

(ii) 7 cusin maigin II > Tairlingis Cú Chulaind isin maigin sin. Except for the word *maigin*, there is less repetition here than in LU.

(iii) atracht duib*néll* trom tiug 'ca forairi I > *i tuarcaib* in dubcheó druídechta *for Lóegaire reme*. Atraigis in *ceó* cétna for Conall II > conus *tarraid* in *dubcheó druídechta* cétna feib tarraid in lucht remi III. Here again there is much <u>more</u> verbal variation than we find in LU. While *dubcheó druídechta* recurs in III, the narrator has expanded the telling of Conall's envelopment by the mist. He varies the mist in some way in every instance. *Néll* does not turn up once in LU.

---

80 The classic exposition of this sort of 'composition by theme' is Albert Lord, *The Singer of Tales*, (Cambridge, Mass.: Harvard University Press, 1960).

81 Mac Cana, 1977, 170.

(iv) *Ro chuir* in gilla na heochu hi férgort bói hi comfocus dó I (word for word as in LU) > *scuiris* in t-ara na heochu isin férgort cétna II > scuiris *Láeg* ha hechu isin férgort cétna III. Both I and II are almost the same in LU, but H introduces *berid* for *scuris* in III. So this version is slightly more repetitive than LU.

(v) Ní cian boí and co n-acca in *scáilfer mór ina dochom* I > Nirbo chian don araid co n-aca *in fer cétna cuici* II > Nirbo chian boí ann co n-acca in fer *cendgarb corpremor* chuice III. Although the variants are not quite the same, the variation takes place the same way in the two versions. The introduction of the epithets, however, is unique to this version (see above), and on this account we would have to say that LU is more repetitive.

(vi) iarfoigis in t-aithech do araid Lóegaire Buadach can dó ⁊ cúich a t[h]igerna I > iarfaigis dó, '*cia occa mbissi aile,*' olse II > '*Cia tussa, a gilla?*' III. These queries differ considerably from the LU version. On the whole, LU is more repetitive here.

(vii) It follows from the questions in vi that the answers here will be different: 'Ní ansa, . . . Lóegaire Buadach' I > 'Oc Conall Cernach. . . .' II > 'Ni mé fuil cin tigerna . . . Cú Chulaind mac Subaltaim' III. Again, LU is more repetitive.

(viii) ro *tógaib* a matán magluirci ⁊ do-breth béim dó ó c[h]luais co caraid I > *la tócbáil* in matáin magluirci boí ina láim ⁊ la *tabairt* béme dó *co riacht in t-ara* II > *tócbaid fair* in matán magluirci ⁊ do-breth béim dó ó chluais co caraid III. The narrator here finds small morphological ways to vary what is essentially a repetition in each case. The Conall episode omits the 'from ear to haunch' formula. This formula in LU is *ó adbrond co hó* 'from ankle to ear' although H reverses it in II and omits it in III. On the whole then, LU is somewhat less repetitive than this version.

(ix) Cnetais ⁊ iachtais ⁊ égmis in gilla I > II > *Garthis* Láeg III. The motif of the charioteer crying out is omitted entirely in the Conall section even though Conall hears 'that' in the next line. On the other hand, three synonyms are employed in the first section, and an entirely new synonym in the third. LU employs *iachtaid* in II and III and *egis* in I. LU is therefore more repetitive.

(x) Imma-comráinic dó ⁊ don scál I > imma-comráinic dó ⁊ don scál II > *fo-cerd cor n-iach n-erred de dochom in scáil* III. The Cú Chulainn section is entirely different from the two preceding, which makes narrative sense. LU employs the same phrase as I and II above for the Conall and Cú Chulainn sections but adds a phrase in the latter. A synonym is employed for Lóegaire. On the whole, LU is more repetitive, especially since our version goes on to expand the Cú Chulainn encounter far beyond what LU offers.

(xi) *Tógbaid in scál a matán magluirci* 7 *do-breth béim dó ó c[h]luais co caraid* I > *Ni bo ferr son dó dano*; for-uaisligther Conall feib ro foruaisliged Lóegaire II > coro foruaislig Cú Chulainn *a bruth* 7 *a bríg* in scáil III. LU omits the overcoming of Lóegaire and has short but different phrases in the other sections. Our version is much expanded. The Lóegaire phraseology is not repeated here but is instead a repetition of the blows the charioteers received; see viii above. II and III employ forms of the same verb. Since LU at this point is offering more of a summary than a fully told narrative, it is hard to compare the versions in terms of repetitiveness.

(xii) iar fácbáil a ech 7 a arad 7 a armgaiscid I > iar fágbáil a *arm* 7 a ech 7 a arad II > *do-breth a n-eochu* 7 *a n-arada* III. The Cú Chulainn section was, of course, going to differ; Professor Mac Cana omits a comparison. The narrator varies the order of the things the other warriors leave behind and substitutes *arm* for *armgaiscid*. LU uses the same verbal noun phrase as I and II above and also works some slight variations.

On the whole, then, the LU version is somewhat more repetitive than the version presented here, and that was to be expected since it is shorter, becoming little more than a summary of the action towards the end as H has to fit the text onto the end of his interpolated leaf. The version of the other manuscripts is more fully told, offering more scope for narrative variety at the level of plot and hence at the level of diction as well. Nevertheless, considering the scope available to the narrator, there is a high degree of repetition; and hence I would claim that both thematically and verbally the 'Giant in the Mist' episode in *Fled Bricrenn* as represented by Eg, L, T (and probably Mael Muire's original text) resembles good oral prose narration to a high degree, more so than LU's more summary version as we have it.

La place de la maladie dans la pensée d'Adomnán — Réalité et symbole*

Nathalie Stalmans

FONDS NATIONAL DE LA RECHERCHE SCIENTIFIQUE,
UNIVERSITÉ LIBRE DE BRUXELLES

PÉNITENCE « médecine de l'âme » et autres métaphores du même type attestées en Irlande dès le VIème siècle[1] n'ont fait que confirmer l'idée largement répandue d'une adéquation dans la pensée médiévale entre maladie et péché individuel[2]. Par l'analyse d'un texte irlandais de la fin du VIIème

---

* Je tiens à remercier A. Dierkens pour sa relecture et ses conseils.

1 Notamment dans les Pénitentiels de Vinnian (§22, éd. L. Bieler, *The Irish Penitentials* (Dublin, 1975), 80) et de Columban (prol., éd. Bieler, *The Irish Penitentials*, 98); dans le Livre de Mulling (éd. F. E. Warren, *The Liturgy and Ritual of the Celtic Church* (1881), éd. J. Stevenson (Woodbridge, 1987), 171–3; voir F. S. Paxton, *Christianising Death. The Creation of Ritual Process in Early Medieval Europe* (Ithaca, 1990), 78–88; dans l'œuvre du Pseudo-Cyprien (*De duodecim abusivis saeculi*, éd. S. Hellmann (Leipzig, 1909) 32–60: 33; voir A. Breen, 'The Evidence of Antique Irish Exegesis in Pseudo-Cyprian *De duodecim abusivis Saeculi*', PRIA 87.4 (1987) 71–101: 75).

2 Pour l'Irlande, voir notamment L. Bitel, *Isle of the Saints. Monastic Settlement and Christian Community in Early Ireland* (Cork, 1990), c. 6. *Spirituales medici*, critiqué dans D. N. Dumville, Compte-rendu de L. Bitel, *Peritia* 9 (1995) 397–401: 397. S'opposant à ce point de vue: J. Kroll et B. Bachrach, 'Sin and Mental Illness in the Middle Ages', *Psychological Medicine* 14 (1984), 507–14; Id., 'Sin and the Etiology of Disease in Pre-Crusade Europe', *Journal of the History of Medicine and Allied Sciences*, 41 (1986), 395–414.

siècle — la Vie de Columba rédigée par Adomnán, abbé d'Iona[3], nous voudrions montrer qu'une telle généralisation est abusive.

La maladie est présente dans les trois livres qui forment la Vie de Columba. Le premier livre concerne des prédictions; la maladie y apparaît de manière fortuite, prélude à une mort prophétisée par le saint. Dans le deuxième livre, celui des miracles de puissance, elle est l'objet d'une guérison. Dans le troisième livre, dédié aux manifestations angéliques, elle est un fléau démoniaque repoussé par le saint[4]. L'œuvre voit le jour à la fin d'un siècle où les épidémies se sont succédé[5]. Adomnán rencontre une attente qu'il se doit de satisfaire, des questions sur l'origine de la maladie et le rôle de Dieu auxquelles il doit tenter de répondre. Il nous permet ainsi de comprendre ce que représente la maladie dans sa pensée et la fonction du miracle dont elle est l'objet.

La maladie atteint tantôt des individus isolés[6], tantôt des populations[7]. Les individus touchés sont tous croyants, certains particulièrement méritants, d'autres dont nous connaissons l'élection après la mort[8]. Les populations attaquées par la maladie sont païennes dans deux récits (II.11, II.33), croyantes dans trois récits, le monastère de Columba étant lui-même attaqué du temps du saint (II.6, II.46, III.8)[9]. La maladie n'est jamais mise en rapport avec l'état de foi, ou un péché

3   Ed. trad. W. Reeves, *The Life of St. Columba* (Dublin, 1857); A. O. et M. O. Anderson, *Adomnan's Life of Columba* (1961, nouv. éd. Oxford, 1991). Trad. R. Sharpe, *Adomnán of Iona. Life of Columba* (Harmondsworth, 1995). Le texte sera abrégé VC; les citations renverront à l'édition des Andersons et donneront les numéros de livre et de chapitre.

4   Au sujet de la structure de l'œuvre, voir J.-M. Picard, 'Structural Patterns in Early Hiberno-Latin Hagiography', *Peritia* 4 (1985) 67–82: 75–77.

5   Les annales d'Ulster mentionnent la peste en 664, 665, 667, 668 (*The Annals of Ulster to AD 1131*), éd. et trad. S. Mac Airt, G. Mac Niocaill (Dublin, 1983), 134, 136, 138). *Non cessante pestilentia et multos (. . .) uicos deuastante*, écrit Adomnán (II.46).

6   VC I.27, I.31, I.32, I.45, I.47, II.5, II.7, II.17, II.18, II.30, II.31, II.32, II.39, III.6.

7   VC II.4, II.6, II.11, II.33, II.46, III.8.

8   L'obéissance de Cailtán, abbé à Diú, est louée (I.31); *ad dominum emigrauit . . . ad dominum feliciter transit* (I.32); Ernán est abbé à Hinba (I.45); *sancta uirgo* (II.5); mère et sœur d'un moine (II.7); *quidam bonae indolis iuuenis* (II.18); *pius minister* (II.30); compagnon de route du saint (II.31); fils d'un croyant (II.32); *cum electis erit pars tua meis in regno monacis, cum quibus in resurrectionem uitae de somno mortis euigelabis* (II.39); les anges emportent l'âme de Brito (III.6). Les récits I.27 et I.47 parlent de laïcs qui se rendent au monastère pour y quérir l'un, un médicament, l'autre, une réponse sur le type de mort qui l'attend; le II.17 n'est pas pris en compte puisqu'il s'agit d'un taureau.

9   Nous ne savons rien de l'une d'entre elles (II.4). Nous trouvons la même idée de population guérie dans *De Locis Sanctis*: *Cuius uidelicet liquoris si etiam paruula quaedam stillula super egrotantes inponatur qualicumque languore uel morbo molestati plenam recuperant sanitatem* (III.3.14, *Adamnan's De Locis Sanctis*, éd. D. Meehan (Dublin, 1983), 110). Aucune cause à la maladie n'y est donnée.

commis. Elle a plutôt pour cause le péché originel que tout homme porte en lui, païen et chrétien indifféremment, et qui le rend vulnérable. C'est bien la raison invoquée par Adomnán à l'arrivée d'une épidémie: *et quamvis utrorumque populorum non desint grandia peccata* (II.46).

Bien souvent, la maladie est évoquée avant la mort. Tout en n'étant pas la meilleure des morts — la « bonne mort » définie par Adomnán est une mort paisible, à un âge avancé, dans son propre lit, entouré d'amis[10] — la mort après un temps de maladie reste un sort enviable, un signe de grâce divine, au sens où elle n'est pas violente et subite[11]. Dans un système de pénitence terrestre où n'existe pas de possibilité purgatoire après la mort, cette mort subite doit être comprise comme un signe de damnation certaine, la pénitence ne pouvant se faire[12]. Inversement, le délai de maladie octroyé doit être mis à profit pour se repentir[13]. La seule exception concerne Columba qui, marque insigne de sainteté, n'a pas besoin d'un temps de pénitence et reçoit dès lors le privilège d'une mort subite et sans maladie[14]. La maladie est donc ici encore liée au péché originel au sens où elle est imposée à l'homme pécheur qui a besoin de ce délai avant la mort.

10 *morte placida in senectute et intra domum suam coram amicorum familiarium turba super suum morietur lectum* (I.10); *morte placida senex inter amicos morietur* (I.13); *in sua super suam plumatiunculam morietur domu* (I.15).

11 C'est de la sorte qu'est caractérisée la mort prédite aux grands pécheurs (VC I.21, I.22, I.36, I.38, I.39, II.20, II.22, II.23, II.24, II.25).

12 N. Stalmans, 'Le jugement de l'âme dans la Vie de Columba', *Cork Conference Proceedings* (Dublin, Four Courts Press, 1999).

13 . . . *qui aliqua ad carnalia medicamenta petiturus pertenentia ad nos venit. Cui oportunius erat veram de peccatis hodie penitudinem gerere, nam in huius fine ebdomadis morietur* (I.27). Le même regret de Columba est exprimé vis à vis d'une perte de temps à des chants de joie peu avant de mourir (I.42). Contrairement à ce qui a été dit (J. Stevenson, 'Literacy and Orality in Early Medieval Ireland', in D. Edel (éd.), *Cultural Identity and Cultural Integration. Ireland and Europe in the Early Middle Ages* (Blackrock, 1995), 11–22: 21–2) ce n'est pas le caractère de l'activité qui est condamné mais le fait de manifester autre chose que du repentir. Dans l'œuvre de Jonas de Bobbio, se confesser trois fois par jour est souhaité, un refus de faire pénitence amenant la damnation (II.19, éd. MGH SS rer. merov. IV 138–140; voir A. de Vogüé, *Jonas de Bobbio, Vie de S. Colomban et de ses disciples* (Bellefontaine, 1988), 56-7). En outre, Columban annonce régulièrement à ses moines le moment de leur mort de sorte qu'ils puissent s'y préparer (A. de Vogüé, *Jonas de Bobbio*, 29–30).

14 *subita emigratione nulla praecedente corporis molestia* (III.22).
Les saints du corpus étudié par M. Lauwers ne sont pas non plus malades avant de mourir, mais par contre leur mort n'est jamais subite: même assassiné, le saint reste en vie le temps nécessaire pour, notamment, confier ses dernières volontés (M. Lauwers, « La mort et le corps des saints. La scène de la mort dans les *Vitae* du haut Moyen Age », *Le Moyen Age* 94 (1988), 21-50: 23-4 et 42).

L'origine de la maladie est en Dieu, maître de tout[15]. Adomnán ne traite pourtant pas le sujet de la même façon qu'il s'agisse d'un individu ou d'une population. Au niveau individuel, les hommes, tous pécheurs et également démunis, sont touchés « au hasard »[16]. La maladie est décrite en termes physiques[17]; elle est guérissable dans les limites de « lois naturelles »[18]. Au niveau collectif, Adomnán précise que Dieu envoie la maladie par impatience et colère vis-à-vis de la nature pécheresse de l'homme (II.46) ou qu'il permet l'action de démons qui viennent infliger des épidémies (II.11, III.8)[19]. Ces démons semblent être, dans son esprit, des créatures concrètes[20].

Nous ne trouvons pas dans la pensée d'Adomnán une dualité implicite: maladie à la fois phénomène naturel et signe de la providence[21], ou une dualité explicite:

15 *Omnipotentia dei omnium dominatur, in cujus nomine nostri omnes motus ipso gubernante deriguntur* (VC II.34).

16 *in hac enim praeterita nocte cassu aliquo Maugina sancta virgo filia Daimeni ab oratorio post misam domum reversa titubavit* (II.5). Ce sera également par hasard que brûlera la demeure des parentes guéries d'un moine (*cassuque post aliquantos contegit dies ut idem viculus cum supradictae domuncula feminae flamma vastante totus concremaretur*, II.7).

17 *coxaque ejus in duas confracta est partes* (II.5).

18 *ab his egrotis quorum vitae terminus supervenerat requisitus idem lapis nullo modo reperiri poterat* (II.33).

19 Au §II.17, c'est le saint qui permet au *magus* d'exercer son « art démoniaque » contre le taureau.

20 La conception du démon chez Cassien influence Adomnán. Quand les démons affrontent les anges, le Christ arbitre est appelé agonothète, selon une expression de Cassien empruntée aux luttes sportives de l'Antiquité et qui confère aux démons une allure anthropomorphique (VC III.6; ils sont décrits physiquement dans III.8: *tetram et nigerrimam daemonum cum ferreis veribus aciem proeliari*. Voir P. Boglioni, « Miracle et nature chez Grégoire le Grand », *Cahiers d'études médiévales 1: Epopées, légendes et miracles* (Montréal, 1974), 11–102: 45 n. 87; B. Merdrignac, Recherches sur l'hagiographie armoricaine du VIIème au XVème siècle, 2 vol. (Saint-Malo, 1985–6), I, 120). C'est une défaillance humaine qui permet au démon de s'introduire. Mais alors que chez Cassien la défaillance est psychologique et le démon, même présenté concrètement, reste un être spirituel qui vient insuffler des idées mauvaises, chez Adomnán la défaillance est celle du péché originel que chaque homme porte en lui et le démon est un être réel, qui, armé, vient éliminer l'humanité. Pour le caractère concret des forces du mal dans les Vies irlandaises, voir J.-M. Picard, 'The Marvellous in Irish and Continental Saints' Lives of the Merovingian Period', H. B., Clarke, M. Brennan, éd., *Columbanus and Merovingian Monasticism* (Oxford, 1981), 91–104: 93–4. De même, pour la matérialité des monstres dans la Vie de Columba, voir J. Borsje, *From Chaos to Enemy: Encounters with Monsters in Early Irish Texts. An Investigation Related to the Process of Christianization and the Concept of Evil* (Turnhout, 1996), 167 et ss.

21 Idée présente chez Bède (W. D. McCready, *Miracles and the Venerable Bede* (Toronto, 1994), 28; *ibid.* 25 n. 45 appliquant a conclusion à la Vie de Columba par Adomnán).

maladie dans certains cas voulue par Dieu, mais naturelle dans d'autres[22]. Vulnérable depuis le péché originel, l'individu peut être « naturellement » attaqué et la population peut subir les effets de la colère divine. Si la colère divine — décrite comme telle ou sous la forme d'une attaque démoniaque — n'atteint jamais un homme en particulier[23], c'est que l'auteur évite qu'un péché individuel puisse être vu comme responsable de la maladie. Les malédictions n'ont d'ailleurs jamais la forme d'une maladie dans l'œuvre[24]. Les hommes sont égaux dans leur état de pécheur, les populations païennes, comme chrétiennes, sont frappées. Il n'y a pas chez Adomnán de conception de phénomène naturel indépendant d'une intention divine: même décrite physiquement, la maladie, due au péché originel, porte le signe de la volonté céleste.

Dieu est également à l'origine des soins apportés aux malades et, de même qu'il utilisait des agents punisseurs sous forme des démons, il utilise ici un agent guérisseur: le saint[25]. Le mode d'action du saint est toujours le même: il bénit un

22 Comme dans les sources étudiées par J. Kroll et B. Bachrach, 'Sin and Mental Illness in the Middle Ages', 507–14; id., 'Sin and the Etiology of Disease in Pre-Crusade Europe', 395–414.

23 Signalons, même si la conséquence est une possession, non une maladie, que dans un cas au moins c'est une négligence qui entraîne l'action d'un démon: un moine n'ayant pas béni un récipient de lait, un démon qui s'y était introduit put y demeurer (VC II.16). C. Stancliffe a montré qu'il s'agissait d'un exemple unique de possession en Irlande à cette époque et un emprunt à Grégoire le Grand chez qui une moniale négligente n'a pas béni une laitue, l'a mangée et fut possédée (Dial. I, 4, 7, *Grégoire la Grand, Dialogues*, éd. A. de Vogüé, II, 42–44). Voir C. Stancliffe, 'The Miracle Stories in Seventh-Century Irish Saints' Lives', *Le septième siècle: changements et continuités. The Seventh Century: Change and Continuity*, éd. J. N. Hillgarth, J. Fontaine (Londres, 1992), 87–115: 108–9). Toutefois, contrairement au récit de Grégoire où le démon est avalé, le démon chez Adomnán quitte le lait avant que celui-ci ne soit bu. Le fait qu'Adomnán n'ait pas emprunté la fin du récit pourrait montrer que dans sa vision, le démon, créature réelle, n'aurait pas pu être ingurgité.

24 Lorsqu'il maudit un individu, Columba lui impose une mort violente et subite (voir supra). Toutefois, quand il prévoit que le péché de cet individu peut être remis, il impose la pénitence ordinaire (II.39) ou même pardonne immédiatement (I.30, I.41). Etre pardonné sans avoir dû accomplir une pénitence devait constituer un miracle, le saint ayant prévu le pardon de Dieu (*cujus veram Christus suscipit penetentiam*, I.30). Par deux fois cependant la malédiction revêtira la forme d'une souffrance physique (voir infra).

25 Au sujet de cette image d'un Dieu distant qui emploie différentes puissances pour l'administration, la punition, la protection du monde, voir J. Daniélou, *Les anges et leur mission d'après les Pères de l'Eglise* (Chevetogne, 1953); C. Stancliffe, *St Martin and his Hagiographer. History and Miracle in Sulpicius Severus* (Oxford, 1983), 218 ss. Dans les Livres des Rois, Elie et Elisée sont également des agents guérisseurs du divin (Kee, *Medicine, Miracle and Magic in New Testament Times* (Cambridge, 1986), 25.

Le Livre des Jubilés a peut-être directement influencé Adomnán. Dans celui-ci, les démons apportent à l'humanité peste et maladie (Jub. 48:5-7) avec la permission divine (Jub. 10:6 et 48: 10), Dieu ayant cependant également enseigné les remèdes aux élus (Jub. 10:10–14).

objet qui, trempé dans l'eau, confère à celle-ci des vertus curatives. Ici encore, l'action respective de Dieu et du saint ne sont pas les mêmes vis-à-vis de populations ou d'individus.

Vis-à-vis des populations touchées, Dieu que l'on avait vu impatient et colérique, s'avère également compatissant. C'est lui qui, mû par la pitié (*deo miserante*), annonce au saint une prochaine épidémie en Irlande, afin que Columba puisse y remédier (II.4) et qui révèle l'existence d'une pierre aux vertus curatives (II.33). Quand le saint parvient au puits empoisonné, Dieu retire aux démons du lieu la permission qui jusque là leur était donnée de rendre la population malade (II.11)[26]. Il révèle au saint, par l'intermédiaire du Saint-Esprit, l'arrivée des démons au monastère (III.8).

Au niveau individuel, l'action de Dieu n'est pas directe. Si, à une reprise, Dieu intervient pour révéler au saint les prières de la femme à la hanche cassée, souvent le saint est mû par sa propre pitié. Il assume alors une fonction qui est bien plus que celle d'un agent. Désespéré par l'agonie de son intendant, ému par le désespoir des compagnons de Finten ou celui des parents de l'enfant, il supplie Dieu qui l'exauce[27]. Dans la guérison du saignement de nez et pour les douleurs ophtalmiques, Dieu n'intervient carrément pas: le saint agit en vertu de son seul charisme. Il pince le nez du premier, cas unique de guérison par contact direct du saint avec le malade, et il bénit un morceau de roche de sel pour les malades des yeux. Notons enfin qu'Adomnán mentionne l'existence de remèdes physiques donnés par les moines[28].

Le caractère moins direct de l'intervention divine dans la guérison des maladies individuelles par rapport aux collectives, n'implique rien concernant l'origine de

---

Les péchés qui attirent le courroux divin tiennent de la nature de homme ou de la condition spécifique d'une génération, ils ne désignent pas les fautes individuelles (Jub. 23: 13–4). La défaite des démons donne à l'individu l'assurance de la disparition des effets du péché et donc d'une vie entière caractérisée par la jeunesse et la force (Jub. 23: 28); cette défaite restaure la santé physique de l'humanité et de la création tout entière (Jub. 23: 29-30). Trad. R. H. Charles, *The Apocrypha and Pseudepigrapha of the Old Testament* (Oxford, 1913), 11–82. Au sujet de l'influence de ce livre, voir Kee, *Medicine, Miracle and Magic in New Testament Times*, 22–3; G. L. Davenport, *The Eschatology of the Book of Jubilees* (Leiden, 1971), 35–40. Pour la connaissance de ce livre en Irlande, voir L. Bieler, *The Patrician Texts in the Book of Armagh* (Dublin, 1979), 20; M. McNamara, *The Apocrypha in the Irish Church* (Dublin, 1984) 20–1.

26 . . . *daemonica deo permittente percussi arte . . . Ex illaque die daemones ab eodem recesserunt fonte; et non solum nulli nocere permisus est, sed . . .*(II.11).

27 Toute la Vie souligne combien Dieu l'honore et tient à lui accorder des faveurs (*honorificantia* I.1, III.16, III.23, le terme étant le même pour caractériser l'honneur dévolu par un laïc à Columba (II.35); *tale praevilegium* I.1, *aeternos honores* III.23; voir également II.25, II.45 etc).

28 *ad carnalia medicamenta petiturus pertenentia ad nos venit* (I.27).

cette guérison. C'est Dieu qui permet l'existence de remèdes, médicaments concrets ou miracles, car s'il veut la maladie, conséquence du péché de l'homme, il la déplore en même temps et ne peut rester insensible aux souffrances causées. Par contre, cette distinction établie entre les acteurs fait mieux comprendre la conception d'Adomnán du rôle de Dieu et du saint. Même si Dieu gouverne en théorie tous nos actes, il intervient principalement dans des miracles majeurs: ceux qui concernent des nations entières ou les événements en rapport avec la mort[29], le règlement de problèmes mineurs étant délégué au saint.

La différenciation que l'on trouve dans le discours d'Adomnán entre péché individuel et maladie, nous renseigne sur les objectifs sociaux et politiques de l'œuvre. Adomnán empêche le rejet social du malade rendu personnellement responsable de sa maladie[30]. Il introduit au contraire les thèmes de la compassion et de la tristesse, la volonté et même le devoir moral de soulager les souffrances[31]. Parallèlement, les guérisons de masse que Columba a permises *in illo tempore*, créent à l'époque d'Adomnán une obligation morale vis-à-vis du saint et appellent à la conversion.

Le message d'Adomnán n'est pas seulement social et politique: il est également eschatologique. Columba guérit au sens où il vient purifier l'homme du péché originel. L'eau fréquemment utilisée pour la guérison est symbole de l'eau du baptême, de la rémission des péchés. La pierre blanche aux vertus curatives flotte *contra naturam* comme une pomme (I.1, II.33); assimilée à une pomme, elle inverse cependant ce symbole du péché originel en guérissant[32]. La maladie elle-même, non par la souffrance qu'elle occasionne mais par le délai qu'elle procure, sert à sauver l'homme; nous constatons que sa durée — et donc la durée de la possible pénitence — est fréquemment de sept jours[33], chiffre symbolique pour une purification de l'âme[34].

29 On trouve Columba démuni face à la mort: il ne mourra pas au moment qu'il souhaite (III.22); la pierre blanche bénie par lui perd sa vertu curative lorsque le moment de la mort est arrivé (II.33); la résurrection de l'enfant est considérée par Adomnán comme un miracle majeur (*quod est majoris miraculi*, I.1).

30 Pour une telle exclusion, voir P. Brown, 'Relics and Social Status in the Age of Gregory of Tours', *Society and the Holy in Late Antiquity* (Londres, 1982), 222–250: 244, R. Van Dam, *Leadership and Community in Late Antique Gaul* (Berkeley, Los Angeles, Londres, 1985), 265 ss; id., *Saints and their Miracles in Late Antique Gaul* (Princeton, 1993), 85–91.

31 *Sed nos eorum miserati subvenire langoribus domino miserante debemus* (II.4).

32 Pour des références à d'autres pommes aux vertus curatives dans l'hagiographie irlandaise, voir D. A. Bray, *A List of Motifs in the Lives of the Early Irish Saints.* (Helsinki, 1992), 96.

33 VC I.27, I.32, II.39. Dans le récit I.31, la durée est d'un jour, bien que nous trouvions également mention de *ante hujus ebdomadis finem*.

34 Pour une telle valeur symbolique dans le Livre des Jubilés, voir G. L. Davenport, *The*

Columba ne se contente pas de guérir l'homme du péché originel: il le protège également. La foi dans le saint suffit à abolir le péché originel de tout homme devenant ainsi invulnérable aux épidémies[35]. Columba punit un moine qui a espionné ses rendez-vous angéliques nocturnes par une « marque de reproche » indélébile dans la figure[36]. Le saint lui confie cependant qu'il a évité une peine d'aveuglement. Si dans la Vie, Columba ne guérit pas d'aveugle, nous le voyons ici empêcher l'homme de le devenir[37].

Ce que promet Adomnán, c'est un monde meilleur, sans péché et sans souffrance. Adomnán nous raconte la bataille livrée entre Columba et les démons porteurs de maladie qui attaquent son monastère (III.8). Le saint a revêtu l'armure de Paul[38] et sa victoire préfigure celle contre l'antéchrist à la fin des temps. Cette

---

Eschatology of the Book of Jubilees, 81 n. 1. Le chiffre sept se rapporte aux offrandes purificatrices dans les *Moralia in Iob* de Grégoire le Grand (*Ipso ergo sacrificiorum numero reconciliati haeretici quid prius fuerint, exprimunt, qui perfectioni septiformis gratiae non nisi redeundo iunguntur*, préf. 17, *S. Gregorii Magni Moralia in Iob*, éd. M. Adriaen, CCSL 143 (Turnhout 1979), 22). Le Lévitique mentionne sept jours de réclusion en cas de suspicion de lèpre (Lv 13:4, 13:21).

35 Il est intéressant de noter que c'est ce même caractère protecteur qui est revendiqué pour leurs dieux par les *magi* (II.32). Au sujet des incohérences de l'hagiographie irlandaise vis-à-vis des *magi* et de l'origine de leurs pouvoirs, voir C. Stancliffe, 'The Miracle Stories in Seventh-Century Irish Saints' Lives', 108–9. Pour la nécessité sociale de considérer favorable-ment les *magi* voir M. McNamara, 'Patristic Background to Medieval Irish Ecclesiastical Sources', *Scriptuiral Interpretation in the Fathers*, éd. T. Finan, V. Twomey (Cambridge, 1995), 253–81: 275; et de façon générale V. Flint, *The Rise of Magic in Early Medieval Europe* (Oxford, 1991), 74ss.

36 La seule autre malédiction physique de la Vie de Columba est celle de la main d'un mauvais évêque qui pourrit et tombe (I.36). W. Reeves a suggéré qu'elle puisse rappeler une malédiction de Job (Job 31:22; W. Reeves, *The Life of St. Columba, The Founder of Hy* (Dublin, 1857), 70). Pour l'emploi des psaumes dans les malédictions dans des textes en rapport avec Iona, voir C. Plummer, *Vitae Sanctorum Hiberniae*, 2 vol. (Oxford, 1910), vol. 1, clxxiv n. 2). Il y a toutefois davantage de chances que ce soit une inversion de la guérison de « l'homme à la main sèche» de Matt. 12.9.

37 VC III.21 (voir l'épisode III.19m très proche).
    On sent ici l'influence de la citation de Jean « Je suis la lumière du mone » (Jn 9:5, 8:12). Cette citation est utilisée par Cogitosus lors de la guérison d'un aveugle (Acta SS Feb 1, 1658, 135–141: 137 col. 1; trad. S. Connolly, J.-M. Picard, 'Cogitosus: Life of Saint Brigit', *Journal of the Royal Society of Antiquaries of Ireland* 117 (1987), 11–27: 16). Kee souligne le symbole de vision spirituelle qui sous-tend la citation évangélique (H. C. Kee, *Medicine, Miracle and Magic in New Testament Times*, 88–89).

38 La mention de l'armure de Paul réfère aux Eph. 6:11–18 où Paul parle de combat contre les forces spirituelles. Chez Ambroise (Hexaemeron V. 10.31), la métaphore est appliquée aux dangers concrets de la mer. Ce passage d'Ambroise a influencé Adomnán dans sa façon réaliste de considérer les dangers de la mer (J. Borsje, *From Chaos to Enemy: Encounters with*

victoire explique l'absence de "jeste" sur le territoire de Columba à l'époque d'Adomnán (II.46). L'analogie: territoire du saint/paradis céleste apparaît, dans les récits thérapeutiques, par l'inversion constante des malédictions bibliques. Si la femme de Loth fut changée en statue de sel pour avoir trop regardé, la roche de sel sert chez Columba à soigner la vue (II.7)[39]. Alors que l'Apocalypse parle de la mer qui se transformera en sang (Apoc. 8:8, mais déjà Ex. 7:21), des hommes qui mourront d'eaux devenues amères (Apoc. 8:11), Columba change le sang en lait (II.17), assainit l'eau empoisonnée et guérit les hommes contaminés (II.11). Columba soigne les « ulcères purulents » comptés au nombre des plaies d'Egypte (VC II.4; Ex. 9:9-10)[40].

Dans la pensée d'Adomnan, la maladie est une réalité qu'il s'agit d'expliquer, à laquelle il faut trouver une cause, une origine, un remède. Ce dernier est le miracle et pour celui-ci deux niveaux de lecture sont possibles. Le premier niveau est celui d'une réalité structurée où les miracles ne nécessitent pas toujours le même déploiement de puissance du saint en fonction de la maladie à soigner. Le second est allégorique[41]. Les démons deviennent l'antéchrist, la maladie, signe du péché

Monsters in Early Irish Texts, 168–9 n. 392). La métaphore paulinienne peut donc avoir ici les deux sens.

39 Le sel qui guérit – que l'on retrouve dans le *De Locis Sanctis* (2.17.4) – doit également être lu en relation avec le verset de Mt (5:13): « je suis le sel de la terre » (T. O'Loughlin, 'The Exegetical Purpose of Adomnán's *De Locis Sanctis*', *CMCS* 24 (1992), 37-53: 52). C'est la seule fois dans la Vie que l'objet semble avoir été utilisé comme tel (nous le trouvons dans la suite du récit, vénéré par les deux femmes guéries) et non pas trempé dans de l'eau qui ensuite produit le miracle par aspersion.

40 Acceptation de la maladie au livre premier où elle précède la mort et où rien n'est tenté contre elle guérison dans le deuxième livre, abolition dans le troisième: nous retrouvons ici l'idée comme quoi la seule progression dans la personnalité de Columba est celle de la puissance qu'il manifeste (J.-M. Picard, 'Structural Patterns in Early Hiberno-Latin Hagiography', 76).

41 Pour une conclusion similaire à propos des guérisons dans l'évangile de Jean, voir Kee, *Medicine, Miracle and Magic in New Testament Times*, 125–6.
   En hagiographie, la puissance du symbole rendait sans doute inutile un déploiement quantitatif de guérisons (*contra* W. Davies qui en tire pour conclusion que les problèmes de santé intéressaient peu la société irlandaise du haut Moyen Age: W. Davies, 'The Place of Healing in Early Irish Society', in *Sages, Saints and Storytellers*, s. dir. D. Ó Corráin, L. Breatnach, K. McCone (Maynooth, 1989), 43–55: 52. Voir le compte-rendu de l'article par R. Black, *CMCS* 23 (1992) 104-5; C. Stancliffe, 'The Mircale Stories', 99).
   Nous n'avons pas trouvé comme le suggère M. Herbert une distinction entre les miracles opérés sur le territoire de Columba, bien documentés, et les miracles produits en dehors, davantage prototypaires (M. Herbert, *Iona, Kells, and Derry. The History and Hagiography of the Monastic Familia of Columba* (Oxford, 1988), 16–17). Il ne nous semble pas qu'il y ait d'oppositon dans la pensée d'Adomnán entre réalité et symbole, mais bien sûr seuls les récits

originel, l'instrument de destruction de l'humanité, le saint le sauveur, son territoire l'anticipation du paradis céleste.[42]

Dans la conception d'Adomnán, Dieu maître de tout peut s'impatienter et décider de ravager le monde. L'auteur a pu lire dans les épidémies de son temps des signes de la volonté céleste[43] et les débuts de la fin des temps[44]. Quoi qu'il en soit, le rôle qu'il attribue à la maladie, la promesse que celle-ci aura disparu du monde nouveau promis par Columba, montre l'importance qu'il attache à ce fléau et l'intensité de son sentiment d'impuissance face à lui. Le seul recours est la miséricorde divine obtenue grâce aux prières de Columba; péché individuel, mérite personnel n'ont pas de pouvoir dans un tel combat.

---

mettant en scène la maladie ont retenu ici notre attention.

42 Dans un article récent, J. O'Reilly a montré combien, pour Adomnán, Columba était impliqué dans l'œuvre de la rédemption universelle ('Reading the Scriptures in the Life of Columba', in *Studies in the Cult of Saint Columba*, s. dir. C. Bourke (Dublin, 1997), 80–106, en particulier 85–89 pour la valeur symbolique d l'œuvre).

43 T. O'Loughlin a montré l'importance sur la pensée d'Adomnán de l'idée d'Augustin comme quoi la création entière porte la marque de la volonté divine, dans ses études de l'autre texte de cet auteur, le *De Locis Sanctis* (T. O'Loughlin, 'The Exegetical Purpose of Adomnán's *De Locis Sanctis*', 37–53; 'The View from Iona: Adomnán's Mental Maps', *Peritia* 10 (1996), 98–122). M. Smyth affirme au contraire qu'Adomnán et ses contemporains ne s'intéressent au monde que pour lui-même (M. Smyth, 'The Physical World in Seventh-Century Hiberno-Latin Texts', *Peritia* 5 (1986), 201–234: 211; id., 'The Earliest Written Evidence for an Irish View of the World', *Cultural Identity and Cultural Integration. Ireland and Europe in the Early Midde Ages*, s. dir. D. Edel (Blackrock, 1995), 23–44: 25).

44 Ce qui expliquerait la prophétie de Maucte à propos de Columba dans la préface de la Vie: *In novissimis saeculi temporibus filius nasciturus est . . . novissima orbis tempora clare inlustrabit* (VC 2ème préface, p. 4).

Sucellos et Valéria Luperca*

Claude Sterckx

INSTITUT DES HAUTES ÉTUDES DE BELGIQUE

UNE ANECDOTE, dans le précieux Livre Jaune de Lecan, a été fréquemment citée car reconnue pour l'une des clés majeures de l'ancienne mythologie celte. Elle raconte comment le Daghdha Eochaidh Ollathair, le dieu jupitérien irlandais[1], a acquis l'un de ses attributs canoniques, la massue à deux bouts:

> Le Daghdha rencontra trois hommes sur sa route, qui portaient les trésors légués par leur père. Il les interrogea et ils répondirent 'Nous sommes trois frères, fils du même père et de la même mère, et nous partageons les trésors de notre père. 'Quels sont-ils?' demanda le Daghdha. 'Une tunique, un bâton et un manteau' répondirent-ils. 'Quel est leur pouvoir?' demanda le Daghdha. 'Le bâton que tu vois a un côté doux et un côté dur. Le premier ressuscite les morts et le second tue les vivants. . .'[2]

---

* Nous remercions John Carey et Marcel Meulder qui ont bien voulu relire ces quelques pages et qui les ont enrichies à travers plusieurs remarques pertinentes, sans pour autant souscrire aux thèses que nous y défendons.

1 Sur cette étiquette voir Sterckx 1985.

2 *Aodh Abhaid Easa Ruaidh mise* = Bergin 1927.402-404. Le massue de Daghdha réapparaît avec son double pouvoir dans *Measca Uladh* 27–28 = Watson 1941: cf. Sterckx 1982: 108. Elle apparaît aussi comme *lorg anfaidh* 'massue de tempête' dans le *Dinnsheanchas métrique* = Gwynn 1903–1935: III 294, ou aux mains de son 'avatar' (?) Mac Roith: cf. Sterckx 1991–1995: III 62.

D'autres anecdotes mythologiques confirment que ce pouvoir de sa massue attribue à Eochaidh Ollathair le rôle majeur de régulateur du cycle vital universel, contrôlant et assurant les passages du Non-Etre à l'Etre et de l'Etre au Non-Etre. Ce sont notamment des descriptions d'un dieu, anonyme mais clairement reconnaissable, transférant des animaux d'un état d'être à un autre.

Ainsi, au cours de leurs errances, le héros Maoldúin et ses compagnons arrivent à une île coupée par un mur de bronze séparant deux troupeaux de moutons, noirs d'un côté et blancs de l'autre, tandis qu'un géant les transfère sans répit d'un troupeau à l'autre:

> . . . et chaque fois qu'un mouton blanc était mis de l'autre côté du mur il devenait noir, chaque fois qu'un mouton noir était mis de l'autre côté du mur il devenait blanc.[3]

L'importance de la massue merveilleuse se reconnaît aussi à travers son caractère pancelte, depuis l'Antiquité gauloise où elle constitue l'attribut canonique d'un dieu majeur, le Jupiter gaulois sous son aspect de Sucellos 'le Bon Frappeur'[4], jusqu'au Moyen Age gallois où ce même dieu se reconnaît à travers plusieurs figures du recueil mythico-légendaire des *Mabinogion* — le Maître des Animaux à la massue duquel tous obéissent[5] et dont on devine qu'il assure là aussi la transformation des 'moutons noirs' en 'moutons blancs' et des 'moutons blancs' en 'moutons noirs'[6] — et même jusqu'à l'Armorique bretonne où le dieu et sa massue se reconnaissent dans plusieurs légendes hagiographiques[7] ou dans des contes populaires encore vivants il y a peu.[8]

Plus clairement encore, l'Armorique a gardé le souvenir de la massue merveilleuse dans un rite fameux, pratiqué au moins jusqu'au tournant de ce siècle.

Il s'agissait, pour les parents d'un moribond, de lui assurer un bon passage dans l'au-delà en imposant sur son front une massue sacrée appelée *mael benniget* 'maillet béni'. C'était, d'après les exemplaires préservés ou dont le souvenir s'est

---

3   *Iomramh Mhaoldúin* = Van Hamel 1941: 35. Cf. Carey 1982–1985 qui cite une série d'anecdotes analogues ainsi que d'éventuels parallèles bibliques qui ont pu inférer. Il faut noter que le 'géant' ne se sert pas ici d'une massue ni d'un maillet.

4   Duval 1976: 62–64; Mac Cana 1983: 66; Sterckx 1985.

5   *Chwedl Iarlles y Ffynon* = Thomson 1968. Cf. Goetinck 1995: 172–174.

6   *Ystoria Peredur ab Efrog* = Goetinck 1976: 47–48. Cf. Carey 1982–1985: XX 277; Sterckx 1985: 99–300.

7   Sterckx 1985. L'hagiographie est un domaine dans lequel l'Armorique a réinvesti un grand nombre de traditions préchrétiennes.

8   Sterckx 1992.

gardé, une masse de pierre[9] conservée soit dans une chapelle du village, soit dans un arbre sacré. Les plus célèbres étaient celles de Cléguérec, de Caurel, déposé dans un if creux, de Quelven, dont le recteur, son dépositaire, n'osait se défaire par crainte de ses paroissiens, du Manéguen en Guénin et, entre tous, de Locmeltro en Guern: un boulet en granit de 42 cm de diamètre recouvert d'une patine rougeâtre. Le nom même de Locmeltro signifie 'la Chapelle du Val du Maillet' et la célébrité de son trésor est telle qu'il est passé en proverbe de dire, à propos d'un vieillard avancé, *mall eo eñ kas da Locmeltro* 'il faut l'amener à Locmeltro'. Ailleurs on dit aussi *ret 'vo mont da vennigo an horz da Gorel* 'il faudra aller faire bénir le maillet à Caurel'.[10]

Ce *mael benniget* est, en Armorique, l'arme de l'Ankou, c'est-à-dire de la Mort. Bien que l'influence étrangère lui attribue parfois la faux ou une pique, ce ne sont là que des déformations tardives et les plus anciens témoignages attestent bien que son arme originelle était la massue.[11]

L'Ankou, comme sa massue, n'est pas exclusivement armoricain. Il se retrouve sous le même nom Anghau au Pays de Galles et Ancow en Cornouailles.[12] Par ailleurs, l'antiquité du rituel est garantie par une notule de Tertullien signalant déjà en Gaule l'usage d'un maillet de la bonne mort dans les combats de gladiateurs,[13] et l'on pourrait aussi relever qu'en Angleterre, au dix-septième siècle, était encore attestée l'existence d'un *holy mawle* 'maillet béni' conservé à l'église et servant aux fils 'à casser la tête de leur père lorsque celui-là atteignait soixante-dix ans'![14] Tout laisse donc croire que l'Ankou se pose en héritier direct de Sucellos, le dieu gaulois au maillet,[15] et en cousin tout aussi direct de l'Irlandais Eochaidh Ollathair, etc.[16]

Le maillet des passages de la vie à la mort et de la non-existence à la vie s'avère bien un phénomène pancelte clairement et surabondamment attesté.

9   Le contraste entre l'appellation 'maillet' et la nature de l'objet rend compte de la distance entre la massue du Daghdha irlandais et le maillet du Sucellos gaulois. On notera les alternances bretonnes entre un marteau, un bâton de fer et une massue (Sterckx 1985, 1992), et le fait que l'antique dieu 'jupitérien' celte paraît porter parfois la massue plutôt que le maillet; cf. Sterckx 1975.

10 Sterckx 1985–196: 15 (avec bibliographie).

11 Le Menn 1979: 18-23.

12 Le Braz 1904: 70, 105.

13 Tertullien, *Aduersus nationes* I 10 47 = Schneider 1968: 90.

14 Thoms 1839: 84.

15 Le Roux-Guyonvarc'h 1950–1953: 166; Le Menn 1979: 22–23.

16 Gricourt 1955: 157–158.

Il a toutefois été bien reconnu que ce phénomène n'était pas exclusivement celte. Le marteau du Scandinave Thor tue ou donne la vie à volonté.[17] La baguette d'or du Grec Hermès 'endort les éveillés et réveille les endormis'.[18] Des faits analogues apparaissent surtout largement dans le monde italien, depuis l'Antiquité étrusque où le passeur des morts dans l'au-delà, Charun, est canoniquement armé d'un grand maillet[19], jusqu'à des rituels catholiques contemporains puisqu'on s'assure encore aujourd'hui du décès et du 'bon passage' d'un pape en lui frappant trois fois le front avec un marteau en argent. Ou l'on pourrait encore évoquer la coutume sarde de *l'accabadura*, accusée jusqu'au dix-huitième siècle de casser la tête des vieillards et de leur écraser la cervelle à coups de bâton lorsque l'âge ou la maladie les rendait impotents![20]

Certes ces parallèles italiens illustrent seulement l'un des pouvoirs du maillet: celui qui assure les passages de la vie à la mort, de l'Etre au Non-Etre. Mais cela ne doit pas étonner: les rites du maillet béni dans le monde celte concernent eux aussi essentiellement sa vertu d'assurer les passages de la vie à la mort.

Essentiellement mais pas exclusivement. Là en effet, quelques faits bien attestés garantissent que le maillet béni avait aussi le pouvoir d'assurer un bon passage du Non-Etre à l'Etre, plus simplement dit de donner la vie.

En Irlande le maillet béni était utilisé exactement de la même façon, par une imposition sur le front, afin d'assurer la vie et la vitalité des nouveaux-nés[21]. Et la coutume écossaise de guérir les malades en les baignant dans une eau où avait été immergé le maillet béni de saint Fillian[22] est certainement un rite similaire où le maillet cette fois ne donne pas la vie mais la restaure en renouvelant la vitalité déclinante des égrotants.

Ce pouvoir vivifiant du maillet n'avait jamais été reconnu dans le monde latin. Il nous paraît néanmoins bien attesté à travers un rituel falérien qui semble avoir laissé jusqu'ici les exégètes à quia:

> On ne sait que faire de la Valéria Luperca de Faléries dont le 35ᵉ des *Parallela minora* parle 'd'après Aristide' dans le 19ᵉ livre de son histoire d'Italie. . .[23]

---

17 Renault-Krantz 1972: 131.
18 Homère, *Ilias* XXIV 343–344 = Mazon *et al.* 1937–1938: IV 141.
19 Grenier 1955–1956.
20 Edwardes 1889: 116–117.
21 Power 1976: 35.
22 Henderson 1911: 320.
23 Dumézil 1974: 355–356.

En voici le dossier maigrement constitué par une notice d'un pseudo-Plutarque:

Une épidémie s'était abattue sur Faléries et y semait la désolation. Un oracle révéla qu'on se libérerait du fléau en sacrifiant chaque année une jeune vierge à Junon. La crainte de la déesse fit qu'on n'osa pas désobéir jusqu'à ce que le sort désignât Valéria Luperca. Celle-là tendait le cou au fer lorsqu'un aigle fondit sur elle, arracha l'arme[24] et déposa sur l'autel un maillet à manche court. Quant à l'arme, l'aigle la lâcha sur une génisse qui paissait à proximité du sanctuaire.

La vierge comprit. Elle sacrifia la génisse et prit le maillet, puis elle parcourut la ville et, de maison en maison, elle guérit tous les malades en les frappant d'un petit coup du maillet et en ordonnant à chacun d'être bien portant; Et c'est de cet événement que dérive encore aujourd'hui l'initiation aux mystères locaux, comme le rapporte Aristide au livre XIX de ses *Italika*.[25]

Cette curieuse notice est confirmée par quelques mots de Jean le Lydien

La vierge comprit la bienveillance de la divinité; elle prit le maillet, parcourut les maisons et guérit . . . d'après le Romain Varron[26],

par des allusions précises au rituel, garantissant son existence, par Denys d'Halicarnasse

Une enfant, appelée canéphore, pure de toute union, accomplissait les cérémonies préalables au sacrifice, puis des chœurs de vierges célébraient la déesse par des chants ancestraux[27]

et par Ovide, témoin oculaire,

Mon épouse étant originaire du pays de Faléries, riche en vergers, nous avons visité ces murs que tu as vaincus, Camille. Les prêtresses de Junon se disposaient á célébrer la chaste fête de leur déesse par des jeux très courus et par le sacrifice d'une génisse indigène[28],

24 Tzétzès ajoute ici *apo tou hiereōs tou dēmou* 'au prêtre officiel'.
25 ps.-Plutarque, *Parallela minora* 35b = Jacoby 1940: 105. Nous remercions ici notre collègue C. Rose pour son aide très précieuse à la compréhension de ce texte. Nous assumons toutefois toute la responsabilité de la traduction ici proposée.
26 Jean le Lydien, *De mensura IV* 147 = Jacoby 1940: 105. La référence à Varron est très peu vraisemblable: Köves 1962: 216.
27 Denys d'Halicarnasse, *Rhōmaikē arkhaiologia* I 21 = Cary 1937–1950: I 66.
28 Ovide, *Amores* XIII = MacEown 1987– : I 217–218.

ainsi que par des monnaies de Valérius Acisculus (ca. 45 avant notre ère) représentant Valéria Luperca et son maillet[29].

L'aspect jupitérien de l'anecdote, qui rapproche le maillet de Valéria Luperca de ceux du Gaulois Sucellos ou de l'Irlandais Eochaidh Ollathair, est dévoilé par son don par un aigle, l'oiseau jovien par excellence.

L'hostilité de Junon envers une vierge mortelle et le rachat de cette dernière par Jupiter suggère une relation éventuelle de l'affaire avec les innombrables fredaines du roi des dieux et les impitoyables jalousies de son épouse trop bafouée.

Mais ce qui nous intéresse le plus ici, le caractère vivifiant du maillet divin, est bien marqué par la vitalité rendue aux égrotants lorsque Valéria Luperca les touche (au front ?) avec cet instrument.

Enfin ce n'est pas ici la place pour discuter si le mythème du maillet de la vie et de la mort est un emprunt des Celtes à l'Italie, de l'Italie aux Celtes ou, plus vraisemblablement, un héritage commun. Dans l'état actuel, nous nous avouons d'ailleurs bien incapable de trancher la question.

OUVRAGES CITÉS

E. Babelon (1886) *Monnaies de la République*. Paris.

O. Bergin (1927) 'How the Dagda got his Magic Staff'. Rajna *et al.*, 1927: 399–406

J. Carey (1982–1985) 'The Valley of the Changing Sheep'. *Bulletin of the Board of Celtic Studies* XXX: 277–280, XXXII: 156.

E. Cary (1937–1950) *The Roman Antiquities of Dionysius of Halicarnassus*. Londres.

G. Dumézil (1974) *La religion romaine archaïque*[2]. Paris.

P. M. Duval (1976) *Les dieux de la Gaule*[2]. Paris.

C. Edwardes (1889) *Sardinia and the Sards*. Londres.

G. W. Goetinck (1976) *Historia Peredur vab Efrawg*. Cardiff.

  (1995) 'Indian Parallels and Belgic Influence on Welsh Mediæval Literature'. *Ollodagos* VIII: 157–182.

A. Grenier (1955–1956) 'Le dieu au maillet gaulois et Charun'. *Studi Etruschi* XXIV: 131–135.

29 Babelon 1886: II 514–519; Köves 1962: 214–229.

J. Gricourt (1955) 'Un *mell benniget* gaélique'. *Ogam* VIII: 155–170.

G. Henderson (1911) *Survivals of Beliefs among the Celts*. Glasgow.

F. Jacoby (1940) 'Die Überlieferung von ps.Plutarchs *Parallela minora* und die Schwinde-lautoren'. *Mnemosyne* III 8:73-144

T. Köves (1962) 'Valeria Luperca'. *Hermes* XC: 214–238,

A. Le Braz (1904) *Essai sur l'histoire du théâtre celtique*. Paris.

G. Le Menn (1979) 'La Mort dans la littérature bretonne du XVème au XVIIème siècle'. *Mémoires de la Société d'Histoire et d'Archéologie de la Bretagne* LVI: 5–39.

G. Le Menn — J. Y. Le Moing ed. (1992) *Bretagne et pays celtiques. Mélanges offerts à la mémoire de Léon Fleuriot (1923–1987)*. Saint-Brieuc.

F. Le Roux-Guyonvarc'h (1950–1953) 'Le *mell benniget*'. *Ogam* II–IV: 164–166.

P. Mac Cana (1983) *Celtic Mythology²*. Londres.

J. C. MacEown (1987–) *Ovid. Amores*. Leeds.

P. Mazon *et al.* (1937–1938) *Homère. Iliade*. Paris.

P. C. Power (1976) *Sex and Marriage in Ancient Ireland*. Cork.

P. Rajna *et al.* (1927) *Mediæval Studies in Memory of Gertrude Schoepperle Loomis*. Paris.

H. Renauld-Krantz (1972) *Structures de la mythologie nordique*. Paris.

J. Schneider (1968) *Le premier livre* Ad natione s *de Tertullien*. Rome.

C. Sterckx (1974) 'Le Géant de Cerne Abbas'. *Antiquité Classique* XLIV: 570–580.

(1982) 'La théogonie celtique'. *Jahrbuch für Anthropologie und Religionsgeschichte* IV: 66–212.

(1985) 'Survivances de la mythologie celtique dans quelques légendes bretonnes'. *Études Celtiques* XXII: 295–308.

(1985-1986) 'Les têtes coupées et le Graal'. *Studia Celtica* XX–XXI: 1–40.

(1992) 'Débris mythologiques en Basse-Bretagne'. Le Menn — Le Moing 1992: 403–414.

W. J. Thoms (1839) *Anecdotes and Traditions Illustrative of Early English History and Literature*. Londres.

R. L. Thomson (1968) *Owein*. Dublin.

A. G. Van Hamel (1941) *Imrama*. Dublin.

J. C. Watson (1941) *Mesca Ulad*. Dublin.

Mimesis and Diegesis in the *Cattle Raid of Cuailnge*

Hildegard L. C. Tristram

FREIBURG

SUMMARY

This paper places the discussion on the prosimetric status of the 'Cattle Raid of Cuailnge' in the wider context of the discourse strategies of medieval Irish prose narrative. The approach advocated is that of functional narratology.

THE NARRATOLOGICAL FRAMEWORK

C LAUDE BREMOND,[1] Roland Barthes,[2] Tzvetan Todorov,[3] Seymour Chatman,[4] Mieke Bal,[5] and other narratologists distinguish between two

1 C. Bremond, 'Le message narratif', *Communications* 4 (1964), 4-32; 'La logique des possibles narratifs', *Communications* 8 (1966) 60-76; *Logique du récit*, Paris 1973.

2 R. Barthes, 'L'introduction à l'analyse structurale des récits', *Communications* 8 (1966), 1-27; 'An Introduction to the Structural Analysis of Narrative', *New Literary History* 6 (1975), 237-72; 'Le discours de l'histoire', *Poétique* 49 (1982), 15-21; 'La mort de l'auteur', in: *Essais critiques IV. Le bruissement de la langue* (Paris 1984), 61-7.

3 T. Todorov, 'Les catégories du récit littéraire', *Communications* 8 (1966), 125-51; 'La grammaire du récit', *Langages* 12 (1968), 94-102; 'Structural Analysis of Narrative', *Novel* 3 (1969), 70-6; *Grammaire du Décaméron* (The Hague 1969); *Poétique de la prose* (Paris 1971); Engl. transl. *Poetics of Prose* (Ithaca NY 1977); *Les genres du discours*, Paris 1978.

4 S. Chatman, 'New Ways of Analyzing Narrative Structure', *Language and Style* 2 (1969), 3-36; 'The Structure of Fiction', *University Review* (Kansas City 1971), 199-214; 'On Formalist-

structural levels of any given narrative: the plot (*fabula* or story) level and the discourse level.[6] 'Plot' is the narrative subject matter and is understood to consist of sequence(s) of events and actions (i.e. 'the what'). Actions are carried out by the characters (or agents), events happen to them. The plot may be expressed by using different words, narrative styles and media. This verbal realisation is termed 'discourse' (i.e. 'the how'). Verbal discourses may be supplemented or replaced by visual and/or aural media. Visual media realisations may be still or moving. In terms of audience response, plots may be 'understood', their discourse realisations may be 'listened to', 'read' or 'watched'. To borrow a metaphor from generative grammar: plot constitutes the deep structure of narrative and discourse the surface structure.

Specific narrative strategies operate both on the plot and on the discourse levels. Various narratological approaches have been proposed since the '60s, when the French structuralists developed recent narratological theory. They drew on the Russian Formalists of the '20s and '30s. Ultimately, all modern approaches go back to classical rhetoric and to Aristotle's *Poetics*.[7] My own approach is that of functional narratology.[8] By 'function' I mean the use to which narrative discourse strategies are put for the purpose of audience appeal.

Structuralist Theory of Character', *Journal of Literary Semantics* 1 (1972), 57–79; 'The Structure of Narrative Transmission', in: *Style and Structure in Literature, Essays in the New Stylistics*, ed. Roger Fowler (Oxford 1975), 213–57; *Story and Discourse. Narrative Structure in Fiction and Film* (Ithaca NY 1978); 'What Novels Can Do That Films Can't (and Vice Versa)', *Critical Inquiry* 7 (1980), 121–40; 'The Circle of Narrative', *Comparative Literature* 39 (1987), 162–68; 'The Styles of Narrative Codes', in: *The Concept of Style*, ed. Berel Lang (Ithaca NY 1987), 230–411; *Coming to Terms. The Rhetoric of Narrative in Fiction and Film* (Ithaca NY 1990).

5 M. Bal, *Narratologie. Essais sur la signification narrative dans quatre romans modernes* (Paris 1977); Engl. transl. *Narratology. Introduction to the Theory of Narrative* (Toronto 1985); 'Notes on Narrative Embedding', *Poetics Today* 2 (1981), 41–60; 'Mimesis and Genre Theory in Aristotle's Poetics', *Poetics Today* 3 (1982), 171–80; 'The Point of Narratology', *Poetics Today* 11 (1990), 727–54.

6 For a short summary of the basics of narratology see H. L. C. Tristram, *Linguistik und die Interpretation englischer literarischer Texte* (Tübingen 1978), 60–71.

7 One of the most recent approaches is that advocated by Monika Fludernik, *Towards a 'Natural' Narratology* (London and New York 1996). See p. 333ff. for the historical connections.

8 The narratological approach has hardly found favour with scholars of medieval Irish or Welsh literature, notable exceptions being Daniel F. Melia, *Narrative Structure in Irish Saga* (Harvard Ph.D. thesis, 1972); Edgar Slotkin ('What Allows Fixed Texts to Enter Gaelic Oral Tradition?', in: *(Re)Oralisierung*, ed. Hildegard L. C. Tristram (Tübingen 1996), p. 61), and B. K. Martin ('Medieval Irish *aitheda* and Todorov's "Narratology"', *Studia Celtica* 10/11 (1975/6), 138–51). In any case, methodological innovations are rare in Celtic studies.

The three recensions of the 'Cattle Raid' share the same basic plot. There is some variation between them — though negligible when compared with the long-term treatment of epic matter in other mediaeval European literatures and their various modes of literarisation.[9] This largely invariable plot (or basic story line) may be termed the narrative 'template' (Gm. *Textschablone*) of the 'Cattle Raid'.[10] The three recensions do differ on the discourse level, but again not so substantially as to constitute completely different texts.[11] In spite of the individual realisations, the basic discourse strategies are the same.

My concern in this paper is not with the story template of the three recensions of the 'Cattle Raid'. Here, I wish to concentrate on the discourse level, as an homage to Professor Proinsias Mac Cana who himself looked at the discourse strategies of medieval Irish narrative at the first Freiburg Colloquium (1987) on the oral and the written media of expression in early Irish literature, albeit from a diachronic stance.[12] My approach in this study is descriptive and ahistorical; I am not interested in developments here.[13] Suffice it to say that I see the origin of the

9   The *Táin's* reception in later centuries differs markedly in that respect from other mediaeval macro-texts with a comparable time depth of transmission, such as for instance the *Nibelungenlied*, the *Chanson de Roland* and Chrétien de Troyes' *Conte del Graal* (see for instance Joachim Heinzle, *Das Nibelungenlied. Eine Einführung* (2nd ed., Frankfurt am Main 1994); 'Zur Funktionsanalyse heroischer Überlieferung: Das Beispiel Nibelungensage', in: *New Methods in the Research of Epic*, ed. Hildegard L. C. Tristram (Tübingen, in press); Barbara Frank, 'Varianten, Fortsetzungen, Neubearbeitungen. Zur Textgeschichte des *Conte del graal* von Chrétien de Troyes', in: *Text und Zeittiefe*, ed. Hildegard L. C. Tristram (Tübingen 1994), 117–48, and Ursula Schaefer, 'Lanval — Eine Geschichte auf dem Weg zum Text', in: ibid., 87–115). I have often wondered why this was so.

10 I owe the term 'template' to Tom Shippey (St. Louis, Missouri). He proposed it in the general discussion at the end of the 1992 Freiburg Colloquium on the long-term transmission of narrative texts in various cultures; cf. my 'Einleitung', in: *Text und Zeittiefe*, ed. Hildegard L. C. Tristram (Tübingen 1994), 19. I use the term 'text' (in the singular) as an abstraction for the various textually recorded 'realisations' (in the plural) of the 'Cattle Raid' template. Furthermore, I distinguish between the *creation* of the extant 'texts' (in the plural) — produced as authorial multiform realisations by the various redactors/scribes distinguishable — and the *re-creation* of the individual textual realisations by the respective reciters/prelectors during performance.

11 No studies on the socio-historical background of the production of the various recensions and versions or on the literary interests of the respective audiences or patrons have come forth so far.

12 Proinsias Mac Cana, 'Notes on the Combination of Prose and Verse in Early Irish Narrative', in: *Early Irish Literature — Media and Communication. Mündlichkeit und Schriftlichkeit in der frühen irischen Literatur*, ed. Stephen N. Tranter and Hildegard L. C. Tristram (Tübingen 1989), 125–47.

13 For the standard hypotheses as to the genesis of the 'Cattle Raid', see Thurneysen,

discourse strategies which constitute the narrative *relievo* of the 'Cattle Raid' in the discourse strategies developed by Hiberno-Latin exegetes in the seventh and eighth centuries. They allowed macro-texts to be formed from smaller text units. The general development was from aggregation to integration.[14] My investigations in this study are both intratextual and intertextual (between recensions), although they are largely based on the first recension, because this constitutes the first attested evidence of the re-writing tradition of the 'Cattle Raid'. Since the basic discourse strategies do not differ between the recensions, therefore, what is said about Recension I holds also for the other two.

In order to analyse the narrative *relievo* of the discourse level, I resort to the classical concepts of 'mimesis' and 'diegesis', also called the 'mimetic' and 'diegetic' mode.[15] 'Mimesis' means the verbal act of 'imitating' or 'showing' the events and actions. In this mode, the narrator presents the narration as if it were not mediated by his use (i.e. choice) of words. He 'imitates' the action by 'showing' it to his audience. The main device of 'imitation' is the use of direct speech set in the mouth of the characters (or agents). In direct speech, first-person and second-person as well as third-person forms may be used. 'Diegesis' means the act of verbal 'mediating' or 'telling' of the events and actions narrated. In this mode, the narrator does not hide himself behind his words. He speaks in his own words, not in those of his characters. He thereby admits that his words mediate the story for his listener/reader. Third-person narrative, descriptions, lists, and indirect speech are common diegetical devices. So are authorial comments, value judgements, corrections and cross-references.

Mimesis affects the audience more directly than diegesis. The difference between these two narrative modes may be compared to different degrees of audience 'distancing': mimetic narrative is emotionally closer to the audience, diegesis is more distanced (or detached). In other terms: 1st and 2nd person narration involves the audience as immediate participants in the action; 3rd person narrative leaves the audience as distanced spectators. Frequent switches between the

---

Heldensage (1921) and the introduction to the three editions of the 'Cattle Raid' by Cecile O'Rahilly (1961, 1967, 1976).

14 Cf. my contribution to the centenary volume of *ZCP* 49–50 (Tübingen 1997): 'Latin and Latin learning in the *Táin Bó Cuailnge*', at 847–77.

15 μίμεσις and διήγησις; cf. Aristotle's *Poetics* 1448a20, the distinction ultimately going back to Plato's *Republic*, bk. 3, 392D–394E; see G. Genette, 'Frontières du récit', *Communications* 9 (1966), 152–63; S. Chatman, *Story and Discourse* (fn. 4 above), 144ff. For a recent critical discussion of the narrative dichotomy between 'mimesis' and 'diegesis' see Monika Fludernik, *The Fictions of Language and the Languages of Fiction* (London 1993), 26–32; also Fludernik, *Towards a 'Natural' Narratology* (fn. 7 above), 333–47.

two modes (and their respective discourse strategies) dynamise the narration. They enhance the narrative *relievo* and avoid monotony. The more mimesis a text contains, the more lively it is. Absence of mimetic switches in basic third-person narrative, a very *recherché* and literary device, is one of the preconditions for a smooth and distanced flow of action, if so desired by the narrator. In dialogic texts and in drama (which is representational in addition) first- and second-person narration predominates.

The 'Cattle Raid of Cuailnge' features a highly complex discourse structure. By this I mean that there are a large number of discourse strategies which give this macro-text[16] a particularly varied narrative *relievo*. For instance, the narrator inverts the chronological sequence of events in the section titled *macgnímrada* 'boyhood deeds'. Here he switches between the chronological pattern (*ordo naturalis*) of the main body of the narrative to an *ordo artificialis* pattern ('flashback') at a particular point of narrative risk. This 'flashback' is realised as direct speech and most effectively placed into the mouths of three characters: Fergus, Conall Cernach and Fiachu mac Fir Febe. Their speeches constitute a narration within a narration ('in-tale structure') or 'diegesis' within 'mimesis'. In themselves, these in-tales also consist both of 'mimesis' and 'diegesis', since the three in-tale narrators also report direct speeches. The technical term for this type of complex narrative technique is 'abysm'. The strategy of using three narrators is technically known as 'gradation' (*gradatio*). While not absent in medieval Irish narrative writing, *ordo artificialis* is, however, rare. The usual pattern is that of an *ordo naturalis* arrangement of plot. I think it is noteworthy that, for instance, the Middle Irish prose adapter of the *Aeneid* undoes the *ordo artificialis* of Vergil's third book and begins his narrative with the destruction of Troy.[17]

A less elaborate flashback than in the *macgnímrada* is, for instance, used by the narrator at the end of the second recension of the 'Cattle Raid', when it was thought necessary to give a reason for the tragic death of Briccriu.[18] A number of prophecies in the 'Cattle Raid', such as the famous prophecy of Fedelm, prepare

---

16 Cf. my 1988 article on 'Aspects of Tradition and Innovation in the *Táin Bó Cuailnge*', in: Richard Matthews and Joachim Schmole-Rostosky (eds.), *Papers on Language and Medieval Studies Presented to Alfred Schopf* (Frankfurt 1988), 1–38, where I chose the English term 'extended written narrative' (for Gm. *schriftlicher großepischer Text*) and 'extended form' (for Gm. *großepische Form*). I have since opted for the term *narrative macro-text*.

17 Cf. Isabel Kobus' 1989 Freiburg M.A. dissertation on *Die mittelalterliche Antikenrezeption am Beispiel der mittelirischen Aeneis-Adaptation 'Imtheachta Aeniasa'*; ("*Imtheachta Aeníasa*": die mittelalterlichen Aeneis-Adaptationen), *ZCP* 47 (1995), 76–86.

18 TBC II LL (O'Rahilly 1967 edition): ll. 4861–70.

the audience for events and actions not yet told.[19] Even if the audience did not know the plot, the narrator made sure that it knew what to expect.[20] In medieval writing, prophecies always came true. Thus between flashbacks and prophecies, the plot is firmly held together in the narrator's effort to create a coherent macro-text.[21]

The discourse of the 'Cattle Raid' is characterised by a shift of audience sympathy (Gm. *Leserlenkung*). At the beginning of the text, the audience's sympathy is clearly lodged with the Connacht party. The action is presented from their viewpoint so that, when Cú Chulainn steps onto the scene (after careful prepara-tion of his entry by means of Fedelm's prophecy and the tripartite telling of the *macgnímrada*), the audience looks at him from the Connacht perspective and shares the Connacht interests. As he is their enemy, his actions are viewed negatively. This Connacht perspective constitutes about one fifth of the whole text. The subsequent sections are characterised by the open conflict between Cú Chulainn, on his own because of the *cess noínden*, and the 'men of Ireland'. It consists first of the mass slaughter of the Connachta and then of accounts of single combats between Cú Chulainn and the Connacht heroes. Here the sympathy slowly shifts from the Connachta to Cú Chulainn. It is firmly lodged with Cú Chulainn when he utters the *M'óenurán* poem (in LU and YBL, part of the *Airg úaim, a Laíg* poem in LL and Stowe), in which he reflects on his loneliness. Audience sympathy is always lodged with the solitary fighter against overwhelming odds, whether he be good or bad. There is another crucial point of narrative risk, when Cú Chulainn is in danger of being overpowered not by his human enemies, but by supernatural powers as personified in the Morrígan. This prepares the audience for the emotionally charged scene of conflict between the foster brothers Fer Diad and Cú Chulainn, which eventually sets Fer Diad in the wrong. For the rest of the text, there is no doubt that the audience's sympathies are lodged with the Ulaid. The shift of point of view in the middle section, between the mass slaughters and the single combats, where the audience's sympathies are balanced between the Connachta and the Ulaid, is brought about by the skilful use of particular discourse strategies. The most important strategy is the careful prepara-

---

19 TBC I (O'Rahilly 1976 edition): ll. 50–113; TBC II (O'Rahilly 1967 edition): ll. 206–275.
20 Other prophecies are TBC I (O'Rahilly 1976 edition): ll. 194–201, 206–9, 294–7, 638–9, 644–5, 1106–9, 1223–6, 1980, 2372–9, 2405–22, 2844–9, 3531–5, 3830–8, 40–84–5; TBC II (O'Rahilly 1967 edition): ll. 673–84, 910–1, 1182, 1285–8, 2380–400, 2422–37, 2813–20, 4617–19.
21 Cf. the article by Michael Reichel on the wealth of 'Fernbeziehungen' in the *Iliad*: 'Narrato-logische Methoden in der Homerforschung', in: *New Methods in the Study of Epic*, ed. Hildegard L. C. Tristram (in press).

tion for Cú Chulainn's appearance 'on stage' as effected by the narrative tension between the flashback technique in the *macgnímrada* and Fedelm's prophecy. Another strategy is by allotting thick clusters of direct speeches to Cú Chulainn.[22] This brings him very much into the foreground.

Sometimes the plot requires the narrator to present two parallel narrative strands. Several verbal strategies for handling such parallel strands can be resorted to. The narrator chooses to alternate between strands and then to mark the transition between them by means of authorial comments such as *A imthúsa ó sin amach nochon iad chestnaigther sund colléic, acht imthúsa Fir Diad* (TBC I (YBL) 2815–6) 'His doings apart from that are not recorded here now, but those of Fer Diad', *Imthúsa Ulad trá ní de leantar sund calléic* (ibid. 3941) 'The doings of the men of Ulster are not described for a while' or *Imthúsa Con Culaind immorro is ed indister sund coléic* (ibid. 3984) 'Doings of Cú Chulainn are now told'. In other instances, the narrator condenses his plot, because he is anxious not to bore his audience with tedious enumerations of single combats: *Acht is emilt engnam cach fir fo leith díb d'innisin* (TBC II (LL) 1857) 'But it is tedious to relate the prowess of each man separately'. Such authorial handling of the discourse level forms part of the larger system of mimetic and diegetic narrative strategies which are characteristic of the complex narrative *relievo* of the 'Cattle Raid'.

THE MIMESIS AND DIEGESIS CONTINUUM

My systematic investigation of the use the narrator of the 'Cattle Raid' made of the mimetic and diegetic discourse strategies uncovered five distinct types, variously realised in the recensions, but, as mentioned above, all following the same basic pattern. Only one pattern is diegetic, four are mimetic. This means that the narrator aimed at strong audience involvement, with varying degrees of emotional immediacy.

1. The narrator's diegetic narration forms the basic grid of the narrative (Gm. *Objektsprachlichkeit*)[23], i.e. the narrator presents the events and

---

22 On the total number of Cú Chulainn's speeches see below fn. 43.

23 The ratio between diegetic narrative and the four types of mimesis amounts to ca 35% to 65% (see below fn. 43). — Extensive narratological analyses of TBC I, based on the O'Rahilly 1976 edition, and of TBC II LL, based on the O'Rahilly 1967 edition, to a minor extent also of the Stowe and O'Curry MS 1 versions, were carried out in the years 1989–1991 by three of my research assistants in the Freiburg Research Project on the oral and the written in the 'Cattle Raid': Dr. Isabel Kobus, Anke Simon M.A. and Tina Hellmuth M.A. The figures given in the following, the line references, line counts, sums and ratios are drawn from their data collections, on which I rely for their accuracy. I wish to thank all three of them for their painstaking and conscientious work as well as for their great patience.

actions of the story by means of 3rd person narration, retarding the action by the use of descriptions,[24] lists or catalogues,[25] enumerations,[26] and reported speeches.[27]

2. The narrator's *mimetic* narration occurs in his own *metatextual* (first-person) enunciations (Gm. *Metasprachlichkeit*), i.e. the narrator himself forms no part of the narrative; he himself is no character in it, but he tells the audience in what way he is telling the story, what he knows and thinks about its subject matter; he interrupts the narration by providing titles,[28] closing formulae of episodes,[29] onomastic passages,[30] and one verse

---

There is, of course, no room here to present the total data collection; only the most important data have been singled out.

24 There are 52 descriptions in 426 lines in TBC I (ed. O'Rahilly 1976), i.e. descriptions constitute 10.24% of the diegetic narration. They consist of descriptions of warriors and messengers, approaching armies, the figures of Fedelm (ll. 30–9) and Láeg (2190–208), Ailill's tent (ll. 140–6) and Cú Chulainn's chariot (ll. 2280–91, 2944–73). Cú Chulainn is the subject of the most elaborate descriptions (ll. 67–78, 428–34, 1651–55, 2215–78, 2341–66, 3847–58). In TBC II LL (O'Rahilly 1967 edition), there are 47 descriptions in 394 lines (i.e. 8% of the total of the text), of which 6 relate to Cú Chulainn and one to the qualities of the Donn Cuailnge (ll. 1320–33). Most descriptions, however, concern the muster of troops.

25 There are 9 lists or catalogues of varying lengths in TBC I (O'Rahilly 1976 edition): the Connacht army's itinerary (115–30), names of warriors killed (935–7), Cú Chulainn's martial feats (1714–9), names of warriors killed (1914–7), names of warriors killed (2319–27), rivers (3147–9), episodes of the 'Cattle Raid' (3155–60), the muster of the Ulster army (3455–97), the muster of the Men of Ireland (3948–81). In TBC II LL (O'Rahilly 1967 edition), there are 8 lists or catalogues.

26 There are 17 enumerations, 10 of them introduced by .i., in TBC I (O'Rahilly 1976 edition), mostly relating to names of warriors, but also to virtues, parts of the body, traits of character and body as well as plants. There are many more enumerations in TBC II LL (O'Rahilly 1967 edition), 82 altogether, due to the rhythmic and alliterative prose style which is fond of chains of synonyms.

27 There are 25 instances of reported speech in TBC I (ed. O'Rahilly 1976). They relate to Cú Chulainn (5 times), Mac Roth (5), Medb (2), Láeg (2), Iliach (2), Culann Cerd (1), Conchobar (1), Cathbad (1), Ibor (1), Lóch (1), Mani Aithreamail (1), 'a certain man' (1), 'the women' (1), 'the learned' (1) and 'every physician' (1). In TBC II LL (O'Rahilly 1967 edition) there are 23 instances of reported speech. Only two of them relate to Cú Chulainn, others to Mac Roth (4), to the men of Ireland (4), Medb (1), Dáire (1), Ailill (1), Fergus (1), Cathbad (1), Dubthach (1), Fer Diad (1), Ferchú Longsech (1, passive), Morrígu (1), 'the hosts' (1), 'the learned' (1), 'the seven underkings of Munster' (1).

28 There are 57 titles of episodes in TBC I (O'Rahilly 1976 edition) and only 16 in TBC II LL (O'Rahilly 1967 edition).

29 There are 11 instances of closing formulae of episodes in TBC I (ed. O'Rahilly 1976): ll. 935–7, 994, 1027, 1523–5, 1684, 1917, 1948–9, 2153, 2563–4, 3363 and 4132, and 22 instances in TBC II LL (O'Rahilly 1967 edition): ll. 276–9, 1214–6, 1332–3, 1695, 1802, 1961, 2093–4, 2320, 2438, 2472, 2509, 2605, 3596, 3758, 3811, 3835, 3861, 3893, 3936, 3980, 4882, 4919.

quotation.[31] He uses abbreviations ('et rel.') for formulaic expressions such as *Tongu do día toinges mu thúath*,[32] comments upon the progress of the narration,[33] refers back to episodes or events already narrated,[34] refers to variant versions[35], to triads or triadic expressions[36], to the 'Cattle Raid' as a tale itself,[37] to other sagas[38], to episodes as in-tales of the 'Cattle

---

30 There are 66 onomastic passages in TBC I (O'Rahilly 1976 edition), i.e. references to the origin of 'contemporary' or former place names. TBC I O'Curry MS I (Ó Fiannachta 1966 edition) has 47 passages. Most of them can be found in E. Hogan, *Onomasticon Goedelicum* (Dublin and London 1910, repr. Dublin 1993). There are 40 instances in TBC II LL (O'Rahilly 1967 edition) and Stowe (O'Rahilly 1961 edition).

31 I have found only one verse quotation in the 'Cattle Raid' texts, that is, the single stanza on the river Cron in TBC I (LU, YBL, Eg. 1782 (O'Rahilly 1976 edition), ll. 1160–3). It is set in no character's mouth and is therefore not to be classed as a speech poem. It also occurs in O'Curry MS I, ll. 334–7, but is there preceded by *ut dixit*, as if the scribe felt the anomaly of the stanza's treatment as a quotation. Quotation poems can, however, be found in many other early Irish texts, in which the narrator wishes to authenticate his narrative by means of quoting some (other) poet's authoritative verse; cf. for instance in the Middle Irish *Sex aetates sunt mundi* (SASM) world chronicle the poems are introduced by:

> *ut poeta dicit* (97), *De quibus poeta dicit* (128), *amail at-beir in fili goedelach sin* (430), *Oengus mac Suibne hoc carmen cecinit de .xii. filiis Iacob* (514), *ut dicitur* (803), *Duan Dublittrech inso forsin panechte* (896).

Line references are to my edition of SASM (Heidelberg 1985).

32 TBC I (O'Rahilly 1976 edition): ll. 735 (cf. l. 742), 808, 938, 1180, 1200, 2559, 2611–2, (2612–3, 2871–2), 3629, 4010, 4018–9, 4099; O'Curry MS I (Ó Fiannachta 1966 edition) 354, 371, 1574, 1638; cf. TBC II LL (O'Rahilly 1967 edition): ll. 1617–8 and 1630.

33 E.g. *Finit a titulrad. Incipit in scél iar n-urd. In scél iar n-urd inso sís* 'Here ends the introductory part. The story in due order now begins. The story in due order' (TBC I (O'Rahilly 1976 edition): ll. 134–5; TBC II LL (O'Rahilly 1967 edition): l. 1217).

34 TBC I (O'Rahilly 1976 edition): ll. 304, 1233–4, 1263, 1523, 2508, 3411; TBC II LL (O'Rahilly 1967 edition): l. 1284.

35 There are 22 references to variant versions of episodes or plot in TBC I (O'Rahilly 1976 edition: ll. 189, 303–5, 825, 873–5, 926–7, 1027–9, 1207, 1413–4, 1487, 1727–8, 1785, 1872–3, 2034–5, 2049, 2054–5, 2316–7, 2464–5, 3445–7, 3523–26, 3538–9, 3903–4, 3928–9. I have found one example in TBC II LL (O'Rahilly 1967): ll. 2322–3 (*Iss ed atberat araile ro fích Lug mac Eithland la Coin Culaind Sesrig mBresslige* (in marg.) 'Others say that Lug mac Eithlend fought along with Cú Chulainn at Sesrech Breslige'). Cf. TBC I O'Curry MS I (Ó Fiannachta 1966 edition), ll. 1346–7: *Itberait aroile do fich Lucc mac Ethlenn la Coin cCulaind Seisrigh mBresleghi*. I have found no references to variant versions in TBC II Stowe.

36 TBC I (O'Rahilly 1976 edition): ll. 325–6, 1214 (cf. 3425, Stowe 3976), 2313–4, 2941–2, 3408, 3448; TBC II LL (O'Rahilly 1967 edition): ll 3927–8, 4011, 4015, 4040–1, 4257–9.

37 TBC I (O'Rahilly 1976 edition): ll. 994, 1844, 1913, 2563, 2735, 2821, 2882, 2942, 3155, 3160, 3392, 3408; TBC II LL (O'Rahilly 1967 edition): ll. 307, 651, 819, 920, 1213, 1214, 1361, 1370, 1395, 1440, 1601–2, 1709, 1802, 1960, 1061, 1992, 2094, 2496, 2498, 2507, 2732–3, 2796–

Raid'[39]; the narrator also provides explanations of names, titles and Old Irish words,[40] background information not immediately relevant to the action[41], and sometimes he also uses Latin words and phrases.[42]

3. The narrator's *mimetic* narration also occurs in the form of the characters' extensive *prose* speeches,[43] i.e. the narrator mediates the speech acts of his characters to his audience by using addresses, monologues and dialogues which show varying degrees of grammatical and stylistic formalisation.[44]

7, 3438, 3584, 3758, 3828, 3870, 3978, 3984, 3988, 4257, 4750, 4807, 4810, 4862, 4868. This type of self-reference gives either the short or the full title of the text, e.g. *Táin* or *Táin Bó Cuailnge*.

38 TBC I (O'Rahilly 1976): l. 2025 (*Táin Bó Regamna*); TBC II LL (O'Rahilly 1967 edition): l. 1990 (ditto).

39 TBC I (O'Rahilly 1976 edition): ll. 2312–3 (*Sesrech Breslige*); TBC II LL (O'Rahilly 1967 edition): ll. 3 and 277 (*comrád chind cherchailli*), 3928 (*Mellgleó nÍlíach*), 2472 (*Tugi im Thamon*), and 4883 (*Aided Bricni*).

40 TBC I (O'Rahilly 1976 edition): ll. 1656–7, 2045, 2312–5, 3011 (*Dáig cúa ainm na claíne isin tsengaidilc* 'For *cúa* is the word for squinting in Old Irish'), 3386, 3452–3, 4126; TBC II LL (O'Rahilly 1967 edition): ll. 3598, 3788, 4452, 4487, 4501, 4519, 4597, 4713, 4729, 4730, 4740, 4741, 4768, 4794, and 4803.

41 TBC II LL (O'Rahilly 1967 edition): ll. 3344–7, 4746, 4775–7.

42 Such as *dixit, dixit carmen, ut dixit, ut praediximus, et reliqua, ut in alis libris inuenitur, secundum alios libros, sic in ceteris, ut ante, et, uel, hic, incipit, finit, amen, finis* etc. Cf. Hildegard L. C. Tristram, 'Latin and Latin Learning' (fn. 14 above).

43 In TBC I (O'Rahilly 1976 edition), there are a total of 279 (direct) prose speeches; they occur in 2719 lines out of the total of 4160 printed lines, the ratio between 3rd person narration and direct speech being ca 35% to 65%. There are 68 speakers (or groups of speakers) altogether. The most frequent speaker is Cú Chulainn: 183 speeches are set in his mouth. Next in number is Fergus mac Róich (104); then come Medb (73), Ailill (64), Láeg (31), Fer Diad (27), Mac Roth (25), Cethern mac Fintain (22), Lugaid mac Nóis (14), Conchobar mac Nessa (13), Fer Diad's charioteer (12), Nad Crantail (11), Lug mac Ethlend (11), Fedelm Banfáith (9), the Morrígan (9), Etarcomol mac Eda (8) etc. In the *macgním-rada* Cú Chulainn is allotted 39 speeches, Conchobor (19), Ibor charioteer of Conchobor (16), Conall Cernach (6), Cathbad Druí (6), the sons of Nechta Scéne (3), Culann Cerd (3), Ailill (1 ?), Fergus (1), Follomon mac Conchobair (1), Mugain the wife of Conchobor (1), 'a man with half a head' (1). In TBC II LL (O'Rahilly 1967 edition) there are 226 (direct) prose speeches and 54 speakers (or groups of speakers); the ratio between 3rd person narration and direct speech is ca 39% to 61%. 161 speeches are set in Cú Chulainn's mouth. Next in number are Fergus with 101 speeches, Medb (92), Ailill (64), Mac Roth (46), Fer Diad (40), Láeg (37), Cethern (18), Fiachu (12), Fíngin (11), Etarcomol (11), Cormac (9), Sualtaim (7), Conchobar (6), Dáire (6), Findabair (4) etc.

44 The direct speeches and dialogues in the 'Cattle Raid' are not reflexes of everyday Middle Irish speech, i.e. of contemporary spontaneous oral speeches. They are stylised in the sense of grammatical 'wellformedness'; cf. Wolfgang Meid, 'Zur sprachlichen Form altirischer Texte, hauptsächlich am Beispiel der *LU-Táin*', in: *Early Irish Literature*, ed. Tranter and

4. The narrator's *mimetic* narration also occurs in the form of his characters' stanzaic-syllabic verse speeches (speech poems),[45] i.e. the narrator presents his characters bursting into verse (with only a very small degree of affinity to everyday speech), when emotional states such as fear, hope, anger, regret and sadness are expressed. There are three basic verse forms: syllabic-stanzaic (*debide* and *rannaigecht*), *ochtfoclach* and *rosc*.[46]

5. The narrator's mimetic narration also occurs in the form of the characters' 'rhetorical speech',[47] i.e. the narrator has his characters use rhythmic accentual and stichic sequences of words, half prose and half verse (sg. *roscad*, pl. *roscada*); the meaning of these pronouncements sometimes is deliberately opaque in order to create a quasi-mantic effect on the audience.[48]

The following diagram tries to systematise these five types of discourse strategies:[49]

Tristram (see fn. 12 above), p. 189ff. In spite of the literary quality of the direct speeches in the 'Cattle Raid', conversations of more than two characters are rare, presumably because of the problem of mapping group conversation onto the linear and two-dimensional medium of writing which the medieval Irish authors had not yet mastered.

45 There are 22 speech poems in TBC I (O'Rahilly 1976 edition), six of which have no *dúnadh*; 29 speech poems in TBC II LL and Stowe, six of which have no *dúnadh*; six poems have been preserved in the fragmentary TBC III (ed. Feargal Ó Béarra, unpublished Galway MA dissertation 1994; translation published in *Emania* 15 (1997), 47–65).

46 I follow Ludwig C. Stern in distinguishing *rosc* from *roscad*, taking the former to designate specifically the type of rhythmic, stichic verse with trisyllabic cadences found twice in TBC I LU, five times in O'Curry MS 1, once in TBC II LL, twice in Stowe, twice in TBC III MS H.2.17 and twice in MS Eg. 93; cf. Stern, 'Ein irisches Leben der heiligen Margarete, *ZCP* 1 (1897), pp. 132–3. Other scholars give the term broader application; thus Liam Breatnach, 'Canon Law and Secular Law in Early Ireland: The Significance of *Bretha Nemed*', *Peritia* 3 (1984), pp. 452–3.

47 In TBC I, 33 rhetorical speeches, all marked by .r., occur in 251 printed lines (O'Rahilly's 1976 edition), i.e. 6.02%. There are only 7 rhetorical speeches in 47 printed lines, marked by .r. in margin, in TBC II LL (O'Rahilly's 1967 edition); this amounts to ca 1% of the total of the text.

48 Cf. Johan Corthals, 'Zur Frage des mündlichen oder schriftlichen Ursprungs der Sagen *roscada*', in: *Early Irish Literature*, ed. Tranter and Tristram (see fn. 12 above), 201–220; Liam Breatnach, 'Zur Frage der *roscada* im Irischen', in: *Metrik und Medienwechsel. Metrics and Media*, ed. Hildegard L. C. Tristram (Tübingen 1991), 197–205. Karin Olsen, 'The Cuckold's Revenge: Reconstructing Six Irish *Roscada* in *Táin Bó Cuailnge*', *CMCS* 28 (1994), 51–69, takes the *roscada*, as earlier researchers did, to be genuine but corrupted survivals of early 'Cattle Raid' realisations.

49 The visual layout (i.e. taxonomy) does not imply a generative principle.

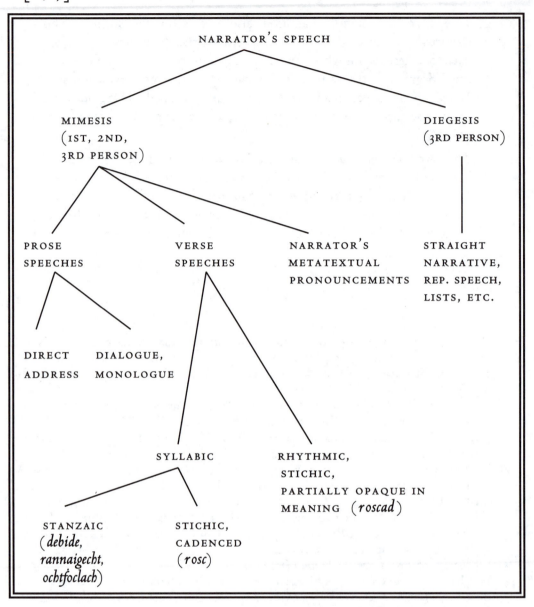

These five types of mimesis and diegesis bring about, as I suggested above, five different types of speech intensities which form a continuum of audience appeal[50].

50 Cf. Roman Jakobson's views on the conative or appellative function of language in his seminal article 'Closing Statement. Linguistics and Poetics', in: *Style in Language*, ed. Thomas A. Sebeok (Cambridge MA 1960), 350–77. Karl Bühler already distinguished between different functions of language within his linguistic model of the ὄργανον διδασκαλεῖον ('organon didaskaleion') in his *Sprachtheorie. Die Darstellungsfunktion der*

This means that, in performance or in the act of reading, they create a gradient of affective distancing between the narrator's voice and his audience. The greatest distance is manifest in the narrator's metatextual, anti–illusionist pronouncements or his 'intrusions' into his narration. He thereby separates himself both from his narration and from his audience. Less distanced is the narrator's 3rd person narration which presents the text as part of the cultural memory shared by both his audience and himself. The prose dialogues take in a middle position between narrative distance and emotional closeness. In spite of their stylised speech, they aim at fictional realism. The verse speeches affect the audience more intensely than the prose ones because of their more immediate aesthetic appeal. Of the metrical forms, *debide* and *rannaigecht* stanzas are less artful than the *ochtfoclach* stanzas which occur in the Fer Diad episode, the most emotional episode of the whole text. The *roscad* speeches and dialogues create the greatest degree of affective closeness to the audience. Their immediacy is brought about by their subcutaneous appeal to the intuitive comprehension of quasi-magical speech. In some respects, the *roscad* speeches and dialogues are close to the Old and Middle Irish charms and some of the incantations.

CONCLUSION

Epic prose, especially when used for macro-form texts, requires special communicative discourse strategies in order to sustain the listening audience's interest over an extended period of time. I would suggest that epic prose is more demanding in this respect than epic verse, because the author cannot rely on the audience's mere enjoyment of verbal aesthetics to sustain their interest. The varied narrative *relievo* of the 'Cattle Raid' texts with their differentiated use of the diegetic and the mimetic modes attests to the narrative skills developed by twelfth-century Irish prose writers to meet this target. It is not enough to characterise these texts as 'prosimetra'. The frequent switches between prose and verse form part of a larger system of narrative switches geared to sustain audience attention. It is as if the 'camera' moved between close-ups, distanced shots, and middle positions, with the narrator frequently intruding by means of different techniques in order to guide his audience's response.

The twelfth century saw the rise of a number of macro-form texts characterised by this sort of diversified narrative *relievo*: the 'Cattle Raid', *Togail Bruidne Da Derga* and *Fled Bricrenn* as well as such texts as the *Agallamh* and *Buile*

Sprache (Jena 1943).

Shuibhne. The ratio between the diegetic and the mimetic modes in these texts may differ, but the implementation of the aesthetic potential of prose narrative is equally well realised. The aesthetic of Irish epic prose had reached a high standard in the twelfth century. Regrettably, due to the political and social changes attendant on the Norman invasions, this very promising stage was not given the chance to undergo further literarisation in the sense of an internalised functional and integrative use of diegesis and mimesis (as in later novel writing).

Trefn Goddrych a Berf yng Ngosodiad Cadarnhaol Cyfieithiad Cymraeg o 'Bestiaire D'Amour'

T. Arwyn Watkins

ABERTAWE

§1.

MAE PEDWAR fersiwn Cymraeg o'r testun Ffrangeg uchod wedi eu cyhoeddi yn Thomas G 1988. Dywed y golygydd (ib. xxv) nad yw unrhyw un o'r fersiynau yn gopi uniongyrchol o'r llall, er bod y pedwar ohonynt yn disgyn o un testun Cymraeg Canol coll. Mae'r hynaf o'r testunau (A) yn perthyn i ddiwedd y bedwaredd ganrif ar ddeg neu ddechrau'r bymthegfed. Mae'r ail (B) wedi ei lunio yn hanner olaf y bymthegfed, a'r ddau fersiwn diweddaraf (C a D) yn chwarter olaf yr unfed ganrif ar bymtheg (ib. xvi–xxii). Mae rhai nodweddion tafodieithol lleol diweddar i'w canfod yn y ddau destun olaf, ond yr hyn sy'n gwneud y testun o ddiddordeb arbennig yw'r ffaith fod y cyfan ar ffurf llythyr personol, ac felly yn ymdebygu i'r rhannau deialog yn rhyddiaith chwedlonol Cymraeg Canol yn hytrach nag i'r rhannau naratif. Adlewyrchir hyn yn y defnydd cyffredin o ragenwau ategol, nid yn unig gyda berfau ond hefyd gydag arddodiaid rhediadol a rhagenwau blaen a mewnol. Daw'r enghreifftiau canlynol o destun C:

. . . am vod i naturiaeth ef ganv . . . 20, kans yna i kan ef . . . 21, pan gano ef . . . 22, i ymgyrhaeddyd a'th drigaredd di . . . 25, idd wyf j megis am hanner nos . . . 26, kans pe bai gennyf j ddim gobaith . . . 27, . . . na vynn ef vrefy . . . 32, ag yna i rydd ef ryw fravad . . . 34, kans nid odwyf j . . . 37, megis i gallwyf j dorri vy newyn . . . 38, ar gerdd i dylyswn j wnaethur hynn 40.

Nid oes cysondeb llwyr; ceir dileu'r rhagenw yn achlysurol lle y buasai'n ganiatadwy ei gynnwys:

idd wyf j yn danfon annerch . . . atoch 1, a bid hysbys gennych . . . 2, megis i gallwyf j dorri vy newyn arnad . . . 38.

Nid oes cysondeb llwyr chwaith rhwng fersiynau. Yn B a D *atochi* sy'n cyfateb i *atoch* yn 1, ac yn D *arnati* a gyfetyb i *arnad* 38. Ond yr arfer cyffredin yn y tri fersiwn diweddar yw cynnwys y rhagenw ategol lle y bo hynny yn ramadegol ganiatadwy.

Peth arall sy'n awgrymu iaith lai ffurfiol yw prinder ffurfiau cwmpasog ar y ferf. Pedair a geir yn C:

ag os ymhell i kar hi i garv yn vawr a wna hi . . . 80, Ag velly kanv yn dda a wna dwy onaddynt . . . 174, a'i hela ef a wnair . . . 248, A ffo a wna yntav yr hyd j gallo . . . 249.

§2. Bwriad yr erthygl hon yw trafod safle berf a goddrych yn y gosodiad cadarn-haol. Mae realeiddiad y cyfansoddion hyn yn y teipiau eraill o frawddeg yn llawer llai amrywiol. Er enghraifft, y drefn gyson yn y gosodiad negyddol yw . . . negydd + Berf rediadol ± rhagenw ategol, neu . . . negydd + Berf 3 un. + Goddrych Enwol. Dyfynnir o destun C:

kans nid odwyf j yn ymgyrhaeddyd . . . 37, kans oherwydd y kyntaf ny ddychon hi roddi i chariad . . . 77, Ag velly ny vedrais j ymweglyd . . . 86, ond ny ad yr ysgidiav yddi dringad 114, Ag velly ny ddelyyd ti vy narostwng j . . . l2o, am nad ynt yn debig . . . ny ddwg hi ddim trwydded yddynt . . . 125, nid oes yddynt ymborth . . . 128, Nid oes meddiginaeth . . . 221.

Gyda ffurf amhersonol, gwrthrych sydd yn cyfateb o ran statws i oddrych berfau personol:

ag velly ny ellir dala yr vn a vo heb wisg kariad 118.

Ychydig weddillion yn unig o destun A sydd wedi goroesi, ac y mae B yn frith o dudalennau wedi eu llurgunio. Felly, seilir y dadansoddiad canlynol ar C, y testun y daeth y dyfyniadau uchod ohono.

I. Y GOSODIAD CADARNHAOL NIWTRAL

§3. Pan fo'r goddrych yn rhagenwol y drefn sylfaenol yw Goddrych + *a* + Berf rediadol, a cheir cytundeb goddrych-berf dieithriad:

> ond mi a ddanfonaf atad ti arwydd . . . 7, Ond mi a baidaf a chanv . . . 42, kans mi a ddwedaf iti . . . 42, a mi a draethaf hynn . . . 61, ag ef a gwilyddia . . . 147, ag ef a gria . . . 225, ag ef heda yn y kylch . . . 232, A mi a glywaf gan rai . . . 244.

Safle dominyddol adferf atodol yw'r slot frawddegol gyntaf. Nid yw ei phresenol-deb yn effeithio ar y drefn:

> kans pan ddarllenir pob llythyr ef a ymchoel yn barabl 10, pan ddel ef i rodio . . . ef a gerdd yn arava ag i gallo 72, ag o damchwaina i wrysgen dorri . . . ef a gny i droed . . . 73, ag os yn agos i kar hi hia gar yn lledradaidd . . . 82, o damchwaina yddi vyned . . . hi a vedr roi esgus . . . 84, pan welo ddyn noeth ef a ffy . . . 93, a phan welo ef dyn dillatog ef a'i kyrch ef . . . 94, kans yr amser gyntaf mi a levesais ddwedvd . . . 101, ag yno ef a eistedd . . . 108, pan ddel yn agos atynt ef a gwsg 178, a phan wypo y vorwyn . . . hi a ddaw ato . . . 178, wrth edrych arnad tithav ti a'm divwynaist j . . . 195, pan glywo ef aroglav . . . ef a ddaw eti . . . 203, kans pei mynyd tithav . . . mi a gyvodwn . . . 227, pei gwnelyd ti . . . mi a debygwn i byddwn vyw . . . 229, Ond pei agoryd ti . . . ti a'm kyvodyd . . . 241, a phan vo ef ymronn deffygio ef a wyr . . . 250, kans pan wybyost di . . . ti a vwraist air teg . . . 257.

Mae'r eithriadau yn brin. Yn y ddwy frawddeg ganlynol adferf + *i* [ə] + Berf rediadol + rhagenw ategol yw'r realeiddiad:

> a chwedy imi ymwisgo . . . i delysyd ti wnaethur llawenydd . . . 133, a phan el ef i hela i gosod ef vorwyn ar i ffordd ef 205.

Mae'n arwyddocaol fod D wedi newid i'r drefn ddominyddol yn achos y frawddeg olaf:

> a phan êl efe i hela ef a esyd y Forwyn ar y Fordd D 205.

§4. Mae'r arfer mewn cymalau cydradd yn gwamalu. Ceir dwy enghraifft o beidio â chynnwys y rhagenw goddrychol (gan ddilyn arfer Cymraeg Canol):

> ag ef a eistedd yn gyverbyn . . . ag a wisg 108, ti a vwraist ag a ddiengaist dithav 257.

a dwy enghraifft o'i gynnwys:

> ag ef a edy yno ysgidiav . . . ag ef a oddyno 110, ef a ddaw eti ag ef a ry i benn
> yn y harffed hi . . . 204 (cymharer: Kans peth anobaithol a vydd kadarn . . . i lef
> ag ef a gefflybir . . . 30).

Cyferbynner â'r rhain y canlynol o'r testun hŷn B:

> ac yna ef a . . . ac a edy yno ddwy essgid . . . 110, Kans dyn anobeithvs a vydd
> kadarn i lef . . . ac a gyfflibir i'r anifeil kadarnaf . . . 30.

§5. Ar ôl adferf gysylltiol mae'r drefn yn wahanol. Y realeiddiad sylfaenol yw
i(dd) [ɔ(b)] + Berf rediadol + rhagenw ategol:

> kans yna i kan ef yn deg . . . 21, ag yna i rydd ef ryw fravad . . . 34, ag am hynny
> i nakaist dithav vinnav 53, ag yna i gollwng hi i digovaint . . . 192, Ag am hynny i
> delaist di vi . . . 198, ag yna i kwsg ef 204, Ag yna i kollais y tri synwyr gorav . . .
> 209, Ag am hynny y delyawn j baido . . . 211, ag yna i dyffro hithav 218, ag yna i
> pigant hwy ef . . . 233, ag yna idd a ef . . . ag i hegyr . . . ag i gollwng ef . . . 236,
> ag yna i tyrr ef y droed honno . . . 261, Ag yna i ffy ef . . . 253.

Ceir eithriadau fodd bynnag sy'n dangos fod y system 'ategol' eisoes wedi dechrau
lledu i'r un gysylltiol:

> Ag am hynny mi a ddanfonaf iti . . . 4, Ag am hynny mi a ddanfonaf atad ti . . .
> 12, Ag am hynny mi a ddangosaf iti gyfran o'm klwyf . . . 16 (cyferbynner: Ac am
> hyny y dangosaf i iti vy ngovid B 17), Ag yna ti a'm lleddaist j . . . 240.

§6. Mae ffurfiau presennol ac amherffaith *bod* yn ddieithriad yn dilyn y drefn
i(dd) + Berf + rhagenw ategol:

> idd wyf j yn danfon annerch . . . 1, a hevyd idd wyf j yn tybiaid . . . 14, ag am
> nad oes . . . obaith . . . idd wyf j megis am hanner nos . . . 25, Ag velly idd wyd
> ti y'm lladd j . . . 104, Kans kyn hynny . . . idd oeddwn heb plyf . . . 132, Ag am
> hynny idd wyf j yn tybiaid . . . 150 Ag velly idd oeddwn j megis kyw . . . 238.

Yn achos ffurfiau *b- bod* y realeiddiad Goddrych + Berf a geir:

> pe bai gennyf j ddim gobaith mi a vyddwn megis y pylgain . . . 27, ag ony bysai
> vy mod j y'th garv ti a vysyd yn tirioni . . . 162.

Mae'n bur debyg fodd bynnag fod y brawddegau cypladol canlynol yn dangos mai'r realeiddiad *i(dd)*+ Berf . . . a geid yn wreiddiol drwy holl ffurfiau *bod*:

pan wybyost di . . . i byost di valch a thraws . . . 90, pan ddauthym j gyntaf . . . i byost di vwyn . . . 95.

§7. Mae'r drefn pan fo'r goddrych yn enw neu'n ymadrodd enwol yr un i bob pwrpas â'r hyn a ddisgrifiwyd uchod am y goddrych rhagenwol:

(adferf atodol) + Goddrych + *a* + Berf:

Kans yr eos a gar i gerdd i hvn yn gymaint . . . 58, a phan vont yn llawn o blyf i mam a'i tad a'i magant . . . 129, kans dechrauad kariad a ddaw drwy edrychiad 141, kans vn a gan gyda thelyn . . . 174, a'r helwr . . . a vwrw drych ar y ffordd . . . 193, a'r helwr kall a edwyn hynny 205, kans pan ddamchwaino yddi gysgv y maen a syrthia . . . 216.

adferf gysylltiol + *i(dd)* + Berf + Goddrych:

ag velly i daw yr helwr kywraint . . . 106, Ag yna i daw yr ap i'r llawr 111, ag yna i daw yr vnikorn . . . 206, ag yna i dala'r helwr ef 207, ag yna i gwila vn . . . 214, Ag yna i daw y tad . . . 224.

(adferf) + *y* + ffurf bresennol/(amherffaith) 3 un. *bod* + Goddrych:

kans ar y gigvran i mae natur arall . . . 137, kans i mae tair amryw vorvorwyn 171, Kans ar vn o'i draed ef i mae rinwedd . . . 247.

Blaenosodir goddrych yn y ddau achos canlynol naill ai am reswm stylistig (mae'r goddrych yn hir a chystrawennol gymhleth) neu oherwydd llediad y system atodol:

Ag velly y kwbl o'r naturiaethav hynn a sydd ar wraig 76, Ag velly yr vn a vo yn gwilad a gymer maen krwn . . . 215.

§8. Gall goddrych enwol flaenoli ffurfiau presennol (ac amherffaith) y ferf *bod*. Y ffurf bresennol yn C yw *a sydd*, sef camddadansoddiad o'r ffurf *ys(s)yd* mewn Cymraeg Canol (cymh. *yssyd* A 4, *yssydd* B 75, *sydd* D 200):

Ag velly y kwbl o'r naturiaethav hynn a sydd ar wraig . . . 76.

§9. Ceir hefyd ddwy enghraifft o ymddangosiad *ef a* fel geiryn yn blaenoli'r ferf yn y drefn Berf + Goddrych. Y gyntaf yw:

> am vod wyneb dyn ag arwydd santaiddrwydd arno . . . ef a gymer y llew i ofn ef . . . 144.

Mae'r ail enghraifft yn wahanol am mai cymal yw'r goddrych, ac o'r herwydd, ni byddai'r drefn Goddrych + *a* + Berf yn dderbyniol:

> kans ef a allai vod peth arnom ni yn dav. . . 170.

§10. Yn achos berf amhersonol anghyflawn mae perthynas y gwrthrych a'r ferf yn cyfateb o ran statws i berthynas goddrych a berf bersonol, ac y mae'r trefnau yn cyfateb:

(adferf atodol) + Gwrthrych + *a* + Berf:

> ag ef a gefflybir i'r anevail kadarnaf . . . 30, a hwnn a gyfflybir . . . i natur kariad . . . 46, a' r dyn dillatog a gefflybir i vn a vo yn karv 116, Kans ymhennydd dyn a gefflybir i synwyr 153.

adferf gysylltiol + *y(dd)* + Berf + Gwrthrych:

> Ag velly i kefflybir kariad . . . i natur y llew 142, Ag am hynny i delyir vy marny j i varw 165.

Mae'r eithriad canlynol yn awgrymu dylanwad y system 'ategol' (cymharer §5):

> ag velly y nos a gefflybir i gariad . . . 24.

§11. Pan gynrychiolir y gwrthrych gan gymal, nid yw blaenosod gwrthrych yn dderbyniol (cymharer §9). Ceir dau ateb cystrawennol i hyn yn y testun:

(i) Ffurf *ef a* + Berf + Cymal Gwrthrychol:

> Ag am hynny ef a vernir vy mod j yn varw 168, Ag velly ef a debygir vod yn bechod i'r vorwyn . . . 180.

(ii) Goddrych/Gwrthrych y cymal + *a* + Berf + rhagenw genidol ôl-gyfeiriol + berfenw'r cymal:

goddrych: kans pob ryw ysgryven a ddangosir i bod yn barabl 8,

gwrthrych: Ag velly y kydnabod kyntaf . . . a ellit i gyfflybv i'r dyn noeth . . . 98, a hynn a ellir i gefflybu at gariad 226.

Mae'r canlynol yn enghraifft o gyffredinoli'r rhagenw gwrywaidd. Cyfeiria'r ffurf *i* o flaen y berfenw at ymadrodd benywaidd, *y sampl honn*:

Ag velly y sampl honn a ellir i gefflybv i ddyn noeth . . . 115.

II. Y GOSODIAD CADARNHAOL PWYSLEISIOL

§12. Defnyddir blaenosod ac israddoli'r ferf i bwysleisio. Mae rhychwant y gosodiad pwysleisiol yn eang yn y Gymraeg. Mae'n cynnwys gwerthoedd semantig yn ymestyn o 'gyferbynnu', 'pennu', a 'gwadu' (na ellir eu mynegi ond trwy flaenosod) i 'hysbysu', 'cyfarwyddo', 'esbonio', 'croesgyfeirio', 'ategu', a 'chymharu'. Am ymdriniaeth fanylach â'r gwahanol agweddau hyn gweler Mac Cana 1991: 62–75, a Watkins 1991: 333–48. Mae enghreifftiau o rai ohonynt yn y rhestr isod. Fe'u dosberthir yn ôl y cyfansoddyn a flaenosodir.

goddrych: Kans natur y blaidd yw os gwr a'i gwyl ef yn gyntaf y blaidd a gyll i rym . . . Os y blaidd a wyl y gwr yn gyntaf y gwr a gyll i rym . . . 43.

gwrthrych: A hevyd achos arall a gevais j . . . 57, Kans llawenydd a digryvwch a gymer hi . . . 190.

gwrthrych berfenwol: ag os ymhell i kar hi i garv yn vawr a wna . . . 80, a'i hela ef a wnair . . . 248, A ffo a wna yntav . . . 249.

ymadrodd adferfol: A ry hir i bvm j heb ystyriaid . . . 60, Ag velly i gwnaethost di a myvi . . . 95, wrth sampl yr helwr i delaist dithav vinnav . . . 119, Ag velly . . . i delyyd tithav wnaethur . . . 130, a ffordd hynny i tynn hi yr amhennydd i maes 139, A chwegwaith i gallai ddyn vyned . . . 149, Ag yn vnwedig ffordd honno i kollais j bedwar synwyr . . . 155, Ag velly idd wyf j yn tybiaid amdanom ni yn dav . . . 182, wrth wrando ar dy gan di i lleddaist di vi . . . 186, Ag velly i delyswn minnav . . . 218, . . . yny gaffo ef ddolur ag yn y dolur hwnnw i lladd ef hwynt . . . 234, ag o'r gwaed hwnnw i hira ef hwynt 237, ag velly i diank ef 255, ag velly i twyllaist di vi 258.

ATODIAD

§13. O ran realeiddiad mae'r gosodiad cadarnhaol pwysleisiol wedi aros yn ddigyf-
newid o'r cyfnod canol hyd heddiw. Blaenosodir y cyfansoddyn a bwysleisir ac
israddolir y ferf. Ond fe fu cyfyngu ar ehangder ei rychwant a lleihad ym
mynychder ei ddefnydd. Hwyrach fodd bynnag i'r datblygiadau hyn fod yn fwy
amlwg yn yr iaith lenyddol nag yn yr iaith lafar.

§14. Yn achos y gosodiad niwtral mae'r olyniaeth yn fwy cymhleth. Mae
tystiolaeth testunau rhyddiaith Cymraeg Canol yn dangos fod rheol wedi datblygu
yn gwahardd ffurfiau berfol rhediadol (ar wahân i ffurfiau *bod*) rhag ymddangos
yn slot gyfansoddynnol gyntaf gosodiad cadarnhaol. Un o ganlyniadau hyn yn y
gosodiad niwtral oedd ymddangosiad Goddrych + *a* + Berf fel realeiddiad
cyffredin ar ddechrau brawddeg ac ar ôl ymadrodd adferfol atodol. Y cwestiwn yw
a ydyw'r drefn hon yn adlewyrchu system lafar y cyfnod. Yn ôl barn yr Athro
Proinsias Mac Cana rai blynyddoedd yn ôl, trefn lenyddol yn unig yw hon:
'. . . one can hardly avoid the conclusion that the "abnormal" sentence of M[iddle]
W[elsh] is essentially a literary syntax which does not reflect the usage of spoken
Welsh' Mac Cana 1973: 115–16. Yr ydym ni o farn wahanol. Mae'n sicr, cyn belled
ag y mae'r goddrych rhagenwol yn y cwestiwn, fod i'r drefn Goddrych + *a* + Berf
ddosbarthiad llafar eang. Ategir y farn hon yn y dyfyniadau canlynol a godwyd o
Awbery 1985: 15–22. Datganiadau 'digymell' ydynt mewn llysoedd barn, a chyn-
rychiolant iaith lafar ardaloedd daearyddol gwasgaredig. Nodir yr ardal a'r dyddiad
wrth ddyfynnu:

> 1623 (Fflint): . . . fo a dynge '. . . he wold sweare . . .'
>
> 1634 (Penfro): . . . he y a agoradd drws yn tu y . . . '. . . shee did open the doore
> of my howse . . .'
>
> 1732 (Fflint): Y hi a fiscarriodd . . .'. . . she miscarryed . . .'
>
> 1635 (Trefaldwyn): ac efe a dyngodd yn anudon . . . '. . . and he did periure
> himself . . .'
>
> 1641 (Trefaldwyn): . . . y fo a forgiodd fond . . . 'hee hath forged a bond . . .'
>
> 1652 (Dinbych): Y hi a wenwynodd fy mab i . . . 'Shee did poyson my son. . .'
>
> 1711 (Brycheiniog): . . . ag hi findws i gwr rhwng coese Rachel . . . ag yno hi
> dunnws i gwr wrth wallt i ben '. . . and she found her husband betwixt the legs of
> Rachel . . . and there she pulled her husband by the hair of the head . . .'
>
> 1739 (Morgannwg): Fe dyngws annudon . . . 'He swore falsely . . .'

1766 (Morgannwg): Mi glywas taw Twm . . . oedd y gwr . . . 'I heard that it was Tom . . . was the man . . . '

Fel y gwelir, y system yw Goddrych rhagenwol + *a* + Berf rediadol. Yr eithriad yw y ferf *bod*, pryd y ceir y drefn *ydd* + Berf rediadol yn y presennol (a'r amherffaith):

1763 (Morgannwg): Y ddwy [ydd wyf] yn credu tau ty di lladdws William . . . 'I do believe that thou didst murder William . . . '

§15. Erbyn hyn erys y drefn uchod yn llafar rhai ardaloedd yn y de-ddwyrain yn unig. Daw'r dyfyniad canlynol o Thomas B 1989: 76.

Mae gan Dde-ddwyrain Morgannwg batrwm hynod . . . gellir yn yr ardal hon ragflaenu berfau â rhagenwau personol sydd yn cytuno â pherson y ferf, e.e. *fi wn, ti wddot, fe ŵyr, i ŵyr, ni wddon, chi wddoch, nw wddon.*

Ac mewn trawsgrifiad o recordiad gan ŵr o Langynwyd, Canol Morgannwg, ceir y canlynol:

Odd yr 'en ffwrn crasu bara yn y wal . . . Wi'n cofio bod jyst y miwn yn y . . . ffwrn . . . O fi welas yn rai ffermydd abothu ma . . . oech chi'n gallu doti citl . . . i sefyll arno fa . . . on' i glŵas a'n gwed . . . Thomas B 1989:146–47.

Ceir Berf rediadol + rhagenw ategol yn achos *bod* (*wi, oech chi*) a Goddrych + Berf yn achos *fi welas* ac *i glŵas*.

Y tu allan i'r ardal gyfyngedig hon cyffredinolwyd naill ai *ef (a)* neu *mi (a)* fel geirynnau cadarnhaol. Mae'r dyfyniad canlynol yn Awbery 1985 yn dangos yr 'hen' system a'r 'newydd' yn yr un frawddeg:

1769 (Dinbych): Yr oeddwn i yn mynd i Gaer . . . a dyma ddyn yn croesi'r ffordd ag wrth ddwad adre mi groesodd y ffordd . . . yr un fan ag a neidiodd . . . ag fe ddweydodd 'Myn Diawl . . .'

Cynrychiola *mi groesodd* y system ddatblygedig a *fe ddweydodd* y system wreiddiol. Yn Watkins 1977–78: 390 dadleuir fod atgof o'r system i'w ganfod yng ngwaith brodor o Sir Gaerfyrddin yng nghanol ybedwaredd ganrif ar bymtheg. Yn neialog *Wil Brydydd y Coed* gan Brutus, ceir Goddrych rhagenwol + *a* + Berf yn bur gyson, ond Berf rediadol + rhagenw ategol yn y naratif.

§16. Yn achos goddrych enwol, yr oedd *ef a* fel geiryn rhagferfol wedi ymddangos eisoes yn 'Kulhwch ac Olwen', testun rhyddiaith cynharaf y cyfnod canol:

> Pan dyuu y thymp idi ef a dyuu y iawn bwyll iti . . . Bromwich 1992: l. 6.

Cychwyn y defnydd, gellir tybio, oedd brawddegau a chymal yn oddrych berf bersonol neu'n wrthrych berf amhersonol. Fel y gwelwyd eisoes, ni byddai cymal yn ramadegol ganiatadwy yn y drefn Goddrych + *a* + Berf. A chan na allai berf rediadol ymddangos yn safle dechreuol brawddeg, defnyddid rhagenw blaen-gyfeiriol fel goddrych neu wrthrych 'gwag'. Gan mai gwrywaidd o ran cenedl fyddai cymal, y rhagenw *ef* a geid fel ffurf flaengyfeiriol:

> ef a vernir vy mod j yn varw . . . 168, kans ef a allai vod peth arnom ni . . . 170.

Cadwyd *ef* fel ffurf sefydlog pan ledodd y system i frawddegau yn cynnwys enwau (neu ymadroddion enwol) goddrychol. O ganlyniad ni cheir cytundeb mwyach rhwng *ef* a goddrych benywaidd neu luosog:

> Ac yna ef a ddaw yr adar jeueigk . . . A 37.

Nid rhagenw blaengyfeiriol yw *ef* mwyach ond rhan o eiryn berfol cadarnhaol. Yn yr enghreifftiau canlynol o Awbery 1985 mae'r goddrych yn fenywaidd. Dilewyd yr *a* ond erys y treiglad meddal:

> 1655 (Trefaldwyn): Fo aeth Jane Roberts . . . 'Jane Roberts went . . .'
>
> 1729 (Llandaf): . . . ah fy gwnnodd yr hen fawd ei mam hi . . . '. . . and the old bawd her mother rose . . .'
>
> 1796 (Penfro): Fe fy Martha . . . yn cysgu gyda modrib . . . 'Martha. slept with my aunt . . .'

§17. Nid yw Goddrych enwol + *a* + Berf fel realeiddiad o'r gosodiad niwtral yn digwydd, hyd y gwyddys, mewn unrhyw ardal erbyn hyn. Gellid tybio ar lefel ar-wynebol fod yr enghreifftiau canlynol yn Awbery 1985 yn awgrymu goroesi ffiniol mewn ambell ardal:

> 1726 (Brycheiniog): Di girn di dorrws y twlle sydd in di hatt di' Thy horns did break the holes that is in thy hatt'
>
> 1755 (Brycheiniog): Shonnet Thomas confessodd wrth i fi bod plentyn idde hi . . . 'That the party agent confessed to the said Sarah that she had a child . . .'

1823 (Fflint): William Thomas a fwrdrodd Robert Lloyd ... 'William Thomas murdered Robert Lloyd ... '

Ond heb gyd-destun ni ellir bod yn siŵr. Gallent yn hawdd fod yn atebion i gwestiynau rhagenwol neu'n esboniadau neu'n groesgyfeiriadau. Byddent felly o fewn rhychwant y frawddeg bwysleisiol.

CYFEIRIADAU

Awbery 1985: Gwenllian Awbery, Ann E. Jones and Richard F. Suggett, 'Slander and Defamation, A New Source for historical Dialectology', *Cardiff Working Papers in Welsh Linguistics* 4:1–24.

Bromwich 1992: *Culhwch and Olwen*, eds Rachel Bromwich and D. Simon Evans, Cardiff, University of Wales Press, 1992.

Mac Cana 1973: Proinsias Mac Cana, 'On Celtic Word-order and the Welsh "Abnormal" Sentence', *Ériu* 24: 90–120.

Mac Cana 1991: Proinsias Mac Cana, 'Further Notes on Constituent Order in Welsh', *Studies in Brythonic Word Order*, eds James Fife and Erich Poppe, Amsterdam/Philadelphia, John Benjamins Publishing Company, 1991: 45–80.

Thomas B 1989: *Cymraeg, Cymrâg, Cymrêg, ... Cyflwyno'r Tafodieithoedd*, Beth Thomas a Peter Wynn Thomas, Caerdydd, Gwasg Taf, 1989.

Thomas G: *A Welsh Bestiary of Love*, Graham C. G. Thomas, Dublin, Institute for Advanced Studies, 1988.

Watkins 1977–78: T. Arwyn Watkins, 'Trefn yn y Frawddeg Gymraeg', *Studia Celtica* 12–13; 367–395.

Watkins 1991: T. Arwyn Watkins, 'The Function of Cleft and Non-cleft ... Orders in Modern Welsh', *Studies in Brythonic Word Order*, eds James Fife and Erich Poppe, Amsterdam/Philadelphia. John Benjamins Publishing Company, 1991: 329–351.

The Feasting Aspects of *Hirlas Owein**

Gruffydd Aled Williams

DEPARTMENT OF WELSH, UNIVERSITY OF WALES, ABERYSTWYTH

MY INTEREST in *Hirlas Owein* — which was to culminate many years later in an edition of the poem[1] — was first aroused some thirty years ago during my time as an Assistant in the Department of Welsh at University College Dublin when Proinsias Mac Cana, paying undue deference to the scholarly pretensions of youth, showed me the typescript of a linguistic note which he subsequently published in *The Bulletin of the Board of Celtic Studies*.[2] In the course of the note he elucidated the syntax of a problematic reading in the poem and demonstrated that textual emendations adopted by two of its modern editors were unnecessary. This early foray did not constitute Proinsias' only engagement with the poem; neither did he confine his attention to strictly textual matters. An article in volume 44 of *Ériu* (1993), 'Ir. *Buaball*, W *Bual*, "Drinking

---

* A revised version of a paper delivered in a session on 'Celtic Feasting in Literary Perspective' at the third International Medieval Congress at the University of Leeds on 8 July 1996. Professor Proinsias Mac Cana was present and delivered a paper on 'Drinking Vessels in Medieval Irish Literature' in the same session.
1 See 'Canu Owain Cyfeiliog' in *Gwaith Llywelyn Fardd I ac Eraill o Feirdd y Ddeuddegfed Ganrif*, Cyfres Beirdd y Tywysogion II, ed. K. A. Bramley et al. (Caerdydd 1994), 191–277. All quotations in the paper are from this edition.
2 '"Dyfod" a "mynd" fel berfau anghyflawn', loc. cit., xxiii (1) (1968), 27–8.

Horn'",[3] devoted considerable attention to the *Hirlas*, described by him as 'the *locus classicus* for the role of the drinking horn in Welsh literature'.[4] This characteristically perspicacious and wide-ranging article stimulated most of the lines of enquiry pursued in this paper. In the few instances where I venture to differ in minor points of interpretation from my former mentor it is entirely in the spirit suggested by the editors' exhortation to contributors to this volume that they should 'choose a topic which you would like to discuss with him' [*sc.* Proinsias], confident that any aberrant observations will receive a characteristically tolerant hearing from one of the most generous spirited of men and scholars.

Hirlas Owein — for reasons which will become apparent later I will not yet translate the first word of the title — is a poem of 150 lines composed in 1156 and associated with Owain Cyfeiliog, prince of Southern Powys.[5] A complete text of the poem is preserved in the Red Book of Hergest (Jesus MS. 111) of *circa* 1400, and a fragment (the last eleven lines of the poem) in the Hendregadredd Manuscript (NLW MS. 6680B) written a century earlier. The poem is conventionally ascribed to Owain on the basis of its Red Book rubric which states that 'Owain Cyfeiliog himself composed it' (*Owein Kyueilyaƀc e hun a'e cant*)[6] together with its mode of presentation as a monologue spoken by the prince. I have argued, however, mainly on the evidence of numerous verbal collocations occurring in the poem which are also found in the work of Cynddelw Brydydd Mawr, the most eminent court poet of twelfth-century Wales, that the poem is wrongly ascribed to Owain, and is, in fact, a lost *œuvre* of Cynddelw's, who elsewhere describes himself as Owain's *pencerdd* or 'chief of song'.[7] I would maintain that Owain is best regarded as a *persona* in the poem, rather than its author in the conventional sense. This view, however, does not rule out a possible role for Owain as the poem's instigator; nor would I deny the possibility of a degree of co-operation between prince and poet in the poem's composition, or, perhaps, in its performance.

Hirlas Owein was composed in honour of members of Owain's war-band following their return from a successful expedition to Maelor in north-east Wales

---

3 Loc. cit., 81–93. All subsequent references to *Ériu* 44 are to this article.
4 Ibid., 87. The poem is discussed on pp. 87–9.
5 On Owain see my introduction to 'Canu Owain Cyfeiliog', 193–8.
6 J. Gwenogvryn Evans (ed.), *Poetry in the Red Book of Hergest* (Llanbedrog 1911), col. 1432.
7 'Owain Cyfeiliog: Bardd-dywysog?', *Beirdd a Thywysogion: Barddoniaeth Llys yng Nghymru, Iwerddon a'r Alban*, ed. Morfydd E. Owen and Brynley F. Roberts (Caerdydd ac Aberystwyth 1996), 180–201. My arguments are summarised in 'Canu Owain Cyfeiliog', 199–206. For recent endorsements of my views regarding the poem's authorship see reviews of *Beirdd a Thywysogion* and *Gwaith Llywelyn Fardd I ac Eraill o Feirdd y Ddeuddegfed Ganrif* by T. G. Hunter and Dafydd Johnston, *Llên Cymru* 20 (1997), 150–1, 153–5.

in 1156 to free Owain's brother, Meurig ap Gruffudd, from prison, an event recorded in *Brut y Tywysogion*.[8] The poem's conception is unique in the context of the Welsh poetry of its day: it consists of a dramatic representation of a feast held at Owain's court at Welshpool, in which Owain greets a servant commanding him to offer the *Hirlas* drinking horn to each hero in turn. The poem fascinatingly combines realistic action and incidental details of the feast with the surreal, for the servant is occasionally commanded to proffer the horn to warriors who perished on the expedition as well as to its survivors. As has often been noted, the inspiration of the poem is the *Gododdin* of Aneirin, pre-eminent amongst Welsh poems in praise of war-bands.[9] Not only is the structure of the poem with its monorhymed odes praising named warriors reminiscent of the *Gododdin*, but Owain's men are explicitly compared to Mynyddog's retinue who went to Catraeth. There are also over a dozen instances of verbal echoes of the *Gododdin* in the poem, including a whole line directly quoted from the earlier work. There is an ideological parallel too, relevant in the context of the present paper, between the poems, in that the concept of *talu medd* ('payment for mead'),[10] so pervasive in the *Gododdin*, is also prominent in the *Hirlas*. Given the evident debt of the *Hirlas* to the earlier poem it is not surprising that Professor Mac Cana has ingeniously explained what he terms 'inconsistencies' in the *Hirlas*'s references to drink and drinking vessels by invoking the shadow of the *Gododdin*.[11] Whether what the *Hirlas* says about such things can be considered authentic or are reflections of literary influence or convention is an aspect I shall consider at more than one point in this paper.

A balanced view of the feasting aspects manifested in the poem requires that they be placed in the appropriate cultural context. The familiarity of Owain and members of his court with the feasting customs and material accessories of contemporary Anglo-Norman England can safely be presumed. An anecdote recorded by Gerald of Wales in his *Itinerarium Kambriæ* tells of Owain dining

8 *Brut y Tywysogion Peniarth Ms. 20*, ed. Thomas Jones (Caerdydd 1941), 102a.

9 I have discussed the relationship between the two poems in detail in 'Canu Owain Cyfeiliog', 206–8. See also Proinsias Mac Cana, *Ériu* 44, 89 who refers to the 'pervasive influence' of the *Gododdin* on the later poem. For references to earlier discussions of their relationship see 'Canu Owain Cyfeiliog', 206, note 66.

10 The concept is discussed by Jenny Rowland, 'OE *Ealuscerwen/Meoduscerwen* and the Concept of "Paying for Mead"', *Leeds Studies in English*, New Series, xxi (1990), 1–12. See also Ifor Williams (ed.), *Canu Aneirin* (Caerdydd 1938), xlviii–xlix; Kenneth Jackson, *The Gododdin: the Oldest Scottish Poem* (Edinburgh 1969), 36. For a recent discussion of the Welsh poetic treatment of mead in general, including the formula *talu medd*, see Marged Haycock, 'Medd a Mêl Farddoni', *Beirdd a Thywysogion*, ed. Owen and Roberts, 39–59.

11 *Ériu* 44, 89.

with king Henry II of England at Shrewsbury (*cum rege apud Slopesburiam in mensa sedens*), jesting with the king, presumably in either French or Latin.[12] Anglo-Norman influence on the ceremonial of Owain's court is pointedly suggested by the terminology of our poem: the horn-bearing servant is consistently referred to as *menestr*, either a borrowing from the Old French *menestre* (*menistre*), or a hybrid form indicating the influence of the French word on an earlier direct borrowing from Latin *minister*.[13] It may be presumed, therefore, that if ancient feasting customs survived in the courts of twelfth-century Powys that they would have existed alongside or merged with innovative practices. Elements of Celtic continuity cannot be entirely discounted, but at best they would have survived in attenuated form within the context of an essentially hybrid culture. Whilst it is possible that the poem may employ literary conventions of ancient origin and may reflect ancient customs, the caveat must be entered that twelfth-century Powys was no island of pristine Celticity; neither was Owain Cyfeiliog a latter-day reincarnation of the so-called 'Hochdorf prince'.

Apart from what *Hirlas Owein* tells us about drinking vessels and drink it conveys also incidental details of the feast which contribute much to the poem's lively portrayal of atmosphere. In a delightfully vivid cameo Owain and his warriors are portrayed (line 140) drinking mead together before a brightly blazing fire and by the light of fine rush candles (*Gwrdd-dan gloyw golau, gwrddlew babir*); as is usual in Welsh court poetry the feast is depicted as taking place at night, doubtless reflecting reality rather than literary convention. Not only the physical setting but also the action of the feast is vividly conveyed. As previously noted, the servant is commanded by the prince to bear the *Hirlas* horn to each hero in turn. The unusual sociology of the poem gives rise to an element of bantering humour, utterly untypical of *Gogynfeirdd* poetry and reminiscent surely of festive actuality. In a direct reversal of the normal convention of Welsh court poetry whereby the poet greets his social superior with due deference, here the prince greets his servant, teasingly mocking him. With regard to one hero, Cynfelyn, described (line 260) as being 'honourably drunk with foaming mead' (*Anrhydeddus feddw o fedd gorewyn*), the servant is commanded to show him due respect should he wish to live another year. Later (lines 79–80), beheading is explicitly threatened should he neglect to serve the warriors with 'the best mead of all' (*[y] medd gorau oll*). The contrast between the anonymous and verbally abused servant and the named heroes is, of

---

12 *Itinerarium Kambriæ* ii, 12, in *Giraldi Cambrensis Opera*, VI, ed. J. F. Dimock, Rolls Series (London 1868).

13 *Geiriadur Prifysgol* Cymru (Caerdydd 1950–), s.v. The word was earlier discussed by Ifor Williams in *Canu Aneirin*, 372–3.

course, deliberate; it serves to highlight the warriors' status and excellence. Interestingly too, there may be a hint that the warriors' status is reflected in the feast's seating arrangement: it is said of them (line 117) that 'they deserve to be in a place of honour' (*Wynt a dyrllydant yn lle honneit*). I would hesitate to claim too much, but in this regard references in Irish tales to the 'champion's seat' (*fochla fénneda*) may well be relevant.[14]

The poem's dramatic action centres around an interesting and seemingly imposing artefact, namely Owain's drinking horn, the *Hirlas* of the poem's title, which is incidentally described at various points in the poem. As the archaeological record is silent as to the existence and nature of contemporary Welsh drinking horns (as it is indeed virtually silent as regards the general material culture of the courts of the Welsh princes) the poem, notwithstanding its difficulties of interpretation, is a source of some value in this regard.[15] What then can be deduced as to the horn's nature and appearance? The first element of the compound which forms its name, *hir* ('long'), is unambiguous. An exhaustive search of contemporary *Gogynfeirdd* poetry and earlier *Hengerdd* has unearthed only two other references to the size of drinking horns;[16] such an emphasis does not seem to have been part of

14 *Dictionary of the Irish Language* (Dublin 1913–76), s.v. *fochla*. Michael J. Enright cites this Irish feature in his recent book *Lady with a Mead Cup* (Blackrock 1996), 270. On the importance of the placement of warriors in the lord's hall see ibid., 147 where, in discussing the *dám* of the Irish warlord, Enright implies a cultural continuum, citing a passage from Posidonius (quoted by Athenaeus) which depicts a hierarchical seating arrangement, largely based on martial prowess, as a feature of the feasts of the Celts of Gaul. On the *fochla fénneda* see also Philip O'Leary, 'Contention at Feasts in Early Irish Literature', *Éigse* 20 (1984), 116–17, note 8.

15 Carol Neuman de Vegvar has some pertinent observations on the validity of the use of literary sources to supplement the archaeological record in this context in 'Drinking Horns in Ireland and Wales: Documentary Sources', *From the Isles of the North: Early Medieval Art in Ireland and Britain*, Proceedings of the Third International Conference on Insular Art, ed. Cormac Bourke (Belfast 1995), 81. Cf. also Proinsias Mac Cana: 'Once we enter the world of medieval literary convention and imagery we must treat all high-flown and pretentious description with a considerable measure of caution, though equally there is enough sophisticated artwork in the archaeological and artistic record of Ireland and Celtic Britain in pre-Christian times to warn against dismissing it out of hand' (*Ériu* 44, 86).

16 In this and similar searches cited in the paper I have used as search-tools the following published microfiche concordances: Marged Haycock, *Concordance to the Book of Taliesin* (Cardiff 1979); Jeremy Boreham and Morfydd E. Owen, *Concordance of Canu Aneirin* (Cardiff 1980); idem, *Concordance to the Black Book of Carmarthen* (Cardiff 1983); Helen J. Williams, *A Concordance of the Poetry in the Red Book of Hergest* (Cardiff 1985); Morfydd E. Owen and Keith Williams, *A Concordance to Llawysgrif Hendregadredd* (Cardiff 1989). *Gogynfeirdd* poetry not found in *Llawysgrif Hendregadredd* and the Red Book of Hergest was manually searched.

Welsh poetic convention. Both of the other references occur in poems by Cynddelw,[17] the likely author of *Hirlas Owein*: the depiction of Owain's drinking horn may thus either reflect a trait of the poet's descriptive technique, or, just as likely, the unusual length of the horn in question. I would maintain too that the *Hirlas* was unambiguously of natural horn. I mention this because Carol Neuman de Vegvar in a recent discussion of Irish and Welsh drinking horns has implied that it may have been of glass.[18] I would counter this by reference to line 75 of the poem, where the horn is described as *Hirlas buelyn*. Welsh *buelyn* (from Latin *bubalinus*) may either be used adjectivally ('made of buffalo or aurochs horn') or substantively,[19] one use, as Professor Mac Cana has emphasised,[20] being as a generic term for a drinking horn, not necessarily one made of buffalo or aurochs horn. In the line in question the lack of initial mutation of *buelyn* is significant; it shows that it is here used adjectivally, 'made of buffalo or aurochs horn' (qualifying *hirlas* which is used substantively) rather than as a noun with *hirlas* used as a preceding adjective.[21] The likelihood of the horn in question being an aurochs horn (*corn bual*) tends also to be confirmed by the poem's title in which the *Hirlas* is specifically associated with Owain Cyfeiliog, implicitly its owner. The stipulation in the Welsh Laws that the king's drinking horn should be of aurochs horn is here of relevance.[22] As the attention given to the *Hirlas* in the poem implies, their size and capacity, notwithstanding any incidental decoration, together perhaps with

17 He refers to the [c]*yrn glas gloewhir* ('?shining bright and long horns') at Tysilio's monastery of Meifod and the [c]*yrn mawr melyn* ('large yellow horns') at the court of the Lord Rhys. See Nerys Ann Jones and Ann Parry Owen (ed.),*Gwaith Cynddelw Brydydd Mawr I*, Cyfres Beirdd y Tywysogion III (Caerdydd 1991), 3.90; idem, *Gwaith Cynddelw Brydydd Mawr II*, Cyfres Beirdd y Tywysogion IV (Caerdydd 1995), 9.228.
18 'Drinking Horns in Ireland and Wales', 85.
19 The actual meanings listed in *Geiriadur Prifysgol Cymru* s.v. are adj. 'belonging to a buffalo; made of buffalo horn'; sb. 'buffalo(es)'; 'buffalo horn(s), drinking–horn(s)'. I follow Proinsias Mac Cana (*Ériu* 44, 81) in opting for 'aurochs ' (= the continental wild–ox, *Bos primigenius*) as being more appropriate than 'buffalo' in this context.
20 *Ériu* 44, 86.
21 The possibility that *Hirlas buelin* is a nominal sentence consisting of predicate + subject is too remote to be seriously considered.
22 E.g. *Llyfr Blegywryd*, ed. Stephen J. Williams and J. Enoch Powell (Caerdydd 1942), 108.5 where *y gorn kyfed* ('his drinking horn/horn of carousal') is listed as one of *Tri chorn buelyn y brenhin* ('the king's three aurochs horns'). Cf. *Llyfr Iorwerth*, ed. Aled Rhys Wiliam (Caerdydd 1960), 42.20–1 where *e korn ed euo e brenhyn* is said to be one of the three horns *a deleant bot en uuelyn* ('which should be of aurochs horn'). See also the various Latin redactions in Hywel David Emmanuel, *The Latin Texts of the Welsh Laws* (Cardiff 1967),127, 200, 284, 370, 465.

their status as coveted imported exotica, would have made such horns objects of attention and admiration at royal feasts.[23]

The second element of the horn's name (*glas*), referring to its colour or surface aspect, is problematical. The *Hirlas* is not unique in being named by colour. A poem in *Agallamh na Seanórach* refers to a drinking horn called *Brec-derg* ('the speckled-red one');[24] the Irish Annals *sub anno* 1197 refer to the plundering of a horn called *Mac Riabhach* ('the swarthy son', or perhaps 'the grey son') from the cathedral church of Derry.[25] In Wales the name *Hirlas* has also been applied to another famous drinking horn, one associated with the Elizabethan adventurer Pyrs Gruffydd (1568–1628) of Penrhyn near Bangor. But this may be a misnomer. This silver-embellished horn, recently described to me as being otherwise 'brownish with a hint of red',[26] is not named as such by the antiquary Thomas Pennant who first

---

23 Aurochs drinking horns found at Sutton Hoo have been calculated to have been approximately 90 cms. in length along the outer curve, to have had a mouth diameter of 9.5–10.5 cms., and to have had a capacity of approximately two litres, see Rupert Bruce–Mitford, *The Sutton Hoo Ship Burial*, ed. Angela Care Evans (London 1983), Vol. 3, I, 325. The value attached to aurochs horns is demonstrated in the Welsh 'Anomalous Laws' where they are classified with gold, silver, treasure, precious stones and garments decorated with orles as valuables to which the king is entitled from the spoil of border-raids, see Aneurin Owen, *Ancient Laws and Institutes of Wales* (London 1841), V.i.17. They were similarly esteemed in Ireland, see Proinsias Mac Cana, *Ériu* 44, 82. The latest aurochs remains from a British site are dated to *c.* 1620 BC but the animal survived into the post-medieval period in continental Europe, the last reported sighting being in Poland in 1627 (*The Sutton Hoo Ship Burial*, 3, I, 408).

24 W. H. Stokes and E. Windisch (ed.), *Irische Texte*, Vierte Serie. 1. Heft (Leipzig 1900), 5.

25 *Annals of Ulster*, ed. B. Mac Carthy, ii (Dublin 1893), 226 (translated, ibid., 227, as 'the gray son'); *The Annals of Loch Cé*, ed. W. M. Hennessy, Rolls Series, i (London 1871), 198 (translated as 'the swarthy son'); *Annala Rioghachta Eireann: Annals of the Kingdom of Ireland*, ed. John O'Donovan, second edition (Dublin 1856), 110. Mac Riabhach is described in these sources as one of the *ceithri corn is ferr* in Ireland, a phrase translated by all the editors of the above texts as 'the four best goblets'. As one of these however is named *cam-coraind/cam-coruinn* it is virtually certain that the vessels referred to were drinking horns (*cam-* being particularly appropriate in relation to the natural curvature of a horn). For a similar interpretation see Raghnall Ó Floinn, 'The Kavanagh "Charter" Horn', *Irish Antiquity: Essays and Studies presented to Professor M. J. O'Kelly*, ed. Donnchadh Ó Corráin (Cork 1981), 271–2. For a further description of an Irish drinking horn where its colouring (*brec, ban, gorm, glas, gel, dub, donn*) is highlighted see Gerard Murphy, 'A poem in praise of Aodh Ua Foirréidh, Bishop of Armagh (1032–1056)', *Measgra i gCuimhne Mhichíl Uí Chléirigh*, ed. Sylvester O'Brien (Dublin 1944), 150 (I am indebted to Professor Patrick Sims-Williams for the last reference).

26 *Ex inf.* Mr. Edmond Douglas Pennant of Penrhyn (letter dated 31 July 1997) who kindly responded to my queries regarding the horn's appearance.

mentions it.[27] Having described the Penrhyn horn Pennant proceeds to discuss horns in general and provides a translation of *Hirlas Owein* prefaced with a reference to 'the *Hirlas*, or drinking-horn'.[28] Later writers may have wrongly taken this to refer to the Penrhyn horn, or, in the case of those with little or no Welsh, may have been misled by Pennant into thinking they were using the common Welsh name for a drinking horn when applying it to the Penrhyn artefact.[29] But let us return to the horn of our poem. The description of Owain's horn as *glas* is paralleled in Welsh by the application of the same epithet to drinking horns in *Gwarchan Tudfwlch* in the Book of Aneirin and in another poem by Cynddelw referring to the monastic community of Meifod in Powys.[30] In addition Professor Mac Cana has cited a parallel instance of *curn glas* in Old Irish.[31] The difficulty with all these examples (as Professor Mac Cana has noted)[32] is that the semantic range of Welsh *glas* and its Irish cognate is wide, embracing the colours blue, green and grey and their intermediate shades. With reference to Owain Cyfeiliog's horn the adjective is usually translated as 'blue',[33] probably because this is its primary meaning in modern Welsh. Carol Neuman de Vegvar is almost alone in translating it (and one of the other Welsh instances) as 'green', and in implying the existence

27 *A Tour in Wales, MDCCLXX*, Vol. II (London 1783), 286.

28 Ibid., 287. The translation is also headed 'HIRLAS OWAIN: *Or, The* Drinking-Horn *of* Owen' (ibid., 288).

29 This is likely in the case of Richard Fenton, *Tours in Wales (1804–13)*, ed. John Fisher (London 1917), 315; also Joseph C. Bridge, 'Horns', *Journal of the Chester Archaeological Society*, 2 (1904), 132–3. Bridge, who discusses the Penrhyn horn in detail, states explicitly that 'The Welsh name for a drinking-horn of this description was "hirlas"' (ibid., 130). For another instance of this usage cf. the illustration of a 'Hirlas Horn belonging to the Clochfaen Family' in J. Y. W. Lloyd, *The History of the Princes, the Lords Marcher, and the Ancient Nobility of Powys Fadog*, V (London 1885), facing p. 464. The ceremonial horn of the Gorsedd of Bards associated with the National Eisteddfod (first used in 1899) was also given the name *y Corn Hirlas*, see Geraint Bowen and Zonia Bowen, *Hanes Gorsedd y Beirdd* (Cyhoeddiadau Barddas 1991), 268–9.

30 *Gwarchan Tudfwlch* has *o gyrn glas med meitin* (*Canu Aneirin*, ed. Ifor Williams (Caerdydd 1938), line 1301). For quotation by Cynddelw see footnote 17 above.

31 *Ériu* 44, 93, note 35: *oc ol meda a curn glas* (from a tale about Mongán mac Fiachna and the poet Eochaid Rígéices).

32 Ibid.

33 E.g. Edward Jones, *Musical and Poetical Relicks of the Welsh Bards* (London 1794), 118, note 9 ('blue, or azure'); Anthony Conran, *The Penguin Book of Welsh Verse* (Harmondsworth 1967), 114 (see also idem, *Welsh Verse* (Bridgend 1992), 149); Joseph P. Clancy, *The Earliest Welsh Poetry* (London 1970), 124, 126. T. Gwynn Jones, 'Catraeth and Hirlas Owain', *Y Cymmrodor* 32 (1922), 47, 53 renders *hirlas* as 'marked with long streaks of blue' and as 'blue-streaked'. The rendering of the *hir* element in the compound as 'streaks/streaked' cannot be justified.

of a Welsh tradition of green drinking horns, possibly tinted.[34] She cites the sole instance (again by Cynddelw!) of a seemingly unambiguous reference to green (*gwyrdd*) drinking horns, *Lledfegin gwin gwyrdd fual*. This may be genuine, though it is conceivable, as *Geiriadur Prifysgol Cymru* implies, that *gwrdd* not *gwyrdd* may be the correct reading here; the line might be translated 'One nurtured on wine from a fine drinking horn'.[35] Professor Mac Cana raises yet another possibility as to the meaning of *glas* as applied to Owain's horn by citing the modern Welsh *arian gleision* ('silver money') and a likely Irish parallel in *Togail Bruidne Da Derga* where a chair is described as being both *glas* and *argidi* ('silvern, made of silver').[36] Does *Hirlas Owein* then mean 'Owain's long and silver-coloured horn'? As we are told in line 76 that the horn is covered with silver (*Ariant a'i gortho*) this seems plausible. Yet against this is the description of the horn in line 16 as being simultaneously '*Hirlas* in appearance and having a covering of gold' (*Hirlas ei arwydd, aur ei dudded*), an odd juxtaposition if 'silver-coloured' is the meaning of *glas*. This objection would not apply if *glas* were assigned a meaning attested as early as the thirteenth century: a Welsh translation of *Imago Mundi* uses *glas* to render Latin *refulgens*.[37] 'Refulgent, bright' would be an appropriate epithet for a horn adorned with both silver and gold. It might be objected that the description of the horn in line 15, *lliw ton nawfed* ('of the colour of the ninth wave') implies a blue or green colour. But no: the poet is here resorting to a conventional comparison inspired by the whiteness and brightness of foam; it occurs often in poetry addressed to women.[38] Cynddelw Brydydd Mawr, the likely author of *Hirlas Owein*, employs it twice in his ode to Efa daughter of Madog ap Maredudd: she was 'of the colour of a wave around an oar' (*liw ton am rwyf*) and

34 'Drinking Horns in Ireland and Wales', 85. The only other instance of the use of 'green' in this context is by the Rev. Richard Williams of Fron who refers to 'the horn so green' in his translation of the poem published in Pennant, *A Tour in Wales, MDCCLXX*, Vol. II, 293. But earlier in the poem he renders *glas* as 'azure' (ibid., 289).

35 *Geiriadur Prifysgol Cymru* treats *gwyrdd fual* as a compound with both *gwyrdd* and *gwrdd* being cited as possibilities for the first element, see ibid., s.v. *gwyrddfual*. The line by Cynddelw is from an elegy to members of the retinue of Owain Gwynedd, see Jones and Owen (ed.), *Gwaith Cynddelw Brydydd Mawr II*, 5.132. The reading *gwyrdd* is retained ibid. The volume's editors are correct in noting (ibid., 11–12) that the meaning ascribed by the *Geiriadur* to the element *bual* in the compound (= 'buffalo; fig. lord') is unlikely and that 'drinking horn' is preferable. Yet the suggestion that the first element may be *gwrdd* remains worthy of consideration.

36 *Ériu* 44, 93, note 35.

37 See Henry Lewis and P. Diverres (ed.), *Delw y Byd (Imago Mundi)* (Caerdydd 1928), 68–9. *Vespero refulgens* is translated as *Venus, glas*.

38 For examples see T. Gwynn Jones, *Rhieingerddi'r Gogynfeirdd* (Dinbych 1915), 27–8.

'of the colour of fair broken foam before the ninth wave' (*Lliw ewynfriw teg rhag ton nawfed*);[39] the latter instance, an elegant variation on the *Hirlas Owain* metaphor, highlights the essence of the comparison. I would maintain, therefore, that the description of the horn in line 15 implies its bright appearance,[40] and goes some way towards confirming 'refulgent, bright, shining' as the likely meaning of *glas* in the name of Owain's drinking horn and in the other instances cited.

Assuming that the *Hirlas* did indeed present a notably bright aspect, it would have been its metal decoration which imparted that quality. As to the extent and artistic design of that decoration we are not informed, the impressionistic nature of the description denying us specific references to likely features such as rim mounts or a terminal. But we are told in line 16 that the horn had 'a covering of gold' (*aur ei dudded*) and in line 76 that 'the silver that covers it is not thin' (*Ariant a'i gortho nid gorthenau*). The apparent contradiction of the descriptions can be resolved by positing a horn adorned with silver but also partially gilded.[41] A specific reference to gilded horns (in the plural) in line 131 (*cyrn buelyn balch oreuraid*) may here be relevant. The possibility — even the likelihood — that other horns as well as the celebrated *Hirlas* may have been used in Owain's feast cannot, of course, be precluded. Yet it is noteworthy that the text at this point seems dislocated and may be corrupt; lines 131 and 130 could well be transposed, in which case the reference cited would follow directly the opening line (129) of the section with its

---

39 Jones and Owen (ed.), *Gwaith Cynddelw Brydydd Mawr I*, 5.29, 46.

40 Cf. the earliest published translation of *Hirlas Owein*, by the Rev. Richard Williams, where *lliw ton nawfed* is rendered as 'That shineth like the sea' (Pennant, *A Tour in Wales*, MDCCLXX, Vol. II, 289). Of later translators only Anthony Conran ('bright as the ninth wave') catches this nuance, see *The Penguin Book of Welsh Verse*, 114 (*Welsh Verse*, 150). If *lliw ton nawfed* does imply the whiteness and brightness of the *Hirlas* the description is paralleled in the thirteenth century English romance of *King Horn* where a drinking horn is described as a *coppe white*, see Joseph Hall (ed.), *King Horn* (Oxford 1901) 64 (L text line 1132). In his notes (ibid., 159) Hall interprets *white* as applied to the horn to mean that it was silver-mounted.

41 Examples of earlier insular drinking horns with mounts and terminals of gilded silver are those of Anglo-Saxon provenance preserved in the Sutton Hoo ship burial and the similar ones recovered at Taplow, Buckinghamshire, see Rupert Bruce-Mitford, *The Sutton Hoo Ship Burial*, Vol. 3, I, 316–46, 384–6, 408. Drinking horns with gold-coloured mounts and terminals, reminiscent of the Sutton Hoo and Taplow horns, are illustrated in the Bayeux Tapestry, see David M. Wilson, *The Bayeux Tapestry* (London 1985), plate 3, strongly suggesting a continuing tradition of such horns in eleventh century England, though none have survived (ibid., 174). For the existence of gold-embellished drinking horns in twelfth century Ireland, see *Annala Rioghachta Eireann*, ed. O'Donovan, II, 1000, *sub anno* 1115; ibid., 1033, *sub anno* 1129 (both references to a *corn go nór* presented to the abbot of Cluain mic Nóis by Toirdhealbhach Ua Conchobhair, king of Connacht).

formulaic verb *dywallaw* which is elsewhere used to command the servant to offer the *Hirlas* to each warrior (*Dywallaw-di, fenestr, fedd hidlaid—melys / O gyrn buelyn balch oreuraid*). If so the plural *cyrn* may well be an error for singular *corn*, and the description quoted applied to the *Hirlas*. Be that as it may, it is the description of the horn as having a silver covering which is of most interest. In Welsh poetry up to the end of the thirteenth century there is no other specific mention of silver in connection with drinking horns; indeed there is only one other reference outside the *Hirlas* (in the *Gododdin*) to silver drinking vessels of any kind. There are, however, 11 references to gold in connection with drinking horns, and a further 16 references to gold in connection with other, sometimes unspecified, drinking vessels.[42] The ratio of gold to silver reflects the relative hierarchic ranking of the metals (compare the *Gododdin* reference cited above which refers to a hero whose mead was 'contained in silver, but he deserved gold');[43] it probably also reflects the conventional nature of poetic description of drinking vessels (which may or may not have its roots in a distant Celtic reality to which archaeology, with its ample evidence of gold-embellished vessels, including drinking horns, bears witness).[44] Welsh poetic convention did not associate silver with drinking horns, so we can be fairly confident that Owain's *Hirlas* was in fact adorned with this metal.

Amongst the drinking vessels at Owain's feast the *Hirlas* horn clearly had pride of place and to be offered drink from it was a distinct mark of esteem.[45] Other

42 For the sources used in compiling the data see note 16 above. The references cited are definite ones. There are a further four possible references to gold in connection with drinking vessels, three of them to drinking horns, though, on balance, I consider them unlikely. With regard to the statistics cited a caveat might be entered that *Aur* (*eur-* in compounds) can occur with a figurative meaning (= 'fine, splendid'), see *Geiriadur Prifysgol Cymru* s.v. With regard to material objects, however, consciousness of the literal meaning would be such that *aur/eur-* would hardly be applied to artefacts whose external appearance was not gold-like (e.g. those of a silvery appearance).

43 *Canu Aneirin*, ed. Williams, 32: *aryant am y ued eur dylyi* (line 798).

44 Proinsias Mac Cana, *Ériu* 44, 92–3, briefly discusses (with further references) the gold-ornamented drinking horns of the continental Celts. On 'Celtic gold' in general see Christiane Eluère, *L'Or des Celtes* (Fribourg 1987). Plates 62, 65 and 92 ibid. illustrate the use of gold to decorate drinking horns. See also idem, *The Celts, First Masters of Europe* (London 1993), 38, 52–3, 70. Cf. also *Fled Bricrend*, ed. George Henderson (London 1899), 74–8, where the metals of the vessels given to Loegaire, Conall Cernach, and Cú Chulainn by Medb (bronze, silver, and gold, respectively) encode her assessment of their relative prominence. (I am grateful to Dr John Carey for providing me with this reference.)

45 Cf. line 74 where the prince commands his servant to offer the horn to the members of his war-band *can anrhydedd* ('with honour'). In another poem (?also by Cynddelw) the men of Owain's war-band are specifically lauded as being *Teilwng medd o fual* ('worthy of mead

references to drinking vessels in the poem are, however, worthy of mention. There are three references to drinking horns in the plural. I have already cited one of them, tentatively suggesting that a singular may be intended, and that the reference may in fact be to the *Hirlas*. Another (line 24) refers to the delight of Owain's warriors in the sound of mead horns (*Bugunad cyrn medd*), whilst the remaining one (lines 54–6) recalls an obscure episode, a contention between two kings said to have occurred 'over drinking horns' (*uch cyrn*) at the feast of some Morfran at Bangor. Apart from drinking horns there are two specific references to other vessels, *trull* in line 53 (from Latin *trulla*), a cup or basin, and *pan* in line 80, a cup, specified as containing mead; not unexpectedly, horns were not the only drinking vessels used at Owain's court (a scene in the Bayeux Tapestry depicting King Harold feasting at Bosham shows horns and a cup being used simultaneously).[46] Two further references remain. In line 103 the servant is commanded to offer drink to a hero from a silver vessel (*llestr arian*). As the verb used is *dywallaw*, elsewhere in the poem associated with the proffering of the *Hirlas*, this may be another reference to Owain's silver decorated horn, although on balance I consider that the use of the word *llestr*, rather than *corn* which is used elsewhere in the poem in referring to the horn, indicates that this is not the case. Lastly, in lines 29–30 the servant is commanded to bring wine 'with bright glass encompassing it' (*a gwydr golau yn ei gylchyn*) to a warrior named Gruffudd. References to glass vessels are rare in pre-*Gogynfeirdd* Welsh poetry, but they occur in the *Gododdin* and elsewhere.[47] Professor Mac Cana tentatively invokes the *Gododdin* to explain the *Hirlas* reference;[48] yet the possibility that we have another glimpse of the material reality of Owain Cyfeiliog's court cannot be precluded.

---

from a drinking horn'), see *Gwaith Llywelyn Fardd I ac Eraill o Feirdd y Ddeuddegfed Ganrif*, 15.42. Cf. Ann Hagen, *A Second Handbook of Anglo-Saxon Food and Drink* (Hockwold cum Wilton 1995), 243, who concludes that to be offered alcohol in a horn was a mark of status, citing an episode from the romance of *King Horn*: 'At her bridal feast a king's daughter is carrying a ceremonial drinking horn round to the guests, but when she is accosted by a man she thinks is a beggar, she offers him instead drink in a large bowl as being more fitting to his condition.' For the passage in question (which features Rimenhild and Horn) see Hall (ed.), *King Horn*, 64–6 (particularly text L, lines 1121–3, 1146–7).

46 Wilson, *The Bayeux Tapestry*, plate 3.

47 *Canu Aneirin*, ed. Williams, lines 797, 1008, 1144; other examples occur in 'Edmyg Dinbych' (ninth or tenth century), see edition by Ifor Williams in Rachel Bromwich (ed.), *The Beginnings of Welsh Poetry* (Cardiff 1972), 164 (line 32), and in a poem about Geraint ab Erbin first preserved in the Black Book of Carmarthen, see edition by Brynley F. Roberts in Rachel Bromwich and R. Brinley Jones (ed.), *Astudiaethau ar yr Hengerdd* (Caerdydd 1978), 290 (line 11).

48 *Ériu* 44, 89.

I come finally to consider the poem's references to drink. There are eleven of them. Mead, with eight citations, predominates. Three of these references (lines 37, 58 and 123) are associated with the concept of *talu medd*, the warriors' metaphorical payment for their mead by fighting for their lord, a key concept in the poem and one whose *locus classicus*, of course, is the *Gododdin*.[49] (In the last of these references the host who went to Catraeth is explicitly cited as the standard to which Owain's warriors are compared.)[50] Three further references to mead are accompanied by qualifiers; the mead is *gorewyn*, 'foaming' (line 26), *[y] medd gorau oll*, 'the best mead of all' (line 79), and *medd hidlaid melys*, 'sweet strained mead' (line 129), the latter being possibly a direct echo of the *medd hidlaid* of the *Gododdin*.[51] There remain three references to other drinks. Wine is mentioned twice; one reference (line 30), already cited, describes it as being encompassed by glass, and another (line 78) mentions *gwin gwinau* ('dark red wine'). The other drink mentioned (line 17) is bragget (*bragawd*). Professor Mac Cana has perceptively noted that the wine and bragget references are preceded by the verb *dyddwg*, rather than *dywallaw* which is usually employed to command the servant, implying that this indicates 'an instinctive gesture of discrimination on the part of the poet'.[52] Not only is there discrimination between these drinks and the more frequently cited and, doubtless, more esteemed, mead,[53] but implicitly too, I think, between the vessels containing them, the *Hirlas* being reserved for mead. As to the various drinks mentioned Professor Mac Cana cites once again the example of the *Gododdin*, where mead, wine and bragget all feature.[54] It is worthy of note, however, that Cynddelw Brydydd Mawr in a long ode to Owain Cyfeiliog portrays the prince's court as one where poets congregate around 'three kinds of drink' (*tri llad*);[55] these are not specified, but may well be the mead, wine and bragget of

49 See note 10 above.

50 Lines 123–7. Earlier in the poem (line 37) Owain's warriors are said to have earned their mead like the men of Belyn (*Taliasant eu medd mal gwŷr Belyn gynt*), a reference to the retinue of Belyn of Llŷn, one of the 'Three Fettered War-Bands of the island of Britain', see Rachel Bromwich (ed.), *Trioedd Ynys Prydein* (Cardiff 1961), 167.

51 *Canu Aneirin*, ed. Williams, line 354.

52 *Ériu* 44, 89.

53 The high value of mead vis-à-vis other drinks is reflected in the laws. In the section on the butler (*trulliad*) it is stipulated that the measure of legal liquor was a full vessel of beer, a half full vessel of bragget, and a one-third full vessel of mead, *Llyfr Iorwerth*, ed. Wiliam, 18.8–10. If mead was not available as part of the food render due to the king, two quotas of bragget were required as a substitute, and, failing that, four quotas of beer, ibid., 96.9–10.

54 *Ériu* 44, 89.

55 Jones and Owen (ed.), *Gwaith Cynddelw Brydydd Mawr I*, 16.18. Maguelonne Toussaint-Samat, *A History of Food*, tr. Anthea Bell (Cambridge MA and Oxford 1992), 37, remarks on

Hirlas Owein. Owain, like many generous hosts before and after him, may well have liked to mix his drinks!

Hirlas Owein's vividness of presentation and dramatic quality make it one of the most remarkable of early medieval Welsh poems. Yet we are not at present concerned with its literary qualities. In terms of its evidence regarding feasting customs and the material objects associated with feasts it may have its ambiguities and difficulties of interpretation. These mostly arise from its nature as a literary artefact rather than a historical document and the consequent impressionistic and generalised nature of its descriptions. Proinsias Mac Cana in his *Ériu* article wisely warned us not to expect what he termed 'pedantic consistency' and 'meticulous accuracy' in the poem.[56] Yet, granted its difficulties and ambiguities, in Welsh terms *Hirlas Owein* remains a source which tells us more than any other about the nature of feasting and drinking and drinking vessels in the courts of the princes. By focusing on whatever detail the poem presents, by elucidating that detail and considering some of it within the context of Welsh poetic practice and literary precedent, I have tried to identify features that may mirror reality rather than literary convention or influence. *Hirlas Owain* is a poem which invites many kinds of exploration. My modest aim has been to explore one of its most absorbing facets without, I hope, transgressing too much the bounds of 'sober' scholarship.

---

the conjunction of mead, wine and beer in medieval feasting. Bragget, which consisted of ale with added honey and spices, might be considered a variant of beer/ale.

56 *Ériu* 44, 88.

Two Middle Welsh Theological Tracts

J. E. Caerwyn Williams

UNIVERSITY OF WALES CENTRE FOR ADVANCED WELSH
AND CELTIC STUDIES, ABERYSTWYTH

THEOLOGICAL TRACTS, whether modern or medieval, do not these days attract much scholarly attention, but, needless to say, they formed an important element in the literary productions of past generations, and Professor Mac Cana's wide-ranging and very productive interest in all aspects of Welsh scholarship is more than an excuse for these introductory notes on two texts, versions of which have been previously published and show that they are important from a lexical if not from a theological standpoint. A case in point is the use of *rhinwedd* meaning 'sacrament'.

TRACT A

Tract A in its best printed version, that from 'Llyvyr Agkyr Llandewivrevi' (see *The Elucidarium and other tracts in Welsh from Llyvyr Agkyr Llandewivrevi* AD 1346 [Jesus College MS. 119] edited by J. Morris Jones . . . and John Rhŷs. Oxford . . . 1894; henceforth LlA) is entitled *Yn ymod hwnn ydysgir ydyn py delw y dyly credv y duw. Acharu duw. Achadw ydegeir dedyf. Ac ym/moglyt rac yseith pechawt marwawl. Ac erbynnyeit Seith rinwed yr eglwys yn enrydedus. Agwnneuthur seith weithret y drugared yr gobrwyaw nef idaw ynteu.* (I use the modern symbols for w, r and s, and, except here, with the words separated), i.e., translated, 'In this way one teaches a man how he should believe in God and love God and keep the Ten

Commandments and avoid the Seven Deadly Sins and receive the Seven Sacraments of the Church and perform the Seven Acts of Mercy in order to be rewarded Heaven for himself.' For obvious reasons I shall use the abbreviated title 'Yn y mod hwnn y dysgir y dyn.' The other printed version is from a slightly earlier MS., Peniarth MS. 5, and unfortunately less faithfully reproduced. It is to be found in *Selections from the Hengwrt MSS. . . Vol. II . . . Edited, with a transla-tion by the late Rev. Robert Williams . . . and the translation continued by the Rev. G. Hartwell Jones . . . London . . . 1892*: henceforth *Hen.* ii.

That 'Yn y mod hwnn y dysgir y dyn' was immensely popular is proved by the numerous copies preserved in Welsh manuscripts. These MS. texts may be listed more or less according to their dating which is based for the most part on Daniel Huws, 'Llyfrau Cymraeg 1250–1400', *National Library of Wales Journal*, XXVIII. No. I Summer 1993, pp. 1–21 and J. Gwenogvryn Evans, *Report on Manuscripts in the Welsh Language*. Volumes I and II, 1898–1910; henceforth RMWL.

THE TEXTS

I   NLW (= National Library of Wales) Peniarth MS. 5, f. xx^v ff.: 1350$^{±25}$. Complete. *[Y]n y mo[d] hwnn y dysgir y dyn py delw, etc.* See *Hen.* ii. Pp. 237–242. A translation is given on pp. 600–603.

II   Jesus College [Welsh] MS 2 (= CXIX), f. 121^r: *c.* 1346. Complete. *Yn y mod hwnn y dysgir y dyn py delw, etc.* See LlA Pp. 141–6.

III   NLW Llanstephan MS. 27, f. 43^v ff.: *c.* 1400. Complete. *Dangos y mod y dylyo dyn gredu y duw holl gyuoethawc. Yn y mod hwn y dysgir y dyn, etc.*

IV   NLW Llanstephan MS. 3, Pp. 408–421: 1400–1425. Defective. *E[n y mod hwnn y dysgir y dyn py delw y dyly credv]*, etc. P. 408 for the most part is illegible.

V   NLW Peniarth MS. 50, Pp. 183 ff.: 1425–1456. Defective. *Y llyuyr hwnn a ddysc y ddyn py ddelw y dyly credu y dduw, etc.*

VI   NLW Peniarth MS. 15, Pp. 32 ff.: 15th century. Complete. *Yn y mod hwn y dysgir y dyn py delw, etc.*

VII   NLW Shrewsbury School MS. XI, Pp. 54 ff.: 1425–1450. Complete. *Yr ymadrawd hwnn a dysg y dyn py delw y dyly credu, etc.*

[Llyfr Gwyn Hergest: *c.* 1461–1483]

VIII NLW Peniarth MS. 191, Pp. 67 ff.: *c.* 1450–1475. Defective. *Yr ymadrawd hwnn a dysc y dyn pa delw y dyly gredu y duw, etc.*

IX NLW Llanstephan MS. 200, Pp. 1 ff.: *c.* 1450–1475. Defective. Lacks an incipit and some of the text's beginning.

X NLW Llanstephan MS. 2, Pp. 350 ff.: *c.* 1450–1500. Defective. *Llyuyr yw hwnn a dysc y dyn pa delw y dyly gredu y duw, etc.*

XI National Library of Wales MS. 5267, ff. 53^v–56^v: *c.* 1450. Complete. *Y llyuyr hwnn a dysc y dyn py delw, etc.*

XII Cardiff Havod MS. 19, Pp. 73 ff.: 1536. The hand of ? dd. ap Ieuan henddyn. Complete. *Llyma val y dyleir kredv i dduw a chadw X dedyf, etc.*

XIII NLW Llanstephan MS. 181, P. 7: *c.* 1556. Defective. A mere fragment.

XIV Cardiff Havod MS. 22, Pp. 7 ff.: 1550–1575. Complete. *Y llyfr hwnn a ddysc i ddyn pa ddelw y dyly ef gredu a charu duw, etc.*

XV British Library [Welsh] MS. 32 (= Additional 31,055), f. 73 ff.: 1594–1596. Hand of 'Syr Thomas Wiliems'. Defective. *Yn y modd hwn y dyscir i ddyn pa ddelû y dyly credu y dduw, etc.*

XVI NLW Peniarth MS. 314, iv, Pp. 1 ff.: 1641. Hand of John Jones, Gellilyf-dy. Complete. *Y Llyfyr hwnn, a ddysc i ddyn pa ddelw, etc.*

XVII Cardiff MS. 36, Pp. 243 ff.: 1717–18. Complete. *Yn y mod hvnn y dysgir py delv y dyly credv y duv, etc.*

XVIII NLW Panton MS. 21, f. 6^v ff.: *c.* 1770. Hand of the Rev. Evan Evans, Ieuan Brydydd Hir. Complete. *Am ddyscu y modd y dyly dyn gredu: Yn y modd hyn y dyscir i ddyn pa dhelw y dyly gredu i Dduw, etc.*

XIX NLW Peniarth MS. 120, Pp. 206 ff.: end of 18th century. Complete. *Hystoria y ddyscu y ddyn pa dhelw y dylei gredu i dhyw. Yn y modd hwnn y dysgir y ddyn py ddelw, etc.*

XX National Library of Wales MS. 9164, Pp. 1 ff.: 19th century. Hand of Gwilym Cowlyd (W. John Roberts, 1828–1904). Defective. Lacks beginning.

XXI NLW Peniarth MS. 319, Pp. 206 ff.: late. Complete. *Yn y mod hvnn y dysgir y dyn py delv y dyly credv y Duv, etc.*

XXII NLW Cwrtmawr MS. 1155, Pp. 12 ff.: late 19th century. Hand of Robert Williams, Rhydycroesau. Defective. *Historia y ddyscu y ddyn pa ddelw a dylei gredy y Dhyw. Yn y modd hwnn y dysgir y ddyn pa ddelw y dyly credu y Dduw, etc.*

CLASSIFICATION OF TEXTS

With so many texts to discuss it is best to divide them roughly as early and late and to begin with the latter, in particular with those texts known to be more or less faithful transcripts of earlier ones.

Thus Text XV in B.L. Additional 31,055 is in the hand of 'Syr Thomas Wiliems' who tells us 'Hynn a sgrivennwyd allan or llyv(yr) Gw(yn) i Rydd(erch),' i.e. 'This was written from Llyfr Gwyn for Rhydderch', i.e. from Peniarth MS. 5 which, together with Peniarth MS. 4, originally formed The White Book of Rhydderch.

Text XVII (in Cardiff MS. 36), the manuscript informs us, was copied 'Ex Codice Didrefnyn' and there can be no doubt as to which volume of the Didrefn Gasgliad this codex was: it was volume 3, i.e. Llanstephan MS. 3. On p. 243 of Cardiff MS. 36 we read the following note: 'Hujus tractatus pag. 2 habetur hac ἐπιγραφή manu D.E. Lh. Ed. Luidio donavit Cl. v. D. Johannes Lloyd de Aber Lhyveni apud Meirioneses,' and on p. 409 (or 2) of Llanstephan MS. 3, 'Ed. Luidio donavit Cl. v. D. Johannes Lloyd de Aber Lhyveni apud Meirioneses.' Note that RMWL II.i.231 describes the material in Cardiff MS. 36, Pp. 243 ff. as 'Ex codice DIDREFNYN ... with variant readings from Jesus College [Welsh] MSS. 2 (= CXIX) and 3 (= XX) and the material in pages 303 ff. as 'A collection of Fables 'Ex Libro cui Titulum *DIDREFNYN* imposuit D. Ed. Lhuyd, nunc (postea) penes D.H. Wanleuim fol. 509b (nunc in Bibliotheca Harleiana asservato)'. Text XVII reproduces Text IV faithfully. The only difference of importance between them is that Text XVII introduces Latin titles, such as 'De amore erga Deum', 'De Decalogo', 'De 7 Peccatis' Text IV is defective, and the lacunae in it are filled in Text XVII from Text II (Jesus College [Welsh] MS. 2 (= CXIX): p. 249 'Saith Rinwedd yr Eglwys', p. 250 'Saith weithred y drugaredd'.

Text XVIII is in the hand of the poet and scholar, the Rev. Evan Evans, Ieuan Brydydd Hir, and it is taken from the lost Llyfr Gwyn Hergest. On Llyfr Gwyn

Hergest, see Thomas Jones, 'Testun Llyfr Gwyn Hergest o'r Bibyl ynghymraec', BBCS X (1939–40) 15–21 and my 'Y Llyfr Gwyn o Hergest a Llanstephan 3', *ibid.*, 120–4. It appears that this is the only transcript we have of a text in Llyfr Gwyn Hergest and as such it is of considerable importance. As Text XVIII follows Text IV more faithfully than any other text in our list we gather that Text XVIII and Text IV fall together.

Texts XIX and XXI are transcripts of Text II, and Text XXII is a copy made by the Rev. Robert Williams, Rhydycroesau, of Text XIX.

Text XVI, in the hand of John Jones, Gellilyfdy, appears to be a faithful copy of an older text. According to RMWL I.1120, it is a 'transcript from Pen. MS. 16', but this cannot be correct as Peniarth MS. 16 does not include our text. We know that John Jones made transcripts from two MSS. containing our text, from Peniarth MS. 5 (= Text I) and Peniarth MS. 50 (= Text V), but it is not likely that Text XVI was copied from Text I: there are too many differences between them and as we know, John Jones was a professional transcriber. It is not impossible that Text XVI is a transcript of Text V in Peniarth 50 if we can assume that it was complete at the time of transcription or that the lacunae were filled from another text.

We can now turn to the older texts. With the exception of Text X, perhaps, all of them are derived from the same original, but there is a closer relationship between some of them than between the others.

Texts II, III and VI fall together. Texts III and VI follow Text II so faithfully that they may be transcripts of it but on the other hand we could expect the same kind of similarity if they were transcripts of the same original.

A comparison of Texts I and II in *Hen.* ii. 237–242 and LlA respectively demonstrates their similarity but the similarity between I and II is not as great as the similarity between II and III and VI.

Text IV, as it is now, is incomplete. It ends in the middle of the description of the sin of gluttony, and there are several pages missing. It does not follow texts II, III and VI closely, but it belongs to the same family.

Text V does not fall with II. Sometimes it agrees with Text I against Text II but it does not follow Text I so closely as to make one believe that it is a transcript.

The texts in the two MSS. Peniarth MS. 191 and Llanstephan MS. 200 are incomplete but it is noticeable that parts missing in one manuscript are found in the other, and as we know that parts of Peniarth MS. 191 have been bound with Llanstephan MS. 200 or *vice versa*, perhaps we should consider Texts VIII and IX as one text, and as falling with Text VII in their readings, and it may be that they are transcripts of the same original, but it is not easy to decide their relationship with the other texts, although they all represent the same original and belong to the same family.

Although Text X begins like the other texts, it differs from them so much that it should not perhaps be considered as one of them. After a certain point, after the sentence:

Gwedy cretto dyn yn fydlawn y duw trwy y pynkeu hynn haws vyd gantaw garu duw a chymryt y ovyn ae wassanaethu trwy uvylldawt . . .

it differs completely from the other texts. Yet it stands comparison with them and that is the reason I have included it among them.

Text XI (National Library of Wales MS. 5267) is not unlike Texts I and II but it cannot be considered to be a transcript of either and although it resembles in its title Text V, it does not fall with it.

Texts XII, XIII and XIV are versions which have been modernised in phrase and language and it is virtually impossible to decide their relationship with the rest. In Text XIV the scribe seems to have taken an older text, perhaps not unlike XII, and to have extended it by adding historical and expository material and by quoting Biblical verses whenever he had an excuse. That is why it seems to be independent of the others.

TRACT B

Tract B in its best printed version, LlA 162–3, begins:

Dangos pywed ydyellir ytat ar mab. aryspryt glan vn duw.

(I use the modern symbols for *w*, *r* and *s*, and, except here, separate the words).

THE TEXTS

I NLW Peniarth MS. 5, ff. l^v–li^r (li torn) 1350±25. Defective. *(P)w bynnac a vynno gwarandav euegyl Jeuan megys y dosparthyssant athravon da truy loes ᵛ mal hynn y gwerendeu.* [K]*Ynn bo perffeithiach no chreadur or byt, etc.*

II Jesus College [Welsh] MS. 2 (= CXIX), f. 136^r–136^v. c. 1346. Complete. *Dangos py wed y dyellir y tat ar yspryt glan vn duw, etc.* LlA 162–3.

III   NLW Llanstephan MS. 27, f. 41ᵛ ff.: *c.* 1400. Complete. *Dangos pa delw y dyellir y tat ar mab ar yspryt glan yn vn dvw, etc.*

IV   NLW Llanstephan MS. 3, Pp. 431 ff.: 1400–1425. Complete. *Llyma dangos val i dichawn y tat ar mab ar yspryt glan vot yn vn duw, etc.*

[Llyfr Gwyn Hergest: *c.* 1461–1483]

V   NLW Peniarth MS. 12, Pp. 157 ff.: 16th century. Complete. *dangos pa ddelw y dyellir y tat ar mab ar yspryt glan yn vn ddvw, etc.*

VI   British Library [Welsh] MS. 32 (= Add. 31,055), f. 167ᵛ ff.: 1594–6. Hand of 'Syr Thomas Wiliems'. Complete. *lhyma dangos val i dichawn y tat ar mab ar yspryt Glan vot yn vn duw teir person, etc.*

VII   Cardiff MS. 36, Pp. 263 ff.: 1717/18. Complete. *Llyma dangos val i dichawn y tat ar mab ar yspryt glan vot yn vn duw Teir person, etc.*

VIII   National Library of Wales MS. 5284, Pp. 41–42: 18th century. Hand of John David from Pentre Vidog. Complete. *llyma ddangos fel y dichon y tad ar mab a yspryd glan fod yr un Duw a thri pherson, etc.*

IX   NLW Panton MS. 21, f. 27ᵛ: *c.* 1770. Hand of the Rev. Evan Evans, Ieuan Brydydd Hir. Complete. *Llyma ddangos fal i dichawn y tat ar Mab ar Yspryt glan fod yn Un Duw tair person.*

X   NLW Peniarth MS. 120, Pp. 232 ff.: end of 18th century. *[Dangos py wedd y dyellir y tat ar mab ar yspryt glan vn Duw, etc.] Hen.* ii, 299–300.

XI   NLW Peniarth MS. 319, Pp. 234 ff.: late. Complete. *Dangos py ved y dyelhir y Tat ar mab ar ysbryt glan vn Duv, etc.*

XII   NLW Cwrtmawr MS. 1155, Pp. 159–160. Hand of Robert Williams, Rhyd-ycroesau. Defective.

CLASSIFICATION OF TEXTS

Text I is defective, because f. li is torn, leaving only an inner strip. The first sentence quoted above as part of the title has been written as such, but perhaps it should be taken as the colophon to 'Evengyl Ieuan', the text which precedes it in the manuscript. Note that in LlA also our text is preceded by *Euengyl Jeuan*

Ebostol. But Text I is different from Text II, sufficiently different to consider it a different and an independent translation of the Latin text which we assume to be the source of *Dangos pa delw*. . . I prefer to think of Text I as a separate translation rather than as a considerably edited version of the same translation as that found in Text II and the others.

Text III falls with Text II in readings. There is enough similarity between these two texts to make it possible to consider Text III as a transcript of Text II, but, of course, transcription from the same original would produce the same correspondence in readings.

Text IV is not very similar to Texts III and IV, but it is fundamentally the same text.

Comparison of Text IV with Texts VI and IX, two transcripts of the text which must have been in *Llyfr Gwyn Hergest*, leads us to conclude that Text IV fell with the text in *Llyfr Gwyn Hergest*.

Text VII is a transcript of Text IV: see the remarks on Text XVII of Tract A: *Yn y mod hwnn y dysgir*.

Text VIII is a transcript of Text VI. British Library [Welsh] MS. 32 was at one time in the hands of John David of Pentre Vidog; see RMWL II. 1653, and he transcribed much of it. After transcribing 'Beibl yn ysgriuennedic yn Gymraeg' (See British Library [Welsh] MS. 32, Pp. III ff.) he wrote in National Library of Wales MS. 5284:

> or lleiaf, llawer or henwau a ysgrifenesid yn llygredig, rhai a Gorectiais i. eraill os gattfydd, a ellir i gwellau wrth y Beibl latin, fel y gwneuthum innau, medd Tho. Williams, y pysygwr o drefryw 1594./A John David o Bentre Vidog ai ysgrifenodd drachefn: 1744.

Texts X and XI are straightforward and faithful transcripts of II and Text XII is a transcript of I.

PROVENANCE

It happens that much could be said of three of the earliest manuscripts in which our theological tracts are found; unfortunately too much for the space here available.

Originally NLW Peniarth MS. 5 was part of the White Book of Rhydderch where it preceded NLW Peniarth 4. It was dated 1300–1325 by J. Gwenogvryn Evans and $1350^{\pm25}$ by Mr Daniel Huws who has described it in detail and analysed it meticulously in *Cambridge Medieval Celtic Studies*, XXI, Summer 1991, pp. 1–21.

Mr Huws confirms that the Rhydderch associated by name with the manuscript was Rhydderch ab Ieuan Llwyd of Parcrhydderch, Llangeitho, some ten miles from the Cistercian Abbey of Strata Florida, and concludes that the abbey had a vital role in its production, 'that it was the midwife if not the mother of the White Book'. He shows that it was written by scribes whom he denotes as A, B, C, D, and E, but argues that the original White Book did not include the quires written by A which stand apart 'on account both of the dimensions of their written space and of their long lines. They also stand apart with respect to their contents which are wholly didactic, or devotional'. Our two theological texts, obviously, belong to this didactic element.

Not very far from Strata Florida is Llanddewibrefi where a collegiate church was established by Thomas Bek, bishop of St. David's 1280–93. At some time in the fourteenth century there was in Llanddewibrefi an anchorite who was also a scribe. It was he who wrote *Llyvyr Agkyr Llandewivrevi* (Jesus College MS. CXIX) at the behest, as a note informs us, of Gruffudd ap Ll(ywelyn) ap Phylip ap Trahayarnn. This Gruffudd ap Llywelyn was married to Elen or Eleanor, daughter of a grandson of Maredudd ab Owain. Maredudd ab Owain had a daughter called Efa: it was for her that Brother Gruffudd Bola translated into Welsh the *Quicumque Vult* (called in Welsh *Credo Athanasius*) as that text informs us. Did he translate more than one religious text for her or for someone else? One would like to believe that he was a member of the religious community at Strata Florida and that as his comments on translating to Efa imply, he was well-versed in the art. The *Quicumque Vult* is found in Peniarth MS. 5. Another text found in that manuscript is the Welsh translation of *Transitus Beatae Mariae*, one of two texts, the other was *Cronicl Turpin*, translated by another cleric, Madog ap Selyf, for Efa's brother, Gruffudd ap Maredudd. It is to be noted that the anchorite of Llanddewibrefi was responsible for other manuscripts besides (see Daniel Huws, 'Llyfrau Cymraeg 1250–1400', *National Library of Wales Journal*, XXVIII, 1 Summer 1993, pp. 1–21, esp. p. 11.

NLW Llanstephen MS. 27, also called *Llyfr Coch Talgarth*, stands comparison with *Llyvyr Agkyr Llandewivrevi* as a rich repository of religious tracts. Fortunately we have the name of its scribe, Hywel Fychan ap Hywel Goch o Fuellt and he has left us five manuscripts and parts of two others: NLW Peniarth MS. 12, Philadelphia (Public Library Company) MS. 86800, Jesus College MS. 57 (= Jesus College [Welsh] MS. 4; RMWL II.i.34) and parts of Cardiff Havod MS. 16 (pp. 101–112) and of Jesus College MS. XCXI (= Llyfr Coch Hergest, Jesus College [Welsh] MS. 1, RMWL II.i.I). A note in Philadelphia MS. 86800 tells us that Hywel Fychan had transcribed one text at the command of Hopcyn ap Tomas and we know from the work of two poets, Dafydd y Coed and Ieuan Llwyd ab y Gargam, that Hopcyn ap Tomas delighted in perusing his manuscripts with poets. Indeed, one can believe that he may have actually perused Llanstephan MS. 27 with these poets. It is interesting that Rhys ap Tomas's name occurs in Llanstephan MS. 27 and it is not impossible to assume that he was Hopcyn's brother and that he also patronized poets and scribes. See my 'Rhyddiaith Grefyddol Cymraeg Canol' in Geraint Bowen (ed.), *Y Traddodiad Rhyddiaith yn yr Oesoedd Canol* (Llandysul, 1974), p. 339.

In these matters it would be rash to be too dogmatic but it seems reasonable to assume that the Cistercian Abbey of Strata Florida was not only a centre for producing transcripts of secular texts (the Hendregadredd MS. cries out to be mentioned), but also a centre for translating texts, expecially religious texts, from Latin into Welsh. There seems to be a general assumption that a Welsh translation was made of the Latin Annals which lie behind the two *Brutiau y Tywysogion* and *Brut Brenhinedd y Saeson*, in Strata Florida. We know that there was a strong nationalist sentiment in some of the Cistercians in Wales and that, together with missionary zeal, would have motivated the translation of religious and theological tracts into Welsh. See my 'Twf Cenedlaetholdeb yng Nghymru'r Oesoedd Canol' in Dewi Eirug Davies (ed.), *Gwinllan a roddwyd* (Llandybïe, 1972), pp. 60–86, esp. 80.